T0319596

One Belt One Road

HARVARD EAST ASIAN MONOGRAPHS 439

One Belt One Road

Chinese Power Meets the World

Eyck Freymann

Published by the Harvard University Asia Center
Distributed by Harvard University Press
Cambridge (Massachusetts) and London 2021

The Harvard University Asia Center publishes a monograph series and, in coordination with the Fairbank Center for Chinese Studies, the Korea Institute, the Reischauer Institute of Japanese Studies, and other facilities and institutes, administers research projects designed to further scholarly understanding of China, Japan, Korea, Vietnam, and other Asian countries. The Center also sponsors projects addressing multidisciplinary, transnational, and regional issues in Asia.

Publication of this book was partially underwritten by the Mr. and Mrs. Stephen C. M. King Publishing and Communications Fund, established by Stephen C. M. King to further the cause of international understanding and cooperation, especially between China and the United States, by enhancing cross-cultural education and the exchange of ideas across national boundaries through publications of the Harvard University Asia Center.

Library of Congress Cataloging-in-Publication Data

Names: Freymann, Eyck, author.
Title: One Belt One Road : Chinese power meets the world / Eyck Freymann.
Description: Cambridge, Massachusetts : Harvard University Asia Center, 2021. | Series:
    Harvard East Asian monographs ; 439 | Includes bibliographical references and index. |
Identifiers: LCCN 2020025777 | ISBN 9780674247956 (hardcover) |
    ISBN 9780674247963 (paperback)
Subjects: LCSH: Yidaiyilu (Initiative : China) | Infrastructure (Economics)—China. |
    China—Foreign economic relations. | China—Foreign relations—21st century. |
    China—Politics and government—2002–
Classification: LCC HF1604 .F745 2021 | DDC 337.51—dc23
LC record available at https://lccn.loc.gov/2020025777

Index by Indexing Partners

♾ Printed on acid-free paper

Last figure below indicates year of this printing
30 29 28 27 26 25 24 23 22 21

To my parents and grandparents

Contents

Part II
Chinese Power Meets the World

Maps, Figures, and Tables

Maps

Figures

Tables

Acknowledgments

It is impossible to write a book such as this without racking up many personal debts.

My first debt is to the generosity and unconditional support of my academic mentors at Harvard and Cambridge Universities. I am particularly grateful to my advisor, Bill Kirby, who took a chance on an unconventional proposal and supported the project to the end. Thank you to Amartya Sen for your humor, wisdom, and ethical example and for continuing to advocate for the project. Thank you to Niall Ferguson and Graham Allison, who taught me the true meaning of mentorship; to Kun-Chin Lin and Hans van de Ven for welcoming me into the community of Chinese scholarship at Cambridge; and to Rana Mitter and Paul Irwin Crookes for doing the same at Oxford. Special thanks also go to Chris Miller, Nara Dillon, Iain Johnston, Pierpaolo Barbieri, and Rush Doshi, who advised me, advocated for me, and instructed me on matters large and small. It has been a true privilege to learn from you.

The field research for this thesis was made possible by two grants from the Harvard University Asia Center through endowments made by Bill Overholt and the Victor and William Fung Foundation. Particular thanks to Bill for your mentorship and sage contrarian advice. The Henry Fund and the Harvard-UK Fellowship made my year at Cambridge possible.

At Harvard, thank you to my brilliant and meticulous editor, Bob Graham, to the board of the Harvard University Asia Center Press, to the two anonymous peer reviewers for their many helpful insights, to Jason

Tranchida for the cover design, to Scott Walker and Ira Anatolevna for the maps and graphics, and to the professors, colleagues, and friends who most shaped my thinking on OBOR and China more generally. These include, among many others, Adam Siegel, Arjun Kapur, Arjun Subramaniam, Cameron Hickert, Gabrielle Chefitz, James Evans, Jasmine Fei Qu, John Park, Julian Gewirtz, Mel Sanborn, Meredith Davis, Neil Thomas, Payam Mohseni, Ryan Neely, Sam Parker, Sugata Bose, Vinay Nagaraju, and Yuan Wang. Caroline Jones; Peter, Sam, Sarah, and Saffy Galison; and Patrick McDonagh were and will always be my second family.

At the Naval War College in Newport, Rhode Island, thank you to Conor Kennedy, Derek Reveron, Isaac Kardon, and Peter Dutton.

In Washington, thank you to Jonathan Hillman and Satoru Nagao for your insights. Thank you to Marc and Andrea Chafetz for your hospitality and good company on so many visits and for offering me a home away from home.

In Beijing, Paul Haenle, Ryan DeVries, Shi Zhiqin, and the Carnegie-Tsinghua team that introduced me to OBOR in 2015. In Hong Kong, Andy Collier, Barry Sautman, David Lague, David Zweig, Ed Tse, Edith Terry, Gavin Bowring, Lee Chiao, Michael McGaughy, and Wendy Hong shared their insights and connected me to others. In Tokyo, Akihiko Sunami, Robert Dujarric, Jonathan Berkshire Miller, and Parker Allen offered guidance and warm welcomes. So did June Park, Changsu Lee, and Hankwon Kim in Seoul. Bill Mellor and Baogang He navigated time zones to Skype with me from Australia.

In England, I am in debt to my colleagues and classmates at Cambridge, particularly Hugo Bromley and Angus Hui; Hajira Mirza, Kasim Khan, and Josh Goldstein at Oxford; and Ben Rhode, Catherine Macaulay, Daniel Yizhe Xie, Dimitris Valatsas, Kerry Brown, Kori Schaake, Nicholas Kumleben, and Shiv Ruparell in London. I have much more to learn from all of you.

In India, Piyush and Dhruv Goyal and the inimitable Sankalp Sharma exceeded all expectations for hospitality and kindness. Thank you also to the other experts who granted me interviews in Mumbai and New Delhi and connected me to their colleagues, including Abhijit Singh, Alok Bansal, Dhruv Katoch, Dhruva Jaishankar, Sachin Chaturvedi, and Simon Mundy.

For helping making sense of China–Pakistan relations from afar, thank you to Abdur Rehman, Akbar Zaidi, Khuzaimah Saeed, Jamil Anderlini, Naubahar Sharif, and Muhammad Ali Zadari.

Thank you Karthik Sivaram, Shanil Wijesinha, and Elizabeth Ferrie for your generosity in illuminating the legal picture and for making introductions in Sri Lanka on my behalf. In Colombo, thank you to Asanga Gunawansa, Duminda Ariyasinghe, Jananath Colombage, Mimi Alphonsus, Nishan de Mel, and Paikiasothy Saravanamuttu. Thank you to Ananda and Nelun for coordinating my trip around Hambantota, and thank you to those who helped and asked not to be identified.

In Tanzania, Togolani Mavura set up meetings on my behalf with people from all across the political landscape. I am deeply grateful for your hospitality and friendship. Thank you to those in Dar es Salaam who spoke to me on the record—Joseph Leon Simbakalia, Uledi Abbas Mussa, Faustine Kamuzora, Deus Valentine, and Zitto Kabwe—to John and to others in Dar es Salaam, Bagamoyo, and Zanzibar who prefer to remain anonymous.

In Greece, thank you to Alexandra Frantzeskaki, Alexis Papahelas, George Xiradakis and his colleagues, Plamen Tonchev, Thodoris Dritsas, Yanni Palaiologos, and Yiorgos Anomeritis. Thanks are due also to Vasilis Trigkas in Beijing and Frans-Paul van der Putten in The Hague.

Thank you to my Greenmantle colleagues Alice Han and Sean Xu for teaching me about China's political economy and how it interacts with the global market.

Those who helped behind the scenes are not forgotten here. Thank you to Andrey Casasola, Chie Ri, Henry Kaempf, Gwen Volmar, Jorge Espada, Matthew Pritchard, Nancy Hearst, Rosie Cortese, and Simone O'Hanlon.

Elizabeth Ferrie, Elizabeth Keto, Finn Freymann, Gil Highet, Hugo Bromley, Kun-Chin Lin, Marc Chafetz, Nathan Hilgartner, Niall Ferguson, Peter Galison, and R. J. Teoh made thoughtful and relentlessly helpful comments on drafts. So did my father, Saxton Freymann, who went far beyond margin comments and created the beautiful and provocative cover art.

I could not have asked for better research partners. This book would not exist without the brilliant and tireless Arthur Abraham, who tracked down and organized thousands of source documents, helped me talk through hypotheses, and boiled down annual reports and vast volumes of official data to their essential points. Nassoro Chakuleja translated many Swahili documents. The inimitable Foteini Alevizou interpreted the Greek sources, clarified many technical and linguistic points, and served as my translator for interviews in Athens and Piraeus. Thank you above all to Ruofei Shen for helping map the Chinese side; for your relentless insight into Chinese politics, history, and law; for teaching me Chinese; and for your friendship. You never failed me.

Thank you to those who chose to remain anonymous and to those I have anonymized out of caution and concern for their safety.

Many other colleagues, family members, friends, and teachers supported me and my research in myriad ways along the way. I cannot name you all here, but I am grateful.

Finally, thank you to my grandparents Marion and Gerald Galison for supporting me unreservedly on this wild and wonderful educational journey, and to my parents, Mia Galison and Saxton Freymann, for talking endlessly through the arguments, contributing to the book in ways too numerous to name, and occasionally proofreading. It stands to reason that any remaining errors must be your fault, so the book, with all my love, is dedicated to you.

Note to the Reader

The principal subject of this book is a grand project known in Chinese as *yidaiyilu* (一带一路). Because *yidaiyilu* goes by several names in English, and the choice of which one to use has political implications, a brief explanatory note is in order.

I use the simplest, literal translation of *yidaiyilu*: "One Belt One Road," which I abbreviate as OBOR. This is the only literal translation. It is also the English-language name the Chinese government used for the first two years after the program was announced. In Chinese, correlative four-character phrases in the form of one-noun-one-noun draw distinctions between two things while implying that together they form a balanced totality. For example, *yifuyiqi* (one husband, one wife) means monogamy; *yixinyide* (one heart, one mind) means united, coordinated, or whole; *yichangyihe* (one call, one harmony) means to echo one another; and *yishouyizu* (one hand, one foot) means a single person or a single effort. In Chinese, the phrase *yidaiyilu* (one belt, one road) therefore has a classical, even epic ring. It conjures an image of China going forth to encompass the world on land and sea, at once opening to the world and binding the world more closely to China, in a manner both balanced and harmonious.

In 2015, the Central Committee's Central Compilation and Translation Bureau issued a decision to change the English-language rendering of 一带一路 from "One Belt One Road" to the "Belt and Road Initiative," or BRI.[1] The new name rolls off the tongue more easily, but it introduces an entirely different set of connotations for foreign audiences. Replacing the classical allusions of OBOR, the word "initiative" suggests that the program is an entirely new undertaking—a fresh, constructive approach to fixing common problems. From 2015 on, most authoritative Communist Party publications have followed the guidance and used BRI. So have most scholars and journalists writing in English. But other prominent Chinese sources publishing in English still do not follow the consistent usage. "New Silk Road," "Belt and Road," OBOR, and B&R are all common. Sometimes, but not always, these names are set off with quotation marks.

Most important, the Chinese language name 一带一路 has never changed, and most references to it in official Chinese texts do not append the word *changyi* (initiative). This inconsistent usage foreshadows two themes that recur throughout this book. The first is that Beijing seems to want to communicate different interpretations of the *yidaiyilu* concept to domestic and foreign audiences. The second is that it has been extraordinarily sloppy in doing so.

The question of which name to use has political implications. The governments in Beijing and Taipei use the number-noun-number-noun syntax to name several important political and legal concepts. The most famous of these is Hong Kong's formal relationship to the Mainland, captured in the phrase *yiguoliangzhi* (one country, two systems). If Beijing were to decide to change the official English translation of *yiguoliangzhi* to the "country and systems initiative," most foreign scholars would continue to use the original translation. This is another reason I follow the US and Indian governments in continuing to call OBOR by its true name.[2]

This book uses the Pinyin romanization system for Chinese names and transliterated words. All Chinese individuals are named with surname first.

List of Abbreviations

ASEAN	Association of Southeast Asian Nations
B&R	Belt and Road; alternative abbreviation of OBOR
CCM	Chama Cha Mapinduzi
CCP	Chinese Communist Party
CCTV	China Central Television
CMG	China Merchants Group
CNPC	China National Petroleum Corporation
COSCO	China Overseas Shipping Company
COVID-19	2019 novel coronavirus
CPD	Central Propaganda Department
CPEC	China-Pakistan Economic Corridor
EAEU	Eurasian Economic Union
ECRL	East Coast Rail Link
HIPS/HIPG	Hambantota International Port Services/Group
HKTDC	Hong Kong Trade and Development Commission
IMF	International Monetary Fund
IRGC	Iranian Revolutionary Guard Corps
LSG	Leading Small Group
LSGPTW	Leading Small Group for Propaganda and Thought Work

MOU	Memorandum of Understanding
MSR	Maritime Silk Road
NDRC	National Development and Reform Commission
OBOR	One Belt One Road
PASOK	Panhellenic Socialist Movement (Greek center-left party)
PPA	Piraeus Port Authority
SCO	Shanghai Cooperation Organization
SEZ	Special Economic Zone
SLPA	Sri Lanka Ports Authority
SOE	State-owned enterprise
TAIPED	Hellenic Republic Asset Development Fund
TANU	Tanganyika African National Union
TPA	Tanzania Ports Authority

INTRODUCTION

The engine grinds, and with a jolt the three-wheeled *tuk-tuk* lurches off the muddy road and climbs onto the expressway. It is a clear morning, and over the din of the straining motor I can hear the cries of monkeys in the trees. Children gawk at us through the windows of the roadside houses. There are no other cars out, so we drive in the middle of the road, swerving every now and then to avoid a sleeping dog. There is no hint of industry here—not a plane in the sky, not a single roof or tower interposing between the thick vegetation that lines the road and the salt flats that stretch to the horizon. Yet the smoothly paved six-lane expressway that slices through this otherwise pristine part of Hamban-tota, Sri Lanka, looks as though it had been built yesterday.

We round a corner. Rising up from the road on the left is a convention center, three floors of glass and steel, its parking lot and helipad deserted. Behind it, a small cluster of wind turbines spin lazily. My driver proudly points out a new hospital, seven stories tall and nearing completion. We pass a concrete dormitory. The sign, in white characters on blue, reads "China Harbour Engineering Company Ltd. / 中国港湾工程有限责任公司" in English and Chinese. A dozen or so Chinese construction workers are milling about outside, smoking cigarettes. To the left is the road to the new international airport, but we turn right instead, toward the $1.4 billion deep water port once billed as the soon-to-be greatest port in South Asia. A few miles away is the second-largest international airport in the country and a large industrial zone, both brand-new. When we arrive, we find that the port is also empty.

What do these white elephants have in common? They all bear the name of Mahinda Rajapaksa, who commissioned them during his term as president of Sri Lanka (2005–15). All but the convention center were built by Chinese workers with imported Chinese construction materials and were financed by commercial loans from the Exim Bank of China. And as of December 8, 2017, the port is controlled by two Chinese state-owned enterprises (SOEs) on a ninety-nine-year lease, with an option to extend.

• • •

Sri Lanka is one of approximately sixty-five countries to have endorsed the One Belt One Road (OBOR) initiative, a program announced by Chinese President Xi Jinping in 2013 to fund infrastructure construction around the world. OBOR is ostensibly the umbrella term for two component initiatives. The first is an overland network, the New Silk Road Economic Belt, intended to link China with other countries on the Eurasian landmass. The second is the 21st Century Maritime Silk Road (MSR), a network of port cities in the South China Sea, Indian Ocean rim, and Mediterranean Sea. Projects funded through OBOR come in many types and sizes: airports, high-speed rail, pipelines, roads, power plants, industrial parks, data centers, undersea cables, and more. On official Chinese maps, Hambantota is now depicted as a key waystation on the MSR, a designation that the Sri Lankan authorities never imagined when they signed the deal to begin construction in 2007.

Analysts have proposed wildly different figures for how much money China has spent on OBOR projects since September 2013. Whatever the precise figures, the project's vision and scope are sweeping. Joy-Perez and Scissors calculate that China spent roughly $135 billion in foreign construction projects between 2014 and 2016 alone.[1] In inflation-adjusted terms, this is more than the United States spent on the Marshall Plan to rebuild Western Europe after World War II.[2] OBOR's strategic and geographic scope continues to expand. Between 2017 and 2019, more than a dozen Latin American countries joined. Chinese government agencies have published guidance documents on a Polar Silk Road to link China to the Arctic and Antarctic; a Digital Silk Road of undersea cables, data centers, 5G telecommunications systems; and an OBOR "space information corridor" to supplant GPS as the world's most advanced satellite navigation technology.[3]

Xi has presented OBOR as his signature foreign policy initiative. Nearly all of his state visits to lower- or middle-income countries in Asia, Africa, Oceania, Latin America, and Europe now culminate in the signing of boilerplate memoranda of understanding (MOUs). These nonbinding agreements typically commit the recipient country to the ideals of OBOR, in particular the virtue of "win-win cooperation," one of China's favorite slogans, and to various collaborative governance and industrial schemes. In return, MOUs announce Chinese pledges of trade and foreign direct investment. Xi actively promotes OBOR at multilateral meetings. He has discussed it at length in addresses to the United Nations General Assembly. In January 2017, days before Donald Trump was inaugurated as president of the United States, Xi closed his keynote address at the World Economic Forum in Davos with an extended pitch for OBOR. Yet this pales in comparison to the publicity OBOR has received within China. In 2016, OBOR was the most mentioned term in the Chinese Communist Party (CCP) mouthpiece *People's Daily.*[4] In a speech in May 2017, Xi described OBOR as the "project of the century." In March 2018, the Nineteenth National Party Congress enshrined OBOR and "Xi Jinping Thought" in the Communist Party constitution.

Investments under the banner of OBOR are deepening China's influence in some of the world's most important industries and geographic regions. By building ports in the Mediterranean, Indian Ocean, and South China Sea, China is cementing its dominance in the global shipping industry and preparing to project naval power far beyond its coastal waters. This has dramatic implications for the long-term security of India and dozens of other countries that depend on the oil, commodities, and manufactured products that travel along the world's busiest sea lanes. By building roads, railways, and related infrastructure across the Eurasian landmass, China is establishing itself as a power broker from Central Asia to Eastern Europe and preparing to challenge the European Union in high-tech manufacturing. By lubricating political relationships with poorer, commodity-producing states across developing Asia, Africa, and Latin America, OBOR is helping China win preferential access to the most important sources of energy and raw materials—and leverage its market power to demand better terms.

FIGURE I.I: Xi raises a glass to OBOR at the Belt and Road Forum at the Great Hall of the People in Beijing, April 26, 2019. Courtesy of Reuters/Nicolas Asfour/Pool.

Any country, company, or institution that deals with the Chinese state must now pay respect to OBOR or face consequences. In April 2019, forty heads of state and leaders of international organizations and representatives from 150 countries attended the Second Belt and Road Forum in Beijing (fig. I.1). Foreign firms and the Hong Kong government host hundreds of OBOR-branded events and conferences. Thanks to these growth pressures from within and without, the initiative continues to gain momentum and scale. In private, many Chinese officials express reservations about whether OBOR serves the national interest or confusion about what goals OBOR is trying to achieve. Yet party-controlled media tolerate no criticism of the leader's legacy project.

For the first five years after Xi announced OBOR in 2013, the United States paid little attention. When China sought out partners to join its Asian Infrastructure Investment Bank in 2014, the Barack Obama administration leaned on its European and Asian allies to join a boycott. But when the United Kingdom and others decided to join in defiance of US pressure, Washington quickly became conciliatory. "Whether you call it the New Silk Road or the Silk Road Economic Belt, now is the moment to work together to restore this region to its historic role as a vital hub of global commerce, ideas, and culture," US Deputy Secretary of State Bill Burns said.[5] This spirit of goodwill seemed to persist into the first months of the Trump administration. In May 2017, the United States even sent a delegation to the Belt and Road Forum. Unsure of what OBOR really was, the United States ricocheted from condemnation to endorsement and back again.

In late 2017, as the Trump administration pivoted to a harder line on China, it reclassified OBOR as a major threat. The administration proposed a new doctrine called the "free and open Indo-Pacific," which implied that China posed much the same threat in the Indian Ocean basin as it did in the South China Sea.[6] Soon after, Secretary of State Rex Tillerson criticized OBOR directly, saying that it "seems to want to define its own rules and norms."[7] This was an unusual statement: in general, US policymakers and official documents pointedly do not dignify OBOR by naming it directly. On Capitol Hill, both political parties became concerned about Chinese lending practices. The *New York Times* published a sensational and somewhat misleading feature on "How China Got Sri Lanka to Cough Up a Port."[8] In October 2018, Trump signed a bipartisan bill to create a new government agency, the US International Development Finance Corporation, to compete with Chinese lending in developing economies. The same month, Vice President Mike Pence condemned China's "debt diplomacy" in a major speech and specifically cited Hambantota as a paradigmatic example.[9]

The United States now assails OBOR as a predatory scheme and pressures its allies in public and private not to join.[10] In a major speech on Africa policy, National Security Advisor John Bolton spoke of OBOR's "predatory practices," which "stunt economic growth in Africa, threaten the financial independence of African nations, inhibit opportunities for US investment, interfere with US military operations, and pose a significant threat to US national security interests."[11] The 2018 National Defense Strategy accuses China several times of practicing "predatory economics."[12] Beijing is trying to build a "treasury-run empire," Secretary of State Mike Pompeo said, and "we intend to oppose them at every turn." When Italy joined OBOR in March 2019, the National Security Council tweeted, "Endorsing BRI [the alternative name for OBOR] lends legitimacy to China's predatory approach to investment and will bring no benefits to the Italian people."[13]

Washington's efforts to build an anti-OBOR coalition have been largely unsuccessful. The only other great power that has embraced the debt diplomacy line is India, which has long had a hostile relationship with China.[14] In contrast, most of America's closest allies are pointedly hedging their bets. Japan has agreed in principle to participate in OBOR, although senior officials admit privately that it may help China tighten its political grip over Southeast Asia. South Korean companies have pressured their government not to criticize OBOR, though the national security establishment fears that it will strengthen the North Korean regime.[15] France and Germany first welcomed OBOR, then grew uneasy as it expanded into Central and Eastern Europe. But they also believe that Washington's China policy is confrontational and unproductive, and they continue to allow Chinese investment in European infrastructure. The United Kingdom has expressed "support" and "enthusiasm" about OBOR for years, though it has not formally joined.[16] Russia has embraced the rhetoric and pageantry of OBOR and welcomed it into its space and energy sectors while quietly working to limit OBOR's expansion into its Central Asian backyard. The bottom line is that despite US fears, there is no organized anti-OBOR coalition or consensus. Nor is one likely to emerge any time soon—particularly if the COVID-19 epidemic leads the United States further into isolation and retrenchment.

•   •   •

Not far from the entrance to the Hambantota port, jutting out from behind the undergrowth, is a fifteen-foot half-completed concrete wall inscribed with Rajapaksa's name. On top rests a large metal globe that is already showing signs of decrepitude. Gazing up at this abandoned monument, I feel a powerful urge to understand. How did this colossal wreck come to be built? Why did China want to buy it? And what does it mean for the future of our world?

PART I

One Belt One Road

CHAPTER I

What Is OBOR?

What is One Belt One Road (OBOR)? Why are the Chinese pushing it so hard? How does it work? Where is it going? Is it true that recipient countries are pushing back? Since 2013, scholars, policymakers, investors, and journalists have debated these questions. This book draws on fresh sources and offers new answers.

The bottom line is a wake-up call for anyone concerned by China's global expansion. Current US policy is to call OBOR out publicly as a predatory exercise in debt diplomacy, while quietly pressuring allies and partners not to join. I find that this strategy is likely to fail because it misunderstands why recipient countries find OBOR so attractive. As a result, OBOR will probably continue to expand until the West either confronts it or acquiesces to it.

What can be done? In foreign policy, as in medicine, diagnosis must come before prescription. This book is not a policy paper but a scholarly work of comparative political economy and area studies for a general audience. It is a guide to the political processes at work "under the hood" of OBOR, based on field interviews on four continents and thousands of documents in Chinese and four other languages. Part I considers where OBOR comes from and how it operates inside China as a propaganda campaign and an administrative effort to marshal the country's resources behind Xi Jinping's pet project. Part II examines why seven very different countries decided to engage with OBOR and how the initiative helped China entrench its political influence in these nations. These include three very detailed project-level case studies of multibillion-dollar port cities in Sri Lanka, Tanzania, and Greece and four broader cases of Russia, Malaysia, Pakistan, and Iran in the context of their respective regions.

The mechanisms behind OBOR are not only poorly understood, they are also relevant to many different audiences—to scholars of international relations, comparative politics, security studies, and Chinese politics and political economy, and to businesspeople, investors, diplomats, policymakers, and concerned citizens. Because of the wide potential audience for this book, I have tried to make the main text as accessible and engaging as possible. Nearly all of the literature review, discussions of theory and methodology, notes on translations, specifics of project funding terms, and other details of interest to specialists can be found in the endnotes rather than in the main text. Finally, the conclusion considers the take-aways for policy.

What is OBOR? I argue that the name elides three different aspects of the same phenomenon. First and most obviously, OBOR refers to the hugely diverse set of overseas investment and construction projects that Chinese firms have undertaken since the early 2010s. Most of these projects have direct or indirect strategic value for the Chinese state. Some secure supplies of natural resources. Others vertically integrate Chinese firms into foreign consumer markets. Others are valuable because they cultivate relationships with politicians and stakeholders in countries where China does business. Yet these infrastructure projects are far less integrated into each other than has been commonly reported. In fact, I argue that the physical footprint of OBOR is less strategically important than are the political relationships that China is acquiring in the process.

OBOR is also a concept or brand for Chinese power on the global stage. By "brand," I mean a set of ideas designed to capture attention, construct ideas about identity and aspiration, and cultivate loyalty. To external audiences, OBOR is China's new national brand: one of an open, peaceful, and forward-looking country willing to undertake joint projects for mutual benefit. Foreign politicians who praise OBOR are rewarded. To domestic audiences, OBOR is a thinly veiled allusion to the imperial Chinese tributary system.[1] Chinese OBOR propaganda juxtapose Xi with Han Wudi (r. 141–79 BCE), one of China's most revered emperors, who has been reinvented in the new party history as the visionary founder of the original Silk Road. They suggest that by resurrecting a New Silk Road, Xi is the heir to this glorious imperial legacy. Just as ambassadors from tributary states once kowtowed before the Chinese emperor, foreigners today come from far and wide to the Belt and Road Forum to pay obeisance. OBOR is not just a foreign policy initiative; it is also a tool for the governance of China.

OBOR's third face is the bottom-up campaign that has emerged to sell the brand. Most of these activities are not coordinated directly by the government or party leadership. Instead, individuals, companies, and institutions—Chinese or foreign—pay lip service to Xi and the OBOR brand while pursuing projects and relationships that (mostly) advance their own interests. A wide range of projects and political schemes therefore fall under the OBOR umbrella. What unites them is a desire to reflect well on Xi and cultivate relationships with foreigners, inducing them to become more friendly to China.

This decentralized management structure explains why the Chinese Communist Party tolerates such diversity and incoherence in OBOR projects. It also means that it is very hard for foreign observers to demarcate the limits of OBOR's reach and distinguish which projects the Chinese state considers highly strategically important from those it considers peripheral. Only since 2017 has Beijing begun to discipline the OBOR campaign into a more organized and systematic national strategy. It has done this largely by putting public pressure on state banks to be more cautious and selective in picking which projects to fund.

How does an OBOR project work? The answer usually depends on what variety of Chinese capital is behind it.[2] A small share of OBOR projects are top-priority industrial policy ventures, such as Huawei's attempt to build 5G mobile telecommunications infrastructure in Western countries. These projects tend to draw disproportionate attention in the international press, enjoy high-level political backing through diplomatic channels, and get close supervision from the party leadership. At the other end of the spectrum are independent investments from people and firms who masquerade as participants in the national strategy to evade capital controls and send money overseas. In between are a wide array of traditional infrastructure projects, usually executed by state-owned enterprises (SOEs). These have presumably been approved by the National Development and Reform Commission in Beijing and are often funded by state policy banks, but they are rarely micromanaged from the top. I focus mainly on this third category. These projects are the closest to what OBOR is most commonly understood to be. They are also the largest group of projects in terms of total funds delivered, and they reveal how Chinese corporations use mundane deals to achieve political objectives.

OBOR is very attractive to political leaders in recipient countries, for two main reasons. First, most OBOR countries are inclined from the outset to partner with China.[3] Public association with China carries few short-term costs and often brings significant short-term benefits in the form of leverage against a geopolitical threat or a demanding patron state. (For Sri Lanka, this is India; for Greece, it is Germany; for Russia, it is the United States, etc.)[4] Second, OBOR projects have the effect of aligning incentives between China and the incumbent party or faction in the partner country.[5] The larger the investment, the greater the incentive to make the partnership succeed. This often entails trading favors to help ruling elites stay in power. Opposition parties and factions in recipient countries therefore have incentives to resist Chinese megaprojects and even cast China as a predatory lender. But once they come to power themselves, the political logic of OBOR begins to work in their favor. Most of the time, they quickly mend fences with Beijing.

China has become very skilled at managing these power transitions. It patiently builds reciprocal political relationships with every relevant stakeholder group in the host country, waiting out periods when the counterparty's behavior is cautious or hostile. Then, at the moment the Chinese side has the greatest leverage, it can press hard for concessions. I find that recipient countries are largely aware that China does this, and they decide to participate in OBOR anyway.

OBOR operates in a more subtle and insidious way than a traditional "public diplomacy" or "soft power" initiative.[6] OBOR refers to a particular model of bilateral diplomatic relationship, lubricated by tribute. Imperial China once used this model to govern peripheral states; Xi wants to restore it in a modern form. By signing documents to signal their acquiescence to the OBOR concept, "member states" implicitly recognize China as the senior partner. China does not demand that they shout about OBOR from the rooftops. In fact, in most of the case study countries in this book, senior officials rarely talk about OBOR per se and are relatively uninterested in how they fit into the broader OBOR scheme. In return, China supports and legitimates the government of the junior partner and initiates joint ventures to build shared economic growth.

In other words, the OBOR slogan can serve as a signal or code for China and host country politicians as they publicly negotiate how to set up a de facto patron–client relationship. Both sides maintain plausible deniability because their concrete commitments are rarely put on paper—at least not in documents released to the public.

Where is OBOR going? If this analysis is correct, it will keep expanding. If there can be a "Silk Road for Health" [健康丝绸之路], a "Silk Road on Ice" [冰上丝绸之路], and a "Silk Road Corridor for Information and Outer Space" [一带一路空间信息走廊], there can be a Silk Road-branded program for just about anything. Within China, the party-state system is united in support of OBOR and the cost of dissent is higher than ever. In recipient countries, the logic for participating is stronger than ever. In the words of Italian Foreign Minister Luigi di Maio, the same week that deaths from COVID-19 peaked in his embattled country: "Those who scoffed at our participation in the Belt and Road Initiative now have to admit that investing in that friendship allowed us to save lives in Italy." In a post-COVID world, the United States may well have lost the ability to contain OBOR's advance, let alone to roll it back.

The Conceptual Challenge

Western scholars and national security professionals have proposed competing explanations of the strategic logic behind OBOR. Some agree with Donald Trump's administration's view that OBOR is a predatory debt diplomacy scheme.[7] Some call it a "grand strategy for Eurasia" that works by linking China with its continental periphery.[8] Some contend that OBOR is a policy vehicle for a more gradualist Chinese grand strategy: establish a presence in every region of the world, convert trading relationships into political partnerships, and eventually become an all-around patron state for friendly countries, serving as the main source of financing, technology, high-end products, and security.[9] Others believe that OBOR is an excuse for China to export its excess labor and construction materials, a subsidy to postpone painful economic reforms in its industrial northeast.[10] Some argue that whatever OBOR's goals, China's infrastructure finance model is a rotten deal for recipient countries, and a global anti-China backlash is inevitable.[11] The main problem with this debate is that few of these motivations are mutually exclusive, and none of the arguments are easy to disprove using publicly available data.

Many commentaries treat OBOR as a blueprint for an emerging international system in which China will play a leading role. Does China want this system to be multilateral, or does OBOR mark the return of a bipolar order in which China and the United States carve out spheres of influence?[12] Does OBOR's success mean that Chinese norms and values will be central to this emerging order?[13] If China can woo US allies with trade and investment, are we entering a world in which America's traditional tools of power projection—security treaties, international institutions, and soft exports like popular culture and democratic ideals—aren't as effective as they used to be?[14] These questions about world order are speculative and hard to answer conclusively. This book does not discuss them directly, although my empirical findings shed some light.

Above all, it is premature to ask these questions while so many of the reports about the basic characteristics of OBOR are either unsubstantiated, misleading, or plainly false. Consider, among other examples, the debate about OBOR's "promised" or "ultimate" size. In the space of a single week in 2017, *The Guardian* wrote that OBOR was worth $900 billion.[15] The *New York Times* reported that it "promises more than $1 trillion."[16] NBC News put the figure at $1.4 trillion.[17] The *South China Morning Post* claimed that it "is expected to require at least $5 trillion in the next five years," and "$2.5 trillion over the next decade" in Asia alone.[18] *Bloomberg* wrote that "estimates of future spending" were "between $4 trillion and $8 trillion."[19] None of these wildly inconsistent figures come from authoritative Chinese sources, but they continue to dominate discussion of OBOR to the highest levels of government. In 2018, when the US-China Economic and Security Review Commission held a hearing on OBOR, one expert witness testified that the program "could include Chinese investments approaching $4 trillion," citing an article in *The Economist*.[20] Notably, the Chinese government has not corrected the record as Western outlets report these figures. Because China is always quick to respond when foreign reports criticize OBOR, it is hard not to read this silence as a deliberate choice—to allow the foreigners to convince themselves that China has bottomless pockets.

Even more misleading are the reports about how much money China has already spent on OBOR. In his speech at the 2019 Belt and Road Forum, China's central bank chairman, Yi Gang, boasted that Chinese financial institutions have provided $440 billion to OBOR projects.[21] Two days later, *Xinhua*, the party mouthpiece, wrote that "China's investment in B&R countries" between 2013 and 2018 "exceeds 90 billion dollars."[22] As of this writing, the American Enterprise Institute's China Global Investment Tracker database calculates $690 billion in Chinese "investments and contracts" in the OBOR framework.[23]

What is interesting here is not the wild variation in headline figures but the fact that the figures are derived from unstated criteria that implicitly define OBOR in specific ways. Should we count funds pledged and disbursed for projects that were already under way when Xi announced the initiative in 2013? Should we count only certain sectors, such as infrastructure construction and heavy industry, or cast a wider net, counting investments in real estate, finance, or technology that have no clear relation to the Silk Road metaphor? What exactly qualifies a country as an OBOR member or partner, such that Chinese investments there should count toward the headline total? Must OBOR projects necessarily be funded by loans from Chinese state-owned policy banks? How can we know whether China actually disbursed all of the promised funds? (Frequently, we cannot.) Tweaking the selection criteria leads to dramatically different conclusions. Appendix B summarizes the criteria and methodological approach that the leading databases of Chinese investment have applied to data collection and shows how this produces very different data sets.

My point is not that OBOR's size is irrelevant but that it is such a slippery concept that headline figures tend to obscure more than they illuminate. Many studies refer to OBOR interchangeably with Chinese foreign policy or foreign investment as a whole.[24] Others aspire after an artificial and illusory precision but do not acknowledge the numerous assumptions inherent in the data collection process. These are conceptual mistakes. OBOR's geographic and financial scope is so vast, its strategic mandate so flexible, and its timeline for implementation so vague that it is hard to assess it separately from China's overall grand strategy. Before any serious discussion of OBOR's strategic implications—let alone what policies are necessary to respond to it—two things must be established. The first is a robust definition of what OBOR actually is, from China's perspective. The second is a working conceptual model to relate the grand strategic and regional levels of analysis to the technical details of individual projects and national contexts. Otherwise, we risk falling into circular logic, projecting onto OBOR whatever we already believe about China.

Three More Common Myths

Before moving on to a discussion of methodology and an outline of the book, three other misconceptions about OBOR need to be addressed. The first is that OBOR is a Chinese scheme designed to trick or coerce recipient countries into debt traps. The second is related: that China has complete control over the implementation of every OBOR project over the course of its life cycle, so the strategic rationale is the main puzzle to be explained. The third is that recipient countries are finally realizing the danger OBOR poses and have begun to pull back. The chapters that follow respond to these arguments in more detail, but it is worth briefly summarizing the key points here.

In a narrow sense, Chinese lending is indeed correlated with debt distress in recipient countries. Sebastian Horn, Carmen Reinhart, and Christoph Trebesch estimate that the world should have seen fifteen to twenty more sovereign defaults between 2011 and 2019, mostly in countries that have borrowed large amounts from China.[25] They hypothesize that China frequently conducts secret debt renegotiations. Luca Bandiera and Vasileios Tsiropoulos of the World Bank propose another model that predicts that OBOR projects will exacerbate medium-term debt sustainability problems in twelve of the forty-three low- and middle-income countries they examine.[26] In Washington, these studies have been read as confirmations of the debt trap narrative.

Yet a closer reading of these studies suggests the opposite conclusion: that China is a relatively accommodating creditor. John Hurley concludes that it "is unlikely that [OBOR] will be plagued with widescale debt sustainability problems," although individual debt restructurings will probably be necessary, particularly in countries that were already carrying unsustainable debt burdens.[27] Agatha Kratz argues that many OBOR recipient countries face debt distress and renegotiate contracts. But China rarely seizes assets. It prefers to refinance lending terms at lower rates and longer durations. Kratz concludes that "despite its economic weight, China's leverage in negotiations is limited."[28] Why has China agreed to renegotiate debt burdens in secret? Perhaps it is willing to offer a premium to avoid sparking news stories that harm its reputation.[29] Chinese officials from Xi on down have also made clear that they do not want to see money wasted on poorly conceived projects. In 2017, Chinese central government regulators ordered the major state policy banks to take more care to fund only creditworthy projects. This was before the Trump administration began to tout the debt trap narrative.

Much of the commentary on the OBOR debt trap also makes the unspoken assumption that projects play out according to China's predetermined plans. This assumption makes little theoretical sense and is not borne out by the facts on the ground. As the case studies in this book clearly show, OBOR projects nearly always face hiccups and political challenges on the path to completion. Recipient countries almost always have the power to press pause, renegotiate, and cancel projects midstream. Yet the academic and policy literature on OBOR pays little attention to the perspective of recipient countries, let alone the subnational stakeholders such as labor unions, local governments, and opposition parties that often make trouble for China after it has sunk large amounts of capital into a project. It is therefore a conceptual error to understand OBOR as a seamless Chinese master plan or as a theater of power competition in which the United States and China are the only two players that matter.[30]

A third popular and seductive narrative is that a recipient country backlash is forming against OBOR. English-language newspapers and think tanks have produced hundreds of articles suggesting that recipient countries are turning away after realizing that partnering with China is not in their interests after all.[31] But the backlash thesis is misleading—it focuses on headlines while ignoring underlying dynamics. Since 2013, over a dozen countries have publicly renegotiated commercial megadeals with China. This book considers five of these cases in great detail: Sri Lanka, Tanzania, Greece, Malaysia, and Pakistan. In each case, local politicians made prominent public stands against OBOR, often with sensational rhetoric, and stalled the implementation of the underlying project. All of these were eventually revealed to be temporary negotiating tactics. In each case, the strategic direction was toward closer partnership with China. Senior officials and stakeholders in these countries almost uniformly express pro-China views and categorically deny that China is pursuing a debt-trap strategy. With the possible exception of Tanzania, each country is more closely aligned with China today than when OBOR was first announced.

Multiplayer Games

To understand OBOR's international effects, we must start to look at it as a global process of realignment toward China, driven largely by countries with economies that are relatively small. This is why the case studies here are narrated almost entirely from the perspective of recipient countries. Top-level officials in these countries are usually far more concerned with short-term local and regional problems than with long-term geopolitical themes. They are constrained—by political opposition, their own patronage networks, economic and financial considerations, civil society, and so forth—in what they can offer China.

Each case begins with a historical review of the relevant country's domestic politics, regional rivalries, and diplomatic and trading relationships with China. It traces the arc of the port project from the perspective of the key decisionmaker (usually the prime minister). To show how other major groups of stakeholders try to influence the project negotiation and rollout, each case draws on interviews with opposition politicians, military officers, union leaders, academics, civil servants, businesspeople, and local residents, as well as official documents and press reports in the local languages. At times, the case study format requires introducing some rather technical points about project and financing terms. This is not because I relish overloading the reader with detail, but because some contractual points are relevant for understanding the playbook China follows when its projects encounter resistance. Together, these sources make it possible to reconstruct why both sides negotiate the way they do, what potential outcomes are considered, and how projects tend to fall into path-dependent arcs.[32]

I selected the three main case studies—Sri Lanka, Tanzania, and Greece—because their original features are similar.[33] All three are ports and adjacent special economic zones along the Maritime Silk Road, on the order of $1 to $10 billion in size. All three were originally proposed by the local recipient government, initiated by a Chinese SOE with explicit political backing from Chinese government officials, and launched before Xi formally announced OBOR in September 2013. In all three, a transition of power occurred in the middle of the negotiation or construction. Thereafter, the new government tried to renegotiate and change the course of the project, creating a temporary diplomatic rupture. All three were rebranded midway through as part of the OBOR scheme. Yet the cases reached very different end-states. Sri Lanka's port ultimately went ahead as planned and became an infamous commercial failure. Tanzania's was put on hold and canceled in all but name. Greece's became a towering commercial success—and China now touts it as a model OBOR project. The project outcomes could not have been more different—yet the OBOR brand helped Chinese interests prevail in all three countries.

What is it like to be a recipient country politician negotiating with China over the life cycle of an OBOR project? This thought experiment illuminates the real political drivers behind OBOR's global expansion. China is undoubtedly adept at playing other countries' political parties and factions off of each other and leveraging its national power as it negotiates. Yet the debt diplomacy argument would suggest that recipient countries will pull away from China as soon as they recognize Beijing's malign objectives. In reality, most developing countries in Asia, Africa, and now Latin America have jumped at the chance to join OBOR and accept Chinese construction projects—not because they systematically underestimate the dangers of debt traps or harbor illusions about China's intentions, but because it is in their leaders' interest to do so. China has mastered the art of helping foreign politicians address their most pressing short-term interests: to deliver economic growth, win popular support, and gain leverage over domestic rivals, neighboring countries, international institutions, and the United States. The cases show how Xi's China is learning to assert itself as a global superpower. They also reveal OBOR to be a story about how countries with smaller or weaker economies are trying to exploit this new reality—with mixed results.

Outline of the Book

This book is divided into two parts. Part I examines OBOR from the Chinese perspective. Chapter 2 traces the OBOR concept back to long before Xi took power and examines why he later falsely claimed to have conceived of the idea himself. Chapter 3 investigates how Chinese Communist Party propaganda materials present OBOR to the public, rewriting history to juxtapose Xi with Han Wudi. Chapter 4 looks at how various Chinese and foreign actors engage with OBOR in uncoordinated and often self-serving ways and how this bottom-up implementation strategy strengthens Xi domestically and internationally.

Part II examines OBOR from the perspective of recipient countries. Three chapters are devoted to the main case studies. Chapter 5 considers Sri Lanka, which went deep into debt to build a port at Hambantota and later sold its stake back to China on a ninety-nine-year lease. Chapter 6 investigates a strikingly similar port city planned for the Tanzanian town of Bagamoyo, which was frozen at the last minute after voters elected an OBOR-skeptic president. Chapter 7 examines the complex case of Greece, the supposed terminus of the Maritime Silk Road, where the Athenian port of Piraeus became an improbable commercial success after a Chinese company took over. Chapter 8 steps back from the granular focus of the case studies and considers four more snapshot cases—Russia, Malaysia, Pakistan, and Iran. From the vantage point of these countries, I consider how OBOR is helping China extend its regional influence in Central Asia, Southeast Asia, South Asia, and the Middle East.

In the conclusion, I argue that OBOR poses a profound threat to US global leadership. Not because most of its constituent projects are security threats (they aren't) but because it represents a working model for a future geopolitical bloc led by China, structured along the lines of a modern tributary system. It is a challenge to which the Western world does not yet have an answer.

CHAPTER 2

Origins

OBOR's Many Fathers

At 10:30 am on September 7, 2013, Chinese President Xi Jinping strode into a lecture hall at Nazarbayev University in Kazakhstan to accept an honorary degree and deliver planned remarks. He spoke first of the long history of friendship between China and Kazakhstan. During the Western Han dynasty, in the second century BCE, imperial envoy Zhang Qian traveled to central Asia twice to establish "friendly contacts" with the kingdoms there. In that spirit, Xi claimed, emerged the Silk Road, a route of trade and cultural exchange that symbolized the friendly ties between China and Inner Asia. "I can almost hear the ring of the camel bells," he said, "and the wisps of smoke in the desert." In closing, Xi announced the creation of a "New Silk Road" or "Silk Road Economic Belt," a sweeping initiative to bind China and Central Asia together via transportation infrastructure, trade, and transcultural "communication."[1] In short, Xi was promising to build a trans-Eurasian network to connect the continent with roads, bridges, airports, pipelines, and trade corridors.

Xi clearly wanted the credit for this New Silk Road concept, and official government communications gave it to him. Xi has stated on numerous occasions that "I proposed [提出] the Belt and Road initiative."[2] Foreign Minister Wang Yi and other senior officials frequently say that "Xi proposed" OBOR. According to the Frequently Asked Questions page on OBOR's official website, "The Belt and Road . . . is a development strategy and framework, *proposed by Chinese President Xi Jinping* that focuses on connectivity and cooperation among countries primarily between China and the rest of Eurasia."[3] Inside China, scholars and government officials understand that Xi's personal involvement is a highly sensitive and important part of OBOR's branding. Every Chinese expert I have spoken with on the record insists that the OBOR concept was entirely of Xi's devising.

Xi's attempt to personalize OBOR was an early indication that he intended to wield power more assertively than his predecessors. Chinese leaders often introduce theoretical concepts in major speeches. In 2002, Chinese President Jiang Zemin spoke of the "three represents" (三个代表): the theory that the Chinese Communist Party must stand for economic growth, cultural development, and the fundamental interest of the majority of citizens.[4] Xi's predecessor, Hu Jintao, promised in 2005 to achieve a "harmonious society" through the "scientific development concept." Like Jiang and Hu, Xi leaned heavily on the advice of Wang Huning, the Communist Party's propaganda chief.[5] Wang was present for Xi's speech in Kazakhstan in 2013. Xi later appointed Wang to serve on the Leading Small Group in charge of supervising OBOR at the highest level. The main difference is that Jiang and Hu attributed their "three represents" and "scientific development" concepts to the party's collective wisdom, whereas Xi claimed OBOR as his own.[6] Xi's concept was more sweeping than his predecessors—it was a bold and open-ended international commitment, not a guideline for internal party governance—and it came within his first year in office. Xi was not just breaching precedent; he was deliberately flaunting the old norm of collective leadership. The subtext of his speech was that power in China now rested in the hands of a single man: himself.

But the New Silk Road strategy was not Xi's idea; in fact, it was not even a Chinese idea. The first country to introduce the New Silk Road to the diplomatic lexicon was the small Central Asian republic of Kyrgyzstan in 1998. Soon after that, the Chinese foreign ministry coopted the phrase. For more than a decade thereafter, the New Silk Road was a contested and flexible slogan in inter-Asian diplomacy and within the Chinese party-state. In the wake of the global financial crisis of 2008, the New Silk Road was one of several potential slogans that Chinese scholars, policymakers, and bureaucratic agencies considered to describe the process of China's internationalization. They considered and rejected an alternative proposal to frame China's overseas investments as part of a Chinese Marshall Plan.

These contextual facts fundamentally challenge the official Chinese explanation of what OBOR really "is." If Xi's goal in announcing the initiative was to reassure the rest of the world that China's intentions were benign, surely the Chinese Marshall Plan would have been a better slogan. So why did Xi choose the New Silk Road concept over the alternatives? In the years since, why has Xi been so keen to take personal credit for the OBOR concept, even though there is publicly available evidence that the concept was well fleshed out before he took power? What can this tell us about the strategic objectives that presumably underlie the whole scheme? The only way to answer these critical questions about the definition and scope of the initiative is to start the clock earlier: decades before Xi's 2013 speech.

This historical view reveals that OBOR has distinct symbolic and substantive dimensions—indeed, it came together as a collision of a slogan and a policy in search of one another. Symbolically, the initiative that Xi hails as the "project of the century" is broadly consistent with China's diplomatic slogans and theoretical frameworks from the late 1990s and early 2000s. The New Silk Road concept came to the forefront of Chinese diplomacy after the global financial crisis of 2008. As the Western financial system stood on the brink of collapse, influential Chinese scholars held a wide-ranging public debate about what role China should aspire to play on the international stage and how to communicate its intentions to domestic and foreign audiences. A historical review of this debate shows that Xi was much more concerned about the domestic audience than the foreign one.

The fanfare surrounding Xi's announcement also disguised the fact that on a substantive level, Chinese infrastructure projects on the ground did not change much after 2013. Hundreds of infrastructure projects that were later rebranded as flagship OBOR projects were already under way. The New Silk Road remained a nebulous, contested, semi-official catchphrase until as recently as 2015. Xi did not take to the stage in Kazakhstan to announce the launch of an organized policy or a coherent strategic vision. He was announcing a plan to call attention to China's ongoing cross-border investments, bring them under a political framework that he controlled, and take credit for both.

Connecting Central Asia

For as long as scholars have written of the historical Silk Road, politicians and economic planners have speculated about rebuilding it.[7] Often, these scholars have been in service to the politicians. The term *die Seidenstrassen*, or "silk roads," was coined in 1877 by geographer and archaeologist Ferdinand von Richthofen, who produced cartographic surveys and planning documents for the German government. "Little doubt can exist," Richthofen wrote in 1869, "that eventually, China will be connected with Europe by rail."[8] As Tamara Chin has brilliantly shown, Richthofen did not conceive of the Silk Road as a historically significant nexus of economic exchange. Nor did he see it as a proud achievement of Chinese culture, for which he had little respect. When Germany seized the Chinese territory of Qingdao in 1897, Richthofen approvingly summed up Berlin's relation to the colonized Chinese as "the relation between a master and his dog." Richthofen continued to advocate for a transcontinental railway line to resurrect the supposed ancient trade routes, but the German government did not act on his advice.[9]

The contemporary notion of the Silk Road entered common discourse between the 1920s and 1940s, thanks to the efforts of Richthofen's student Sven Hedin.[10] With backing from Lufthansa and the governments of Nazi Germany, Sweden, and China, Hedin conducted further cartographic studies in Central Asia in 1933 and 1934 and advocated for transcontinental highway and airline routes. He invoked a creative and inaccurate historical narrative to persuade the Chinese government in Nanjing to adopt his Plan for the Revival of the Silk Road. This included, among other things, a massive highway into Central Asia. Hedin's 1938 book *The Silk Road* claimed that the ancient Silk Road began in 138 BCE when "the great Emperor" (Han Wudi) sent an emissary (Zhang Qian) to the Western regions.[11] This claim had no factual basis in Chinese historiography. When Chinese papers first reported on Hedin's proposal, they called it the "so-called Silk Road" (所谓丝路) to express their skepticism. But the concept stuck. In the decades after the communist victory in the Chinese civil war, the party mouthpiece, *People's Daily*, periodically referred to the Silk Road (丝绸之路) to refer to relations with Afghanistan, Pakistan, and Iran. In 1971, the *People's Daily* traced the origins of the Silk Road to Han Wudi, just as Hedin had done.[12] As we will see in chapter 3, Hedin's origin myth for the ancient Silk Road has become the foundation of OBOR propaganda today.

Central Asian states introduced the term "New Silk Road" in the early 1990s to describe their desire for a harmonious regional order. In the nineteenth century, Britain and Russia had competed in a great game for hegemony in Central Asia. Following the collapse of the Soviet Union in 1991, every country in the region had an interest in managing the dangerous power vacuum and preventing history from repeating itself. The weaker post-Soviet states were particularly keen on setting up overlapping multilateral institutions that could set norms of regional governance. In October 1992, Kazakh President Nursultan Nazarbayev proposed the Conference on Interaction and Confidence-Building Measures in Asia. The group's stated purpose was to establish a joint security agreement between China, Russia, and the other post-Soviet states on the principle of mutual noninterference. The same year, seven Central Asian states (Afghanistan, Azerbaijan, Kazakhstan, Kyrgyzstan, Tajikistan, Turkmenistan, and Uzbekistan) applied to join the Economic Cooperation Organization, which had accomplished little after it was first founded in 1985. Among this alphabet soup of fledgling groupings, the most successful was the Shanghai Cooperation Organization (SCO), inaugurated in 2001.

The SCO became the most important regional grouping because it included China, a rapidly growing and increasingly assertive regional power. In the mid-1990s, China began to prosecute its long-standing territorial claims in Central Asia.[13] Kyrgyzstan was particularly wary of China's intentions. Beijing used military aid, transportation infrastructure, and trade deals—whatever it took to secure rights to land and water.[14] In a secret 1999 agreement, the Kyrgyz government agreed to trade approximately 340 square miles of sparsely populated glacial terrain in the Naryn and Issyk-Kul provinces to China. A prominent Kyrgyzstani politician who criticized the move was arrested, leading hundreds of protesters to launch hunger strikes in January 2002. These ultimately led to riots that toppled the government. For most Central Asian member states, the purpose of forming the SCO was to preserve regional stability by constraining China's potentially expansionist tendencies.[15]

Central Asian diplomats argued that the historic Silk Road could be a model for peacefully engaging China in multilateral cooperation. In November 1998, Ishenbay Abdurazakov, the state secretary of Kyrgyzstan, introduced the New Silk Road concept in a speech to students at Johns Hopkins University. "In our memory, the Silk Road has a symbolic meaning," he declared. "It has, throughout several thousand years, played a role not only as a commercial path, but it has also played a role as a connecting bridge between people and civilizations."[16] After the talk, Abdurazakov distributed copies of a booklet by Kyrgyz President Askar Akayev titled "The Diplomacy of the Silk Road." The pamphlet, which was published in English the following year, formalized many of the principles that China later ascribed to OBOR: a call for strengthening regional institutions and an emphasis on mutual noninterference and peaceful conflict resolution. "Our country is deeply convinced that along the entire length of the modern-day Great Silk Road, no serious problems or contradictions of an antagonistic nature are to be found between the countries falling within its orbit," Akayev wrote, gushingly. The pamphlet made for an ironic counterpoint to Xi's claims of authorship two decades later. The New Silk Road was not originally a Chinese idea but a rhetorical ploy from China's neighbors to enmesh it in international institutions and contain Beijing's potential for territorial revanchism.

In the early 2000s, China began to take an interest in Central Asian transport infrastructure. This was a time of deep, ambitious, and painful economic reform. Premier Zhu Rongji had recently authorized the layoffs of tens of millions of workers from inefficient state-owned enterprises (SOEs) ravaged by the 1997 Asian financial crisis. Before the private sector could absorb them, China had to make even more reforms before it could join the World Trade Organization in 2001. Western countries were ramping up pressure on Beijing to abandon its currency manipulation policies, and China's economic planners realized that the country might have to plan to spend some of its foreign currency assets. Against this backdrop, the State Council announced a policy of "Going Out" (走出去) in 1999.[17] SOEs were instructed to invest abroad. Zhu, an economic reformer, hoped they could secure their own supplies of raw materials and acquire new technologies to compete on the global market.

The "Continental Bridge"

Because Central Asia was an obvious investment destination for Chinese SOEs, Chinese policymakers appropriated the Silk Road concept to show that the policy could be mutually beneficial. According to a report of a meeting with Turkmenistan President Saparmurat Niyazov on November 17, 2000, Chinese President Jiang Zemin promised, "We are willing to strengthen cooperation with the Central Asian countries in the field of transport, give full play to the unique advantage of the 'Eurasian Continental Bridge' and transnational road transport cooperation, establish a sound cooperation mechanism, and work together to revive the modern 'Silk Road.'"[18] In 2004, according to Wei Jianguo, the vice minister of Commerce, the Continental Bridge initiative was written into Beijing's development strategy for its western provinces. In September of that year, *China Daily* wrote about progress toward the Eurasian Continental Bridge. The accompanying map of the "New Silk Road" curiously left out nonparticipating South and East Asian countries (fig. 2.1).

The purpose of China's new Eurasian Continental Bridge was to bring raw materials to the Chinese market. China saw Central Asia as a breadbasket of natural resources, with Kazakhstan the biggest prize: oil and gas in abundance, the world's second-largest reserves of uranium and zinc, and vast deposits of chromium, copper, and manganese. The other Central Asian republics are rich in other resources, particularly water and timber.[19] China's imports from Kazakhstan increased by a factor of fifteen between 2000 and 2010. Bilateral trade in fuel products increased even faster, rising from 13 percent of China's total imports from Kazakhstan to 52 percent in less than a decade.[20] From the perspective of China's national interests in securing supplies of raw materials, the Going Out strategy succeeded spectacularly.

But the Continental Bridge was not, as Chinese statesmen claimed on their trips abroad, a serious plan to build a large-scale overland rail link to Europe. Oceanic shipping remained a far more economical alternative. China invested minimal resources in building the promised rail transit corridor.[21] Almost seven years after the announcement of the Continental Bridge, Dutch and Chinese officials celebrated a single cargo train traveling the distance from Antwerp to Chongqing.[22] Meanwhile,

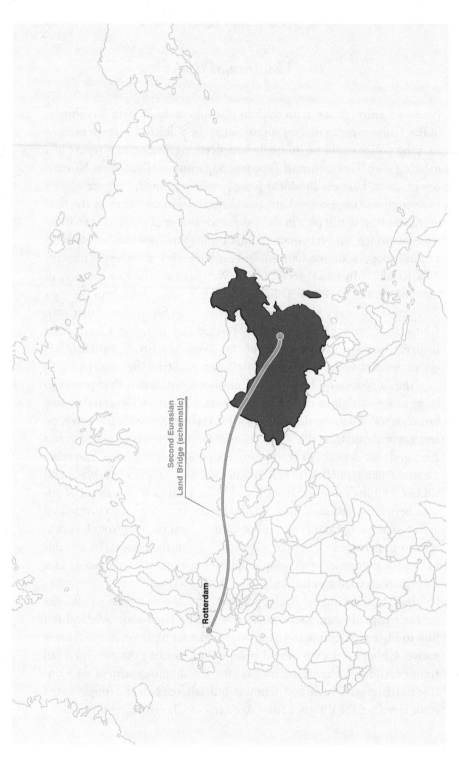

FIGURE 2.1: The "China–Europe Land Bridge." Based on a map originally appearing in *China Daily* on February 2, 2004. Courtesy of Ira Anatolevna.

Second Eurasian
Land Bridge (schematic)

Rotterdam

Chinese SOEs were dramatically increasing their holdings in the global container shipping industry. The percentage of total global container traffic passing through Chinese-owned or -invested ports increased from 19 percent in 2000 to 42 percent in 2010 and to 67 percent in 2015.[23] This was a pattern that China repeated after Xi announced OBOR in Kazakhstan in 2013. As we will find in the Russia case in chapter 8, China still has made few serious steps to rebuild any ancient overland routes to Europe.

As the Continental Bridge and New Silk Road concepts attracted more press toward the end of 2004, other Chinese government agencies began to appropriate the slogan. Looking closely at official documents, one can clearly see that this was a bottom-up phenomenon. Bureaucrats used the phrase of their own accord, probably not entirely clear on what it meant, in the hope of winning funding and central government approval.

A good example is an editorial written in August 2004 by Yang Guoqing, deputy general director of the Civil Aviation Administration. Yang wanted to liberalize commercial air transport between western China and Central Asian countries, so he called it the "Asia-Europe Continental Bridge." He also called for the establishment of a "Eurasian Continental Bridge regional economic cooperation air transport seminar discussion mechanism," which probably would have brought new funding to his agency if it had been approved.[24] Between September 5 and 7, 2007, Yang convened his counterparts from eight Central European countries in Ürümqi to "discuss the creation of a New Silk Road in the sky" (空中新丝路).[25] Yang was unsuccessful. The New Silk Road in the Sky was not mentioned again for several years—probably because the People's Liberation Army Air Force asserted its authority over the nation's airspace.[26] Still, Yang's conference illustrates the point nicely: the New Silk Road concept was nebulous and was probably used more frequently by enterprising bureaucrats in peripheral agencies than at the highest levels of the party-state in Beijing. After all, the New Silk Road slogan did not refer to any actual policy. Its function was to echo the rhetoric of senior leaders and thereby imply that one's preferred policy carried an official imprimatur.

Encountering Resistance

Meanwhile, China struggled to articulate its investment-based diplomatic model outside Central Asia. Under Jiang's successor, Hu Jintao, China became the world's largest importer of copper, iron, and most nonferrous metals. Many of these resources were sourced from Africa, which saw its trade with China increase at a compound annual rate higher than 30 percent between 2000 and 2010.[27] But the Hu administration's experimental attempts to tie these new economic relationships to politics and ideology came off as flat-footed at best. In a speech in Addis Ababa in December 2003, Premier Wen Jiabao spoke of his affection for "brotherly African nations."[28] "China-Africa friendship and cooperation under new historical conditions," he said, could become a "paragon of South-South cooperation," except that "hegemonism is raising its ugly head." Hu was echoing the rhetoric of the 1955 Bandung Conference to suggest that an increasingly dominant China would again take the lead in the Third World. The language of China and Africa as brothers also alluded to Mao's "Three Worlds theory," which suggested that China was the leader (and Africa a follower) in a struggle to find a third way between the United States and the Soviet Union.

But China's Cold War pitch to the developing world had lost its salience. Hu was no Mao, waving a little red book and riling up the crowd. He was a technocrat so awkward and cautious that he famously used cue cards in meetings. China was no longer the country of the Cultural Revolution, bent on exporting its ideology to the world. On the contrary, as far as economic relations went, China increasingly resembled a Western country, pursuing its national interests through unapologetically transactional deals. As Deborah Bräutigam showed in her landmark 2009 study *The Dragon's Gift*, in nearly every Chinese-funded infrastructure project in Africa, some Chinese firm was a clear beneficiary.[29] Just like Central Asia, the main strategic goal of Chinese projects was more often than not to bring raw materials to market.

A growing number of infrastructure projects that Hu announced in his travels across Asia were also confronting grassroots opposition. Projects were hitting roadblocks even in authoritarian countries where China and the local government were equally invested in moving forward. For example, a scheme to construct a $28 billion, eighty-four-mile Kra Canal through Thailand has been under discussion since 2005, if not earlier. If it is ever completed, the canal would represent a huge geopolitical achievement for China by providing an alternative to shipping goods through a narrow chokepoint in Malacca. But opposition by local residents led the Thai government to stonewall. It now seems unlikely that the project will go through.[30] In other cases, local residents resisted projects because they perceived the terms to be too one-sided. For example, the government of Myanmar approved the Myitsone Dam project in 2007 and authorized the relocation of thousands of local residents. Under the scheme, the state-owned China Power Investment would build and operate seven dams for fifty years, exporting over 90 percent of the electricity across the border to China. In defiance of harsh pressure from the government of Myanmar, local residents protested their impending evictions. The dam became a national issue in Myanmar, and discussions with China Power Investment ground to a halt. Four years later, the prodemocracy activist and future president Aung San Suu Kyi announced her opposition, and the proposal was scrapped for good.[31] The Myanmar government has still not released the original contract.

Under Hu, China's overseas investment schemes began to encounter pushback abroad. China's acute need for raw materials justified a growing commercial presence in source countries. But China lacked a foreign policy doctrine that could explicitly link these economic commitments to structured political relationships. And then the financial crisis came, and China saw an opportunity.

Financial Crisis or Opportunity?

The global financial crisis marked a turning point in Chinese economic policy. On November 9, 2008, the State Council announced a $586 billion stimulus package. Of these funds, 38 percent were earmarked for domestic infrastructure, including the equivalent of $50 billion for rail construction in 2009 alone.[32] Beijing tried to invest its way out of the crisis by relaxing restrictions on borrowing by provincial and local governments. Infrastructure spending accomplished several domestic policy goals simultaneously. It kept the government from having to lay off workers in the bloated industrial materials sector, created new construction jobs, and expanded transportation links to its poorer interior and western provinces. The plan worked. As the world's developed economies fell into recession, China's gross domestic product grew an astonishing 8.7 percent in 2009 and 10.3 percent in 2010.

After 2008, Chinese policymakers began to ask whether the country's banks could export this investment-based stimulus model abroad. Two issues received particular attention. First, if China were to make an overt play for global economic leadership, how would the United States respond? Second, might overseas investments lead China to overextend itself strategically, just as the Soviet Union had done? The need for a new strategic concept to guide growing overseas interests had already been established. The main question now was what kind of international commercial power China wanted to be. How should Beijing justify to domestic audiences the need to spend enormous amounts of capital overseas? How should Beijing help Chinese firms deal with political disruptions to their overseas investments? How should China prepare for the possibility that the United States would respond defensively? By contrast, there was no discussion about how to articulate a friendly version of Chinese soft power for Western audiences. Their approval or disapproval was not seen as a major concern.

The need for a new national strategy became even clearer in 2011, when Chinese elites were swept with sudden fear that the Barack Obama administration planned to adopt a "containment" strategy against China. In a speech in Chennai in July 2011, Secretary of State Hillary Clinton proposed that the United States lead its own effort to build a New Silk Road:

> Let's work together to create a new Silk Road. Not a single thoroughfare like its namesake, but an international web and network of economic and transit connections. That means building more rail lines, highways, energy infrastructure, like the proposed pipeline to run from Turkmenistan, through Afghanistan, through Pakistan into India. It means upgrading the facilities at border crossings, such as India and Pakistan are now doing at Waga. And it certainly means removing the bureaucratic barriers and other

impediments to the free flow of goods and people. It means casting aside the outdated trade policies that we all still are living with and adopting new rules for the 21st century.[33]

Clinton expanded on her vision two months later at a New Silk Road ministerial meeting in New York:

> For centuries, the nations of South and Central Asia were connected to each other and the rest of the continent by a sprawling trading network called the Silk Road. Afghanistan's bustling markets sat at the heart of this network. Afghan merchants traded their goods from the court of the Pharaohs to the Great Wall of China. . . . As we look to the future of this region, let's take this precedent as inspiration for a long-term vision for Afghanistan and its neighbors.[34]

The Americans convened another meeting in November to pressure their allies to sign on. Clinton raised the issue in meetings that autumn with the leaders of Pakistan, Tajikistan, and Uzbekistan. It seemed that the United States was turning its attention from the Middle East to China's neighborhood, and it saw trade and investment as the keys to strategic success.

The Chinese did not realize that Clinton's proposal was not serious. As Shen Weizhong of the Ministry of Foreign Affairs told an audience in Budapest in 2014, "When [the] United States initiated [the New Silk Road plan], we were devastated. We had long sleepless nights."[35] In reality, even the State Department's bureaucrats considered the New Silk Road scheme to be half-baked and unrealistic.[36] The newly elected Republican Congress had no interest in funding it. The Obama administration's "pivot to Asia" strategy, which Clinton announced in an essay in *Foreign Policy* magazine later that year, proved to be equally lacking in substance.[37] From a Chinese perspective, however, the United States was demonstrating the desire—if not yet the means—to encircle China strategically by courting its neighbors and major trading partners. China needed a new national concept for foreign trade and investment more urgently than ever before. This was a key issue in the policy debates leading up to the Eighteenth Party Congress in November 2012.

"China's Marshall Plan"

Weeks before the Party Congress, influential Peking University economist Justin Yifu Lin published an editorial titled "Promote Global Economic Recovery through the 'New Marshall Plan'" (新马歇尔计划):

> Changes in the international economic sectors are accelerating. Developed countries will fall into a relatively long period of economic weakness. If developing countries can take full advantage of their potential to avoid the shortcomings of their own systems, then their economic weight in the world will increase rapidly. . . . In view of this, I put forward the "New Marshall Plan" in order to provide developed countries a chance to carry out their own structural reforms. That is: increase the export demand of developed countries through investments in global infrastructure. This kind of investment will lead to a win-win situation. Developed countries can take this opportunity to carry out structural reforms and escape financial crisis, while developing countries can eliminate their infrastructure bottlenecks and gain opportunities for faster development. Given that the developed countries still have the power of reserve currency and monetary stimulus, it is better for them to increase employment by printing money and investing in global infrastructure construction than to print a large amount of money and buy government bonds in the hope of stimulating consumer demand.[38]

Although Lin spoke in jingoistic terms about the virtue of the Chinese economic model, the subtext was more restrained. His argument hinted at a real fear that the global economic crisis had permanently dampened consumer demand in developed economies. If he was right, China's export-dependent economy was in deep trouble. Yet Lin also implied that it would be a mistake for China to respond to economic weakness in the West by brashly claiming the mantle of global leadership. Rather, the best platform for proposing the Chinese Marshall Plan to other countries would be the G20. China should channel its funds through the World Bank, not its own financial institutions. Lin argued that China's successful response to the financial crisis proved that the world should learn from its economic model. But his strategic proposal was cautious, low-key, and multilateral—the opposite of the bold, flamboyant vision for OBOR that Xi ultimately adopted.

Lin was not the first prominent Chinese thought leader to propose a multilateral Chinese Marshall Plan. Three years earlier, Xu Shanda, a former top tax official and party elder, had argued for his own Chinese Marshall Plan to export excess capacity and capital.[39] Xu wanted China to establish a fund named the "harmonious world plan" (和谐世界计划) or "shared development plan" (共享发展计划). He proposed endowing the fund with $500 billion in initial working capital and using it to provide state-to-state loans to "friendly" developing countries for infrastructure construction. Xu identified three existing organizations as potential channels for processing applications and disbursing funds: the China-Africa Cooperation Forum, the SCO, and the Association of Southeast Asian Nations Free Trade Area.[40] In short, Xu and Lin basically agreed on the economic mechanism for what a Chinese Marshall Plan should be: China should export its national savings to help the world economy invest its way out of financial crisis. But this process should take place within existing international institutions, they argued, so as not to antagonize the West.

There was a key difference between Lin's and Xu's proposals for a Chinese Marshall Plan: whereas Lin was concerned about jump-starting global growth, Xu saw it as a way to achieve domestic economic objectives. The loans should be for specific commercial or infrastructure projects, Xu argued. Interest rates should be concessionary—that is, lower than in regular commercial loans—but higher than US Treasury bonds after taking risk into account. Foreign governments should be able to "voluntarily apply" for the project loans and assume responsibility for repayment. All project construction and procurement should be carried out through Chinese enterprises, which would create jobs in China. "The fund will help accelerate the pace of internationalization of the Chinese renminbi, reduce foreign exchange reserves and avoid the risk of long-term USD depreciation," Xu concluded. "The core content is: the state bears the loan risk, enterprises export excess capacity, and the RMB is internationalized."

In 2010, Xu wrote an editorial in the party mouthpiece *Global Times* titled "Making a Perfect Chinese 'Marshall Plan'" (做好中国版"马歇尔

计划"). He pointed out that his idea could also help fix the growing over-capacity problem in China's heavy industrial sector.[41] "Just like the American 'Marshall Plan,' if Chinese foreign exchange can be converted into purchasing power for emerging markets, plenty of Chinese excess capacity will be released when developing these market resources," Xu wrote. The initiative could both "expand domestic production capacity and increase domestic employment." China was already engaged in infrastructure construction around the world, of course. Xu was advocating for the same thing, but on a much larger scale and in a more coordinated fashion. Two years before Xi took power, Xu had fully sketched out the economic model for a project resembling OBOR. His views could not have been far from the mainstream, or else the *Global Times* would never have published his recommendations in such detail.

Unfortunately for Xu, comparisons to the Marshall Plan were politically problematic. Chinese senior high school students learn that the Marshall Plan was not an act of US generosity but an exemplar of hegemonic Cold War realpolitik. As the standard textbook puts it: "In order to help Western Europe restore their economy, the United States began to implement the European economic assistance program proposed by Secretary of State Marshall so as to support *and control* Western European countries. At the same time, the United States, UK and other Western countries also tried to use the Marshall Plan to draw Eastern European countries over to their side, but were rejected."[42] By contrast, Xu, who had attended graduate school at the University of Bath in England, was clearly referring to the Marshall Plan as it is known in Western political discourse: a goodwill gesture offered by the wealthiest country to emerge from a devastating war—indeed, even a case study in foreign policy idealism.[43] But according to the Communist Party's official historiography, the Marshall Plan was an imperialist trap for vulnerable countries. Xu's and Lin's proposals never gained traction.

Xi Rejects the Marshall Plan

Why did Xi Jinping ultimately accept most of Xu's policy recommendations but reject his branding? One possible explanation is that Xi and his advisers were familiar with the official history of the Marshall Plan and believed that developing countries would interpret a Chinese Marshall Plan as a Cold War–style hegemonic scheme. Another explanation is that they feared domestic Chinese audiences would struggle to understand the notion of a Chinese Marshall Plan, having learned in school that the original plan was hegemonic. Neither explanation is persuasive. More likely, Xi dismissed the Chinese Marshall Plan slogan because it sounded derivative and insufficiently nationalistic, just as he dismissed Lin's and Xu's recommendations that China pursue this economic policy within existing international institutions. To Xi, the main political value of OBOR was as a watchword of his own authority. The irony, of course, is that if Xi had framed OBOR as a Chinese Marshall Plan and implemented it as Lin had recommended, he would have gone a long way toward persuading US and European audiences that China's intentions were benign.

While Western media have frequently drawn comparisons between OBOR and the Marshall Plan, official Chinese sources have consistently taken pains to argue that the policies are not analogous. In June 2015, *Qiushi*, China's most influential journal of international relations theory, published an essay titled "The 'Belt and Road' Is Definitely Not the Chinese Version of the 'Marshall Plan.'"[44] The author, Wang Yiwei, is a professor at Renmin and Fudan Universities and one of China's most prolific academic commenters on OBOR. Wang noted five key differences between OBOR and the Marshall Plan: context, objective, participants, content, and implementation. The most important difference, he argued, was the difference in strategic objectives. "Economic 'Trumanism' ultimately existed to serve the global hegemony of the United States," he wrote. This "made it easier for the United States to control (控制) and occupy (占领) the European market."

In Wang's interpretation, OBOR is different from the Marshall Plan because it does not seek gains for China at the expense of anyone else:

> During the special historical period after World War II, the "Marshall Plan" played a certain role in stabilizing the situation in Europe and restoring the European economy. However, the American hegemonic plot behind it is obvious. The Cold War is over now. The "One Belt and One Road" initiative proposed by China completely abandons the old framework of a

Cold War mentality of zero-sum games, and conforms to the new trend of peace, development, cooperation and win-win. The meaning and significance of "One Belt and One Road" goes far beyond the "Marshall Plan." There is no historical or factual basis for comparing the "Belt and Road" with the Chinese version of the "Marshall Plan."

Instead, OBOR is "a platform (平台) for countries to work together," and a "public good (公共产品) that China provides to the international community." OBOR is different from the Marshall Plan not because of its size or approach to construction projects and economic strategy, but because it promotes a win-win foreign policy that eases tensions in great power competition. The onus is therefore on the United States to desist from hegemonic behavior. Wang's line of argument was clearly aimed at a Chinese audience; it would surely fail to convince a Western one.

Meanwhile, the Chinese bureaucracy continued to use the metaphor of the New Silk Road to describe China's international vision, but they did so in an ad hoc and uncoordinated fashion. For example, on a tour through the Persian Gulf states in January 2012, Premier Wen Jiabao spoke of the ancient Silk Road that linked Chinese and Arab people together and promised that China would endeavor to re-create it. "Now we are building a new 'Silk Road' (新的"丝绸之路"), he declared, "which is a road of friendship, a road of political mutual trust of China and the Arab people, a road of commercial integrity, a road of unity and mutual aid, and a road for the exchanges of different civilizations and culture."[45]

Wen expanded on his vision in a speech in Urumqi in September 2012, less than two months before the National Party Congress when Xi was promoted as the new General Secretary. Addressing the Second China-Eurasia Economic Development and Cooperation Forum, Wen extolled the virtues of mutual noninterference and win-win and declared that "a multidimensional silk road consisting of roads, railways, air flights, communications, and oil and gas pipelines is taking shape."[46] With the leaders of Kyrgyzstan, the Maldives, Cambodia, Kazakhstan, and Tajikistan in attendance, Wen spoke again of the Silk Road as the proof of concept for the Continental Bridge that China had promised its central Asian neighbors eight years before.

Marching Westwards

As the Party Congress approached, Wang Jisi, China's most prominent foreign policy commentator, offered his own proposal for the new national strategy: "marching westwards" (西进).[47] Wang published his piece in the *Global Times* weeks before the Eighteenth Party Congress convened in November 2012, clearly hoping to influence the discussion. His proposal was less radical than Xu's, although it echoed some of his themes. It also drew a connection between China's growing need for a larger geopolitical footprint and its economic reform priorities. "The logic of 'marching westwards' . . . reflects the complex regional quagmire China is in," Wang wrote, in a reference to the US pivot. "As Washington rebalances to Asia, the relation between the United States and China has become increasingly contentious and 'zero-sum.'"

Although the maritime Asia-Pacific would remain a site of competition, Central Asia would become newly open to engagement with China, Wang wrote. The US withdrawal from Afghanistan would create a strategic vacuum, which China would inevitably have to fill. This could be the basis for win-win with the United States, Wang argued, because the United States is "desperate for China's assistance in stabilizing Afghanistan and Pakistan."[48] Finally, Wang argued, "marching westwards" could also be a win-win for the Chinese economy. It could dovetail with the "Grand Western Development" (西部大开发) strategy that Beijing had intermittently used over the previous decade to build infrastructure in the western provinces. With the imprimatur of Wang and the *Global Times*, a new policy toward Central Asia seemed inevitable by late 2012.

Xi emerged from the Party Congress in November 2012 as China's new paramount leader. But the debate over Wang's proposal continued during Xi's first months in power, playing out in the pages of the *Global Times* and the party's leading theoretical journals. This was a sign that the Chinese strategic community remained deeply divided. Xian Xiao, for example, argued that China should prioritize its neighbors first and avoid spreading its resources too thinly. After a pro forma line praising Wang, Xian launched into a devastating critique. "What does 'West' refer to?" he asked. "From the perspective of distance, first the western neighboring countries, followed by the Middle East countries which are moderately far, and then the distant African countries."[49] Xian's concern was that Wang's theory set up a slippery slope that would lead China to "march" all over the world, hopelessly overextending its limited resources.

Another critique of Wang's proposal argued that "marching west-wards" would antagonize the other great powers. An essay by Zhang Jiye, published in the *Global Times* in 2013, identified three particular risks that China should guard against: a deterioration in relations with Rus-sia, India, and other great powers; excessive "westward marching" into hazardous areas (like the countries of the Middle East); and the risk that excessive westward marching would burden China with responsibilities too great for it to bear: "With the international situation complicated and volatile and the game between major powers increasingly fierce, the road to China's 'westward development' is by no means a smooth one. China's top priority is not to take a big 'step in,' but rather to judge strategic risks and construct a strategic plan to fully grasp its 'westward move.'"[50] In short, many Chinese foreign policy intellectuals were deeply concerned about the risks of an OBOR-like venture. "Marching westwards" could be doubly dangerous: directly, by creating incentives to spread Chinese resources too thin and fund unnecessary foreign projects; and indirectly, by inviting backlash.

Xi's Answer

Xi's "One Belt One Road" announcement speech in Kazakhstan was not proposing a new idea; it was settling a long-standing debate. OBOR com-bined aspects of Wang's strategic vision with the more benign New Silk Road slogan. It specifically rejected the proposals to brand China's over-seas projects as a Chinese Marshall Plan, though it would later follow some of Lin's and Xu's technical recommendations for project financing. Above all, the choice of the Silk Road metaphor implied that Xi would not base his foreign policy on a Western model. As China strove to become a global commercial power, it would look first to its own imperial history.

In a sign of things to come, the historical references in Xi's speech had little connection to his specific policy proposals. The speech itself could have been delivered in a half-dozen other central Asian countries.

It was clearly not directed to Kazakhstan in particular—a fact that must have come as a surprise to the Kazakh dignitaries present. (In his subsequent remarks, President Nazarbayev ignored Xi's references to the Silk Road and spoke only of bilateral relations.) The pageantry surrounding the event also suggested that Kazakhstan had not been aware that the summit was supposed to be Silk Road–themed. The main photo op for Xi and Nazarbayev was staged in front of a giant screen depicting the Chinese and Kazakh flags side by side, without any visual references to Silk Road history (fig. 2.2). Nazarbayev University was also a strange location for a Chinese leader to announce an initiative rooted in the memory of a glorified past. Astana is a planned city, established as a garrison town by Cossacks in 1830. Today it is Kazakhstan's political capital, known for its futuristic architecture and monuments to Nazarbayev. Why did Xi not give his address in Almaty, Kazakhstan's largest city and cultural capital, which was a waystation on Eurasian trade routes for two thousand years? Perhaps it was because Xi was primarily speaking not to a Kazakh audience but to a Chinese one.

FIGURE 2.2: Xi Jinping and Kazakh President Nursultan Nazarbayev on Xi's trip to announce OBOR, September 7, 2013. The ceremonial events during the trip gave no visual hint that they were launching a major multilateral initiative. Photograph courtesy of Reuters/Shamil Zhumatov.

The following month, in a speech to the Indonesian parliament, Xi announced a Maritime Silk Road to complement the Belt across continental Eurasia.[51] This time Xi drew on the history of Zheng He, the fifteenth-century eunuch admiral who led seven missions into the South China Sea and Indian Ocean between 1405 and 1432. "His visits left nice stories of friendly exchanges between the Chinese and Indonesian peoples," Xi claimed, "many of which are still widely told today." Xi also cited the "spirit of Bandung," referring to the 1955 conference of nonaligned states that convened in Indonesia to inaugurate a new era of postcolonial world politics. These principles were "peaceful coexistence" on one hand and "seeking common ground while shelving differences" on the other. In closing, Xi pledged China's commitment to invest in countries along the Maritime Silk Road, which would extend down the Chinese coast into the South China Sea, through the Malacca Straits and along the Indian Ocean rim, and finally through the Suez Canal to terminate at the Greek port of Piraeus. With these two speeches, OBOR became China's official policy.

After more than two decades without a coherent concept, the question of a how a rising China would describe its proper mode of engagement with greater Asia was finally settled. Scholarly fears about the potential pitfalls went unheard. Instead, Xi determined that China would undertake a bold and unapologetic initiative to restore itself as a major global power. OBOR would not seek to antagonize the United States, but it would not bend over backward to accommodate it. Instead, claiming Chinese history as its guiding light, OBOR would propose an entirely new model of economic and political partnership. China would seek win-win opportunities everywhere, and it would partner with any willing country.

Conclusion

The New Silk Road was an established slogan in the Chinese diplomatic lexicon long before Xi Jinping visited Kazakhstan in 2013. The roots of what we now know as OBOR trace back to the 1990s, when the countries of Central Asia began to form multilateral organizations to preserve regional stability and security. Toward the end of that decade, the Chinese government began to encourage state-owned firms to internationalize themselves, "Going Out" to secure their own supplies of natural resources. This process was haphazard and largely driven by firms and local governments with little central oversight. By the time of the 2008 global financial crisis, influential Chinese scholars and policymakers recognized that the country's overseas projects needed more oversight and conceptual coherence. Yet an internal debate raged about what exactly the organizing concept should be: a Chinese Marshall Plan? A westward march? A New Silk Road? Many different actors in the Chinese system took part in this debate. Above all, different elements of the Chinese bureaucracy appropriated the New Silk Road slogan to brand their own projects and proposals and create the misleading impression that they were acting with Beijing's imprimatur.

When Xi took to the stage in Kazakhstan, he was communicating something very different to Chinese and foreign audiences. By taking personal credit for a slogan that Chinese officials already knew and used, Xi was asserting his own political authority over the language that the Chinese Communist Party uses to communicate with itself. By declining to commit to a headline amount of new aid or investment, Xi was signaling to listeners at home that OBOR would not only refer to new projects, but would also claim credit for projects that were already ongoing or completed. By choosing the Silk Road as his historical touchstone, Xi was invoking the grandest memories of Chinese imperial history and placing himself—and his adopted home province of Shaanxi—as the heir to that legacy. To the Kazakh audience assembled, Xi's speech may have sounded like the usual diplomatic boilerplate. But to an internal Chinese audience, it was a bombshell—a signal that the time had come for China to ascend the world stage as a wealthy, powerful, and virtuous country.

CHAPTER 3

Emperor Xi

Making the Past Serve the Present

At the beginning of the propaganda film, a little girl in pajamas is sitting up in bed, waiting to be tucked in.[1] She cradles a stuffed animal as the gentle light of the bedside lamp catches her blonde hair. Her father opens the door.

> Time for bed, sweetie.
> OK, Baba.
> Baba's going to be gone a few days, and I'll miss you.
> Why?
> I'm going to attend a forum in Beijing on the Belt and Road Initiative.
> What's that?

He walks over and sits down on her bed. It is time for a bedtime story.

• • •

Chinese attempts to pitch One Belt One Road (OBOR) to Western audiences often take the form of painfully flat-footed propaganda.[2] This film is an illustrative example: the first of a five-part English-language video series released in 2017 by the state-controlled overseas media organization *China Daily*. Over the course of five "bedtime stories," the playful and inquisitive Lily learns about the benefits of globalization. Her earnest father extolls China's contributions. Lily concludes by saying how much

想法是中国提出的 但它属于全世界
It's China's idea. But it belongs to the world.

FIGURE 3.1: A Western father tells his daughter "Belt and Road bedtime stories" in a propaganda film for English-language audiences. Film still from *China Daily*, "The Belt and Road Initiative and globalization | Belt and Road Bedtime Stories series," May 2017, YouTube.

she hopes the world can see what she does: that Xi Jinping's plan to restore China's ancient trading heritage is an unalloyed good (fig. 3.1).

Chinese propaganda materials are windows into the political and historical narratives that define and drive OBOR. They explain why Xi Jinping has so assertively promoted the New Silk Road concept as his own idea. They suggest what the average apolitical Chinese citizen is likely to know about OBOR, and therefore how the OBOR concept relates to other big ideas in Chinese political discourse.[3] But propaganda materials are not designed exclusively to inform and influence individual citizens. The official slogans and images that define OBOR in China also function as signals to the sprawling parallel bureaucracies of the Chinese Communist Party (CCP) and the Chinese state.[4] Companies, local governments, and government agencies look to propaganda for clues about what the central authorities expect from them.[5]

Chinese OBOR propaganda celebrates Xi for restoring China's historic status on the global stage. They stress the parallels between OBOR and the ancient Silk Road to suggest that OBOR is restoring an old, morally superior international order, not inventing a new one. In this international order, China manages its interactions with other countries through token economic exchanges. China supports its junior partners by sharing its "wisdom and experience," leading cooperative projects, and sharing superior products and technologies. In return, partner countries acknowledge China's senior status by voicing gratitude, offering gifts, and praising the tributary order. The propaganda strongly suggests that this harmonious model of international relations serves China's economic and political interests without disadvantaging any other country. Xi is thus portrayed as a visionary leader for launching a world-historical transformation and as a virtuous traditionalist for restoring China to its rightful position at the center of the global system. Thus, the Chinese government's efforts to drum up domestic support for OBOR are intrinsically linked to Xi's individual project of building narratives that sustain his cult of personality. Branding is not adjacent to the story of what OBOR is. From the perspective of Chinese propaganda, it *is* the story.

The Chinese government has put remarkably little effort into producing OBOR propaganda for English-speaking audiences.[6] In the materials that have been publicly released, the hero cult of Xi and the bold historical claims so central to the domestic propaganda are conspicuously absent. One possible explanation is that Beijing is wary of triggering Western alarm about rising Chinese power. But the fact that China has made many of these materials available in some form with English translations indicates that it considers the narrative about China's rise to preeminence as describing a basic fact, not as a politically sensitive or provocative idea that needs to be hidden from foreigners. A better explanation is that the OBOR vision has little to do with the West directly. The Chinese government simply does not perceive reassuring Western audiences to be a high priority. Ultimately, the primary political function of OBOR propaganda is to calibrate nationalist ideology at home.

This is all clearly relevant for policymakers and concerned citizens everywhere. How the OBOR concept is perceived within China limits Beijing's options for modifying or repackaging it in the future. Furthermore, if the core domestic purpose of OBOR is to create narratives that legitimize Xi personally, then the initiative has considerable staying power. The more established the OBOR slogan becomes, and the more thoroughly its associated policies become institutionalized, the more clearly self-interested party members will see that Xi and other elites have personal stakes in seeing it succeed. This will create strong incentives to praise OBOR, support expanding its scope, and publicly defend it against perceived foreign threats—even if none of these sycophantic policy proposals prove to be rational or beneficial by themselves. More important, if this analysis is correct, then foreign efforts to pressure China to roll OBOR back are unlikely to succeed. There is little the West can do to untangle the OBOR brand from Xi's own.

This chapter analyzes three types of OBOR promotional materials directed at different audiences and unpacks the metaphors and historical claims embedded in them.[7] First, it examines domestic propaganda, in particular "One Belt One Road," a six-hour TV series aired on CCTV in September 2016. This documentary is the Chinese government's most authoritative single exposition of OBOR, how it operates, and what it hopes to achieve. Next, the chapter reviews how China has revised its national history and civics textbooks for secondary school students since Xi came to power. Apart from a flagrant disregard for historical accuracy, the clear narrative pattern to these revisions shows a political interest in reframing the historical Silk Road as a deliberate, visionary achievement of renowned emperor Han Wudi. These changes legitimate Xi by presenting him as a latter-day successor to Han Wudi. They also bring the official history of the Silk Road into parallel with Xi's contemporary policy objectives. Finally, this chapter considers some recent propaganda materials for English-language audiences, which feature a completely different and far more benign storyline about OBOR and why China is promoting it. The "Belt and Road Bedtime Stories" cast Xi's China as a peace-loving power that respects difference and seeks to protect the existing international system by promoting globalization and free trade. I argue that this last narrative is not at all persuasive.

Domestic Propaganda

All across the world, children dream of prosperity and opportunity. Karina is a dreamy girl who lives in a small town in Kyrgyzstan and loves to study history class because studying the Silk Road makes her "[feel] her eyes are being opened to the exciting outside world." Karina lives opposite the railway station in her town. Only passenger trains stop there, and they pass through rarely. Karina dreams of one day traveling on

I want to take a fast train and see what's out there.

FIGURE 3.2: Karina, a schoolgirl in Kyrgyzstan who wants to achieve her dream through the New Silk Road. Film still from China Central Television, "The Belt and Road EP 1 Common Destiny | CCTV," September 2016, YouTube.

one herself. At sunset, dreamy, uplifting music plays as she dances on the tracks (fig. 3.2).

This scene comes from the second episode of "One Belt One Road," a six-part documentary series aired on China Central Television (CCTV) in 2016. The documentary is the closest thing to an authoritative explanation of what OBOR is and how it works, geared toward general Chinese audiences. It first ran on CCTV1, the most important channel on Chinese television, which broadcasts the CCP's official version of the day's news every evening. It has since been replayed on other CCTV channels. Production value is extremely high compared with CCTV's other specials. To film it, camera crews visited dozens of OBOR countries, filming Chinese infrastructure projects and interviewing local residents and officials about their passion for China. The series boasts a range of interviews with foreign dignitaries whom CCTV could almost certainly not have booked without high-level political backing. These include Vladimir Putin and Henry Kissinger; former French, Italian, and Australian Prime Ministers Jean-Pierre Raffarin, Romano Prodi, and Kevin Rudd; and several other current and former world leaders. A version of all six episodes with subtitles in Chinese and English is available on the

YouTube channel of China Global Television, essentially the Chinese equivalent of Russia Today.[8] (YouTube itself is blocked in mainland China.) With a few subtle exceptions that I explore below, the English-language version renders the original narration with great accuracy. But the series was viewed only 96,000 times on YouTube in the two years after it was posted—a pitiably small figure that indicates that the Chinese government has made little effort to promote the series overseas.

"One Belt One Road" is organized around a guiding narrative: that China's Silk Road history is glorious and Xi has initiated a world-historical transformation to restore it. For most of world history, the series claims, countries across Eurasia prospered together thanks to the "Silk Road spirit" of communication and the booming trade in Chinese products. After a few ignominious centuries in the shadow of the West, China has re-emerged as the world's most dynamic economic and technological power and is finally ready to re-create the Silk Road order for the benefit of humanity. As the de facto leader of the developing world, China has an obligation to become the leading global provider of public goods and share access to its technology and markets. OBOR will resolve the inequalities and contradictions let loose by the relatively recent rise of the West, and will help disadvantaged people and countries achieve their dreams. In return, the recipients will acknowledge China's preeminent status and show their gratitude through friendship, praise, and token gifts.

CCTV's History Lesson

The first episode of the CCTV series, "Common Fate," begins with a reverent reenactment of Xi's announcement speech in Kazakhstan.[9] After the promo, the narrative kicks off in Astana, "where the civilizations of East and West meet." Gentle orchestral music swells as the camera pans across an empty lecture hall. The music is restrained and anticipatory. Ethereal octaves turn to stirring suspended chords—Chairman Xi is about to speak. Finally, the shot cuts to footage of the speech itself. "Shaanxi, my home province, is at the starting point of the Silk Road," Xi says. "As I stand here and reflect on history, I can almost hear the camel bells echoing among the mountains and see the wisps of smoke rising from the desert. It all reminds me of home." In this historic speech, the narrator intones, Xi "for the first time proposed reviving the ancient Silk Road." The rest of the episode is devoted to a whirlwind tour of world history leading up to that seminal day. "Reviewing history can focus our minds on the present and the future," the narrator says as the music swells again. In the next scene, the documentary begins to lay its first dubious historical claim: that the historic Silk Road was a Chinese invention.

In ancient Greece, the audience meets a mute Eratosthenes, portrayed by a Western actor in a toga, laboring by candlelight over a map of the known world. But Eratosthenes underestimated the size of the Earth. His map had no place for East Asia. It was only later, thanks to trade, that "European eyes were opened" to the lands to the East. The realization that there was another empire in the Far East that could make a product as remarkable as silk "transformed the ancient Romans' understanding of world geography," the narrator says. The scene shows a crowd of blond Roman aristocrats scrambling to caress a silken shroud. The staging allows for only one interpretation: that the Europeans were the lucky beneficiaries of the Silk Road, which in time became the only way for them to fulfill their desire for Chinese products.

Next the film credits the creation of the Silk Road to Emperor Han Wudi. Back in the imperial court, we meet loyal emissary Zhang Qian and Han Wudi, whose reign "ushered in a Golden Age of Chinese history and in its relations with other countries." The reenactment shows the emperor solemnly handing a sword to the kneeling Zhang, and then cuts to images of Zhang leading his train of horses across the desert. Several minutes are devoted to Zhang, the loyal emissary who "opened a way for the Chinese people over the vast landmass they called the Western Regions." Within the first ten minutes of the film, the juxtaposition of Xi and Han Wudi allows for no doubt about the historical parallel. In the course of this hour-long special about Chinese history, they are the only two Chinese leaders mentioned by name.

Obviously this characterization of Silk Road history is historically inaccurate. As Valerie Hansen shows in *The Silk Road: A New History*, there was never a single standard "road" across the Eurasian continent.[10] The so-called Silk Road was a dispersed network of trade routes that rose and fell over the centuries. Each route was dominated by its own amalgamation of linguistic, political, and religious subcultures. Furthermore, trade routes across most of Asia had existed for hundreds of years before Zhang Qian's western voyages, mostly through the domains of the Persian empire. When the Han moved its capital west to Chang'an (modern-day Xi'an), it did not "found" anything new but connected to existing networks of trade. As we saw in chapter 2, even the Chinese term for the Silk Road, *sichouzhilu* (丝绸之路), is a literal translation of a nineteenth-century German neologism.

The rest of the CCTV episode acknowledges these facts in passing, at several points implying that the Silk Road was indeed more of a metaphor than a physical road. But it still insists that "in time, the Silk Road and Maritime Silk Road became associated with a particular spirit" that defined global history from the Han dynasty in the third century BCE through the early Ming dynasty in the late fifteenth century. The Silk Road spirit was part and parcel of transnational trade. It "embraced values of peace and cooperation, openness and inclusiveness, mutual learning and mutual benefit." To visualize this point, the documentary uses the leitmotif of men in Turkic hats leading loaded camels over dunes. "Often the motivation was the pursuit of wealth," the narrator acknowledges, but trade also spoke to a timeless human desire to connect with others and learn from them. This spirit, it is claimed, was a Chinese gift to the world and provided the dominant model of world order for over a millennium.

From ancient Rome onward, the West was captivated by the Silk Road, which symbolized China's benevolence and its centrality to world affairs. The film takes pains to put this in both economic and technological terms. Amid images of Chinese technology, wealth, and power, the narrator notes that "in Europe, by contrast, techniques of iron-making lagged far behind." When the West ultimately developed and became powerful, it was only because of technologies it acquired from China through Silk Road trade. These were China's so-called four great inventions: the compass, gunpowder, paper, and printing.

China's centrality to world affairs is a key theme in "Common Fate." One of the interview subjects, Professor Liu Yingsheng of Nanjing University, even claims that Western powers undertook their voyages to the Americas only because they were enraptured by Marco Polo's reports of his journey to China. "European merchants realized that if you wanted to be rich, head east, go to China," Liu says. Intriguingly, this is one of the points where CCTV's English subtitles modify the meaning of the narrator's statement in Chinese. In the English translation, Liu hedges his words: "The reason Europeans undertook voyages to the East and Americas, was partly because of Marco Polo." In Chinese, he leaves no room for doubt. "Why did Europeans sail to the east? Why was America discovered? The driving force *was* the story that Marco Polo brought back to Italy." In this account, the Silk Road was never a true two-way street connecting nations of equal status. It was the pathway through which countries across Eurasia learned about China and acquired treasured Chinese goods.

Then the West rose, ushering in a dark period in global history. A reenactment shows dozens of black ships spewing smoke into the darkening sky as they converge on a small port, as the narrator speaks of the malignant European model of "colonial expansion and trade monopoly." The music turns to a minor key and becomes increasingly stern and anxious through the following scenes on European rule. At one point, the camera cuts to a shot of a black locomotive running the viewer down. The shots of European mass production are frightening, managing to make technological progress seem like a grim and unfortunate development. As the Western capitalist model spread its tendrils across the globe, it laid low the peaceful and mutually beneficial trading system that China had underwritten for millennia. This was when "the Silk Road reached its lowest ebb," the narrator says. China "faced a struggle for survival."

Fortunately, Western hegemony proved to be an unsustainable model for global governance. "Eventually the Western colonial system entered its twilight period," the narrator says. To illustrate the wave of decolonization after World War II, the film shows long camera shots of South Asian men singing joyous music, banging drums, and dancing in a public square in front of stone colonial buildings. Then the subject turns to the founding of the People's Republic of China in 1949. The narrative pace rapidly accelerates, and the music bursts into swelling, major harmonics.

Up to this point, the film has focused on China's commonalities with other colonized nations. It inaccurately reframes the Bandung Conference, the 1955 gathering of nonaligned countries, as a meeting about economic development. Skipping over the rest of the Maoist era, the film jumps ahead to images of Chinese industrialization in the 1980s under Deng Xiaoping: people banging hammers, water mills, factories. The narration pivots from sweeping statements of historical themes to a barrage of statistics. There are graphs displaying China's growing GDP, a graph showing China's rapidly growing foreign exchange reserves, and an icon to show that China is now the largest trade partner of 126 countries. Images of heavy industry turn to footage of workers packing new laptops into boxes, assembly lines of robots manufacturing cars, rocket launches, airplanes, and high-speed rail. To contrast with the victorious climax, the film then shows darkened images of Times Square and Wall Street in the rain, their sidewalks strewn with trash.

The World Looks to China

The CCTV narrator says that the rest of the world is "attempting to follow the example set by China." Former Australian Prime Minister Kevin Rudd confirms the point. The next segment of the episode runs through several examples of Arab countries looking to China for guidance and leadership. In Mecca, the new urban metro system was built by a Chinese company. Video shots move from China joining the World Trade Organization in 2001 to the Beijing Olympics of 2008 to the Shanghai World Expo of 2010. "China for its rejuvenation is depending on the world, while the development of the world depends on the rise of China," the narrator says. "The destiny, interests, and responsibilities of China and the world are becoming more closely interwoven." The images and music send an unsubtle message: developing countries, tired of Western rule, are clamoring for China to fix the global order and guide them on a path to development.

Having risen to preeminence, China is answering the call by restoring the ancient Silk Road system. The images and narration strongly imply that forty years after Deng Xiaoping began the policy of Reform and Opening Up in late 1978, China has emerged as the world's preeminent technological power. This is represented visually through stories about China installing infrastructure and high-tech industrial facilities around the world, as well as testimony from prominent foreign officials and experts. The film mentions no explicit benefits that China will draw from OBOR, except perhaps the vague promise of prosperity. Instead, it frames China's new global role in terms of status, virtue, and responsibility. Through OBOR, the narrator says, "China can help improve the global system of governance, bolster the representation of developing countries in global affairs, and pass on its wisdom and experience."

The West is not an important player in this story. The documentary series does not once mention the World Bank, the International Monetary Fund, or other international institutions. There are no images of cities or technology in the United States or Western Europe other than the dreary and desolate images of New York City mentioned above. On the contrary, the only purpose of the interviews with the Western leaders is to validate the narrator's claims about China's economic growth, technological sophistication, and leadership on the world stage. Former French Prime Minister Jean-Pierre Raffarin has a Chinese calligraphic inscription framed on the wall behind him and a copy of Xi's book *The Governance of China* on his desk.

The next five episodes of the CCTV series shift from a world-historical scale to stories about people whose lives have been transformed by OBOR. The organizing theme of these later episodes is that lack of infrastructure is the main barrier preventing regular people from achieving their dreams. These dreams are culturally specific to each recipient country and are always packaged in the form of human subjects. The film profiles a disproportionate number of schoolgirls, including Karina from Kyrgyzstan and a group of girls from Pakistan who dream of getting an education and leaving their hometown. In Vientiane, Laos, we see a newlywed couple posing for wedding photos at the train station—the country portrayed as so backward that even antique trains are technological marvels. In Saudi Arabia, we meet Ahmed, who has left his family's business to work with a Chinese company building a rail link that will allow more Muslims to complete the *hajj*. CCTV thus portrays China primarily as a benefactor and partly as a collaborator. Lifted by Chinese beneficence and technological guidance, partner countries can build infrastructure that meets local communities' most urgent needs and helps ordinary people achieve their highest aspirations.

Performing Gratitude

According to the documentary, the spirit of OBOR can already be seen in the genuine bonds of affection forming between Chinese workers and their foreign hosts. The trope of Chinese workers sharing meals and toasts with their local partners, laughing together, and meeting each other's families recurs frequently in CCTV's other OBOR propaganda.[11] Episode 2, "Road of Connectivity," ends with a lengthy anecdote about a friendship between two electrical technicians from China and Mongolia. At dawn on a frigid winter morning, we meet Wang Congxin, director of the Yarant Power Station in Xinjiang province. His Mongolian colleague, Ayouxi, is waiting for him at the border and embraces him as stirring music plays. Both men speak in loving terms about each other.

Still, Wang and Ayouxi's relationship, like all other Chinese–foreigner friendships portrayed in the CCTV series, is based on an obvious status inequality. Wang has crossed the border at the break of dawn on a Saturday not for a purely social visit but because the Mongolian village's electric grid has broken down, plunging the village into darkness. The broken component is obsolete and cannot easily be replaced. So Wang finds a Chinese factory to make a single unit, enabling him to restore power. Their "primitive existence on the grassland" is "transformed" by Chinese technology.

What the Mongolians lack in technical prowess, they make up for in gratitude. To show his thanks for the Chinese engineer's generosity, a herdsman, Maktel, invites Wang and Ayouxi to spend Christmas with his family. In a joyful scene, Wang and Ayouxi join Maktel's family for an evening of eating, drinking, and festivities in the family's yurt. "Without electricity, we had no life," Maktel says, raising his glass as his eyes fill with tears (fig 3.3).

After watching the dozens of anecdotes in the six-hour series, a credulous viewer would conclude that China today is the main driver of global progress. The Chinese government's external communications relentlessly claim that OBOR is a multilateral initiative. But this documentary for Chinese audiences does not provide a single example of a multilateral exchange along the Belt and Road. Nor does it mention any independent interactions between two OBOR countries that does not include China. This contradiction speaks to the fundamental tension in the narratives that the Chinese government has used to describe OBOR. On the one hand, the stated purpose of the initiative is to help powerless countries open up to the world. On the other hand, the unspoken rationale is that history is calling on China to reclaim its rightful status and that OBOR

FIGURE 3.3: A Mongolian herdsman, Maktel, praises OBOR. Film still from China Central Television, "The Belt and Road EP 1 Common Destiny | CCTV," September 2016, YouTube.

is the proper means to get there. As the narrator says, "History has shown that a country can open to the world once it is powerful, and that its power will only grow after it opens."

Rewriting Textbooks

How, then, does Xi Jinping conceptualize the historical model of Chinese leadership that he is promising to resurrect? Several middle and high school history and civics textbooks have been revised since Xi took office in 2013.[12] These materials are in use nationwide, and nearly all schoolchildren in China must study them. The textbooks tell us what the average Chinese citizen is likely to know about the objective facts of Silk Road history and therefore how he or she is likely to interpret the New Silk Road metaphor in a civic context.[13] A close look at the revisions shows that the CCP is engaged in a comprehensive effort to revise the official history of the Silk Road, rewriting it from scratch when the old facts are politically inconvenient. Predictably, these changes back up OBOR's key historical claims and implicitly glorify Xi.

The CCP has long treated history education as an ideological battleground. In August 1991, not long after the violent crackdown on protesters at Tiananmen Square, China's National Education Commission issued a general outline for the new patriotic education curriculum for high schools. "History education reform is China's fundamental strategy to defend against the peaceful evolution plot of international hostile powers," the outline informed school administrators. "Strengthening education on China's [pre-1949] history and national conditions is of strategic significance."[14] To drive home the point, the CCP's Propaganda Department established "patriotic education bases" across the country, renovating historic sites that memorialized China's "century of humiliation" by outside powers and its rise to international might and wealth under communist rule. Changes in the history curriculum were integrated into the national university entrance exam, the *gaokao*, forcing all ambitious students to demonstrate mastery of this material. Xi's administration clearly sees political and historical education in similar terms. The difference is the brashness with which recent textbook revisions have rewritten the facts.

Just as the CCTV documentary does, the textbook revisions portray the overland Silk Road as a strategic initiative launched by Han Wudi (fig. 3.4). They also create nearly from scratch an extensive section on the Maritime Silk Road, which they describe as an imperial policy to demonstrate Chinese wealth and power and thereby win the friendship of foreign states. The claims here are even more historically tenuous. Most important, the textbooks point out that the ancient Silk Road conferred specific geopolitical and status benefits to imperial China beyond material gain. The changes have a common feature: they bring the history of the ancient Silk Road more closely into parallel with Xi's New Silk Road concept.

Before Xi, the standard textbooks used in China described the formation of the Silk Road as a diffuse phenomenon that "formed" over time. The 2001 textbook for middle schoolers begins the lesson by introducing the Huns, or Xiongnu tribes, who had threatened China from the north and west for centuries. In the late second century BCE, the Hun

FIGURE 3.4: Reenactment of Han Wudi sending Zhang Qian to open the ancient Silk Road. Film still from China Central Television, "The Belt and Road EP 1 Common Destiny | CCTV," September 2016, YouTube.

threat emerged again. "Relentless" Hun attacks from the "Western regions" to the central plains left the Han rulers helpless and "utterly passive." In the first century CE, Han Wudi's successors established a permanent imperial presence in the Western regions and fought a series of bloody battles to turn the local tribes into tributary states. The textbook drives home the point with a guiding question just above the section on the Silk Road. "How did the Silk Road form?" it asks.[15] In the 2016 version, the question is rewritten as: "Who opened the trade route for silk? And when?"[16]

In the 2001 textbooks, the story of the Silk Road formation is largely the bloody story of how the western province of Xinjiang became integrated into China more than a century after Han Wudi's death. According to the old textbooks, this was accomplished not through peaceful trade but through conquest and brutal acts of shock and awe. At this time, the Han dynasty did not have a strong garrison presence along its western periphery. The whole region lived under the enduring threat of invasion and sacking by the Hun armies roaming the Central Asian steppe. When Ban Chao, the envoy of the Eastern Han dynasty to the western regions, arrived at the court of Shanshan in modern-day Xinjiang in

79 CE, he learned that the Huns had retaken territory and rebuilt their alliances with other regional powers. At first, the king of Shanshan gave a "warm reception" to Ban Chao and his attendants. But "after a few days, the king's attitude suddenly became cold" because a Hun envoy had arrived at court. Seizing the moment, Ban Chao told his followers: "Nothing ventured, nothing gained. Our plan now can only be to attack the Hun camp by night!" Without delay, "under the cover of the midnight wind, [Ban Chao] and his 36 followers set fire to the Hun camp and beheaded their messenger." Ban Chao's act of ruthlessness proved that China did not fear Hun retaliation. "Thus," the 2001 textbook read, "the King of Shanshan decided to break up with the Huns and devoted his heart and soul to the Han Dynasty." The 2016 textbooks removed this story. Instead, they recast Ban Chao as a gentle, peace-loving diplomat.[17]

When the textbooks were revised in 2016, they made many other factual and structural changes to present the Silk Road as Han Wudi's grand strategic vision and create obvious juxtapositions with Xi's vision for OBOR (table 3.1). For the first time, the Silk Road was pulled out to be its own discrete lesson. The section heading was renamed from the dry "Han-Western Links and the Silk Road" to the more exciting "'Silk Road' of Communication Between Chinese and Foreign Civilizations." The old version had glossed over the political situation in the western regions when Zhang Qian set out, saying only that the western kingdoms were enslaved by the Huns. The 2016 version dramatically raised the stakes, stating that the Huns invaded Han territory.

In this light, Han Wudi's decision to send Zhang Qian on his journey is recast as a brilliant strategic decision—China's first organized attempt to study the Huns and build a coalition to fight them. As the textbook puts it, "Emperor Han Wudi realized the importance of the western regions and decided to recruit envoys to the western regions and contact the Darouzhi [a Central Asian tribe] to launch a converging attack on the Huns." The 2016 textbooks suggest that Zhang's trip had a clearly defined political purpose: learn about the enemy and tell potential partners about the Han dynasty's wealth and power. Han Wudi and Zhang Qian are rendered as national heroes—Han Wudi for his sweeping strategic vision, and Zhang Qian for his patriotism and loyal execution.

Over the long run, Han Wudi reasoned, deepening political and economic relations with the Central Asian states would separate the Huns

Table 3.1
Summary of Revisions to Chinese Middle School History Textbooks

Difference	2001 Version	2016 Version
Lesson title	"Han Dynasty-Western Region Links and the Silk Road"	"A 'Silk Road' of Communication Between Chinese and Foreign Civilizations"
Reason for Zhang Qian's mission	Small nations in Western Regions were controlled and enslaved by the Huns; Zhang's specific objectives not specified	"The Han Dynasty was invaded by the Huns" and Han Wudi wanted to recruit allies for a joint counterattack
Characterization of Zhang Qian	Neutral, passing summary of Zhang Qian's journeys	Detailed descriptions of Zhang Qian's journeys added, including commentary on his personal courage and patriotic enthusiasm
Description of the Han dynasty's administration of Western Regions	Stresses that Xinjiang has been a part of China since 60 BCE, and primary political theme is territorial unification of China	Adds considerable detail on the Han dynasty's methods of controlling and administering the Western Regions; notes that the Han dynasty controlled more territory than present-day China
Formation of the Maritime Silk Road	"After Han Wudi's time, businessmen from Western Han Dynasty used to do overseas trade and opened up the maritime transportation line, which is the historic Maritime Silk Road"	Credited to Han Wudi ("Han Wudi also vigorously opened up maritime traffic, and the Han Dynasty successively opened up many sea routes")
Route of the Maritime Silk Road	Went south, toward India and Sri Lanka	Also went to Korea and Japan
Destination of the Maritime Silk Road	India and Sri Lanka	Europe

Sources: Ministry of Education, *Zhongguo lishi* [Chinese History], 2001 and 2016.

from their allies. Once the whole region became dependent on trade with China, the security problem would resolve itself. The revised textbooks suggest that the process was peaceful and that expanded trade tipped the scales. In other words, Chinese students today learn in history class that

"communication" between the Han court and the Central Asian kingdoms was all it took to divide China's enemies and induce them to submit to Chinese rule. A 2005 high school textbook defined the tributary
system thus:

> In ancient China, foreign trade was under the control of the government,
> and tribute trade, which consisted of tribute and reward, occupied an
> important position. This kind of tribute trade tended to give much and
> receive little in return. The money paid by Chinese buyers to the foreign
> sellers was always several times higher than the offered price.[18] Its purpose
> was not to obtain maximum economic benefits, but to promote state power,
> strengthen ties with overseas countries, and satisfy the ruler's demand for
> special exotic treasures.[19]

The tribute system sounds a great deal like OBOR in the CCTV
documentary.

Inventing the Historical Maritime Silk Road

The textbook revisions had another task: to create an historical backdrop
for the Maritime Silk Road that Xi had promised to re-create. In the old
textbooks, the Maritime Silk Road (MSR) was mentioned only in passing. It formed spontaneously "after Han Emperor Wudi's time," the
2003 edition read. "Businessmen from Western Han Dynasty used to do
overseas trade and opened up the maritime transportation line, which is
the historic Maritime Silk Road." The road crossed the Indian Ocean,
reaching "the southern Indian peninsula and Sri Lanka island . . . at its
furthest." In fact, the 2003 high school textbook specifically confirms
that the ancient MSR did not extend to the Mediterranean.[20] The revised 2016 textbook made out the historic MSR to be older and much
longer, including a route to Korea and Japan and an Indian Ocean route
that extended all the way to Europe. (The textbook did not elaborate on
how this was possible before the construction of the Suez Canal.) The
most important new claim was that the MSR was formed on the instructions of Han Wudi himself, who is presented as a strategic genius

for "vigorously open[ing] up maritime traffic. The Han Dynasty successively opened up many sea routes."[21]

The rest of the lesson focuses on making a national hero of Zheng He, the Ming dynasty navigator who made seven great voyages in the early fifteenth century. Chinese historians have framed his legacy in a variety of ways over the years. Zheng He fell into obscurity in the late imperial period. Chinese nationalists rediscovered him in the early twentieth century, casting him as a symbol of China's lost status as a naval great power. Famed turn-of-the-century nationalist intellectual Liang Qichao praised Zheng as the "great navigator of the motherland."[22] In recent decades, Zheng has made a powerful return in Chinese official history, not as a symbol of national boldness but as an icon of China's supposed long tradition of peaceful commercial exchange. Still, until very recently, Zheng's legacy remained a matter of scholarly debate. At a 2005 conference in honor of the 600th anniversary of his voyages, historian Wu Haiying agreed with the old account: that Zheng's most important quality was his patriotism and valor. Fellow historian Yang Huaizhong disagreed, arguing that Zheng was remarkable because he brought fortune and peace to the countries he visited, while Western navigators brought only death and disaster.[23] The latter interpretation sums up the new official line in China's history textbooks. The new textbooks add even more details about Zheng's heroism and virtue and about his legacy of "non-cheating, non-bullying" exchanges.[24] Hagiographic paragraphs about Zheng's great deeds also serve the function of filling space in the revised textbooks. Otherwise, the MSR section would appear much shorter than the section on the overland Silk Road. This would not do, given Xi's insistence on presenting the "Belt" and "Road" as parallel, sister initiatives.

Perhaps because the MSR concept rests on shaky historical ground, lower-ranking Chinese officials have been known to exaggerate or misrepresent the history of Zheng He's voyages to justify current-day projects. In 2018, at an event in Australia, the deputy editor-in-chief of *China Daily* claimed that "historical records show Captain Zheng He had a short stop at Darwin in the early 15th century. Australia was right on the route of the Maritime Silk Road."[25] There is no factual basis for this claim. Perhaps Wang understood on some level that the official historical claims about Zheng He are designed to be politically useful and not strictly accurate. Still, it is hard to think of a more cynical way of putting history to work for political ends.

External Propaganda

For three years after Xi announced OBOR at his speech in Kazakhstan, China made no serious effort to publicize OBOR in the West. Since then, Chinese media have produced a few English-language propaganda materials, but their efforts have been half-hearted at best. The Chinese government also describes OBOR very differently to foreign audiences than it does to domestic ones. There is no hint of the implicit claims about China's technological superiority and recipient countries' gratitude. The message is solely about abstract values: globalization, free trade, free movement of people, and win-win. Propaganda speeches, articles, and audiovisual materials take pains to present these ideals as benefits of the current international order that must be sustained, not deficiencies or inequities that need to be corrected. Foreigners are therefore told that China wants to uphold the global status quo as it rises, not disrupt or overthrow it. The implication is that the United States and its allies are no longer responsible guardians of the international system, so China is reluctantly stepping up as a "responsible great power" to protect global trade and international institutions.[26]

At various points, the Chinese government has instructed domestic media not to report on OBOR in ways that might frighten foreigners. Before the all-important May 2017 Belt and Road Forum in Beijing, the central government imposed a moratorium on university-sponsored academic conferences relating to OBOR. A few weeks before the forum, a guidance document for journalists clarifying how to navigate the "minefield" of OBOR reporting went viral on WeChat.[27] Although the article was posted under a pseudonym, it was widely interpreted as reflecting official guidance because it cited senior officials from the China Association of Journalists and the CCP-affiliated newspaper *Guangming Daily*.

The pseudonymous WeChat guidance corrected several common "errors" in press reports about OBOR. The first was the use of "non-standard figures." "The Chinese government has never defined the scope of the 'Belt and Road,'" the article said, and media should not publish irregular maps suggesting arbitrary limitations on the number of countries that can or will join. The second error was the overuse of military language to describe OBOR projects, including the word "strategy" (*zhanlüe* 战略), which has aggressive connotations in Chinese. According to the article, these allusions "will make people stay away from [OBOR], and even stay away because of fear."

The guidance document cautioned against overstating OBOR's positive effect in enabling Chinese firms to outsource their excess capacity (mindful of the Trump administration's complaints about Chinese industrial policy), warned that media should not equate OBOR projects with foreign aid, and reminded journalists to focus on people-to-people connections, not just economic benefits for OBOR countries. Journalists were urged not to "put too much emphasis on OBOR's 'Chineseness,' especially in reports for foreigners." "The starting point of the Silk Road is China," it read, "but countries of the world have to work together to turn 'mine' into 'ours,' to use 'China' lightly and use 'them' heavily, and to emphasize the United Nations." Finally, it clarified that journalists must use OBOR's new English-language name: the Belt and Road Initiative. The Chinese-language name, which directly translates to "One Belt One Road," would remain unchanged.[28]

In line with these directives, external OBOR propaganda offers a very different historical account of the ancient Silk Road than the one now taught in Chinese history textbooks. Rather than a Chinese invention to bring prosperity, harmony, and order to the world, the Silk Road is interpreted as an expression of the universal human desire to have free trade across borders.

This is how Lily's father introduces the historical Silk Road in episode 1 of the "Belt and Road Bedtime Stories," the 2017 English-language series produced by *China Daily*.[29] First, he must make an apology—he is leaving for a few days to attend an important conference, the Belt and Road Forum in Beijing. When Lily asks what the conference is about, he tells her about the caravans and merchant ships of the ancient Silk Road, which carried giraffes and all kinds of other wondrous products:

A few years ago, China's President, Xi Jinping, proposed making new routes like the old routes, but even *bigger*. It's called Belt and Road Initiative. More stuff can move around the world more easily. And people can travel around the world more easily and build things countries need.

That's good, Baba!

So this forum is a chance to tell the world about the Belt and Road, like I'm telling you.

As Lily's father describes the initiative in terms that his young daughter can understand, it is clear that he is oversimplifying somewhat. (When she asks innocently if OBOR is "like countries sharing?" he answers energetically in the affirmative.) Yet his body language and vocal inflection suggest that the very thought of OBOR fills him with inspiration. As he speaks, he gestures by moving around toys on a map of the world labeled entirely in Chinese.

The reason for the father's enthusiasm comes into focus later in the series, as it becomes clear that OBOR touches his family directly. At the beginning of episode 2, Lily is drawing a picture of a train when her father enters the room. The lines, colors, and motifs of her drawing are remarkably similar to the children's illustrations of trains shown in the CCTV documentary, complete with the same smiling sun:[30]

You said the Belt and Road wasn't just about moving stuff from country to country? What do you mean?

Okay, I'll tell you. Countries make deals about buying and selling things. And they visit each other's countries, and even go to each other's schools.

Like how I'm American and I go to school in Beijing?

A lot like that, but the United States hasn't joined the initiative.

Is that because it's too far away?

Actually, any country can join, anywhere.

How?

They make agreements with China and the other countries.

But it's a Chinese initiative, right?

It's China's idea. But it belongs [*sigh*] to the world.

This exchange neatly captures how Chinese media describe the Silk Road spirit differently to foreign audiences. The CCTV series for Chinese audiences portrays the archetypal beneficiary of OBOR as a young person in a developing country who aspires to connect to the globalized world and access economic opportunity. For Western audiences, on the other hand, the protagonist is Lily, a wide-eyed American child who is awed by China and happy to learn that China welcomes her family in the spirit of friendship and openness. China watchers will note the bitter irony of Beijing boasting of its openness to the free movement of people. Chinese families are still bound by the *hukou*, or household registration system, which restricts them from legally moving within their own country in search of better work or economic opportunities. But if Lily's father understands that domestic OBOR propaganda would never mention the concept of open borders, he does not let on. As he explains it to Lily, OBOR is a gift from China, who expects no repayment. It is only out of pride or ignorance that the United States could have refused to join a program that is so tautologically good.

In the next two episodes, Baba explains to Lily the value system that China wants to promote through OBOR. In episode 3, he draws a picture of a globe with children of different races ringed around it, holding hands. As she colors in the drawing, her father explains how OBOR will "increase globalization." Lily is puzzled. She doesn't know the word. "Globalize-lation?" she asks, "What's that?" So, her father begins another lecture:[31]

> That's where people from different parts of the world cooperate. They buy and sell things to each other, and they visit and even live in other countries.
>
> Like we live in China?
>
> Exactly, globalization is why *you* were born *here*.
>
> But why does globalization happen?
>
> It's good for people! We live happier lives when we cooperate. That's why countries want to join the Belt and Road. And that's why they're holding a forum in Beijing, so that more people can understand it.

Lily's father continues his lesson through three more short videos, sometimes while playing a ukulele. Each time he tries to put his daughter to bed, she squeals and demands more stories about the ancient trade routes. First, he tells her that "globalize-lation," which she continues to mispronounce, has come under threat because "some countries are moving away . . . So the Belt and Road is an opportunity to move globalization forward."[32] In episode 4, he explains that OBOR will pay for itself by supercharging economic growth across the world.

"I hope that other people understand, like me," Lily says, with great feeling, in the last video in the series.[33]

"So do I," her father sighs. "I really do."

Conclusion

Chinese government propaganda defines OBOR differently for domestic and foreign audiences. For the domestic audience, the OBOR brand juxtaposes Xi Jinping's current policy with the ancient Silk Road, using history to justify why China is investing overseas. For the first time since the imperial period, China is ready to reclaim its historical mantle—not only as the architect and defender of trade links across Eurasia but also as a first-rate, technologically advanced, and truly global power. The propaganda presents OBOR in such glowing terms that no country opposing it could possibly seem to be acting in good faith. The textbook revisions actively change the official history of the ancient Silk Road, too, bringing it into alignment with the government's description of the current OBOR policy. This does more than raise the profile of OBOR within domestic Chinese political discourse. It elevates Xi by comparison, embedding him into the OBOR concept, and brashly suggesting that he deserves to be mentioned in the same breath as Han Wudi, perhaps the most venerated emperor in Chinese history.

To Western audiences, the "bedtime stories" seem tone-deaf and even slightly ominous—but still relatively benign. Since it would be hard to imagine a clumsier or more transparent piece of propaganda, it is easy to dismiss the video as a bunch of empty slogans—"win-win," "globalization," "mutual benefit," and so on. Why, then, are these five short videos the Chinese government's best effort at explaining OBOR to ordinary people in the English-speaking world? In contrast, the OBOR concept has been omnipresent in Chinese-language media, topping the list of policy buzzwords in the *People's Daily* year after year. It is clear enough that the Chinese government is not particularly concerned with persuading voters in Western democracies that OBOR is not a threat. Yet the film suggests something else—that even the Chinese propagandists can scarcely contain their cynicism. OBOR "is China's idea, but it belongs to the world," Lily's father tells her. In the West, only a child would ever believe it.

CHAPTER 4

The Emperor's New Brand

Promoting OBOR at Home and Abroad

Thousands of Chinese and foreign businessmen have donated blood to OBOR to "bring together the blood of nations," the Chinese headline read.[1] On July 15, 2017, a blood drive was held in Yiwu, coorganized by twenty-eight companies and organizations, including the Bank of China, the local chamber of commerce, business groups from Taiwan and Sudan, and a Yemeni businessman.[2] The newspaper recorded that more than 200 foreigners representing more than thirty countries donated blood, including Malaysia, Canada, Ukraine, India, Russia, Sudan, and Syria. But, they noted, "it is understood that most of the foreign investors who participated in this blood donation activity came from OBOR countries."

The article went on to boast about the city of Yiwu's commitment to OBOR. "At present, Yiwu is actively integrating into OBOR's national strategy" (国家战略), it read. "In accordance with the five requirements of 'national policy communication, infrastructure connectivity, trade smoothness, capital finance, and shared human feeling,' Yiwu is accelerating the transformation and upgrading of cities and markets and striving to promote steady growth of exports." At the same time, Yiwu is "vigorously cultivating and developing" its import trade and "has become the home of businessmen from around the world." In conclusion, the article claimed that Yiwu was integrating the spirit of blood donation—the "manifestation of human love"—into its civic society, which would help "promote it as an international trading city."

Since Xi Jinping announced OBOR in Kazakhstan in 2013, nearly every public and private institution in China has publicly embraced it. Provincial and local governments have submitted OBOR-branded development master plans for building roads, ports, airports, power plants, and industrial parks. Universities have founded OBOR programs for international exchange and have opened more than a hundred think tanks and centers devoted to studying and promoting OBOR. Private companies and trade organizations have sponsored thousands of conferences and promotional events like the Yiwu blood drive. Foreign companies and businesspeople have participated, too, doing their part to ensure that these events have adequate photo opportunities and receive media attention in China and overseas. Finally, of course, there are the overseas OBOR infrastructure projects initiated by Chinese companies. These OBOR proposals and projects share a common denominator: they are brazen schemes to attract press coverage in Chinese official media and thereby win political favor.

Bizarrely, most people involved in organizing these events freely admit (off the record) that they do not clearly understand what OBOR is, how it is supposed to work on an administrative level, how its constituent projects are supposed to link up with one another, and what strategic policy objectives it is trying to achieve. They know that OBOR is a high-priority national initiative closely linked to Xi Jinping. They grasp the major themes and priorities: cross-border investment, people-to-people cooperation, joint ventures with foreign companies, "connectivity," and so forth. Yet in the vast majority of cases, the people who lead these OBOR-branded plans, projects, and events receive little to no direct oversight from Beijing.

How does the Chinese party-state manage OBOR administration on the ground and sustain the illusion that it is a vast, intricate, and tightly coordinated master plan? In Hans Christian Andersen's parable of the Emperor's New Clothes, when the emperor proudly reveals his new "clothes," his ministers make a collective decision not to challenge him in public. They praise the clothes in effusive terms, either because they want to curry favor or because they fear that their inability to see the clothes means that they must be foolish. Similarly, the real protagonists of the OBOR story are the Chinese government ministries, Chinese Communist Party (CCP) organs, local governments, state-owned enterprises (SOEs), private businesses, and academics who sustain the illusion that the implementation of OBOR is highly centralized and systematic, rather than ad hoc and bottom-up. Foreign people, companies, and governments also participate in constructing this OBOR myth whenever they parrot the Chinese government's claims about what OBOR "is," assuming that Beijing's plans play out as intended. The analogy is imperfect in only one respect. In Andersen's tale, the emperor himself is the first person taken in by the swindlers. Today, it is not clear whether Xi believes that OBOR is in fact a world-historical project that will assure his place in the pantheon of Chinese political history or whether he, too, is in on the con.

To recognize that OBOR operates as a campaign to promote Xi's personalized brand is not to deny its strategic importance. On the contrary, this view of OBOR reveals several fascinating and sometimes alarming insights about how the CCP is taking its unique style of power politics global. By declining to micromanage OBOR projects, dictate project terms, and so on, the Chinese government has freed up its companies to take responsibility, experiment, and adapt their practices to local contexts. This hands-off approach to governance also tells the firms in question that OBOR is first and foremost about loyalty and political relationships, not transnational connectivity or profitable investments. The megaprojects built under the OBOR umbrella are not ends in themselves but means for firms and foreign governments alike to build patronage relationships with China. In the most desired end-state, all those who participate in OBOR will eventually learn that it pays—politically and financially— to be friendly to China and acknowledge China's status.

Performing Party Loyalty

The CCP has long used campaigns and organized performances of ideological loyalty as governance tools. During the Cultural Revolution, Mao Zedong's Little Red Book functioned as both a weapon and a shield. Party cadres strove to outdo each other in their race to praise Mao and avoid being branded as counterrevolutionaries. The tradition of using branded campaigns to spur grassroots action outlived Mao himself. It also survived China's transition from a planned to a partially market-driven economy, which rendered most of the old Marxist slogans obsolete. When German political scientist Heike Holbig interviewed dozens of scholars from the elite Central Party School in 2009 and 2010, she was surprised to find that most of her interview subjects no longer took party ideology literally. Instead, Holbig argues, party language has evolved to serve a very different function: "as a set of practices and incentives for . . . proper performance."[3]

Holbig calls this phenomenon "ideology after the end of ideology." In her rather cynical view, official slogans and descriptors like "Marxist-Leninism"—which Xi still embraces—are not historical relics that persist because they are inconvenient to retire. Rather, the CCP preserves them precisely because they bear so little resemblance to lived experience. When a young cadre from Shanghai praises Marx, what he really does is perform his loyalty to party rule and his submission to the party's "monopoly over truth."[4] Mandatory classes and training exercises in elite party schools teach the importance of ideological rituals, as Dutch anthropologist Frank Pieke has brilliantly captured. The "content," Pieke argues, matters little in comparison to the "performative tasks that ideological work fulfills among the ruling elite."[5] When the Party periodically amends its official theoretical positions, cadres at all levels are expected to adhere strictly to the new usage rules.

Today, the CCP uses propaganda and ideological innovations—what it calls "thought work" (思想工作)—to continually update its claim to political legitimacy and police potential challenges to its authority. China's propaganda bureaucracy sends guidance (指导) from the top down; direct supervision (领导) and most of the work of producing and censoring content is outsourced to lower-level and peripheral agencies. Anne-Marie Brady describes how this process works in her classic study, *Marketing Dictatorship*. Ultimate oversight over the propaganda system lies with the Leading Small Group on Propaganda and Thought Work (LSGPTW). The LSGPTW operates essentially as a board of directors and is currently chaired by Wang Huning, a member of the Politburo Standing Committee and one of Xi's most influential advisers. Beneath the LSGPTW is the Central Propaganda Department (CPD), which has a staff of several hundred. Writing in 2008, Brady argued that "the CPD's leadership role over China's propaganda system is mostly on moral grounds, with little legal standing. Yet its effective power is very strong; it is in charge of overseeing a vast and complex interconnected system of control."[6] Brady compares the CPD to the Vatican in medieval Europe. Its influence is vast, but diffuse and indirect. It polices the behavior of lower-level actors more through the fear of punishment than through the promise of reward.

As a result, Beijing does not need to micromanage the country's vast media ecosystem to promote OBOR; it merely provides the guidance, and the bureaucracy takes care of the rest. The CPD appoints the most senior officials in the major newspapers, TV and radio stations, and on-line news networks. It has extensive influence in academia and think tanks because it funds most social science research in China. Xi has dramatically increased propaganda budgets and placed several of the key state propaganda agencies under direct party control.[7] At the same time, he has preserved and strengthened the incentive structures that keep party and state officials in line all the way down the chain of command.[8] For most functionaries on the lower and middle rungs of the party-state, the hardest part of the job is coping with uncertainty about Beijing's expectations. When the directive comes down to "promote OBOR," officials and institutions have to decide how to interpret what this ambiguous guidance means. If they misstep, they could bring the hammer down on their own heads.

Vision and Action

After Xi announced OBOR's launch in 2013, the Chinese bureaucracy delayed several years before taking the first step toward institutionalizing it. It was not until March 2015, more than eighteen months after Xi's speech, that the Chinese government finally published a policy document laying out OBOR's theoretical objectives and high-level structure. Everything about the document was clunky, starting with the title: "Vision and Actions on Jointly Building Silk Road Economic Belt and 21st-Century Maritime Silk Road."[9] The document had all the markings of a highly authoritative policy paper. It was released jointly by the National Development and Reform Commission (NDRC), which supervises Chinese industrial policy and SOEs; the Ministry of Foreign Affairs; and the State Council. In short, every major power base in the Chinese state approved it. However, even the most cursory look made clear that "Vision and Actions" was a guidance document directed at an audience of Chinese officials, not a statement to explain OBOR in language comprehensible to foreigners. The NDRC faithfully published versions in six languages on its website, but the translations were literal renderings of the original Chinese text, loaded with generalities and officialese.

Every official would have to read "Vision and Actions" carefully for clues about what they personally could do to contribute to OBOR's success. This was not a straightforward task, because the document was ambiguous and obviously written by a committee.[10] More than half of the text is devoted to abstract statements about the positive benefits of OBOR. For example, there is a lengthy passage about the Silk Road spirit, which is defined as a "historical and cultural heritage shared by all countries around the world." The document contains no maps, diagrams, figures, lists of projects, budgets, or project criteria. Apart from some general instructions about how each region in China should participate, it provides hardly any detail about the timeline or process for implementing OBOR's goals. There is no mention of the $1 trillion price tag widely reported in the *New York Times* and many other Western news outlets.[11] If the "Vision and Actions" document was the Chinese government's first step toward implementing OBOR through the country's major institutions, it indicated that the debate about the country's strategic future was still far from being resolved. In fact, the document seemed to invite different branches of the party-state, still squabbling over ownership of the New Silk Road concept, to compete to shape OBOR in their own image.

"Vision and Actions" did clarify the government's objectives on a few important points. One of the five defining principles is that "the Initiative follows market operation." OBOR "will abide by market rules and international norms," it reads, "give play to the decisive role of the market in resource allocation and the primary role of enterprises, and let the governments perform their due functions." To a Western reader, this principle reads as contradictory. By definition, a state-led infrastructure program follows political imperatives, not market operation. To a Chinese audience, the instruction to "give play" to market forces was a clear warning to firms not to throw money at unprofitable or unviable projects in the name of fulfilling OBOR obligations.

The document strongly implied that OBOR's political objectives outweighed its economic goals. This had several important practical implications for Chinese firms and bureaucrats working on OBOR projects overseas. First, "deepen[ing] political trust" at all levels was presented as a priority of paramount importance. "Vision and Actions" instructed Chinese government officials to "give full play to the bridging role of communication between political parties and parliaments, and promote friendly exchanges between legislative bodies, major political parties, and political organizations of countries along the Belt and Road." Second, for OBOR to succeed over the longer term, China would have to build relationships with all important political factions in the countries where it does business—not just the current ruling parties. This instruction shaped China's approach to the case studies discussed in part II of this book.

"Vision and Actions" made clear that the top priority in overseas OBOR projects would be to achieve "policy coordination" between China and recipient governments.[12] This was an important clue that OBOR's strategic objectives are about political influence and go far beyond the financial success or failure of the underlying projects. A few lines later, the document suggested that OBOR was a new kind of bilateral diplomatic relationship between China and recipient countries, not a multilateral platform. "China will work with countries along the Belt and Road" to do various things, it reads. By implication, a project cannot be part of OBOR unless China is directly involved. In summary, "Vision and Actions" laid out a low-profile and highly flexible mechanism of political control. Micromanagement would not be necessary—as long as ultimate power over OBOR projects and political relationships still rested with Beijing.

"Vision and Actions" was intended as a starting point, not a detailed roadmap. The Chinese observers I interviewed—for their safety, on the condition of anonymity—acknowledged that it is highly ambiguous in places. Yet they stressed a common theme: any Chinese official reading "Vision and Actions" when it was first handed down would have known that to misinterpret even one line could bring career catastrophe. This was not a diplomatic or foreign policy document, nor was it intended as a primer for foreign audiences. It was a study document for officials and party members across China. Sure enough, the system answered the call.

Crowdsourcing Strategy

Since 2015, the Chinese party-state has embraced OBOR in ways more creative than Xi could have expected. All of the major central government department and provincial ministries are independently pushing their own interpretations of OBOR to compete for funds. The Ministry of Culture has requested OBOR funding for its existing soft power programs in the culture and entertainment industries.[13] The Ministry of Education has proposed setting up five hundred think tanks and research centers dedicated to OBOR and is seeking funding for more than 100,000 scholarships for students from OBOR countries.[14] Chinese provinces have also submitted their own OBOR master plans, though some have been more successful than others in getting them approved. François Godement has shown that the provinces originally depicted in official maps as the starting points of the overland and maritime Silk Roads—Xinjiang and Fujian provinces—have received far less central funding for infrastructure projects than have wealthier coastal provinces that traditionally wield more political influence in Beijing.[15]

OBOR has become a useful branding theme for conferences across China, including in industries that have nothing to do with infrastructure or connectivity. In August 2017, beauty industry executives from Taiwan and mainland China held their annual "cross-strait youth health and beauty industry seminar" in the coastal city of Fuzhou. The theme was "'One Belt, One Road': Beauty All the Way."[16] In October 2017, China's largest industry association of kitchenware manufacturers held an OBOR Green Development Forum in Xingfu, Shandong province. In his keynote speech, Wang Bingsen declared that manufacturers of kitchen utensils should "fully understand the situation, actively respond to national policy requirements, and firmly grasp the national strategic deployment" of OBOR.[17] Local governments and party officials have actively encouraged these kinds of events, presumably because they attract media attention and photo ops. From the OBOR International Invitational Football Match to the countless OBOR-branded art shows, it is usually local officials and party cadres, not the corporate sponsors, who coordinate the promotional strategies.[18]

Private companies, both Chinese and foreign, have learned to perform obeisance to OBOR. Nearly every major Western company operating in China—including Wal-Mart, Boeing, Allianz, Samsung, and Microsoft—has publicly praised OBOR and presented itself as a potential partner or contributor.[19] HSBC has plastered pro-OBOR advertisements in dozens of Western airports. Sumitomo Group, a Japanese conglomerate, was recognized in *Xinhua* for "taking advantage of the OBOR initiative . . . actively deploying in the provinces, cities and overseas markets along OBOR to enhance the competitiveness of the Group."[20] Sun Jie, CEO of Ctrip, one of China's largest travel companies, has said that "Ctrip is responding to the [CCP's] call with practical actions, from actively deploying [business in] countries along OBOR to promoting one hundred poverty alleviation travel routes."[21] Tsingtao Brewery, China's second-largest beer producer, justified a joint venture it initiated in Sri Lanka by claiming that it will "gradually enhance the brand influence of Tsingtao Brewery in South Asia and lay an important foundation for OBOR."[22] Bank of China, the country's second-largest bank, has promised to "deepen the construction of the 'OBOR' financial artery and become OBOR's preferred bank."[23] None of these press releases provide evidence that the companies deviated from their preexisting business strategies to meet OBOR policy requirements. This would not be the point. The companies and the Chinese government understand that these statements are performances of good favor toward Xi's pet project.

Two types of companies are particularly concerned with proving their loyalty to OBOR: private companies in political or financial difficulty, and Hong Kong–based organizations that depend on access to the mainland market. These branding efforts are not official, but they indicate how far vulnerable institutions will go to demonstrate loyalty to the OBOR brand. For example, not long before it declared bankruptcy, the Chinese bike-share company Ofo boasted that its "'Singularity' big data platform has improved the smart city transportation system" and thereby "taken 'Intelligently Made in China' overseas under the guidance of OBOR." Ofo's executives must have been thrilled that the Chinese government reposted their report on OBOR's official website.[24] In September 2018, the Law Society of Hong Kong held a conference with the theme of "The ABC to Building a Smart Belt and Road: Law and Artificial Intelligence, Blockchain, and Cloud" (fig. 4.1). It is not clear what any of these things had to do with OBOR—but that was not the point. The Hong Kong government advertised the event on its website.[25] As one senior representative from a major conglomerate told me in August 2018, "we can only speculate what the Belt and Road is all about. All we know

Friday, 28 September 2018
Hong Kong

For online registration and details:
www.hklawsoc-beltandroad.com

FIGURE 4.1: Promotional poster for an unofficial OBOR conference, "The ABC of Belt and Road." Courtesy of the Law Society of Hong Kong.

is that the government wants us to show that we support it, so that's what we are doing—as loudly as we can."

At times, even senior CCP officials have explicitly called OBOR a brand. On December 18, 2018, more than one thousand eminent Chinese politicians, businesspeople, journalists, and scholars attended a ceremony in Beijing for the 13th Influential Brander Summit.[26] Gu Xiulian, vice chair of the Standing Committee of the Tenth National People's Congress, kicked off the festivities. At the ceremony, awards were granted to the top ten national Chinese brands. A special OBOR Outstanding Brand Contribution trophy (品牌年度人物峰会) was awarded to China Enterprises Development Holdings Group.[27]

The proliferation of the OBOR brand has turned the slogan into a trope—one that might have made for a popular meme if it were less politically sensitive. One image circulated on Chinese social media featured a satirical advertisement for an escort service, crudely stenciled on a concrete wall. "Marry a foreign chick," it read. "Civil and diplomatic endorsement. OBOR Project." Below it was a blurred-out phone number.[28]

The Case of the Missing Data

Of course, the fact that independent actors are trying to twist OBOR for their own purposes does not itself prove that OBOR is strategically confused, nor that politics is paramount and the underlying projects don't matter. Could OBOR actually be a tightly controlled and highly organized investment policy run out of Beijing, with a public relations component left to the grassroots? The lack of official sources makes it impossible to rule out this possibility. Nevertheless, the circumstantial evidence suggests that OBOR is not primarily a detailed master plan for infrastructure connectivity. If it is, then Beijing is executing it neither methodically nor very effectively.

What does the Chinese government claim it is actually building? For the signature initiative of China's paramount leader, OBOR has a curiously low profile on the non-Chinese internet. OBOR did not even have a foreign-language website until March 2017, when the Belt and Road Portal was launched. This website was "developed under the guidance of the Office of the Leading Group for the Belt and Road Initiative and hosted by the State Information Center." It "aims to promote information sharing among enterprises, social organizations, and citizens of the countries along the Belt and Road routes."[29] The portal is now available in English, Spanish, French, Russian, Arabic, and Chinese.

The Belt and Road Portal presents itself as a one-stop shop for information about OBOR, but it is nearly useless for serious corporate, financial, or academic research. The website's prominently marked Data section consists of a single interactive calculator that generates bar graphs of annual data between 2010 and 2015. The menu of available statistics is bizarre, almost comically unrelated to OBOR's stated goals. The thirty-nine indicators available range from the consumer price index (a measure of inflation) to the population of women in the country. Statistics are available for China and sixty-three "B&R countries." The Belt and Road Portal has a separate section on International Cooperation, which contains "country profiles" for China and all sixty-three countries. Yet these do not contain any reference to OBOR projects. Instead, the profiles consist of three paragraphs summarizing each country's generic economic statistics: its population, growth rate, and GDP per capita.[30] Nowhere on the site is there a list of OBOR projects by country. Nor is there any data about the most important question of all: how much money China has actually spent.

In fact, the only relevant data set available on the Belt and Road Portal undermines the CCP's narrative about OBOR. If OBOR were actually a "$1 trillion infrastructure connectivity plan," we should expect the data to show an *acceleration* in the value of Chinese overseas contracted projects after Xi announced the initiative in 2013. But the official data on China's "contracted amount of overseas investment projects" from 2010 to 2015 shows no such acceleration in outbound funds. This confirms the argument in chapter 2 that one of OBOR's original functions was to repackage previous investments under a new name. It also corroborates the argument that OBOR's strategic purpose is more political than commercial. If not, why would China not publish far more detailed, reliable, and compelling data to support its claim that all this new "connectivity" is paying dividends?

Mapping the Unmappable

Official Chinese maps released by government offices and party-controlled media depict OBOR's physical footprint in staggeringly different ways. The most charitable way to interpret this is that the central government has a master plan that the media do not reveal to the public. A more plausible explanation is that there is no coherent master plan for linking individual OBOR projects into an integrated network. The following section discusses five maps of OBOR published by various official media sources, each of which is closely linked to the Chinese government and CCP. I had new maps drawn to re-create the key features of the originals while making them more legible for non-Chinese speakers. Standardizing the format makes it easier to see the important differences in how the original maps render OBOR's routes and key hubs. Interested readers can find the original maps (in Chinese) by following the references in the Appendix.

The most obvious inconsistency between the official Chinese maps is how they depict the routes of the overland Silk Road Economic Belt and Maritime Silk Road. The most common rendering follows the outline of the Xinhua map (fig. 4.2): an overland route from Western China (near Xi'an) to Rotterdam and a sea route from South China (near Fuzhou) to the European Mediterranean coast (Venice or Athens). Yet the termini are not consistent. Figure 4.3 is based on a map produced by the Hong Kong Trade and Development Commission (HKTDC), an institution linked to Beijing and the Hong Kong government. This map also breaks the Belt and Road into several differently colored component routes. There is no consistent labeling of what these constituent initiatives might be. HKTDC included the Bangladesh-China-India-Myanmar economic corridor, while Xinhua left it out. The HKTDC map also tacks an eastern maritime leg onto the Maritime Silk Road, passing through eastern Indonesia and down to northern Australia. This raises the question: are these ancillary projects parts of OBOR? Are they administered separately?

Other maps of OBOR reveal the preferences of the state entities that produced them. For example, for years the State Oceanic Administration and China's northeastern provinces have been pushing for the central government to open "blue economic passages" through the Arctic. As a "near-Arctic power," they argue, China is entitled to use Arctic resources and shipping lanes and should invest in maritime infrastructure links to the Russian far north.[31] Figures 4.4 and 4.5 offer more detailed images of potential Arctic routes. The latter is based on an OBOR development plan published by the municipal government of the landlocked northeastern city of Changchun. The bureaucrats who drew this route clearly wanted funding from Beijing to link Changchun to a nearby port and turn it into a trans-shipment hub for Arctic maritime trade. These maps certainly do not reflect a coherent official definition of OBOR. Instead, they suggest that lower-ranking officials understand OBOR to be a flexible concept. Municipal and provincial governments strive to show how they could contribute to the advancement of OBOR's vaguely defined objectives, and the ones that do this most effectively are rewarded. The "routes" drawn on the maps are simply useful abstractions.

Perhaps a better way to conceptualize OBOR is as a metaphor for a network: a constellation of nodes or hubs with various types of connectivity between them, as CCTV did (fig. 4.6). After all, many official maps explicitly label the major nodes. Xinhua rendered the overland Silk Road as a series of hubs between Xi'an in the east and Rotterdam in the west (fig. 4.2). Most of the pins dropped in this map are in national capitals—

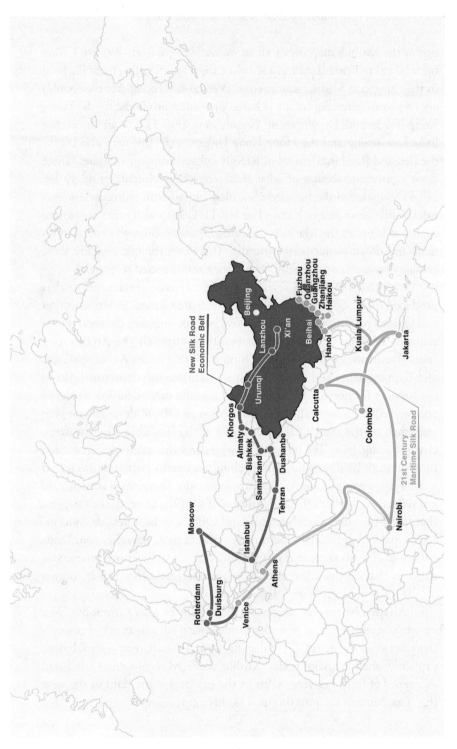

FIGURE 4.2: OBOR's traditional shape, based on a map from Xinhua reproduced on Belt and Road Portal. Courtesy of Ira Anatolevna.

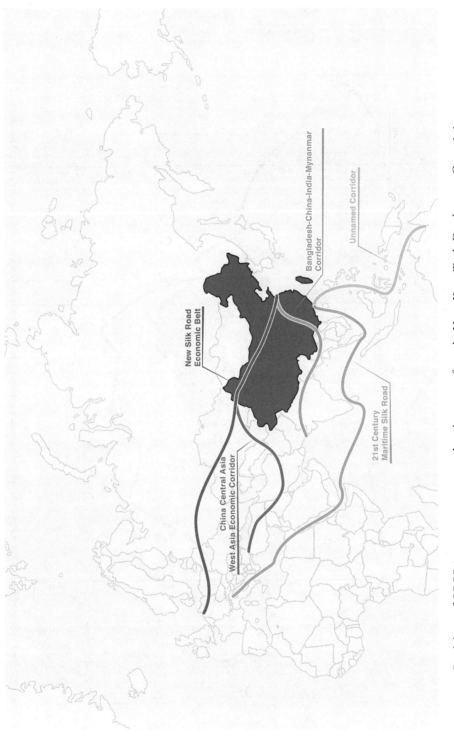

FIGURE 4.3: Breakdown of OBOR into component routes, based on a map from the Hong Kong Trade Development Commission. Courtesy of Ira Anatolevna.

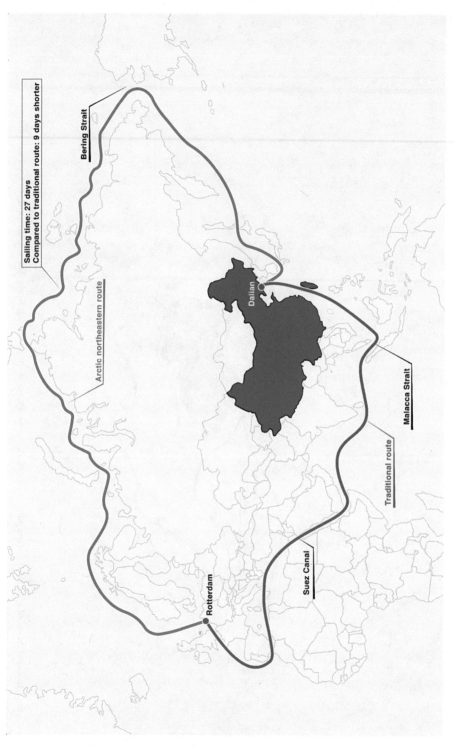

FIGURE 4.4: The Maritime Silk Road as a loop around the Eurasian landmass, based on a map from Sohu. Courtesy of Ira Anatolevna.

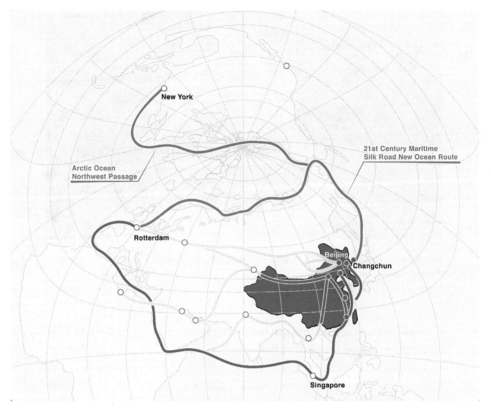

FIGURE 4.5: "New Ocean Route," based on a map from the Changchun New Area Government. Courtesy of Ira Anatolevna.

Dushanbe, Tehran, Moscow—but not all are. Along the Maritime Silk Road, the map marks six Chinese cities as hubs, including the relatively minor cities of Fuzhou, Hankou, and Beihai. Along with the national capitals of Jakarta, Kuala Lumpur, Colombo, and Athens, it also marks Venice, the hometown of Silk Road explorer Marco Polo, and the relatively little known Kenyan port of Mombasa. To try to understand what China is really building, is the correct approach not to connect the dots but to pay attention to the dots themselves?

Not so—Chinese map makers select OBOR hubs as arbitrarily as they draw their routes, with no relation to the size or strategic significance of construction projects. Pakistan, for example, has accepted far more

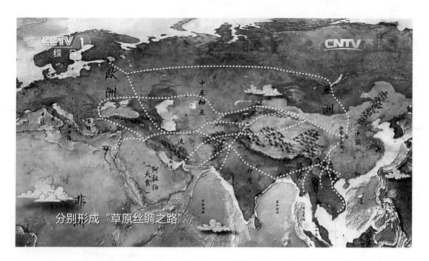

FIGURE 4.6: The overland Silk Road Economic Belt depicted as a network rather than a route. Still from China Central Television, "The Belt and Road EP 1 Common Destiny | CCTV," September 2016, YouTube.

Chinese infrastructure investment than any other country. Yet the Xinhua map includes no pins in Pakistan. The Xinhua map highlights the Italian port of Venice, rather than Genoa, which has received far more Chinese investment. It seems probable that the selection of which cities to highlight as hubs does not indicate waystations or infrastructure junctions. They simply reveal the mapmaker's arbitrary political classification of which partner countries and cities are most important.

There are two ways to explain the variation between these maps. The first is that the Chinese state does have a detailed master plan for OBOR that is secret from the public and even possibly from the mapmakers in the CPD. However, in light of all the other evidence—Xi's fixation with branding the initiative, the bizarre inconsistencies in official data, and the exceptionally ambiguous "Vision and Actions" document—the simplest explanation is that OBOR is not really a developmental master plan at all.

"Known Unknowns" of OBOR Administration

The curious lack of useful data on the Belt and Road Portal would not be a problem if it were easy to get data on OBOR from other sources. Unfortunately, OBOR's structure makes it extremely hard to make even the roughest of estimates about the size and scope of the initiative. Foreign researchers who want to study OBOR as a traditional policy program have to surmount six barriers preventing them from getting reliable data.

First, the Chinese government has never defined OBOR's boundaries. There is no official roadmap document that gives hard figures for how much China plans to spend, on what, and over what time frame. Articles and press releases from CCP newspapers and state agencies offer contradictory information about what countries are "members" of OBOR and which overseas projects count as OBOR projects. Nowhere has the Chinese government published a set of criteria to distinguish projects as "in" or "out" of OBOR. Because OBOR is still in its early stages and has only recently begun to receive critical attention, its future direction is inherently unknowable. Perhaps Xi and his associates have even grander ambitions for OBOR in the longer term, after China becomes wealthier and amasses more influence. If so, then the current slate of OBOR projects could be nothing more than a foundation or trial run for more strategically significant projects in the pipeline.

Second, the Chinese government systematically uses arithmetic games to overstate the size of OBOR projects. A Chinese promise to invest $2 billion in a project may include several hundred million dollars for projects that have already been funded, plus an unknown amount of private sector investment that is "projected" to follow after the infrastructure is built—all rounded up to the nearest billion. Nor does the Chinese government update its official data in light of progress on the ground. That is, it does not always acknowledge whether the funds that have been pledged are ever actually disbursed.

Third, very little is known about how the Chinese party-state supervises and administers OBOR at the highest levels. Xi has established a Leading Small Group (LSG) responsible for OBOR issues. This group is chaired by Han Zheng, a member of the Politburo Standing Committee and the seventh-ranked official in the CCP hierarchy. Han previously oversaw construction of the Three Gorges Dam. Hu Chunhua, a Politburo member whom some analysts have identified as a potential successor to Xi, is in charge of OBOR's trade aspects. Wang Huning, the CCP's leading theoretician and Xi's close confidant, is said to be closely involved. Xi himself is also clearly an important player. It is unclear how hands-on the OBOR LSG really is.[32] LSGs are closer to governing boards than active management bodies. Their purpose is to provide strategic direction and coordinate an interagency process; their members, who are among the most powerful people in China, are too busy to engage with minutiae. Most of the specifics of project implementation almost certainly fall to the NDRC, the powerful agency that oversees industrial policy and domestic infrastructure construction.

Under the highest level, almost nothing is known about how the Chinese government administers OBOR on a day-to-day basis. Western scholars do not know which agencies or people in the NDRC have the most influence over key strategic and project management decisions. They do not know the size of OBOR's operational or managerial budget; how many dedicated staff in Beijing are working on OBOR's organization, funding, and planning; whether OBOR administrators have the formal power to command the largest state-owned banks to fund their projects; or what institutional relationships the OBOR LSG has formed with the other powerful party committees. Rumor has it that as of early 2018, the NDRC had only a skeleton staff dedicated to OBOR supervision. Apart from this type of unverified account, nearly nothing is known about what role central planners play in OBOR projects.

Fourth, most OBOR deals are designed to prevent outside researchers from collecting or inferring this information from other sources. Many of the most prominent OBOR projects are funded by sovereign loans from China to another government. First, a Chinese policy bank such as China Exim or the Silk Road Fund lends a tranche of money to a recipient government or a company the recipient controls, such as an airport management company. The recipient government then turns around and uses the funds to hire one or more Chinese contractors for the construction. Most of the time, the contractor is a Chinese SOE that does not release public financial disclosures. Because most of the money loaned goes straight onto the balance sheet of the Chinese contractor, it is hard to track spending on ongoing projects. In some cases where Chinese firms use a "build-operate-transfer" contract, it can take decades before the public learns just how profitable or unprofitable the project is. Even the global investment community is kept in the dark. In many recipient countries, the finance ministry or central bank does not factor in hidden debts to China when publishing official economic data.[33]

As we will see in the case study chapters, Chinese firms are very clever about negotiating tax exemptions in countries where they operate. The structure of these tax breaks is often highly technical. Local news organizations in recipient countries often do not consider them to be newsworthy. Even in cases where the details of tax concessions are publicly available, they are often very hard to find. For countries that accept Chinese infrastructure investments, such as Pakistan and Greece, tax concessions are often the biggest long-term cost. Very little of this information is made public, so scholars and commentators rarely note their importance.

Without project-level data, researchers have no way to identify which deals would have gone ahead even in a world where OBOR did not exist, and which deals were possible only because of OBOR-linked political pressure or financial support from Beijing. This is not simply a question of separating out the investments made by SOEs from those made by private firms. On one hand, it may seem that SOEs would be most likely to take on risky and unprofitable projects. After all, most SOEs enjoy explicit or implicit government backing, which gives them what economists call a "soft profit constraint." That is, compared with private firms that cannot count on government bailouts, SOEs tend to have a greater appetite for financial risks that could potentially push their balance sheets into the red.[34] On the other hand, SOEs would obviously rather make money than lose it. SOEs have a track record of thousands of profitable deals all over the world going back to the 1990s. In fact, SOEs may be more likely to be at the front of the queue in getting government approval for strategically important and potentially lucrative projects abroad. In contrast, private firms have the most to lose if they fall out of the CCP's good graces. Executives I have interviewed at private firms operating in China speak about participating in OBOR as the "cost of doing business." Since China imposed strict capital controls in late 2015, SOEs and private firms now need official permission to make large overseas investments. All firms that want to pull money out of China now have incentives to

brand their projects as part of OBOR, whether or not they have coordinated the investment with the government in advance.[35]

Fifth, recipient governments have little incentive to be transparent
about the details of their contracts with China, even when there is no
corruption involved. Stories about delays, cost overruns, tax concessions,
local opposition and protests, and the viability of Chinese-funded infrastructure projects make excellent fodder for domestic political opposition.
Recipient governments fear that embarrassing news stories will make
them appear weaker or less attractive partners to the Chinese. Media coverage can turn local opposition to the project into a national issue, which
could scare China away. Perversely, these incentives lead many recipient
governments to deny that they are quarreling with China—even as they
push back aggressively in private.

Sixth, individual employees of the government and civil service have
nothing to gain—and often a lot to lose—from helping foreign researchers access documents and information. This is particularly true in countries with weak or nonexistent protections for whistleblowers, and in political environments where procurement and tender processes usually
come with bribes and kickbacks. Even when the process is unimpeach-
ably clean, it is entirely understandable that a local functionary would
decline to help a foreign researcher. The individual instinct to stay out of
trouble is just as powerful in democratic countries as in autocratic ones.
One lawyer at a Colombo firm representing the Sri Lankan government
in negotiations with China Harbour Engineering Company assured me
that I had "no chance" of obtaining complete copies of official contracts,
even though by law they ought to be publicly available. I was lucky to
meet generous and brave civil servants in every country where I conducted
case study research, some of whom bore personal risks to help me. I have
anonymized many of them.

Conclusion

When Xi launched OBOR in 2013, it seemed that his goal was to resolve
the debate about how China should understand its sprawling overseas investments by proposing a single guiding concept. This chapter has ar-

gued that he succeeded, but in a different way than most observers expected. Xi has personalized OBOR, fleshed out the concept into a brand with different meanings for domestic and foreign audiences, and tightened his grip over the propaganda system. In so doing, he has shrouded himself in a set of ideas and slogans that are both ubiquitous and extremely flexible.

OBOR is not administered as a policy in any traditional sense. There still seems to be no central office for coordinating it, no single budget for funding it, no agreed-on map for tracing it, and no official set of criteria for defining its purview. Instead, OBOR is governed principally through an incentive structure in which numerous companies, local governments, and bureaucratic agencies operating in China try to show that their activities are in service to the national interest. This explains why Beijing has been content to let OBOR participants use the slogan as they please—for kitchenware and cosmetics, for blockchain and beer—despite the risk that this cacophony will dilute or taint the OBOR brand. Xi has mobilized thousands of independent actors to promote his ideology of Chinese power, compete to prove their loyalty, and understand themselves in relation to his governing concept. The campaign has also enabled Xi to sustain some useful myths: that the Chinese investment into the developing world rapidly accelerated after he took power, when in fact the trend of steadily increasing investment extended back nearly a decade earlier; that China has a vision to reconnect the world, moving inexorably forward; and that under his enlightened leadership, every component of the Chinese system moves as one.

The political purpose of the OBOR campaign is therefore to strengthen Xi's political authority inside China and extend the political influence of the CCP overseas. This is accomplished every time an individual or institution tries to show their loyalty to OBOR and frame their activities as compatible with Xi's guidance. The governing logic behind OBOR is thus precisely that of the tributary system. The exchange of money and gifts is not an end in itself. It is a means toward establishing and cultivating a relationship between patron and client. What matters most is the performance of submission—in this case, to the emperor's new brand.

PART II

Chinese Power Meets the World

CHAPTER 5

Strategic Promiscuity

Sri Lanka Flirts with OBOR

It is late afternoon. Off the side of the road near the Hambantota salt flats, about a mile from the blue and white barracks where the Chinese construction workers live, a small group of local men and women gather around a market shop, chatting and drinking tea. Through a translator, I ask some of the assembled group why they think China wants to invest in their village. A housewife in her late thirties frowns a bit and offers a simple answer. "The same thing that the British wanted, and Dutch, and the Portuguese," she says. "When I am gone, when my children are gone, the port here in Hambantota will still belong to China."

Starting in 2007, the Chinese government provided loans to build the Magampura Mahinda Rajapaksa Port in Hambantota (fig. 5.1). The Sri Lankan government contracted the China Merchants Group, a state-owned enterprise (SOE), to build it. The first stage of the port opened for business in November 2010 and has been unprofitable ever since. Hambantota is only twenty nautical miles from the main commercial sea lines connecting the Persian Gulf to the Straits of Malacca, but for the first five years after the port was built, it failed to attract transshipment business from the Port of Colombo, 150 miles further up the coast. The first time I visited (January 2017), dozens of Sri Lankan port employees milled around idly on the dock. The Sri Lanka Ports Authority (SLPA) had to redirect money from the profitable Colombo port because Hambantota's meager revenues did not come close to covering its debt service payments.

I returned to Sri Lanka in January 2018, weeks after the other shoe dropped. The Chinese government agreed to pay $1.2 billion—essentially

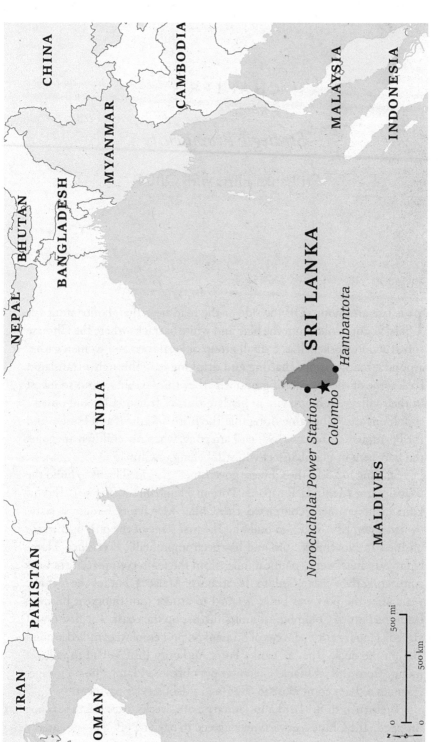

MAP 5.1: Map of Sri Lanka, courtesy of Scott Walker.

canceling the debt Sri Lanka had taken out to finance the Hambantota port zone. In return, Sri Lanka agreed to hand over the port and its ancillary infrastructure on a ninety-nine-year concession to a Chinese-controlled joint venture. The Sri Lanka Ports Minister Arjuna Ranatunga vehemently opposed the deal, arguing that it would compromise national sovereignty. Following the agreement, dozens of port employees organized anti-China protests, fearing correctly that they would be laid off. China was blasé about the potential blowback. One commentator in a prominent Chinese newspaper asserted that China now had the right to use Hambantota as a military base. *Xinhua* even tweeted—in English—that the "handover" was "another milestone along path of #BeltandRoad."[1]

The US policy community responded with fear and alarm. In May, Sam Parker and Gabrielle Chefitz published a widely cited report through Harvard's Belfer Center about China's "debtbook diplomacy," basing their Sri Lanka case study on the then-unpublished research I present in this chapter.[2] In June, Maria Abi-Habib of the *New York Times* published an exhaustively reported 4,000-word cover story titled "How China Got Sri Lanka to Cough Up a Port." Abi-Habib's most damning finding was a document showing that China Harbour Engineering Company had funneled $7.6 million into the 2015 Sri Lankan election. By autumn, the top China experts in the US government were persuaded that Hambantota was the tip of the spear. In October 2018, US Vice President Mike Pence accused China of "us[ing] so-called 'debt diplomacy'" to expand its influence around the world.

Pence singled out Sri Lanka. Describing Hambantota as a typical OBOR project, his speech suggested that the whole OBOR scheme is a cover to expand China's political and military influence:

> Today, [China] is offering hundreds of billions of dollars in infrastructure loans to governments from Asia to Africa to Europe and even Latin America. Yet the terms of those loans are opaque at best, and the benefits invariably flow overwhelmingly to Beijing. . . . Just ask Sri Lanka, which took on massive debt to let Chinese state companies build a port of questionable commercial value. Two years ago, that country could no longer afford its payments, so Beijing pressured Sri Lanka to deliver the new port directly into Chinese hands. It may soon become a forward military base for China's growing blue-water navy.[3]

Pence's speech at the Hudson Institute marked a shift in the United States government's view of OBOR. At the Asia-Pacific Economic Cooperation Summit in Papua New Guinea the following month, Pence argued that Asian countries should partner with the United States since China's predatory lending is proof of its malign motives. "Know that the United States offers a better option," Pence said. "We don't drown our partners in a sea of debt. We don't coerce or compromise your independence. The United States deals openly, fairly. We do not offer a constricting belt or a one-way road."[4]

This chapter challenges Pence's diagnosis in five important ways. First, China did not have to deceive or pressure Sri Lanka to seek funding for the port or sign up for OBOR. As a small state seeking to maximize its autonomy and security in a multipolar world, Sri Lanka has always resisted relying too heavily on any one patron, particularly India. One local analyst calls this "strategic promiscuity"—a hedging technique in which Sri Lanka encourages other countries to compete for access and influence.[5] Second, the Hambantota project was never going to be commercially viable without billions of dollars of investment in ancillary infrastructure, which Sri Lanka knew it could not fund by itself. Third, the Chinese government and China Merchants Group were patient and flexible in using the project to build political relationships in Sri Lanka. In the end, they won equity control on a ninety-nine-year lease and restored relations with the new government, which had come to power on a largely anti-China platform. Fourth, most observers in Sri Lanka's educated elite believe that the Hambantota project is still fundamentally in the national interest. And fifth, Sri Lanka's strategic promiscuity strategy is working. Recently announced investments from Singapore, Oman, and India will transform the Hambantota region in the next decade, counterbalancing Chinese influence in the process.

These findings suggest that the US strategy of trying to expose China as a predatory lender is unlikely to succeed. If even the *Sri Lankans* are happy with the outcome of their dealings with China, then OBOR can be a successful diplomatic tool almost anywhere—even if the underlying infrastructure projects turn out to be commercial failures. What OBOR actually offers politicians in small countries is more valuable than profits or losses on any individual project. OBOR empowers political elites in partner countries to leverage their relationship with China to pursue their own objectives.

How to Write a Case Study

Chapters 5–7 are case studies of Chinese port projects in Sri Lanka, Tanzania, and Greece, presented from the perspective of stakeholders in the recipient countries. Based on extensive elite interviews, public documents, and various written sources in Chinese and the local languages, I seek to explain why recipient countries accept Chinese loans and infrastructure development contracts and then trace how the projects are negotiated and rolled out. Each case begins with a review of the historical context, since history and collective memory are profoundly important in shaping how decisionmakers perceive foreign threats and their potential strategic choices for dealing with China. The case then traces the subsequent implementation of the initial project plan through the lens of domestic politics, considering factors such as protests, civil society activism, elections, elite patronage networks, and direct and indirect financial pressure.

I am interested in two clusters of questions. The first deals with explaining the recipient government's behavior. Why did Sri Lanka accept the funds? To what extent did it have agency in structuring the terms? Why did the Hambantota project not go according to plan? How do influential Sri Lankan stakeholders assess the strategic risks and benefits of inviting greater Chinese investment and influence in their country? How did pressure from the domestic political opposition and other countries in the region influence the Sri Lankan government's decisionmaking? The second group of questions concerns the behavior of the various actors on the Chinese side. Why were Chinese firms drawn to this project, and what contractual terms did they demand? In the case studies that follow, publicly available sources and interviews in English and the local languages shed more light on these questions than Chinese documents, which are heavy on boilerplate and light on specifics.

Ancient Maritime Ties

The first direct contact between China and Sri Lanka came around six hundred years before the beginning of the Hambantota port. In 1405, at the height of the Ming dynasty, eunuch admiral Zheng He embarked on the first of seven voyages to the "Western ocean." On his third voyage, Zheng visited Sri Lanka for the second time. He landed in Galle, on the west coast of the island, and presented a tablet brought from Nanjing with a votive inscription in Chinese, Tamil, and Persian, along with offerings to Buddha. Zheng's fleet returned in 1410 or 1411 on his way back to China. For reasons that are not fully clear, Zheng deposed the usurper Vira Alakeshvara from the throne of Kotte and brought him, his wives, and several of his advisers back to Nanjing as prisoners. Zheng then installed Parākramabāhu VI on the throne. The new Sri Lankan king visited China twice, in 1416 and 1421, to pay tribute to the Yongle emperor.[6] There are no records of diplomatic interactions between China and Sri Lanka for several centuries thereafter.

Sri Lankan politicians played up the history of Zheng's voyages to justify their interest in the Hambantota project, just as Chinese officials have done elsewhere. In one official Sri Lankan publication in 2007, local politicians pointedly describe the Hambantota project as the restoration of an ancient port. According to Asanga Gunawansa, one of Sri Lanka's most influential attorneys, Rajapaksa's "vision was to develop a site that he claimed had historically been a Silk Road port."[7] The oldest known shipwreck in the Indian Ocean is in fact located at Godavaya, near Hambantota. The area was a trading entrepôt from the second to the seventh centuries. Roman and Sassanian coins and shards of Chinese pottery have been found there, although they did not arrive on Chinese vessels.[8] The outcome of this debate surely has little direct bearing on China–Sri Lanka relations today, but it illustrates that observers in both countries tried to draw from remote historical legacies to legitimate contemporary policy choices.

Sri Lanka Guards Its Sovereignty

Over three waves of colonization—Portuguese, Dutch, and British—Sri Lanka (or Ceylon) preserved a unique cultural and political heritage. The British governed Ceylon separately from the Indian subcontinent.[9] Even after the fall of the Kingdom of Kandy in 1815, the British operated a highly competent civil service staffed largely by Ceylonese officials. Ceylon continued to rely on Britain after it won statehood in 1948. Under the new Soulbury constitution, Ceylon remained entirely dependent on Britain for its defense and external relations. The Royal Air Force maintained an airfield at Katunayake; the Royal Navy kept its naval base at Trincomalee. The island nation was too small and vulnerable to go its own way in strategic matters. Yet British dominance in the security domain didn't mean that London could sustain its political influence in Colombo.

After independence in 1948, Ceylon first sided with the Anglo-American geopolitical bloc. It reaped substantial economic benefits from doing so—subsidized commodity purchasing arrangements, technical assistance for agriculture and health care, and dollar credit lines from Australia, New Zealand, Canada, the United States, and West Germany. At the Bandung conference in 1955, Ceylonese Prime Minister Sir John Kotelawala stood apart from the other delegates by criticizing Soviet expansionism as imperialism in a new guise. "Are not these colonies as much as any of the colonial territories in Africa or Asia?," Kotelawala asked, speaking of the Eastern European countries that had fallen under Soviet influence. "Should it not be our duty openly to declare opposition to Soviet colonialism as much as Western imperialism?"[10] These statements created a public rift between Kotelawala and Indian Prime Minister Jawaharlal Nehru, who favored a more pro-Soviet form of nonalignment.

While Ceylon aligned strategically with the West, it quietly sought ways to partner with communist China. Between 1951 and 1952, global rice prices rose 32 percent, and prices of other agricultural commodities collapsed, including Ceylon's leading exports: rubber and coconut oil. The new communist government in mainland China faced the inverse problem. A UN embargo in 1950 and subsequent US trade actions cut off Beijing's rubber suppliers in Malaya. Without rubber, Mao could not achieve his goal of rebuilding the country's industrial capacity. Bilateral trade between Ceylon and China fell almost to nothing in 1950 after the embargo was imposed.

In 1952, Ceylon disregarded repeated warnings from Washington and struck a barter agreement with Beijing. Known as the Rubber-Rice Pact, the deal was periodically renegotiated to adjust relative quantities according to changes in market prices. After a preliminary exchange was successful, Colombo and Beijing formalized and extended the deal in January 1953. Washington cut off the flow of development aid to Ceylon, but the 40 percent premium that Beijing paid for rubber made the trade-off worth it. Ceylonese administrations of both political parties kept some version of this barter deal for two decades. From the Sri Lankan government's perspective, pragmatism trumped ideology.[11] The Hambantota port deal six decades later sprang from the same tradition of Sino-Lankan cooperation in the face of international condemnation.

In 1956, S. W. R. D. Bandaranaike was elected prime minister of Ceylon, promising to take the country into nonalignment abroad and socialism at home. In 1958, the Bandaranaike government signed an economic cooperation agreement with the Soviet Union, accepting a $24 million loan to construct sixteen industrial projects. Concerned that the West would lose Colombo to communist influence if it did not keep up, the World Bank offered several large development loans. But Colombo's most lucrative economic relationship was still the one with Beijing. By 1968, the People's Republic was the largest source of Sri Lankan sovereign loans.[12] In 1972, with Bandaranaike's wife, Sirimavo, now prime minister, Sri Lanka opened formal diplomatic ties with both China and the Soviet Union.

Holding Back India

Sirimavo Bandaranaike also distanced Ceylon from India. She changed the country's official name to the Socialist Republic of Sri Lanka to please the Sinhalese nationalists and changed the national language from English to Sinhala. These policies angered the Tamil minorities on both sides of the water. In 1971, Bandaranaike allowed Pakistani warplanes to use Sri Lankan airbases for refueling in the Indo-Pakistani War. Sri Lanka's move to balance geopolitical pressure from India had long-term repercussions and later informed the Hambantota deal.

As Moscow and Beijing competed for Sri Lanka's affections, gifting it with military equipment, loans, and technical assistance, US foreign policy analysts fretted that Bandaranaike was pulling Sri Lanka into dependency on the communist bloc. As George Lerski noted in 1974, even Moscow feared that "Peking was plotting to turn Sri Lanka into China's bridgehead on the Indian Ocean."[13] Lerski noted that the Sri Lankan opposition had accused Bandaranaike of plotting to form a new party with

Chinese funding. But Washington had once again underestimated the centrality of the strategic balancing principle to Sri Lankan foreign policy. Soon after Lerski's article was published, Sri Lankan voters turned the country back toward the West. Relations with India improved, but relations between Colombo and Beijing remained warm. Chinese naval vessels called at Colombo on their first journey into the Indian Ocean in 1985. The relationship with China gave Colombo leverage to manage the other powers competing to fold it into their spheres of influence: the Americans, the Soviets, and the Indians.

If the global Cold War had illustrated that being a small state had its benefits, the Sri Lankan civil war proved that it also carried risks. Starting in the 1970s, driven by a fear of losing influence, India began to offer covert training to Tamil rebel groups in the north of Sri Lanka. When civil war erupted between the government and the Tamil Tigers in 1983, India found itself in a political quandary. On one hand, instability in Sri Lanka, a stone's throw across the strait from Tamil Nadu, was a security headache for New Delhi. On the other hand, Indian Tamil leaders were sympathetic to the plight of Sri Lanka's Tamil minority, making direct intervention politically complex. In the 1987 Indo-Sri Lanka Peace Accord, Colombo agreed (under heavy pressure from New Delhi) to devolve more powers to the Tamil-dominated provinces in the north, withdraw the national army, and allow an Indian peacekeeping force to deploy in majority-Tamil areas to enforce a ceasefire agreement. This soon expanded into an active Indian military operation on Sri Lankan soil. The accord proved a failure on both sides: a humiliating invasion of sovereignty for Colombo and a strategic miscalculation-*cum*-domestic political disaster for New Delhi. India withdrew in March 1990 after losing 1,200 troops. The following year, a Tamil assassin murdered Indian Prime Minister Rajiv Gandhi. For Colombo, the lesson of the intervention was that Indian meddling threatened Sri Lanka's national interest. India was a giant next door that had to be held at bay.[14]

The Rise of Rajapaksa

After India's withdrawal in 1990, the Sri Lankan civil war entered an even more destructive phase. The Sri Lankan army pushed the Tamil Tigers into to a few remote bastions in the north. In 2005, the hard-charging left-populist Mahinda Rajapaksa was elected president. Rajapaksa delivered on his promise to bring the war to a speedy end by using scorched-earth tactics to annihilate the last Tamil Tigers. More than forty thousand people were killed in the government's final offensive.[15]

The other half of Rajapaksa's promise was economic renewal. His economic plan-*cum*-manifesto, Mahinda Chintana, called for rebuilding Sri Lanka's shattered economy with massive investments in infrastructure and industrial development.[16] The ten-year plan promised 8 percent annual real GDP growth by "integrat[ing] the positive attributes of market economic policies with the domestic aspirations by providing necessary support to domestic enterprises and encouraging foreign investments."[17] It recommended dozens of new infrastructure projects, including port expansions in Colombo, Galle, and Trincomalee and the construction of a port, coal plant, and water processing facility at Hambantota.

Rajapaksa's growth targets would have been wildly unrealistic even if there were not a war still going on. The national budget would have had to meet ambitious growth and fiscal revenue targets to afford even the projected increases in debt service. It is possible that Rajapaksa's economic advisers failed to plan that far ahead, or that the Mahinda Chintana was fundamentally a political prop. More likely, they expected that Colombo would simply roll over its old loans into new ones. Before the war, Sri Lanka had not struggled to attract sovereign credit. What the Rajapaksa administration could not anticipate was how deeply the shock of the global financial crisis two years later would disrupt its access to its usual sources of financing.

In the first three years of Rajapaksa's administration, with the Tamil Tigers in retreat and the end of the war seemingly in sight, India and China positioned themselves for the aftermath. The two powers competed for Rajapaksa's favor. In 2006, India provided military helicopters and brought in the Indian navy to blockade the Tigers' northern strongholds, but it refused to provide more lethal assistance. In 2008, India and Sri Lanka signed a Comprehensive Economic Partnership, and India extended $200 million in reconstruction aid. But this aid had strings attached, and it overwhelmingly benefited Tamil-dominated areas in the north. These conditions irritated the Sinhala majority, concentrated in the relatively undeveloped south of the country. In 2007 China signed a $37 million ammunition and ordnance deal. It gifted Sri Lanka several F7 fighter jets, antiaircraft guns, and JY-11 radar. Solicited and unsolicited Chinese proposals flooded in to fund power plants, steel mills, and road construction all over the country. China also defended Rajapaksa in the UN Security Council, blocking US resolutions to censure him for war crimes. As Paikiasothy Saravanamuttu, director of the Colombo-based Center for Policy Alternatives, told me, it was thanks to Chinese obstruction that "no proposal to punish Sri Lanka ever got to New York."[18]

New Delhi saw Rajapaksa as a strategic headache: chauvinistic, inclined to resist diplomatic pressure, and divisive in ways that were sure to agitate the Indian Tamil population. As the war wound down, however, India calculated that it had no choice but to engage with Rajapaksa. As Indian National Security Advisor Shivshankar Menon recalls:

> India's policy options in the situation were limited. *We recognized that a victorious Rajapaksa would be less dependent on India* and therefore less responsive. A consummate politician who had risen through the political ranks, pragmatic and practical to the core, *Mahinda Rajapaksa by 2009 had a firm grip on all the levers of power in Sri Lanka*, standing head and shoulders above his potential rivals. In effect, *Sri Lanka is an aircraft carrier parked fourteen miles off the Indian coast.* This is the perpetual dilemma of India's Sri Lanka policy: we must engage in order to defend our interest in keeping Sri Lanka free of antagonistic outside influences while also trying to prevent the growth of Tamil extremism and separatism that could affect Tamil Nadu.[19]

According to Indian Lt. Gen. Dhruv Katoch, the Indian navy played a critical role in bringing the war to an end by blockading the sea lines across which the Tigers had supplied themselves with provisions from Tamil Nadu. "No one talks about it, but it's true," he admitted. "If you want to win a war, you have to isolate the battlefield."[20] Indian analysts believed that geography would carry the day, and that Sri Lanka would stay out of China's sphere. They were wrong.

Sri Lanka Turns toward China

The United States also recognized 2007 as a turning point. Western countries had suspended development aid in condemnation of human rights violations committed by the Sri Lankan army in the final phase of the war. But in a 2007 cable from the US embassy in Colombo, later released by Wikileaks, a State Department analyst warned that this hardline anti-Rajapaksa position would no longer be tenable after the war. Rajapaksa was preparing to unleash a wave of government spending enabled by his plentiful choices of foreign financing. Sri Lanka had quit its International Monetary Fund (IMF) structural adjustment program in 2003, abandoning plans to reform or privatize its bloated state-run industries. "As Sri Lanka taps into new sources of assistance," the cable argued, "Tokyo and other Western donors are at risk of losing leverage with the Rajapaksa government, making it harder for us and others to prod the government toward a peaceful solution to Sri Lanka's ethnic conflict, and address such concerns on human rights and corruption."[21] Rather than bow to Western pressure, Colombo would simply become more reliant on its fastest-growing source of financing: China. Intriguingly, the State Department cable was "skeptical" that "giant packages" promised by China would "fully materialize." Still, Washington's view was that as Rajapaksa reorganized Sri Lankan politics around "patronage," no US money would mean no US influence.

The State Department memo proved prescient. Indian and US pressure on Rajapaksa pushed him further into the arms of the Chinese. Rajapaksa had little patience for India, which he believed was eager to intervene in Sri Lankan internal affairs when convenient but would not fund his postwar reconstruction schemes. He neither recognized nor cared for the political headache the Tamil issue posed for New Delhi. Menon puts a finer point on it: Defense Minister Gotabaya Rajapaksa was "sensitive to Indian concerns," but his brother Mahinda was "compliant with Chinese demands, having built a political machine on Chinese money."[22] (In November 2019, Gotabaya was elected president on a pro-China platform. All subsequent references to Sri Lankan politicians will use the titles they held at the time.)

This review of Sri Lankan diplomatic history has three major lessons. The first is that beneath its instrumental political alignments with one or another foreign power, Sri Lanka has a strategic culture that is fiercely resistant to external interference. As a small island nation on India's doorstep, Sri Lanka long ago learned to cultivate alternative sources of investment and technology and to leverage its relationships with other foreign powers to achieve strategic balance. The brief period in which Colombo invited India to intervene in its civil war was a singular exception to this historical rule. The second characteristic is that Indian strategists consider Sri Lanka to be essentially a geographic extension of their own country and are therefore deeply troubled by the prospect of a foreign military presence there. New Delhi has no choice but to engage diplomatically and militarily with Colombo. The third lesson is that China sees Sri Lanka as a strategically situated small state that has historically resisted political domination by outside powers. For all of these reasons, Sri Lanka has consistently been willing to strike deals with China, provided that the price is right.

Floating Hambantota

It was Sri Lanka's idea to build a port at Hambantota. According to Adm. Jayanath Colombage, the former commander of the Sri Lankan navy, government officials had discussed the idea on and off ever since the British era.[23] Whether this claim is true—I could find no textual evidence for it—it is clear that the proposal was under active discussion before Rajapaksa took power. In 2002, the Sri Lankan government negotiated a $400 million port at Hambantota with two Canadian firms, but the plan fell through.[24] Rajapaksa included a proposal for a port at Hambantota in his Mahinda Chintana development plan in 2006. Around this time, the Sri Lankan government invited Japan and other major donor countries to bid to fund the project, but Tokyo declined.[25] In November, Minister of Southern Region Development Ananda Kularatne told the press that construction of a major international deepwater port at Hambantota was a top priority for the government.

It was also clear as early as 2002 that Rajapaksa's patronage network stood to profit if the Hambantota port went ahead. Canadian contractor SNC Lavalin was hired to conduct the feasibility study.[26] Although the full study was never made public, press reports at the time note that it recommended that Phase I of the project would have to include container operations or else the port would struggle to attract business from the more developed facilities in Colombo. Rather than accept these findings, Sri Lankan government officials tried to bury the report. After it was leaked to the press, they denied its contents. Rauff Hakeem, Port Development and Shipping minister, called the report "useless and not acceptable to the government." A task force that Hakeem appointed called it noncomprehensive, unbankable, and even a violation of contract. A representative of the SLPA claimed it was "based on already available information and not on primary research." Further sources criticized the decision to hire SNC Lavalin as "political machinations," arguing that a French company would have been far preferable.[27] This reflexively negative response to an independent feasibility study was the first hint that the local power brokers had their own reasons to build a port at Hambantota. China did not enter their calculus until much later.

This was not the last feasibility study that the Sri Lankan government ignored because its findings were inconvenient. Less than two years later, Ramboll, a Danish consultancy, projected that it would cost $33 million to build a bunkering facility at Hambantota, assuming that the "work is carried out to normal industry standards by reputed international suppliers and contractors."[28] In March 2005, Ports Minister Mangala Samaraweera submitted a Cabinet paper requesting a $100 million loan to finance the bunkering project. Corruption, it seemed, was not a side effect—it was the whole point.

This was how Rajapaksa ran the whole of Sri Lanka: through a system of patronage and family control. Each Rajapaksa brother oversaw a major Cabinet portfolio and region of the country. The prime minister himself saw Hambantota as a personal priority. Not only would the port bring prosperity to his home district, the promise of a new economic base served his ethnonationalist agenda of bringing the center of the Sri Lankan economy from the west coast to the Sinhala-dominated south. Mahinda's brother Basil, the powerful Minister for Economic Development, also played a role. It was Basil—nicknamed Mr. 10 Percent by those that alleged he was a notorious embezzler—who oversaw the design of the Southern Development Plan. In short, Hambantota was a politically and personally useful vanity project that ticked several boxes for the Rajapaksa family. Nor did it hurt that (according to Saravana-muttu), the port would lubricate the relationship with China. Partnership with Beijing offered an "international political insurance policy" for Rajapaksa's regime, Saravanamuttu told me, "an insurance policy backed by a bottomless wallet."[29]

Enter China

To develop Phase I of the Hambantota port, Sri Lanka invited all of its major donors to submit funding proposals. The IMF, World Bank, and Asia Development Bank considered the project in their reports on Sri Lanka's infrastructure needs. Multiple interview subjects, including Dhruva Jaishankar, the son of India's national security advisor and an accomplished scholar in his own right, confirmed to me that the port had been offered to India in or around 2006. Delhi declined the deal because of budget constraints and because it was concerned that the project was not creditworthy.

After the alternative funding sources failed to pan out, China submitted its proposal. The original proposal came not from the Chinese government but from China Merchants Group, a state-controlled conglomerate listed in Hong Kong. China Merchants indicated that if Sri Lanka accepted its proposal, the China Exim Bank would make the necessary loans available. In July 2006, Mangala Samaraweera, then foreign minister, visited Beijing to discuss terms. The visit produced a joint communiqué that "welcomed increased participation by Chinese enterprises in infrastructure and development projects in Sri Lanka."[30] A coal power plant at Puttalam, a highway in Colombo city, and the harbor and bunkering facility at Hambantota were identified as the three priority projects. The port was a "go."

Sri Lankan observers hoped that China's investments elsewhere in the Indian Ocean region would make their own country more valuable as a strategic regional hub. In 2008, a feature article in the newspaper *Island* highlighted the now-defunct Chinese plan to build a canal in Thailand linking the South China Sea and Indian Ocean. By circumventing the Straits of Malacca, the Kra Canal could potentially shift the main sea lines connecting East Asia and the Middle East northward, creating new opportunities for Sri Lanka to reinvent itself as the primary transshipment hub for South Asia:

> Singapore's inevitable loss could be Sri Lanka's gain. Kra Canal will place Hambantota port directly on the Asia-Europe sea route, even more than the existing route. Beside India, the hinterland of Hambantota could be Bangladesh, Myanmar and even Indonesia and the Philippines. Currently cargo from India and Bangladesh to the Far East is trans-shipped mostly via Singapore. Kra Canal is bound to divert that cargo to Hambantota.[31]

Accepting Chinese loans for port construction seemed to be a good way to align the countries' incentives. But this argument did not acknowledge that China was also negotiating to build very similar ports in Gwadar, Pakistan, and Chittagong, Bangladesh. Even if the Kra Canal had gone through, the Hambantota port was bound to face stiff competition for transshipment business. China was hedging its bets by playing all sides. Having burned his bridges with India and the United States, Rajapaksa had no such luxury.

Clearing the Way for China

The Chinese proposal for Phase I of the Hambantota port then went through a secretive approval process. The regulators and relevant parliamentary committees conducted little to no oversight. According to Nishan de Mel, director of Verité Research and a leading analyst of Sri Lankan politics, "Parliament during the Rajapaksa administration did little apart from passing laws, regulations, and the budget. Due diligence and project approval and management responsibilities were principally in the hands of the Cabinet"—that is, the Rajapaksa family. Parliamentary committees were particularly toothless.[32]

Under Basil Rajapaksa's oversight, the Ministry of Economic Development became a super-ministry that involved itself in any projects it liked. As one State Department cable put it, "Basil advises the President on an array of topics despite his limited education and lack of relevant work experience."[33] In theory, the government could not approve free-hold land grants—which would give the holding company nearly total, permanent control—without approval from the Ministry of Lands and the Urban Development Authority. But that agency was under the control of Gotabaya Rajapaksa, the defense minister and another of the prime minister's brothers.[34] (In 2019, Gotabaya was elected president and appointed his brother Mahinda as prime minister.)

Discussions with China Development Bank and China Harbour were finalized, and construction began in 2007. Although the operational contract was never made public, the terms of the loan implied that the SLPA expected Phase I to become profitable soon after opening. Eighty-five percent of the funding for the $361 million project was drawn from a $307 million loan from China Exim Bank, with the SPLA contributing the rest. The interest rate was 6.3 percent, repayable over fifteen years with a four-year grace period. This was a lower rate than Sri Lanka could have borrowed on the capital market, but it was a commercial deal, not a concessional loan. China demanded a high interest rate because it needed compensation for taking on the risk.

The Chinese later pointed to this negotiation as proof that it had not foisted the Hambantota project on the Sri Lankans—and the evidence backs up their claims. As one *Xinhua* report pointed out, Sri Lanka first sought funding from the international development agencies and turned to China as a lender of last resort.[35] When "the Sri Lankan team did try to seek a preferential loan from China," the report argued, "the quota of China's preferential loans to Sri Lanka had been used" for "other projects." In the decade prior to June 2015, China Exim Bank loaned over $6 billion to Sri Lanka, three-quarters of this total at preferential interest rates of 2 percent. For the Hambantota project, China Exim offered a choice of two loan structures at commercial rates significantly higher than 2 percent.[36] This was evidence that the Sri Lankan government was dead-set on going ahead with the Hambantota project, even at a higher rate.[37] It also showed that China had demanded compensation for taking on the higher risk, pointedly refusing to offer its usually generous funding terms. In sum, the Hambantota port originated as a Sri Lankan project that China went along with to placate a corrupt ally, not a predatory pie-in-the-sky scheme that China used to trick a gullible Sri Lankan government.

China's reasons for offering the loans were political. Funding Rajapaksa's vanity project was a small price to pay for the strategic headache it would create for India. From a commercial or military perspective, Hambantota could be a useful transshipment or resupply hub in China's growing network of Indian Ocean ports, even if it stood no chance of growing into a lucrative "new Shenzhen." From an institutional perspective, the China Merchants Group and China Harbour saw that building the port would be a good way to win the Chinese government's good favor. Beijing had clearly indicated that deepening economic relations with Sri Lanka was a national priority. Indeed, when one of China's deputy ministers of transportation visited Hambantota in 2009, he praised China Harbour for forging ties with the Sri Lankan government through "perseverance and tenacity."[38] The Chinese players had their own interests in pursuing the deal and supporting Rajapaksa's government. But if China's goal from the beginning had been to engineer the failure of the port, it would have offered more tantalizing terms when Sri Lanka first invited it to bid.

Sri Lanka Doubles Down

Why Sri Lanka chose to recommit to Hambantota after 2008 is a different question. With the onset of the global financial crisis, it no longer made sense to build a multibillion-dollar deepwater port and industrial complex from scratch in the remote and disconnected Hambantota region. The port of Colombo was growing quickly, thanks to investments from none other than China Harbour. The fact that Rajapaksa remained committed to Hambantota proved that his political interests trumped any concerns about profitability.

Facing a debt crisis in 2008, Rajapaksa decided to borrow more from abroad and invest his way back to growth. The crisis began when outbound capital flows caused the Sri Lankan rupee to collapse. Imports became more expensive in local currency terms, and inflation jumped to 23 percent. The rising price of imports blew up the trade deficit. The central bank burned through half of its foreign exchange reserves. Nearly all of Sri Lanka's external debt was denominated in US dollars, which now cost more in rupee terms. But with tax revenues falling, the government had to borrow more to service the debt. Public sector credit rose 46 percent in a single year. By the following year Rajapaksa had no choice but to turn to the IMF, which offered a $2.6 billion bailout in exchange for reductions in military spending and tax reforms. Over the next two years, as Hambantota Phase I construction progressed, Sri Lanka issued dozens of requests for proposals to develop an adjacent industrial zone and held at least thirteen separate negotiations. As the ancillary projects piled up, the government again looked to China for funding. As the financial crisis deepened, it became even clearer that Sri Lanka's debt was fiscally unmanageable. To make itself whole, China would eventually have to renegotiate the construction and operation contracts to swap its debt for equity. China must have recognized that Sri Lanka was not managing its finances responsibly.

Still, China had political reasons to continue lending. This was the height of the financial crisis, where Chinese economic planners had allocated hundreds of billions of dollars for infrastructure at home, in a building frenzy that included many projects just as unfeasible as Hambantota. Since China Merchants and China Harbour would supply all of the labor and materials for the construction, the loans to Sri Lanka doubled as domestic economic stimulus in China. This was an illustration of the Chinese investment-driven economic model that Justin Lin and other Chinese scholars boasted of (discussed in chapter 2).

President Mahinda Rajapaksa's borrowing binge spun out of control (figs. 5.1 and 5.2, table 5.1). Sri Lanka took out a $77 million loan to expand the bunkering facility at Hambantota. It pushed through approval of the Shangri-La Hotel, a 35,000-seat cricket stadium, and a South Korean–funded twenty-seven-acre convention center, complete with a helipad and 1,500-seat performance hall. In 2009, China Exim approved another loan for approximately $210 million to fund China Harbour's construction of an international airport nearby. This would be the second-largest airport in the country and would also bear the name of the president. When Phase I of the port was completed in 2010, Sri Lanka's leading dignitaries attended the opening ceremony. The politicians' speeches spoke of a plan to turn Hambantota from a town of 11,000 inhabitants into the second-largest city in the country. The Sri Lankan government

FIGURE 5.1: Phase I of the Hambantota port, January 2017. Photograph by the author.

hid most of this debt in off-balance-sheet financing vehicles, even as official statistics showed the central government's public debt declining.

Today, the Colombo elite disagree as to why Rajapaksa doubled down on this vision. Some point to corruption. Others shake their heads, musing that "someone didn't do the math." Asanga Gunawansa, a leading Colombo lawyer involved in renegotiating the contracts after Rajapaksa left office, admitted that Hambantota was a "terrible mistake made by a political leader without a proper feasibility study."[39] After Mahinda Rajapaksa had spent hundreds of millions of dollars and branded the Hambantota project with his own name, it would have been bad politics to abandon it.

Colombo Springs Ahead

Meanwhile, China was much more interested in the port of Colombo, which had the clear potential to become massively profitable for both

FIGURE 5.2: Office building beside Hambantota port, January 2017. Photograph by the author.

sides. In 2006, the Sri Lankan government had contracted Hyundai, the South Korean conglomerate, to build a 6.8-km breakwater around a 19-meter deep harbor astride the city. This was a vast footprint, large and deep enough to dock the world's largest container vessels. In 2009, Sri Lanka sought bids to develop one side of this breakwater, which China won. Today, the Chinese-built container terminal is the only side of the breakwater open for business. In 2011, China Harbour submitted another unsolicited proposal to develop real estate nearby. Dubbed Colombo Port City, the project would take up 233 hectares of reclaimed land and cost an estimated $1.4 billion. Negotiations over the terms of this development began in 2012 and continued until 2014. During this time, the Colombo port's shipping business was booming. This was important context for the Hambantota project. If Hambantota was bound to lose money, China reasoned, perhaps it could recoup the losses by negotiating better terms on its Colombo investments.

Table 5.1

Chinese Loans for Infrastructure in Hambantota District, 2007–2014

Date Committed	Funding Source	Loan Amount (US$ millions)	Interest Rate	Maturity	Project
2007	China Exim Bank	$307	6.3 percent	15 years, 4-year grace period	Port Phase I
2009	China Exim Bank	$77	Unknown	15 years, 3-year grace period	Bunker facility
2009	China Exim Bank	$210	6.3 percent	20 years, 5-year grace period	Mattala Rajapaksa International Airport
2012	China Exim Bank	$253	2.0 percent	15 years, 5-year grace period	Hambantota Hub Development Project
2012	China Exim Bank	$809	First two tranches at 2 percent, final tranche of $51 million at LIBOR	19 years, 6-year grace period	Port Phase II
2013	China Exim Bank	$147	6.3 percent	20 years, 5-year grace period	Port Phase II supplementals
2014	China Development Bank (CDB)	$100	LIBOR 6-month rate	15 years, 3-year grace period	Road construction in Matara and Hambantota districts
2014	China Exim Bank	$412	Unavailable	15 years, 5-year grace period	Road connection between port and airport

Source: Collected from Dreher et al., "Aid, China, and Growth"; China AidData data set.

Note: LIBOR is a floating benchmark rate used primarily for lending between banks. In this context, it was a concessional rate for the Sri Lankan government, which would have paid a far higher rate if it had issued bonds instead.

While the Phase I development at Hambantota floundered commercially, the Colombo port met with increasing commercial success. In 2014, then the Hambantota port's busiest year on record, Colombo handled eighty-four times more cargo.[40] By 2016 the Colombo port had become the world's twenty-fifth busiest port by total container weight handled. The SLPA could afford to subsidize Hambantota's operations only by redirecting revenue internally from the Colombo operation.[41] Why did China and Sri Lanka continue to invest in Hambantota at all, given that the Colombo port already offered a broader and better quality array of services? The answer, as before, was Sri Lankan politics.

Sri Lankan negotiators continued to push for more money for Hambantota, and China finally acquiesced. In January 2011, Phase II of the Hambantota port was announced. The planned expansion was massive. Upon completion of the final phase, the physical footprint was to be larger than the Colombo port. It would include four 100,000-ton container berths, a 100,000-ton oil wharf, two 30,000-ton branch line berths, a harbor basin separating Phase II from the planned Phase III site, an offshore manmade island, and a shipyard. All of this would cost Sri Lanka an additional $810 million.[42] This time, China Exim offered the loan on concessional terms—at a highly favorable 2 percent interest rate. This was bizarre, seeing that Phase I had generated almost no business at all. But it was not a new predatory lending scheme under the aegis of OBOR. The new loans were announced three years before Xi made his speech formally launching the Belt and Road.

Negotiating the Handover

On September 16, 2014, Xi Jinping arrived in Colombo. It was the first visit by a Chinese leader in twenty-eight years (fig. 5.3). Over the course of his two-day visit, Xi took part in an "in-depth exchange of views with President Mahinda Rajapaksa and other leaders and people from various sectors of Sri Lanka on bilateral relations and issues of mutual interest."[43] The two presidents watched the opening of the Norochcholai power station, which had been completed with the help of Chinese loans. They also

FIGURE 5.3: Sri Lankan President Mahinda Rajapaksa (center) shows the way to Chinese President Xi Jinping (right) at a welcome ceremony at the Presidential Secretariat in Colombo, September 16, 2014. Courtesy of Reuters/Dinuka Liyanawatte.

signed more than twenty deals covering infrastructure, power, transport, and culture; agreed to strengthen their strategic cooperative partnership; and announced the beginning of negotiations for a bilateral free trade agreement. The following day, Xi called for expedited progress on the Hambantota port and other joint projects in a meeting with the Sri Lankan prime minister. He "encouraged and welcomed" Sri Lanka's participation in OBOR and invited it to join as a founding member of the Asian Infrastructure Investment Bank. Xi met with members of the Sri Lankan parliament and spoke of Sri Lanka as China's "all-weather friend."[44] Before departing, he visited Colombo International Container Terminal to launch the construction of Colombo Port City. China claimed that all of these preexisting projects fell under the umbrella of OBOR.

By formalizing the investment partnership as a political arrangement within OBOR, Chinese negotiators skillfully used Xi's 2014 trip to their advantage. In the final hours before Xi arrived in Colombo, the Sri Lankan government yielded to China's demands on the new concession agreement for Hambantota Phase II. Under the framework deal, a joint venture between China Harbour and China Merchants would take a thirty-five-year operational lease on four of the seven berths to be built in Phase II.[45] The two countries would share the cost of building Phase II, with the SLPA contributing $212 million. Other elements of the agreement remain murky, and the full contract has never been made public.[46] Still, the headline figures proved the strength of China's negotiating position. China would get operational control of the port and take more than half of any profits, and the SLPA's share of equity would be reduced to 35 percent. Rajapaksa was too deeply committed to the project to walk away. Facing acute time pressure in the lead-up to Xi's planned visit, his choice was ugly: yield to China's demands for more equity or risk China walking away, leaving Sri Lanka with the unprofitable Phase I of the port and a billion dollars of debt. Faced with this choice, Rajapaksa relented. Sri Lanka would double down.

The announcement of OBOR raised the stakes in the middle of the game. What secret concessions might Rajapaksa have offered China to close the 2014 deal over Hambantota Phase II? The concession agreement for Colombo Port City, which was struck in the same week, suggests two answers to this question: land grants and tax concessions. Under the Colombo Port City concession agreement, China Harbour assumed responsibility for all construction activities. In return, it received twenty hectares of the reclaimed land indefinitely on a freehold basis, plus eighty-eight additional hectares on a thirty-five-year lease with the option to extend for another ninety-nine years.[47] China Harbour also won a twenty-five-year waiver on all income taxes and import tariffs on machinery. As a cherry on top, Sri Lanka gave China special concessions to use the renminbi as the currency in the Port City zone in a nod to Beijing's desire to internationalize its currency.

China drove a hard bargain on the contract for Colombo Port City. If Sri Lanka defaulted on its obligations or unilaterally terminated the deal, it would be liable for 200 percent of China Harbour's net construction costs. China Harbour could walk away with no penalty at any time. Since China Harbour and the SLPA negotiated the Hambantota and Colombo Port City deals in parallel, it is reasonable to assume that the contents of the agreements were similar. If anything, the Chinese had more leverage in the Hambantota negotiation. Unlike the fast-growing Colombo port, Hambantota had no prospect of paying for itself if Phase II were never built.

Many Sri Lankan government officials were angry at the concessions that Rajapaksa had made to China during Xi's visit. The day after the two agreements were signed in the presence of Rajapaksa and Xi, the *Sunday Times* reported that anonymous sources in the Ministry of Finance were dismayed about the terms. The External Affairs Ministry denied, unprompted, that it had been involved in the negotiation. The Attorney General said he did not know whether his office had signed off. The *Sunday Times* concluded that it was "not possible for the Cabinet to have seen and approved the document before it went through."[48] In conclusion, the 2014 operational agreement for the Hambantota deal was almost certainly much less favorable to Sri Lanka than what the press reported.

A New Government Renegotiates

When Rajapaksa lost his reelection bid four months later, the Hambantota and Colombo Port City agreements were thrown into doubt. China had actively supported Rajapaksa's reelection. As the *New York Times* later found, China Harbour gave his campaign $7.6 million through backdoor transfers.[49] On the other side, India, the United States, and the United Kingdom quietly backed the opposition. As one senior Sri Lankan political figure put it to me, India's main problem with Rajapaksa was that he was "too close to China." But voters were angry for a different reason: "not because Rajapaksa had taken loans from the Chinese, but because he had failed to make the projects profitable." After the election, the new Sri Lankan government expelled Indian intelligence operatives for interfering in the election against Rajapaksa.[50] Once again, Sri Lanka found itself caught between larger and even more meddlesome powers.

The new president, Maithripala Sirisena, immediately froze OBOR projects across the country. Everything was stalled, from construction of the bunkering and transshipment operations at Hambantota Phase II to the Lotus Tower and Colombo Port City real estate developments in the capital. Beijing was furious. Behind closed doors, Chinese businessmen and diplomats pressured the Sri Lankan government to resume construction. When direct political pressure failed, Beijing let its state-owned enterprises play the bad cop. By February 2016, the Chinese joint venture was demanding $143 million in damages for Colombo Port City alone.

India was pleased with the election result that it had helped engineer. According to Adm. Jayanath Colombage, at the time the commander of the Sri Lankan navy, the new government's plan was to hope "that India and the West would come back in and salvage us."[51] But India misread the new Sri Lankan president. New Delhi interpreted Sirisena's decision to freeze Chinese construction projects as a repudiation of OBOR, rather than an invitation for New Delhi to make a counteroffer. But Colombo could not afford to wait, since the bill for Rajapaksa's borrowing spree was coming due. "When the Indians and Americans didn't bite, we had to go back hat in hand to the Chinese and negotiate from a position of weakness," Colombage recounts. "In the next round of negotiations, the Chinese demanded guarantees that we would not be able to withdraw unilaterally [from joint projects]. And at that point, having lost our credibility as a committed partner, we had to provide that guarantee."[52] Colombage thinks that Sirisena misinterpreted India's strategic interest in Sri Lanka. New Delhi wanted to see Sri Lanka free of foreign influence, but it was not willing to pay for the privilege. "India has strategic objectives, but not strategic patience or strategic capability," Colombage concluded. "China has all three."[53]

By 2016, the Sri Lankan government had no choice but to swap its equity in the Hambantota port for a reduction of its debt burden on harsher terms. That summer, China and Sri Lanka struck a framework deal that would raise the Chinese joint venture's stake in Hambantota to 80 percent. But Sri Lanka's complex domestic politics added yet another set of internal constraints. Allies of Rajapaksa, now in the minority, criticized the Sirisena government for selling national infrastructure to foreigners—even though Rajapaksa himself had negotiated the 2014 concession agreements. The Sri Lankan effort to renegotiate with China backfired spectacularly.

The Sri Lankans were internally divided. Ports Minister Arjuna Ranatunga feared that a deal would compromise national sovereignty and security and began to leak details of the ongoing negotiations to the press.

"We are hoping they [the Chinese] will take at least 70 percent of the debt in this swap," Ranatunga told a reporter in October 2016, "and we are talking to the Chinese on this basis for Hambantota's development.[54] This contradicted other reports that China was opposed to renegotiating the debt. Ranatunga also claimed that the Chinese had demanded a 199-year concession and had compromised for 99 years. He admitted that the SLPA was sustaining the Hambantota port with funds pulled from Colombo. Most of all, Ranatunga railed against the framework agreement. "If we give this particular excuse for [the Chinese] to create another ports authority [to run Hambantota], then the SLPA would be in trouble," he told an interviewer in April 2017.[55] Ultimately Ranatunga's demands were not realistic. Sri Lanka no longer had any leverage over the Chinese. Sirisena removed Ranatunga from office the following year, before the final deal was struck.

Announcing the Handover

The Sri Lankan government announced the renegotiated deal in July 2017.[56] In a nod to Indian and US concerns that a new agreement could allow China to militarize Hambantota, the Sri Lankans claimed that they had won "strict prohibitions to prevent any form of military-related activities." The SLPA promised that the Sri Lankan navy, Defense Ministry, and national police would take joint responsibility for the port's security. The Chinese joint venture would make three payments to the government of Sri Lanka totaling $1.12 billion. This would almost fully relieve the government of Sri Lanka from the debt it had taken on to finance Phases I and II of construction.

The Sri Lankans used pseudo-arithmetic to misrepresent the terms. According to the announcement, SLPA "will hold a share of 50.7 percent and China Merchants Ports 49.3 percent." A legal analysis of the public disclosures makes clear that the Sri Lankan government's claims were misleading. In fact, the port was broken into two holding companies. The Chinese would take an 85 percent stake in the outer shell, known as Hambantota International Port Group (HIPG), which had "the sole and exclusive right to develop, operate and manage the Hambantota Port."[57]

HIPG would then take a 58 percent stake in the inner shell, Hambantota International Port Services (HIPS), which would have the "sole and exclusive right to develop, operate and manage the Common User Facilities, for the operation of the Hambantota Port." These facilities included the fifteen thousand acres of industrial zone surrounding the port itself and control of the port's security. The SLPA would hold the remainder of the equity: 15 percent of HIPG and 42 percent of HIPS.

In fact, the deal gave China total control over *both* of the Hambantota holding companies. According to an updated and substantially more detailed disclosure released by China Merchants on December 8, 2017, a shell company incorporated in the British Virgin Islands and owned by China Merchants would appoint the leadership teams of both Hambantota companies. The Chinese-controlled entity gets to nominate eleven board members, and the SPLA only two.[58] Despite Sri Lanka's evasions and protestations, it had handed China total control (fig 5.4). Nor was there any public written agreement to restrict Chinese military use of the Hambantota port. If such an agreement had existed, the Sri Lankan side surely would have every incentive to release it.

During the negotiations, there were a series of strikes on the ground in Hambantota. The first was organized by the port employees. These were mostly unskilled young men from nearby villages who had been recruited under a staffing scheme from 2007 and could see that they would probably be laid off under a new agreement. The port workers detained two Japanese vessels. In October 2017, Mahinda Rajapaksa's son Namal was arrested outside the Indian consulate in Hambantota, protesting the impending sale of Mattala airport to India. Video recordings showed him chanting anti-Indian slogans and criticizing the Sirisena government for accepting too low a price. This was political gamesmanship and had no effect on the high-level contractual negotiation between the Sri Lankan and Chinese governments.

Embracing OBOR

Concurrently with the Hambantota handover, Sri Lanka decided to embrace OBOR more fully and explicitly than before. In 2017, Sirisena—

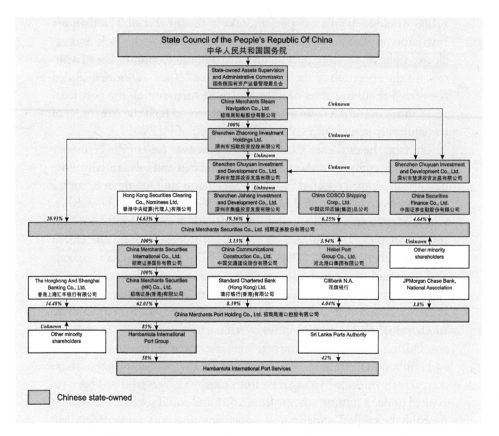

FIGURE 5.4: Ownership structure of Hambantota port after December 2017 handover. Compiled from public records. Courtesy of Ruofei Shen and Ira Anatolevna.

who had frozen all Chinese projects on taking office—signed two OBOR memoranda of understanding and committed to partnering with China to implement the country's long-term development plan. He also sent his prime minister to attend the OBOR summit in Beijing. Both Sirisena's party and their Chinese partners played down their previous disputes as a "temporar[y] . . . twist" in an otherwise amiable relationship, denied that any coercion had taken place in the negotiations, and blamed the rocky period in relations on the former government's "errors." The Chinese embassy heaped praise on Sirisena and claimed that "OBOR has become mainstream consensus in Sri Lankan society."[59] As Sri Lanka Central Bank Governor Ajith Nivard Cabraal put it, in comments widely reported in the Chinese press: the *New York Times* report accusing China of "debt diplomacy" at Hambantota is "what Trump calls 'fake news.'"[60]

Today, the Hambantota project is a relatively minor issue in Sri Lankan domestic politics, and most elites are still excited about the economic growth and political flexibility that OBOR can offer. It is unclear how many Sri Lankans—including in the security community—are aware that the Chinese joint venture's controlling stake in HIPG gives it full operational authority over security for the Hambantota industrial zone. It is not clear whether these facts would have much of an effect on Sri Lankan domestic politics even if they came to light. Hambantota barely figured in the elections of 2018 and 2019. In another demonstration that most Sri Lankans do see China as a threat, the Rajapaksa family has returned to prominence. Mahinda, the former president, joined Sirisena's government as prime minister. In November 2019, Gotabaya Rajapaksa was elected president on an unapologetically pro-China platform. He met publicly with Chinese officials closely linked to Xi Jinping and promised to "restore the relationship to where it was" under his brother. "I suppose the thinking was if we upset China, the West would come to us with endless bags of gold," Rajapaksa's campaign spokesman said, "but the bags of gold never materialized."[61]

Does China plan to militarize Hambantota? Immediately after the handover, it seemed that it did. Less than three weeks after the final agreement was signed, *Global Times* published an essay explicitly proposing that Hambantota be used as a naval base. Zhou Yongsheng, a professor at China Foreign Affairs University's Institute of International Relations, was quoted extensively.[62] "India has always had strong influence over the decision-making of many South Asian countries on foreign policy, including Nepal, Bangladesh and Sri Lanka, treating them like its backyard," Zhou said. "Such an overbearing mindset will not work anymore . . . The lease agreement is a reasonable commercial arrangement, but even if China someday would leverage the port for any military activities, it is totally understandable." On the other hand, now that Hambantota has drawn intense scrutiny and criticism in the international press, it is probably no longer worth the reputational damage for China to try to militarize it. For the foreseeable future, Hambantota will benefit the Chinese navy only insofar as it is a well-located supply depot.

China is working hard to make Hambantota a commercial success, with the help of Singapore, India, and Japan. After China won the ninety-nine-year lease on Hambantota, the Indian Aviation Authority negotiated its own four-year lease concession on the $210 million Chinese-built airport that sits empty near the Hambantota port.[63] Japan approved a forty-year concessionary loan to expand the Colombo port. China Merchants and Sinopec, a Chinese oil giant, announced new investments in the Hambantota area. The number of ships calling at the port nearly doubled in 2018, though absolute levels of traffic remain very low. In March 2019, companies controlled by the Indian and Omani governments won approval to build a $3.85 billion oil refinery at Hambantota.[64] In October 2019, a Singaporean company won approval to build a $20 billion oil refinery there. If this project is implemented as planned, it will be larger than all of China's projects in Sri Lanka put together. These deals have shown Sri Lanka that strategic promiscuity works brilliantly. Embracing OBOR in spite of the US backlash has not only helped Sri Lankan politicians' private interests, it has also created a global bidding war to finance the country's infrastructure development (fig. 5.5).

Conclusions

Sri Lankan elites are remarkably sanguine about the geopolitical ramifications of the Hambantota affair. I asked Asanga Gunawansa, the prominent Colombo lawyer, what he found mysterious or unclear about China's motivations. "Nothing about Chinese behavior presents a puzzle," he responded. "They are businessmen who want influence, that's all." Is China trying to bully Sri Lanka? I pressed. "Absolutely not," Gunawansa replied. "They are clever. When a trader is trying to sell you something, he will always try to make you feel you're smart. But do we fear a loss of sovereignty because of our dealings with China? Not at all. We fear the Indians more than the Chinese."[65] Gunawansa also dismissed my question about the risk that China could turn Hambantota into a military base. "That is India's security problem, not Sri Lanka's," he said. "If the

FIGURE 5.5: A Sri Lankan worker walks through the Colombo Port City construction site as Chinese dredging ships work in the distance, October 2017. Courtesy of Reuters/Dinuka Liyanawatte.

Indians want to prevent that from happening, they can make a bilateral agreement with us."

Some experts believe that rivalry between India and China will destabilize the region and that Sri Lanka should intermediate. "Sri Lanka has to convince India that we want to do business with both of them—and that is non-negotiable," Saravanamuttu tells me. "Eventually, a natural division of spheres of influence in Sri Lanka seems to present itself: India in the north, particularly in the Tamil areas, and China in the south." Saravanamuttu does not believe that war between China and India is at all likely. He is more concerned that India's defensive response to China will destabilize the Indian Ocean region and slow Sri Lanka's economic development. "Whether the elephants make love or war," he says, "it is the grass that suffers."

• • •

Duminda Ariyasinghe's office in the World Trade Center building has a terrific view over Colombo harbor. Dressed in a pressed suit and red tie, the charismatic director of the Sri Lanka Board of Investment leans back and forth over his wooden desktop. Ariyasinghe tells me about his vision for Sri Lanka as a "South Asian Singapore." He believes that Sri Lanka can become an upper-middle-income country if it turns itself into a regional trading hub. The former Harvard Kennedy School fellow is a fan of the late Singaporean prime minister Lee Kuan Yew. Lee brought order to an ethnically divided city-state, Ariyasinghe says, and showed the world that Singapore was open for business.[66] Sri Lanka should do the same.

The conversation turns from Singapore to China. We discuss the country's economic and political history. Ariyasinghe praises Ezra Vogel's biography of Deng Xiaoping, the visionary leader whose Reform and Opening Up policy began market reforms in China.[67] I mention that I have done academic work on US–China relations after the Tiananmen massacre in 1989. Ariyasinghe asks whether I think the Chinese Communist Party would have collapsed if it had not used force against the demonstrators. "That is what Deng understood," he says. "Leaders have to think for the long term. If the government had not cracked down, would the Chinese economy be where it is today?" There is a pause and we both look out the window, where Chinese cranes can be seen building Colombo Port City.

The time comes for me to go. "Since ancient times, our relationship with China has been economic," Ariyasinghe concludes. "I firmly believe that China's reason for being here now is also economic. Chinese projects move fast. They see opportunities for profit all around them." He smiles. "As far as I can see, it's a win-win."

CHAPTER 6

The Skeptical Bulldozer

Tanzania Turns Away

The beach seethes with activity. About fifty yards offshore, a line of fishing boats float at anchor. Dozens of men wade toward shore, the water up to their waists or shoulders, balancing great trays of fish on their heads. When they reach the beach, they lay their loads down on tables, where the fish are sorted. The smaller ones are piled by the thousands onto tarps for drying in the sun. The whole market smells of them. The larger fish are cleaved and cleaned on the spot. More than a hundred men and women crowd around the fish tables on the narrow, dirty strip of beach (fig. 6.1). There are fruit stands higher up, and women grilling chicken. On the dirt road leading to the water is a stall where two young men are playing slot machines. One of them tells me that the machines are Chinese-owned.

From the fifteenth century through the late nineteenth century, Bagamoyo was one of the main trading hubs on the East African coast.[1] On a terrace bisecting the market are more than a dozen iron and concrete posts where slaves from the interior used to wait in neck braces before being sent to Zanzibar for auction. In the Arab-built fort, which the Germans later turned into a garrison, my guide shows me rooms where prisoners were held without food or water for up to five days at a time. When the Germans took the territory of Tanganyika (now the mainland portion of Tanzania) in 1884, they chose Bagamoyo as their capital. They bought out the Omanis and converted the slave barracks into official buildings. The Germans built schools, abolished slavery, and fought with local chiefs who had profited through the slave trade. But the locals remember that

FIGURE 6.1: Fish market in Bagamoyo town, December 2018. Photograph by the author.

the Germans practiced their own kind of brutality. Today, the German "Hanging Place" in Bagamoyo is marked with a concrete monument. A hand-painted sign reads: "HERE IS THE PLACE WHERE GERMAN COLONIALISTS USED TO HANG TO DEATH AFRICAN REV-OLUTIONARIES WHO WERE OPPOSING THEIR OPPRESSIVE RULE." In the 1890s, the Germans moved their capital down the coast to Dar es Salaam, and Bagamoyo fell into decline.

• • •

In 2013 the Tanzanian government and China Merchants Group announced plans to restore Bagamoyo's former position as the largest port in East Africa—this time not for slaves but for containers and dry bulk. The week after Xi Jinping assumed the presidency of China, he visited Tanzania (map 6.1) to make the announcement in person. As Xi and Tanzanian President Jakaya Kikwete looked on, the Tanzanian finance minister and the chairman of China Merchants signed a framework agreement. The

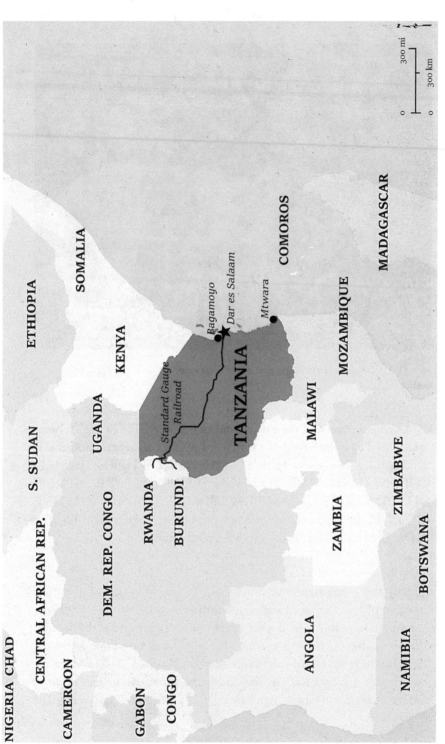

MAP 6.1: Map of Tanzania, courtesy of Scott Walker.

press release claimed that the goal was to turn the coastal area north of Bagamoyo town into a "new Shenzhen," the hub of a $10 billion Special Economic Zone (SEZ). Just before he left office two years later, Kikwete returned to Bagamoyo for a groundbreaking ceremony. He told reporters that construction would be completed within three years: that is, by 2018.

Kikwete's deadline has come and gone, and the beach where the port is planned stands empty except for a few local fishermen and their hollowed-out canoes. In the port zone, whole villages of local residents have yet to be resettled or compensated for their property. Looking out across the harbor, it seems obvious that a large island will have to be eliminated and the sea floor dredged before ships of any size can reach the shore.

In its scale, design, and construction schedule, the plan for the Bagamoyo port is strikingly similar to Hambantota. On the ground, the differences could not be more obvious. In Hambantota, the newly paved main road to the port passes by two large dormitories for Chinese construction workers and several official buildings. In Bagamoyo, the port site is five miles north of town on a dirt road studded with potholes the size of small craters. The locals I spoke to told me that Bagamoyo town does not have a single Chinese resident. Since John Magufuli replaced Jakaya Kikwete in 2015, relations with China have hit their lowest point since Tanzania won its independence in 1961. Some Tanzanian officials privately told me that they don't believe the port will ever be built. In June 2019, as he geared up for his reelection campaign, Magufuli condemned the Chinese financing offer as "exploitative and awkward" and said that "as a country we have been played with, and we need to change."[2] China appears to have written off the Bagamoyo project. Chinese press reports and statements from the local embassy rarely mention it anymore. Tanzania is not one of the sixty-three OBOR countries listed on China's official Belt and Road Portal website (see Appendix A for the current list of OBOR countries).

Why, then, do Tanzanian officials forcefully deny that the Bagamoyo port project is dead? Why has a senior Tanzanian politician told the press every few months since 2015 that construction is scheduled to start any day? The current and former government officials who granted me interviews on the record spoke about Bagamoyo in strikingly similar language. They insisted that there was no change in Tanzania's plans for Bagamoyo after Magufuli assumed the presidency. They told me that relations

with China are better than ever, reeled off lists of other Chinese investments in the country, and extolled the virtues of win-win economic cooperation. Several of the more senior officials even boasted that Tanzania is a major OBOR hub. If the Bagamoyo port is stalled or canceled,
and if Tanzania is not part of OBOR, what can explain these statements?

Because of the tense political environment in Tanzania, it is impossible to document the negotiations with the same level of detail as in the
Hambantota case. The Chama Cha Mapinduzi (CCM) party has won
every national election since independence, so all national politics is driven
by opaque intraparty maneuvering. Magufuli has cracked down violently
on the free press and political dissent.[3] As a result, it is little surprise that
no proper investigative research has been done in English or Swahili and
that the local press has covered the issue cautiously.[4] The Tanzanian and
Chinese governments do not discuss their ongoing negotiations over contract terms. Several current and former government officials granted me
interviews, on and off the record, but other interviews and the Chinese
documents contradicted some of their claims. There were also safety and
ethical issues involved in researching this case. Tanzania has never been
entirely safe for journalists. Conditions have worsened further in recent
years.[5] Still, Bagamoyo is a worthy case study because in other respects it
is similar to Hambantota. To protect the safety of my sources, I cite some
of their information and commentary without attribution. Where my interview subjects offered me irreconcilable accounts, I allow them to
speak for themselves.

Deep Freeze: A First Cut of the Case

Like Hambantota, Bagamoyo was a fully home-grown idea. Also like
Hambantota, its starts and stops were driven from beginning to end by
Tanzanian domestic politics. The Tanzanian government first began to
discuss the prospect of building an SEZ in the area in 2005. The original
concept was to build an industrial park and supporting services (banks,
transit, residential areas) and *maybe* a port, if funds allowed. The Tanzanian government hired foreign consultancies to run feasibility studies. It
pitched the idea to its major donors, but no investors came forward. Fi-

nally, in 2012, a few months before Xi was set to visit, Chinese government officials submitted their own proposal in a private meeting with Tanzanian leaders. The Chinese proposal committed in principle to funding the entire $10 billion project. But they wanted China Merchants Group to build the port first, just as it had done at Hambantota. The risk was that the port would struggle to pay for itself until the ancillary infrastructure and industrial zone were completed. In the meantime, Tanzania would be on the hook for debt payments.

The Tanzanian president jumped at China's offer to help him fulfill his long-standing vision. The political optics were excellent (fig. 6.2). Bagamoyo is Kikwete's hometown, just as Hambantota was Rajapaksa's. There was a stronger argument for building a port in Bagamoyo than in Hambantota. Sri Lanka had capacity to spare at the Colombo port. In contrast, Tanzania faced an urgent congestion crisis at its main national port in Dar es Salaam. Although the most urgent priority was to improve efficiency at the Dar es Salaam port, there were natural limits to how much that port could be expanded, since it crowds up against a densely populated urban neighborhood. Sooner or later, Tanzania would need a second international port. Bagamoyo's favorable geography and proximity to the capital made it an excellent candidate.

Bagamoyo likely would have turned into a second Hambantota if Kikwete had not been term-limited and left office before construction began. When Magufuli was sworn in in November 2015, the Tanzanian government had not yet acquired even a fraction of the land for the port and SEZ. Magufuli was a nationalist, unmoved by the argument that China was a patron that had to be courted. A fiscally prudent pragmatist, he quickly saw that the looming overcapacity crisis at the Dar es Salaam port was a far more urgent development priority. Above all, Magufuli was an observant politician. He recognized that the Bagamoyo and Standard Gauge Railway projects were the flagship achievements of his predecessor, and he wanted to leave his own mark. Shortly after taking office, Magufuli halted negotiations with China on all projects. The government did not say how this decision affected Tanzania's formal relationship with OBOR.

Magufuli did not want to provoke a major diplomatic incident by scrapping the Bagamoyo project. He was playing to a domestic audience, not an international one. In time, like his Sri Lankan counterpart,

FIGURE 6.2: Tanzanian President Jakaya Kikwete (right) accepts a large key from Xi Jinping in Dar es Salaam on March 25, 2013. Courtesy of Reuters/Thomas Mukoya.

Maithripala Sirisena (who came to power in the same year), Magufuli recognized the inescapable logic of continuing his predecessor's cooperation with China. Starting in the second half of 2016, relations gradually began to warm again. Magufuli brought in more Chinese investments to the Dar es Salaam port, restarted negotiations on Bagamoyo, and brought in Chinese funds for a white elephant of his own: a new airport in his isolated rural hometown. In the meantime, members of Magufuli's government praised OBOR even more enthusiastically than Kikwete's once did, and played down the president's more provocative statements in the press. If Magufuli's decision to freeze Bagamoyo hurt relations with China, these senior Tanzanian politicians seem to think, perhaps praising OBOR can heal it.

Legacy of Cooperation

Tanzanian politicians' view of China, like that of their counterparts in Sri Lanka, is rooted in their personal experience and shared ideas about their country's history. Before 1961, the land that is now Tanzania was dominated by foreign powers in succession: the Omanis, the Germans, the British. Since independence, Tanzanian leaders have skillfully forged a brand of nationalist ideology based on principles of self-reliance and religious pluralism. This has helped the country escape the sectarian violence that plagued some of its neighbors. In the first decades after independence, China saw Tanzania as one of its closest strategic partners in the developing world and showered it with aid and political honors. The older generation of Tanzanian leaders remembers this. A sense of trust and admiration for China is deeply embedded in the country's political discourse.

Tanzania's experience with colonialism was shorter and less brutal than its neighbors', but still left it with little interest in Western-style politics or economic models. Germany won control over much of East Africa at the Berlin Conference of 1884. After the defeat of the Central powers in World War I, the territory, known as Tanganyika, became a British protectorate. British colonial administrators took an extractive approach to governance. Thousands of Tanganyikan citizens were conscripted to serve in World War II. After the war, an ill-planned British scheme to grow groundnuts in unsuitable soil conditions devastated the Tanganyikan economy.[6] After Tanzania earned its independence in 1964, its politics moved toward left-wing nationalism. Tanzania joined the global nonaligned movement, collectivized agriculture, and adopted import substitution economic policies in the hope of becoming self-sufficient.

From the very day Tanzania declared independence, it has enjoyed a special relationship with China. The founding father of independent Tanzania, Julius Nyerere, was a visionary nationalist who fiercely opposed US and Soviet influence. As relations between China and the Soviet Union worsened in the 1960s, China poured aid into Africa. Tanzania became the leading recipient.[7] In 1964, following a visit from Chinese Premier Zhou Enlai, Tanzania negotiated a barter trade agreement similar to Sri Lanka's "Rubber-Rice" deal.[8] In 1967, China began work on the Tazara railway, a $1 billion, 1,160-mile line that connected landlocked Zambia to the Tanzanian coast.[9] The line was China's single largest foreign aid project before OBOR. It is an important part of Tanzania's national infrastructure network to this day. In fact, Col. Joseph Simbakalia, the director-general of Tanzania's Export Processing Zone Authority, specifically told me that one reason for locating the SEZ at Bagamoyo is that the Tazara rail line passes close by.[10] Every Tanzanian official I spoke with, without exception, mentioned Tazara as irrefutable evidence that Tanzania can trust China to deliver on its promises.

Chinese patronage of Tanzania paid political dividends for both countries. Nyerere embraced socialism and pan-Africanism and looked to China as a potential model for development in his own country. He visited China thirteen times during his time in office and modeled his system of agricultural collectivization, or *ujamaa*, on the Maoist system, not realizing it had led to mass starvation during the Great Leap Forward. "We are using hoes," Nyerere mused. "If two million farmers in Tanzania could jump from hoe to the oxen plough, it would be a revolution. It would double our living standard, triple our product. This is the kind of thing China is doing."[11] Nyerere also modeled Tanzania's ruling party—Tanganyika African National Union, later reorganized as the CCM—after the Chinese Communist Party (CCP). In 1971, Nyerere repaid China for its financial and political support by helping deliver the votes to restore Beijing's seat on the UN Security Council.[12]

China pulled back from Africa after Deng Xiaoping rose to power in 1978. Deng canceled most Mao-era programs to support revolutionary activities in the developing world and dramatically cut down foreign aid in favor of fledgling market reforms at home. Without a patron, Tanzania had no choice but to liberalize its economy. In 1985, Nyerere stepped down from the presidency rather than oversee market reforms. His successors took out loans from the International Monetary Fund (IMF) and other international donors and privatized some of the largest state-owned enterprises (SOEs). By the 1990s, Tanzania's economy was growing—but nowhere near as quickly as China's, which was growing meteorically. Diplomatic engagement with Beijing continued in the background, but the countries' interactions were largely symbolic.

In the 2000s, China began to pay attention to Africa again. Jiang Zemin's "Going Out" strategy (discussed in chapter 2) encouraged Chinese SOEs to secure their supplies of raw materials around the world and build the infrastructure necessary to bring it to market. Africa stood alongside Central Asia as one of the most promising regions for this kind of investment. In the mid-2000s, the Chinese government began to create political forums to coordinate its engagement with African countries. Just as it would do ten years later under the OBOR framework, China claimed to support regional and multilateral organizations while making most of its deals bilaterally. China established the Forum on China-Africa Cooperation in 2006. Then it began to sign strategic partnership agreements with African countries, including Tanzania. The annual volume of trade between China and the continent increased more than 100-fold between 1980 and 2010. By the time Xi first visited Tanzania in 2013, China had transformed itself from an economic nonentity into the largest trading partner of almost every African country.

China's return to Africa has brought great economic benefits to Tanzania. Growing Chinese demand has supported the country's most important industries: tourism, gold, coffee, and cashews. China has offered funding and technical expertise to begin tackling some of the country's greatest infrastructure bottlenecks, which include poor roads and a nearly total lack of electrification in rural areas. When large natural gas reserves were discovered off Tanzania's southern coast, a Chinese firm built the pipeline to the capital. Chinese firms have built modern army barracks across the country, installed a fiber-optic communications network, and begun construction on a $4.2 billion Standard Gauge Railway from the Tanzanian coast into the mineral-rich Democratic Republic of the Congo.

China is also showing a growing interest in African governance and security issues. China fully funded the construction of the African Union's new headquarters in Addis Ababa, Ethiopia. Since 2012, China has provided more UN peacekeepers than the United States, Russia, France, and the United Kingdom combined, most of whom are deployed on the African continent.[13] In July 2017, China opened its first overseas military base in Djibouti on the East African coast.[14] China benefits in several ways from involving itself in African political and military affairs. Peacekeeping operations offer practical training for Chinese military personnel, protect the million Chinese nationals who now live on the African continent, and remind countries in the region that China is a major power, all without antagonizing the United States.[15] China sees its African resource supply lines to be strategically important and—unlike in Central Asia or the Middle East—cannot be sure that the United States or Russia would intervene to prevent the major commodity exporters from turning into failed states. Regardless of China's objectives, it's a fact of life for most governments in sub-Saharan Africa that Beijing's shadow now looms larger than Washington's.

Conceiving Bagamoyo

Dr. Joseph Simbakalia, a retired army colonel who has run Tanzania's industrial policy for almost two decades, is a very impressive man. Though it was late in the afternoon on a Friday, he spoke to me energetically for more than two hours as a professor would—guiding me from topic to topic with an astonishing mastery of detail. As he spoke, he brandished a Samsung tablet to support his points with graphs, documents, and slides. Simbakalia has a modern and well-kept office in a walled-off compound on the outskirts of Dar es Salaam: the country's first SEZ. On the wall outside, a simple, all-text promotional poster reads, "Tanzania: an Investment Gateway to the World." It has four bullet points: "Fiscal incentives," "Non fiscal incentives," "Quality and timely service," and "World class infrastructure."

Simbakalia began our conversation by seeking to persuade me that the Bagamoyo scheme was originally and always a Tanzanian idea. In the late 1990s, he told me, Tanzania set out to replicate the model of southern China and Southeast Asia, which had rapidly built up their manufacturing bases by establishing tax-advantaged SEZs. In 2003, Tanzanian President Benjamin Mkapa met Japanese economist Soichi Kobayashi, who became an influential outside adviser on Tanzania's development strategy. Kobayashi persuaded Mkapa that "export processing zones" alone were not enough. The country should build bigger and broader zones that could accommodate secondary industries, such as financial services and retail. Kobayashi's idea was to build several SEZs along the coast. In early 2006, Simbakalia recalls, the government first began to discuss the prospect of a major development at Bagamoyo.[16] The original plan centered on an industrial park surrounded by commercial and residential areas, "and maybe a port, if funds allowed."

The Tanzanian government commissioned a series of independent studies, which confirmed that a port would be a useful addition to the proposed SEZ. In 2008, the Tanzania Ports Authority (TPA) contracted a Dutch company to draw up a capital investment plan for the whole country. It included Bagamoyo on the list of potential port sites. Later, Tanzania contracted a German firm, Hamburg Port Consulting, to do a feasibility study for Bagamoyo. In July 2012, the Danish firm COWI A/S was brought in to do a master plan for the Bagamoyo SEZ. Simbakalia sees two takeaways from this historical background. First, "the idea for the port was homegrown, and the Chinese didn't enter until later." Second, the consultants found that "the SEZ in a worst-case scenario was designed to function without a port attached." If true, this meant that Tanzania began the tender process in a strong position. It had a clear sense of what it wanted and needed, unadulterated by foreign influence, and had no pressing need to yield to any lender's proposed terms. "If you are a lender and you go to another country that has no ideas, they will take anything you offer," Simbakalia told me. "But Tanzania has its own ideas. Maybe that's why it has taken so long to negotiate the details of the Bagamoyo port."

Tanzania's port bottleneck was on the verge of becoming a serious economic problem. By 2013, the port of Dar es Salaam, which handled 95 percent of Tanzania's foreign trade, was operating at 90 percent capacity. Because of a combination of corruption, inefficiency, and aging capital equipment, it was one of the most dysfunctional ports on the East African coast.[17] When the TPA published its twenty-year strategic plan in 2009, four out of the five strategic recommendations related to reforming and expanding the Dar es Salaam port.[18] Only one of the recommendations was to build a second, back-up port. Bagamoyo was one of the four possible locations named on that list.[19]

Kikwete's government acknowledged that upgrading and expanding the Dar es Salaam port was the government's most urgent infrastructure problem. In public statements, Tanzanian officials clarified that the Bagamoyo project would not come at the expense of Dar es Salaam. The year after Xi visited and the framework deal for Bagamoyo was signed, Kikwete struck a separate $565 million deal with the World Bank and other international development agencies to modernize the Dar es Salaam facility. The renovation would nearly double the port's annual capacity from 15 million tons to 28 million tons while revamping the port's operations. This renovation resolved the short-term bottleneck. It was no longer an urgent necessity to build a new port at Bagamoyo.

The Bagamoyo location had both pros and cons. Proponents of Bagamoyo countered that the Dar es Salaam metropolitan area was already expanding to the north. Less than two hours' drive from the capital, Bagamoyo was also located not far from the Standard Gauge Railway, which Tanzanian planners hoped could one day connect to a trans-African rail network. On the other hand, the seabed along the Bagamoyo coast is not well suited to docking large vessels. The proposed site was located more than five miles from Bagamoyo town. The site would require substantial ancillary investment because it lacked rail and other infrastructure links to the capital. Perhaps most important, Bagamoyo is located hundreds of kilometers from the estimated 53 trillion cubic feet of offshore gas deposits in Tanzania's southern Mtwara region. "If you're going to have two major ports," one anonymous analyst told Reuters when Bagamoyo was announced, then isn't the place to have [one] in the south, where the gas is?"[20] Nevertheless, every current and former Tanzanian official I interviewed argued that the benefits of Bagamoyo's location outweighed the costs. If China continued to fund the expansion of Africa's railway network, Simbakalia claimed, Bagamoyo could one day become the premier transshipment hub on the East African coast.

Tanzania's Only Best Friend

Tanzanian President Jakaya Kikwete's enthusiasm for China seemed to know no bounds. Lü Youqing, the Chinese ambassador to Tanzania, captured this spirit best in a remarkable undated essay (likely written sometime in 2017). In it, Lü recalls briefing Kikwete in December 2012 on Xi's recent promotion to CCP general secretary at the Eighteenth National Party Congress. Kikwete's response was so comically over the top—outrageous and perfectly illuminating about the zeitgeist leading up to Xi's trip to Tanzania four months later—that the essay is worth discussing at some length.[21]

Lü's narrative begins in late December 2012, when he arrived at the presidential palace for a routine meeting with Kikwete. After the conversation, Lü mentioned that his embassy had a copy of Xi's remarks from the Party Congress. After Christmas, Lü says, he would be very happy to share them.

"Why wait until the end of the vacation?" Kikwete insisted. "Let's talk about it tomorrow morning!"

Lü demurred. The vacation had been planned. The presidential entourage and their families were packed and ready to depart for the Christmas holiday. But Kikwete's mind was made up. "I am the President of Tanzania, and I make the final decision," Lü reports him as saying. "Tomorrow morning it will be. You need to prepare it this evening."

At 9 am on the Christmas holiday, Lü and his staff returned to the nearly empty palace to brief Kikwete on "Xi Jinping Thought" and the CCP's latest innovations in policy and Marxist theory. "President Kikwete focused completely," Lü recalls. He peppered the Chinese delegation with questions about the minutiae of the discussions at the Party Congress and "highly praised the great achievements" of China's contributions to world peace. When Lü turned the discussion to Xi himself, Kikwete's enthusiasm grew even more pronounced. He noted that Xi was "promoted step by step from the grassroots level, making numerous achievements at each stage, and thereby setting an example for Tanzanian politicians." Kikwete drew a parallel to his own experience and exclaimed: "I can't wait, I want to see General Secretary Xi right now!"

Lü reserves the most salient details for the end. Beyond praising Xi, Kikwete also made clear that he intended to "pay special attention to China's core interests." When the conversation turned to foreign policy, Kikwete "stood up and pulled me to the globe on the other side of the reception room." One by one, he demanded to be shown the places Lü named: from Taiwan to Tibet, from the Diaoyu [Senkaku] Islands to the South China Sea. One by one, Kikwete pledged to support Beijing as it sought to safeguard its interests. He insisted to Lü that the Dalai Lama would never be allowed to come to Tanzania on his watch—or anywhere in Africa, if he could help it. "The entire briefing and interaction continued for more than three hours, from 9 am to 12:30 pm," Lü recalls. When he finally bid the Chinese visitors farewell, Kikwete told them to remember something: that "Tanzania has many friends in the world, but China is its only *best* friend."

This remarkable essay from the Chinese ambassador, written up several years into Xi's term in office, says more about China than it does about Tanzania. It does not matter much whether these recollections are strictly accurate. The general thrust cannot be too far from the truth, or Lü would not have dared to publish his essay for general audiences and run the risk of being contradicted. The essay reveals that the depictions of grateful and obedient OBOR recipients that CCTV portrayed in its 2016 documentary series are very real. Lü noted Kikwete's self-debasing performance without comment, suggesting that Chinese diplomats would not find such a performance to be wildly out of the ordinary. Above all, Lü's essay is a performance of his own loyalty to Xi. Although the essay is nominally about Kikwete's passionate affection for China, it implies that Lü deserves credit for persuasively touting Xi's achievements. The essay clearly illustrates the argument of chapter 4. From the perspective of any individual functionary or organization in the Chinese system, the practice of foreign policy is, first and foremost, about looking good to the authorities back in China.

Kikwete had his own reasons for the boot-licking performance: he needed Chinese help to leave a legacy. In February 2013, Kikwete was term-limited in the upcoming election. Even so, he announced a new national development strategy called Big Results Now. The plan aimed to replicate Malaysia's development model with targeted investments in six sectors: energy, agriculture, water, education, transportation, and resource mobilization.[22] Though the master plan did not say so directly, it was understood that the lion's share of the funding would need to come from Beijing.

The Announcement

The following month, Xi visited Tanzania, less than two weeks after he was sworn in as president. He first gave a speech in Dar es Salaam about the long history of economic and political cooperation between China and postcolonial African countries. In it, Xi tacitly acknowledged that the growing presence of Chinese-manufactured goods in African markets risked crowding out local firms. To compensate, he promised that China would redouble its efforts to invest in African infrastructure, broaden technological transfers, and expand its purchases of African products. Xi did not mention OBOR in this speech—it was not until later that he announced his vision for OBOR in Kazakhstan, using many of the same rhetorical flourishes.

In the speech, Xi pledged financial and technological support for a $10 billion deepwater port and SEZ near Bagamoyo. On March 24, 2013, as Xi and Kikwete looked on, the chairman of China Merchants Group, Fu Yuning, and Tanzanian Finance Minister William Mgimwa signed a framework agreement. China Merchants Securities Ltd., a separate branch of the China Merchants conglomerate, promised to issue $10 billion in corporate bonds to finance the project. It was the first time China Merchants had used such a financing mechanism, and the firm still boasts about it on its website.[23]

The framework agreement called for the Bagamoyo development to take place in three phases. On completion of Phase I, which was expected to take three years, Bagamoyo would be capable of receiving large container ships with volumes of up to 8,000 twenty-foot containers. Phase II would build a network of roads and rail links, an export processing facility, and an SEZ. All of this would take a decade to complete. The government of Oman signed on as a potential investor in Phase II, promising to erect a "state-of-the art fertilizer factory" among other investments.[24] By the time Phase III was completed, the new facility at Bagamoyo would exceed twenty times the cargo capacity of the Dar es Salaam port. It would also far surpass the Kenyan port of Mombasa, currently the largest in East Africa.[25] This was a massive potential legacy for Kikwete, whose hometown was in Bagamoyo district.

When the framework deal was signed in March 2013, construction on Bagamoyo was planned to begin as soon as January 2015. The Kikwete administration was clearly in a rush to set the project in motion in advance of the election that October. In January 2014, China Merchants signed a formal agreement with the Tanzanian government describing the details of the plan. By August, Tanzania's ambassador to China, Abdulrahman Shimbo, announced that construction would begin ahead of schedule.[26]

The Chinese rhetoric that followed was boastful and unrestrained. Although they did not explicitly call Tanzania an OBOR country, Chinese news articles repeatedly pointed out that the Bagamoyo site could be expanded further into a mega-port after the first two phases had become commercially successful.[27] Lü explicitly said that China Merchants would guarantee a repeat of its past successes. "This is a mega project," Lü said. "It is [*sic*] a huge work to turn Bagamoyo into Shenzhen of Tanzania."[28]

The Bulldozer Ascendant

On October 25, 2015, John Magufuli was elected president of Tanzania, replacing Kikwete. Magufuli's rise to the top of the CCM was accidental and unexpected. He had been selected as a compromise candidate between the party's two most powerful factions. Because Magufuli had no power base of his own, party elites expected that he would be weak and pliable.

Magufuli set them straight. After winning an election marred by irregularities, he quickly established a reputation for fiscal discipline. He scaled back government expenditures that he deemed unnecessary—including his own motorcade. He conducted surprise inspections of government facilities. He publicly shamed officials who had mismanaged public funds and fired some of them on live television. Among other changes, in February 2017 Magufuli fired the TPA's acting director, Madeni Kipande, for running a corrupt procurement process in the Dar es Salaam port expansion. For this, Magufuli earned a new nickname: "The Bulldozer."[29]

Magufuli did not reflexively oppose all commercial deals with China, nor did he pull out of OBOR—Tanzania's association with the initiative was not clear anyway. In June 2017, Magufuli signed a $154 million deal with China Harbour Engineering Company, the same SOE that had led the way in Colombo and Hambantota, to oversee the Dar es Salaam port expansion. Tanzania could afford it. The IMF had repeatedly found that Tanzania was at low risk of debt distress. Even factoring in the prospect that it might binge-spend on infrastructure at Bagamoyo and elsewhere, Tanzanian public finances were solid.[30]

But Magufuli put Bagamoyo on the back burner. The Tanzanian government had not yet cleared the local residents from the land—a necessary step before China Merchants Group could move in and begin construction. In the decentralized and corrupt context of Tanzanian local politics, this proved to be a much more arduous task than Kikwete had anticipated. By January 2016, nearly three years after Xi attended the signing ceremony for the framework agreement, a Tanzanian newspaper reported that 2,183 displaced residents had been compensated but the resettlement process was not yet close to complete.[31] Construction had not yet begun.

Magufuli was skeptical that the Bagamoyo project would justify the massive debt. Tanzania was a poor country, and $10 billion accounted for nearly a quarter of national GDP. Magufuli's skepticism about debt-funded infrastructure schemes set him apart from most other leaders in the East African region. While Kenya and Ethiopia accepted unsolicited proposals from China Road and Bridge Corporation to expand their railway networks, Magufuli held out until the Chinese offered much better terms.[32] In January 2016, Tanzanian media reported that the government had halted discussions on Bagamoyo and would prioritize Dar es Salaam and a new port facility at Mtwara, near the offshore gas fields.[33] According to interviews, Magufuli's administration concluded that it should concentrate its spending on the Dar es Salaam port.

Magufuli's skepticism about Bagamoyo was driven more by domestic politics than by specific fear of China's intentions through OBOR. Insecure about his limited power base in the party, Magufuli prioritized the personal consolidation of power—cracking down on corruption, one senior adviser told me, so as to concentrate the gains in his own small patronage network. Political dissidents were arrested and silenced; the office of one opposition group was bombed. In 2017, Tundu Lissu, an opposition member of parliament and one of Magufuli's most prominent critics, narrowly survived an assassination attempt in his own front yard.[34] Some of Magufuli's interventions in the economy have also had negative effects on Tanzanian growth. For example, he imposed excise taxes on containers arriving at the Dar es Salaam port, leading the major shipping firms to divert to other ports, mainly in Kenya. In this light, Magufuli's decision to hold back a flood of Chinese investment may illustrate nothing more than a general instinct to hold outsiders at bay while he consolidated power.

China's Take on Magufuli

China saw Magufuli as a rash and unpredictable partner. China's State Administration of Taxation's 2016 guide for Chinese residents in Tanzania described Tanzania's domestic political situation variously as "somewhat volatile" and "extremely fragile."[35] The 2015 election "may have a certain degree of impact on the continuity of economic and trade policies," the document read. "After the election, all political powers in Tanzania 'need a certain breaking-in period,' and the possibility of political "friction" cannot be ruled out. In addition, Tanzania's official red tape and corruption have caused unnecessary problems in bilateral economic and trade cooperation."[36] China resolved to dial down pressure on Tanzania to join OBOR formally and proceed with negotiations on Bagamoyo.

The Chinese tax manual stated that Magufuli's election had dramatically raised the political risk to investments in Tanzania. The country's fiscal and tax policies are "not clear and stable," it claimed. "The legal system is not sound enough and implementation is weak; policy changes from time to time." Customs enforcement is "relatively chaotic, especially when dealing with relevant investment projects." Officials frequently collude with customs management companies to "jointly extort investors." Companies that do not properly "coordinate" their activities with the correct legal and political authorities often see their investments "failed or aborted." Tanzania, of course, had always had its share of corruption.

What was new was that Magufuli, the new president, was now wary of Chinese influence.

The Chinese sources also pulled back from suggesting that Bagamoyo was an OBOR project, lest Magufuli attack OBOR itself. In 2017, Lü published his revealing essay in Chinese official channels and the major Tanzanian newspaper *The Citizen*. Lü defended China's ostensible goal of "peaceful development" and discussed OBOR in detail. He closed by inviting Tanzania to send a delegation to the Belt and Road Forum in Beijing later that month, with the implication that China would reward Magufuli with a flood of new investment if he showed receptivity to the concept:

> Tanzania was invited, not only because it is a historic and natural part of the Maritime Silk Road, and it is a landing point of the Belt and Road in Africa. More importantly, Tanzania was invited because of its special traditional friendship with China built since history. . . . It is fair to say that China-Tanzania capacity cooperation has born early fruit which has laid a sound foundation for the bilateral cooperation under the framework of the Belt and Road Initiative.[37]

The article went on to list several Chinese–Tanzanian joint projects, including a railway, a gas pipeline, and a ceramic factory, but the Bagamoyo port was not among them. The omission indicated that negotiations on the port were stalled and that the Chinese side did not believe that public pressure would move Magufuli.

The softer touch did not work, either, so China began to take a harder line. Magufuli declined Lü's invitation to send a Tanzanian delegation to the Belt and Road Forum in Beijing. Ethiopia, Kenya, and Djibouti were all represented. Thereafter, Chinese state media criticized Magufuli for his isolationist tendencies and claimed that his actions were damaging the bilateral relationship. In one suggestive bulletin from January 2018, the African edition of the *People's Daily* reported that Magufuli had decided (again) not to attend an African Union summit in Addis Ababa. It is unclear why this was relevant to China, since no senior Chinese officials planned to attend. Still, the article noted dryly that the Tanzanian Foreign Ministry "did not explain the specific reasons why Magufuli will once again be absent."[38] "Some people are questioning Magufuli's decision," the article continued. "They said that the president's failure to attend major conferences with other heads of state would undermine Tanzania's influence on the international stage and result in a reduction in domestic investment, aid funds, and trade." Cumulatively, the article portrayed Magufuli as ungrateful, irrational, and blind to history. "Although Tanzania has long been the country that receives the most development aid from China in Africa, funding for the construction of the Tanzanian Standard Gauge Railway project has become a great problem," it read. "This year, China will hold another major meeting of global leaders. It is still unclear whether President Magufuli will attend."

The View from Bagamoyo Town

What do the residents of Bagamoyo say? To most, the stakes are intensely local: about the economy, the state of the fishing and tourism industries, and a few hundred families' emotional connection to their land. Bagamoyo is a beautiful town that looks as though it is slowly falling to pieces. The old town is marked by grand Omani and German buildings in various stages of collapse. Most have extraordinarily beautiful antique wooden doors, intricately carved with geometric patterns and African and Islamic symbols. Next to the grand German-built administrative building, now empty and run-down, enormous trees blossom with crimson flowers. If you stand on the ramparts of the fort at night, you can see the lights of Zanzibar on the horizon to the east.

My guide, John, is twenty-eight years old.[39] He gives tours to pay his way through university and hopes to work as a professional safari guide one day. His English is sometimes hard to follow, but he is highly intelligent and has no end of opinions about local politics. His gestures are expressive, and he grabs hold of my arm to punctuate important points. John estimates that out of every ten residents of Bagamoyo district, seven prefer Kikwete to Magufuli. Not only is Kikwete the town's favorite son, he is a singularly charismatic politician who is famous for remembering the names of thousands of his constituents.

John supports the proposal to build a port at Bagamoyo. He accosts several friends and passersby on our walk around town, interrogating them on my behalf to prove his estimate correct. There appears to be common agreement that a port will bring investment and tourism to the region. John's question is "why the Chinese have to be the ones to build it." He has heard that the Chinese demanded terms that would give them full control and exemption from taxes for a hundred years. If this is the case, John thinks that Tanzania must resist. However, as long as the government negotiates properly, he has no doubt that the port could be a great windfall for the local economy.

No Chinese people live in Bagamoyo district, but Chinese visitors come frequently on Fridays and Saturdays, mostly men between the ages of twenty-five and forty-five. They speak Swahili slowly and do not like to speak English. John has taken several of them to the port location on the outskirts of town. He tells me that Chinese visitors generally ask the same questions I do: when the port construction will begin, why the government has delayed acquiring the land, and when the local residents will move out. John doesn't know what his clients talk about when they confer in Chinese, but he thinks that they are particularly puzzled about why the Tanzanian government struggled so much to acquire the land. He shrugs. The Chinese are good customers, and they always pay well.

The site of the Chinese port is outside of Bagamoyo proper, in the villages of Mlingotini and Mbegani. It is only five miles north of town, but the drive takes us over half an hour because the dirt road is in such poor condition. The area has been depopulated. We visit in late afternoon when the heat has subsided, and the sun shines through the palm trees and casts a warm light on the wide, overgrown fields. At least half of the houses we pass are abandoned. Some have had their windows and even roofs stripped out, and each is marked in red spray paint with a number and a check mark. Still, it is clear that the government is far from done clearing the land. We pass over a hundred local residents as we make our way down the road: children playing and walking home from school, women standing outside fruit stands, men carrying loads.

We pass the school (still in use), a few shops, and an abandoned mosque. Finally we reach the village that sits astride the site itself. We walk down to the water, passing some grazing goats. Two fishermen sitting on the sand are cleaning their nets. They greet us politely and return to their conversation. John and I walk the length of the beach together until a wall of mangroves blocks our path. There are a few dozen canoes

FIGURE 6.3: Planned site of the Bagamoyo port, December 2018. Photograph by the author.

and fishing boats and a boarded-up hotel. Across the water is an island in the middle of the harbor about half a mile wide. It will clearly have to be eliminated entirely. The color of the water indicates that the sea floor is shallow here: massive dredging will be required before any large ship can enter the harbor (fig. 6.3).

Walking back down the beach, John tells me that Magufuli is "50-50" on the whole affair. Most Tanzanians see the port and SEZ scheme as Kikwete's legacy project, he explains. People from the interior of the country generally oppose it, on the grounds that Tanzania already has ports at Dar es Salaam and Tanga and the money should be spent on social services instead. When Magufuli entered office, John says, he wanted to cancel the port project right away. But "China paid off his cabinet and they convinced him to change his mind. Everyone knows this." We ask some passersby who seem to agree. John thinks that Chinese businessmen are "liars" and only get their way through corrupt methods. The Omanis offered better terms, he believes. He says that the only way the Chinese could have gotten the contract was through bribery and dirty tricks.

On the way back to town, John and I stop to talk to a few women selling produce at small shops along the road. The school day has just finished, and children run around us, the shyer ones waving through the windows, the bolder ones approaching to say hello. Their mothers tell us that they think Chinese construction on the port will go ahead eventually. They assume this because the national government has continued to compensate local residents in the port area to move. However, the women complain that corrupt local officials have skimmed off of the payments earmarked for the villagers. Some residents have received as little as 500,000 shillings, about US$230, to abandon their homes. The holdouts have refused to move until they are paid in full. In this remote town, politics seem a world away. No one has heard of OBOR, nor do they much care why Chinese investors are interested in their sleepy village. But this much is clear: unless the government commits new funds to make the local residents whole, it could be many more years before the land is free for development.

The View from the Opposition

Hours before my flight out of Dar es Salaam, a friend informs me that he has arranged an evening interview with Zitto Kabwe, the leader of the opposition Alliance for Change and Transparency–Wazalendo Party. I wait for him in the lobby of a hotel outside the government district. Zitto is wearing a simple white tunic in the Tanzanian style, and I recognize him immediately by his dignified gait. He strides to the elevator, makes eye contact with me, and gives the smallest of nods. I walk into the elevator alongside him, and we find a quiet corner in the bar upstairs. Zitto lives in constant fear of arrest. He has tired eyes and wears the expression of a man who can never afford to let down his guard. To me, however, he is warm and unhurried. He orders a gin and tonic and invites me to turn on my recorder.

I begin by asking Zitto to describe the political culture under Magufuli. "The civic space is narrowing," he says, letting each word fall with a heavy weight.

It has been narrowing every day. Today I saw my colleague, a member of parliament and another opposition leader, who has been in jail for the last three weeks. Another, female member of parliament is also in jail. The accusations are politically motivated, and they are also supposed to be bailable—and yet, there she is. There is a sense of fear in the population. Journalists have disappeared; one member of the parliament survived an assassination attempt last year. People don't feel as free as they used to.[40]

I ask Zitto if he fears for his own safety. "Of course I am taking precautions," he says, "but I know that if they want to make a move against me, they have the means. In the meantime, I have to do my job." He reminds me that he is not the only one living in fear. Members of the ruling CCM "praise Magufuli in public, but when you meet them privately they freely admit that things are not okay. There is a sense of fear inside the ruling party, too." I heard similar things from other sources who asked to remain anonymous in this book.

Anticipating my next question, Zitto acknowledges up front that Magufuli is popular with the general public and is likely to perform well in the 2020 presidential election. "There is a feeling among the population that the president is delivering on development projects," he acknowledges, citing the railway and Magufuli's purchase of new jets for the national airline. Only when pressed does he clarify that he thinks these projects are wasteful and are partly responsible for the sluggish economy. Zitto is a refreshing interview subject because he responds to questions rather than pivoting back to talking points. "People see Magufuli as a crusader against corruption," he says. He pauses for a moment, considering. "There is *some* truth in that."

The discussion turns to Bagamoyo, which Zitto supports wholeheartedly. "It is bad luck that the project did not start before Kikwete left" in 2015, he says. "Kikwete had already agreed with the Chinese government to construct Bagamoyo and the Standard Gauge Railway" through a build-operate-transfer agreement, a type of public–private partnership.

This would have brought an inflow of foreign currency and investment and would probably have averted our current economic downturn. Remember: Bagamoyo is not just about the port. It's about the port and infrastructure that will turn Tanzania into the transport conduit for all of its landlocked neighbors. Kikwete was clear on what he wanted from China. His projects were all strategic: the gas pipeline, the modernization of the Army, the fiber optic network.

In Zitto's description, Bagamoyo is a fully Tanzanian project. It will be completed with outside funding that just happens to be Chinese.

Zitto agrees that "Magufuli backed away" from China for domestic political reasons after he won the 2015 election. Whether his motivations were "conscious" or "unconscious," Zitto does not care to speculate. "Perhaps he thought that these big projects somehow advantaged Kikwete's people, and he wanted to cut them off." Perhaps Magufuli was influenced by Western propaganda—"there were also whispers about China and debt traps, and Magufuli may have listened to them." In any case, the result was a "decision early on to frustrate all of China's projects." Only recently has Magufuli's attitude toward China begun to warm again, returning to the historical norm in Tanzania, since election season is approaching. "We are always being told that the project will get done," Zitto says. "We don't know when, but we are sure it will happen—once Magufuli has total control over it."

I raise the issue of Hambantota and OBOR's strategic implications. Does a Chinese project as massive as the Bagamoyo port really pose no danger to Tanzanian sovereignty? Zitto laughs gently. "I don't have any sovereignty concerns," he says. "I wonder if anyone in Tanzania would buy this Western propaganda. We have a very long history with China. They are not going to invade our country. We heard these same narratives in the 1970s, when the Chinese came to build the Tazara railway. The nightmare predictions didn't come true. What I do understand is that China is pursuing its own *interests*. We must also pursue our own interests."

I try again. Why is China's track record of building similar white elephant projects not relevant to the discussion? Zitto cuts me off. "Who proposed that port in Sri Lanka?" he retorts. "Sri Lanka did? Then the viability of the project is up to Sri Lanka. If you're the leader of a country and you suggest to a lender a white elephant project, it's your fault! I understand that China has some responsibility to study the project, or whatever. But I have a very strong view that Bagamoyo is not a white elephant project. There will be no Sri Lanka here."

Magufuli's Strongman Turn

In spring 2019, as Tanzanian politics began to turn into its election year cycle, Magufuli intensified his repressive policies and nationalist rhetoric. Crackdowns on journalists and opposition politicians ramped up. The space for free discourse online rapidly closed. In May, Reuters quoted the director general of the TPA, Deusdedit Kakoko, criticizing the Chinese approach to the Bagamoyo negotiations. "They shouldn't treat us like schoolkids and act like our teachers," Kakoko said.[41] He complained that China was demanding tax exemptions and compensation for losses incurred during construction. Even tax calculations would have been outsourced to China Merchants' offices back in China, so completely would the firm control the port's throughput. In June, Magufuli criticized China's demands for Bagamoyo as "exploitative and awkward." "They want us to give them a guarantee of 33 years and a lease of 99 years, and we should not question whoever comes to invest there once the port is operational," he said. "They want to take the land as their own . . . These tough conditions can only be accepted by mad people."[42] Several international news outlets reported that he had "halted" negotiations or "suspended [them] indefinitely."[43] The implication was that the Bagamoyo port was formally dead.

Within days, however, senior members of Magufuli's administration were insisting to the press that negotiations would continue. "There's a negotiation . . . ongoing between the government and the investor [China Merchants]," said Mbelwa Kairuki, the Tanzanian ambassador to China. "Some of the issues that the investor is proposing don't make sense, but we hope that through engagement . . . we will get to understand better. The good thing is the investor is ready to engage, and the government is willing to as well."[44] Kairuki also lambasted the "Western media" for reporting that the Bagamoyo project was a "debt trap." "This is pure investment," he said. "This is investors bringing capital. The government is not bringing a single cent. So how can it be a debt trap? Maybe an investment trap. And what's wrong with investment? Investment brings jobs, it brings capital, it brings technology, it brings everything." In October, the Tanzanian government issued a performative ultimatum to their Chinese counterparties, demanding five major concessions on project terms.[45] As of this writing, it seems that the project is no more or less frozen than it was the day Magufuli took office.

Conclusion

Tanzania's preference for China goes beyond mere national interest. Togolani Mavura, a rising star in Tanzanian politics who previously served as Kikwete's speechwriter but has positive things to say about Magufuli, waved his hands with great feeling as he explained this to me. "African leaders feel nervous meeting with an American president," he said.

> They go all the way to Washington to get as little as five minutes of face time. Imagine what it feels like to prepare for those five minutes. Then you arrive—cold faces, cold handshakes, and it's all over. The Chinese know that it's the small things that make all the difference. The Chinese diplomats don't just speak Swahili; they speak the *Tanzanian* dialect. Their leaders are warm when you meet them in person. On state visits they are always more generous with their time. The Americans don't give you a siren and clear the streets of the capital for your motorcade. The Chinese always do.[46]

While the branding of OBOR projects portrays China as a benefactor, Chinese diplomats have mastered the art of showing public respect for recipient countries' national pride.

Magufuli's turn toward strongman isolationism has undoubtedly strained relations with China, though as of this writing they have done no permanent damage. Apart from Magufuli, there has been almost no daylight between Dar es Salaam and Beijing since Tanzania won its independence in 1961. Among the senior Tanzanian civil service, the collective memory of Chinese assistance in the 1970s runs deep. All but one of the current and former officials I interviewed forcefully defended Magufuli's policies toward China. They also insisted, however implausibly, that there was no discontinuity between Kikwete's and Magufuli's policy approach toward the Bagamoyo port. Senior officials of all major factions and parties laugh off criticism about Chinese debt diplomacy as a transparent and even somewhat pathetic piece of "American propaganda." Although the senior officials all know about the Hambantota case, none of them express concern that Tanzania could fall into the same trap.

The recent rupture in the relationship has everything to do with Tanzanian domestic politics and almost nothing to do with OBOR. Since the early 2000s, Chinese development investments have played an increasingly important role in lubricating Tanzanian domestic politics by creating opportunities for patronage and graft. Only one of my senior interview subjects believed that Magufuli had ideological reasons for halting the Bagamoyo project when he took power in 2015. Most argued that the decision was entirely practical: an attempt by a new president with no established power base to cut off his predecessor's most powerful foreign patron. Magufuli is certainly not reflexively anti-Chinese. One morning in December 2018, shortly after the Donald Trump administration had launched a global effort to persuade foreign governments to ban or regulate Chinese telecom Huawei, I was waiting for an interview in the lobby of a Dar es Salaam hotel where a Huawei event was being held. Magufuli's motorcade pulled up. He paused to smile for the photographers and then followed several Chinese businessmen into the conference room.

Bagamoyo is a perfect counterpoint to the Hambantota case. Both projects were three-phase plans to transform the presidents' hometowns from sleepy fishing villages into thriving international port cities. Both required linking the new ports to much more expensive—but less clearly planned—infrastructure in adjoining SEZs. The plans were originally conceived by their host governments in the mid-2000s, adopted by the China Merchants Group, and finally given official backing when Xi visited. Both were designed to be secondary to the main national port (Colombo and Dar es Salaam, respectively), which raised questions about how they could be profitable in the short term. And both were disrupted after national elections in 2015. Yet the Hambantota and Bagamoyo projects could not have turned out more differently. Hambantota became a commercial failure known around the world, and a cause célèbre for critics of OBOR. Bagamoyo never made it past the planning phase. The two ports' fortunes diverged because of timing and domestic politics.

The Bagamoyo case also illustrates how China arbitrarily applies and removes the OBOR label based on conditions on the ground and relations with the recipient government. The senior Tanzanian officials I interviewed, including Uledi Mussa, the former chief negotiator on Baga-moyo, and Faustine Kamuzora, the permanent secretary for policy and coordination in the prime minister's office, told me emphatically that Bagamoyo *is* part of the Maritime Silk Road route.[47] Even after Magu-fuli harshly criticized China and all but canceled negotiations, the About the Embassy page of Tanzania's embassy website in Beijing contains a let-ter from the ambassador claiming that "Tanzania is also among the first countries to support the visionary One Belt, One Road initiative."[48] On the other hand, Bagamoyo does not appear on any Chinese OBOR map I have seen. Lü scrupulously avoids suggesting in his articles and pub-lic speeches that Tanzania is an OBOR member. Nor is Tanzania listed as one of the sixty-three OBOR countries in the Data section of the Belt and Road Portal.[49] This further corroborates the argument that OBOR is in no way intended to describe physical routes over land and sea or even a network of major infrastructure hubs. Joining OBOR is often a major event, marked with pomp and ceremony. When convenient, the brand is liberally applied. Yet the invocation of the OBOR slogan is al-ways discretionary and always political. When a recipient country gets cold feet, China is content to let it wait on the margins, neither in nor out, believing that in time it will return to the fold.

CHAPTER 7

The Eagle's Nest

China Prevails in Greece

At the last stop on the Athens metro, the gentle breeze carries the smell of salt. On the hill overlooking the Aegean Sea, there are shops selling olives and small tchotchkes of the Parthenon made of faux limestone. Gigantic container vessels float placidly in the cerulean waters. At the passenger terminal, thousands of tourists spill out of cruise ships and onto the pier, wielding selfie sticks and blinking in the midday sun. The outbuildings and warehouses of Piraeus Port sprawl along the rim of the bay. In the distance, a long line of orange gantry cranes blend against the Mediterranean scrub on the bare hills beyond. And then, looking closer, they come into focus—monuments to all that is ancient here and much that is new.

Athenian general Themistocles recognized the strategic value of Piraeus 2,400 years ago and ordered the construction of walls and fortifications. As the historian Thucydides recalled in the *History of the Peloponnesian War*, Themistocles was doubly prescient—both "because the geography of a place with three natural harbors is excellent, and because of the great start which the Athenians would gain in the acquisition of power by becoming a naval people. He was the first to venture to tell them to stick to the sea and forthwith began to lay the foundations of empire."[1] After centuries of neglect during the Ottoman era, the town of Piraeus restored its ancient name in 1835. Its strategic location astride the Attic peninsula helped the port grow rapidly. Soon it was Greece's second-largest city and one of the country's most important industrial regions. In the twentieth century, Piraeus remained a major hub of the Greek economy, which after World War II leaned ever more heavily on the shipping industry (map 7.1).

There is perhaps no better monument than Piraeus to Greece's last decade of turmoil, hardship, and resurrection. In 2006, when Prime Minister Konstantinos Karamanlis first visited Beijing to seek investments in Greek ports, the shipping industry based at Piraeus was the engine of the booming Greek economy. Four years later, the Piraeus port was ground zero for the collapse of the global shipping industry. As the shippers fell on hard times, the Greek economy cratered. The country required three bailouts to escape from default. Domestic terrorists mailed bombs to prominent public officials. Politicians in Berlin and at the EU Commission in Brussels spoke in whispers of the unimaginable—a Greek exit from the euro. So dire was Greece's situation that the whole project of European integration seemed to be in doubt.

The restructuring of the Greek economy over the past decade has been a messy and halting process. Waves of workers' strikes, a revolving door of governments and cabinets, and start-and-stop negotiations make this by far the most technical and politically complex case in this book. The whole episode played out under the microscope of the international press and financial markets, which left day-by-day accounts in several languages. Today, the smoke has cleared. Greece is once again stable and growing, albeit from a much poorer baseline. But the ancient port of Piraeus has a new owner: COSCO (China Ocean Shipping Company), a vast and opaque conglomerate directed by the highest levels of the Chinese state.

Since 2008, Chinese investment has turned the port of Piraeus into an astonishing commercial success. COSCO signed a lease for the port's two largest piers in 2008. Seven years later, it bought out the Greek state's controlling equity stake in the port's holding company, Piraeus Port Authority (PPA). Under COSCO's management, the Piraeus port has returned to profitability and posted nearly a decade of double-digit annual profit growth. The port is now the sixth largest in Europe. COSCO has expanded the port's warehousing facilities, improved its connections to rail transshipment links, and brought new business to its profitable passenger terminal.

Chinese media describe Piraeus as a crowning achievement of the OBOR concept, and they are not wrong. Win-win economic cooperation has brought political benefits to both countries. The remaining Greek

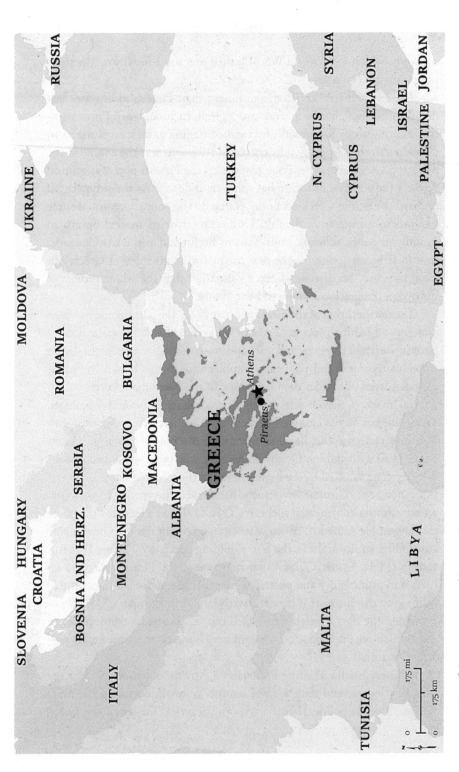

MAP 7.1: Map of Greece, courtesy of Scott Walker.

critics of privatization—the unions and a few holdout leftist politicians—
have been shut out of the mainstream discourse. All of Greece's major
political parties are now pro-China. Greek politicians proudly speak of
their country as China's "gateway to Europe" and unapologetically block
EU resolutions critical of Beijing. Athens is learning to use its connection to China as leverage when it negotiates with Brussels and Berlin.

Behind closed doors, leading Greek officials, scholars, businesspeople, and journalists of all political stripes admit that Greece got the short
end of the Piraeus deal. "Beggars can't be choosers," a prominent Greek
public figure told me. "The Chinese were the only ones willing to invest
here during the economic crisis." Yet even he believes that the Greek government "could probably have gotten a better price." Politicians also
"should have sought firmer commitments" about the design of the contract, he told me. Chinese "innuendo" suggested that a deal on the port
would trigger many side benefits that never materialized. Other Greek
observers blame themselves for buying into China's charm offensive. "The
Chinese play football with their hands," a prominent scholar told me.[2]
"We should never have allowed ourselves to believe otherwise."

COSCO achieved in Piraeus what China Merchants promised to do
in Hambantota and Bagamoyo. Indeed, the three cases have much in
common. All three are ports along today's Maritime Silk Road. All three
were first conceived by the recipient government before Xi Jinping came
to power and were later rebranded as part of OBOR. In all three countries, the Chinese shipping and construction firm acted as a quasi-
representative of the Chinese state. Just like in Hambantota and Bagamoyo, China's engagement in Piraeus began with high hopes and grand
promises. The local government quelled the first waves of grassroots opposition. Both sides doubled down on their commitments, and China became even more aggressive in pressing for faster engagement after Xi
took power. The Piraeus port became a contentious issue in national elections. After taking power, Greece's new leaders froze negotiations, then
reconsidered after weighing the cost of walking away.

There are significant differences between this case and the others.
Greece is an EU member, a NATO ally, and a former Marshall Plan beneficiary. Though Greece is one of the poorer members of the Eurozone,
it is a high-income country by global standards, with a GDP per capita
five times as large as Sri Lanka's and twenty times as large as Tanzania's.
Sri Lanka and Tanzania benefited from Chinese trade and development

assistance during the Cold War; Greece had almost no relationship with Beijing until 2002. Hambantota and Bagamoyo were greenfield investments—long-term schemes to build secondary ports in disconnected regions. Piraeus was already the largest port in Greece when COSCO took out its first lease agreement. Chinese media no longer care to mention Hambantota or Bagamoyo, but they frequently describe Piraeus as a model for OBOR projects around the world.

Yet Piraeus resembles Hambantota and Bagamoyo in the ways that matter most. By the time Xi took power in 2013, COSCO had already been involved in Piraeus for five years. COSCO privately communicated that it wanted to buy out the port. The behavior of COSCO and the Chinese state was entirely consistent before and after China started to present Piraeus as an OBOR project. It was originally the Greek government and later the European institutions leading the bailouts—not China—that first pushed to privatize the port. Finally, the Greek government's approach to China was strategically incoherent and highly inconsistent, except in one respect: it followed directly from the immediate demands of domestic and regional politics. Piraeus is indeed the consummate OBOR project. It was not just a financial win-win; it was a political win-win, too.

Four other aspects of the case are noteworthy. First, Piraeus proves that Chinese overseas projects can become massively commercially successful. While Greece was mired in years of economic pain and political turmoil, COSCO quietly modernized the port's infrastructure and tightened its operations, saving hundreds if not thousands of local jobs. Second, Greece has since become the cornerstone of an emerging pro-China bloc in the EU, largely because Greece believes that its partnership with China strengthened its hand in negotiating bailout agreements with Germany and the International Monetary Fund (IMF). Many prominent Greeks believe that the Chinese saved Greece from expulsion from the Eurozone in 2015. Third, China systematically benefited from the twists and turns in Greece's chaotic domestic politics. Greece tried three times to renegotiate with COSCO. Each time, their moves backfired and further strengthened COSCO's grip. Fourth, China used Piraeus to lock in tax-advantaged "gateways"—or backdoors—into the European market. If Piraeus is part of a Chinese geoeconomic strategy, the most important feature may not be overland transportation or trade but market access.

Origins of Partnership

"Now that everyone is happy, and most importantly rich," Greek shipping tycoon Henry Viafas wrote in 2004, "let us take our monthly tour around paradise."[3] Six years later, Greek papers led with very different stories: unemployment lines, violence in the streets of Athens, and intimations of a catastrophic "Grexit." For most Greek citizens living through this period, the debate over privatization of the Piraeus port was first and foremost a domestic issue, a matter of pride, ideology, and national sovereignty. The global financial crisis was an inflection point in China's relationship with Greece. It was, in a sense, a period of transition from partnership to patronage.

For most of the postwar era, Greece was a fully integrated member of the West. As a NATO ally and an anchor of US foreign policy in the Mediterranean, Greece was one of the original beneficiaries of the Marshall Plan. The United States saw Greece as a bulwark against leftism in Europe and integrated it into European institutions. Greece joined NATO in 1952 and the EU in 1981. It was part of the first group of countries to adopt the euro. When Greece and China met, it was on the battlefield. Between 1950 and 1953 there were over a thousand Greek troops stationed in Korea, fighting Chinese and North Korean forces at Scotch Hill and Outpost Harry.[4] Athens opened diplomatic relations with Beijing in 1972, shortly after Richard Nixon's visit to China, but trade and bilateral diplomatic exchanges were negligible until the 1990s.

By accidents of history and geography, at the end of the Cold War Greece had economic structures complementary to China's. The Greek economy is dependent on international trade, but is also dominated by the state. In the 1990s, Konstantinos Mitsotakis's New Democracy party tried to privatize some of the country's most bloated state-owned enterprises (SOEs). The Greek left responded in force, and market reforms were slow and halting. Plagued by inefficiency, the Greek economy became increasingly dependent on the shipping industry, which stayed competitive through political connections and tax advantages.[5]

Greek shippers profited massively from the rise of Chinese manufacturing in the 1990s. Trade between China and Europe increased more than 130 times over between 1979 and 2006, most of it transported on

Greek vessels.[6] The shipping magnates who dominated Greek politics pressed for deals to access Chinese funding and build their vessels in Chinese shipyards. Thanks to China, "Greek shipping is having a golden age which we have never seen before," Petros Aivazidis of the Hellenic Chamber of Shipping said at the height of the boom. "Rates now are five times what they were a couple of years ago. People are paying hundreds of thousands of dollars a day for ships." The result was an orgy of speculation. "Ship values are now very high," said Aivazidis, "but still Greeks are trying to buy any ship because they don't want to miss out."[7] By 2006, the world's shipyards were working at capacity to meet the insatiable Greek demand. Back orders for new ships took up to five years to fulfill.

COSCO was a natural partner for Greek firms trying to break into the Chinese market. Founded in 1961, it had begun to internationalize itself in the 1980s, long before other SOEs looked abroad. In 1993, COSCO's Singaporean affiliate became the first Chinese SOE to be listed on a foreign stock exchange. COSCO then diversified into logistics and ship-building and repair, benefiting from state monopoly protections.[8] By 2004, at the dawn of China's relationship with Greece, COSCO had amassed a fleet capacity of over 35 million deadweight tons, making it the largest shipper in China and the second largest in the world. The company was also immensely profitable—unusually so for an SOE. Today the firm has a fleet of over a thousand vessels and carries more cargo by weight than any other shipper in the world. It owns and operates forty-six container terminals worldwide.[9]

COSCO operates as an extension of the Chinese state, which sees the shipping sector as an important part in its national growth strategy.[10] In the 1990s, when China first began to push its SOEs to international-ize, COSCO was one of fifty-three firms chosen for special backing.[11] Other Chinese documents indicated that COSCO had "high national security value." COSCO's top managers are approved or appointed directly by the State Council.[12] COSCO's chairman and chief executive officer double as the firm's party representative and deputy, a somewhat unusual arrangement that allows the party to supervise the firm directly. COSCO is therefore privy to high-level party discussions, and has some leeway to "translate" general guidance into specific operations. This structure gives COSCO an advantage in getting government approval to make the most desirable overseas investments.

The Road to Crisis

By the early 2000s, both Greece and China had clear national interests in building a bilateral relationship centered on the shipping sector. In 2000, Chinese President Jiang Zemin visited Athens. It was the first-ever trip by a Chinese head of state to the Balkan region.[13] Two years later, Greek Prime Minister Costas Simitis led a delegation of Greek shipping magnates on a weeklong trade mission to China. Not only did Beijing agree to allow access to its shipyards, it took steps to endear itself to the Greek people. In August 2005, China's Minister of Affairs, Li Zhaoxing, backed the Greek position (against Turkey) on the issue of Cypriot independence. The Greek press lauded China's show of support, even though China had used hedged language in its original statement.[14]

Relations between China and Greece remained primarily economic through the 2000s. Greece's center-right government wanted to turn the country into China's main transshipment hub in the Balkan, Mediterranean, and Black Sea regions.[15] The New Democracy party also hoped that Chinese investment could give it cover to take on the labor unions and begin privatizing the moribund state sector. In 2006, Karamanlis visited China, signed various accords, and announced a new "strategic partnership." For the first time, the two sides discussed a possible Chinese investment in the Piraeus port.[16]

Around that time, Chinese observers detected a souring in European policy toward Beijing. Trade frictions were growing, with the EU opening antidumping investigations into Chinese products. Some EU countries sharpened their criticism of China's human rights practices. In 2009, Zhao Huaipu, professor at the Diplomatic Institute of International Relations, concluded from two EU policy documents that "although the general tone is still constructive," the EU's "tone and approach" toward China increasingly "included disappointment and dissatisfaction."[17] This insecurity partly explains why COSCO intensified its interest in Greece in 2010. Concerned that the window of good relations might be closing, China wanted to establish a bridgehead for distributing its products in Europe.

By 2010, the global financial crisis and its aftereffects had had a catastrophic impact on Greece's finances. In 2008, the country's public debt had amounted to 109 percent of its GDP. By 2016, it was 180 percent—in spite of three bailouts and draconian cuts to the Greek welfare state. The IMF, European Central Bank, and European Commission—collectively known as the troika—demanded that Greece cut the minimum wage by 19 percent and restructure its pension system as conditions for the bail-out funds. Consumer spending collapsed, and the Greek economy fell even further. By July 2015, ratings agency Standard and Poor's argued that a Greek exit from the euro was more likely than not, even though prom-inent economists such as Paul Krugman predicted that this would cause the common currency to disintegrate.[18]

Many European citizens empathized with the plight of the Greek people, but the politics in Brussels was such that leniency was impossi-ble. Wealthier countries in Northern Europe and less-indebted countries in Eastern Europe feared that giving Greece a free pass would open the door to further cash transfers to Portugal, Italy, and Spain, which were also facing debt crises. Nor could Greece be allowed to leave the Euro-zone and default on its debts, lest it be the first domino to fall in the col-lapse of the European banking system. By process of elimination, the EU's leading states agreed to keep Greece in the Eurozone—but to make it into an example for others.

As Greek politics soured on Europe, voters fled to ideological ex-tremes. By 2012, 81 percent of Greeks believed that the troika was "inter-ested only in safeguarding the interests of big corporations." Thirty-six percent favored leaving the EU, despite the prospect that this would bring even deeper pain.[19] Popular goodwill toward Berlin and Brussels was shat-tered. Membership of the far-right, neofascist party Golden Dawn swelled to its highest level in decades. As Greece was convulsed by un-certainty, pain, and anger, China plotted its advance.

Leasing Piraeus

Greece began privatizing Piraeus in 1999. That year, the government formed the PPA, a government-owned holding company charged with managing the port's operations.[20] The concession agreement from the gov-ernment gave PPA exclusive use of the port's fields, buildings, and other infrastructure for a period of forty years.[21] In 2003, PPA was listed on the Athens Stock Exchange. In 2006, on a visit to Beijing, the Greek finance minister announced a public tender process for a concession, or lease, of Piers II and III. The announcement came shortly after he had met with COSCO's chairman, Captain Wei Jiafu.[22]

Predictably, Piraeus port employees were outraged that the government had decided to privatize the port without consulting them. The unions feared that if foreign investors entered the scene, pay cuts and layoffs would follow. In November 2006, port employees protested a municipal council meeting about the lease of Pier II and the planned Pier III. Over the next two years, the workers did everything possible to obstruct the privatization process. They refused to work overtime, weekends, or holidays. They carried out frequent shorter strikes. The Dutch dock workers' union gave financial support to the striking Greek workers, fearing that COSCO would make the Piraeus port more competitive and draw business away from the Port of Rotterdam.[23] This obstruction came on top of the broader slowdown in global shipping that coincided with the negotiations. The results were ugly for PPA's finances. Container traffic fell by 75 percent, and the Piraeus port booked losses of €10 million in the first half of 2008.

By 2008, the strikes, which had started as local labor disputes, had grown into a national political issue. Syriza, the still marginal far-left opposition party, jumped on the protests as an opportunity to criticize the New Democracy government. When PPA sued the unions, Syriza's leaders showed up at the court hearings. Among them was Alexis Tsipras, the party's charismatic young leader. "The strike of the port's employees is neither illegal nor abusive," Tsipras declared at one court hearing. "The government's intention to concede [the use] of strategically important infrastructure to private companies is both illegal *and* abusive. We will stand by the employees during their fight to defend the public nature of our country's infrastructure."[24] No one then present would have believed that seven years later—as prime minister—Tsipras would approve the sale of a controlling interest in the port to COSCO.

Syriza was opposed to privatization as a general principle. Tsipras accused the government of "hand[ing] over the keys of the Piraeus Port to Chinese people, along with the keys of the Maximos Mansion," Greece's presidential palace. He called on the government to cancel the tender.[25]

But Syriza was more interested in aligning itself with the unions than with defending national sovereignty. Its core complaint had nothing to do with China, but rather that the government was handing the port over to "*private* speculative interests."[26]

The Panhellenic Socialist Movement (PASOK), the main center-left opposition party, also opposed the deal for tactical reasons. "We are choos[ing] to give away our telecommunications to a German company, to give away our Olympic Airlines to the Arabs, and to concede our ports to a state-owned Chinese company," the party's press representative protested.[27] Prominent PASOK members referred to China's "colonial strategy" in an attempt to drum up popular anger. But PASOK's main goal was to score political points. The New Democracy government pressed ahead with the lease agreement. COSCO signed the contract in November 2008. The deal was set to take effect the following October. Chinese President Hu Jintao flew to Athens for the signing ceremony.[28]

Meanwhile, the Greek shipping industry faced an unprecedented crisis. Greek shippers owned a fifth of the world's fleet. In a matter of months, as the global financial crisis began to affect trade volumes, it became apparent that there was a glut of supply for cargo vessels. Dry cargo rates fell by more than 90 percent. Vessels that could earn $150,000 a day in May 2010 fetched less than $7,000 a day by November. And prices were expected to fall even more, because as many as 10,000 new ships were still on their way to market. Some shippers, unable to afford insurance, chose to ground their ships. Others ordered vessels in transit to slow to half speed, as there would be nothing to reload once they arrived at port. Greek shippers feared that the Piraeus strikes would drive away what little business remained.[29] In a matter of months, the stakes of discussions with COSCO had risen higher than the Greek government had ever expected.

What was China's objective? For the Chinese government, the deal offered an opportunity to acquire a friend in Europe, where the politics seemed to be turning increasingly hostile. For COSCO, Greece's desperate situation offered an attractive opportunity to lock down an entry point to the European market for an affordable price. COSCO had no competitors for the leasehold on Piraeus. The Greek government was desperate to raise funds and willing to offer attractive tax concessions. In the longer run, a closer relationship with the Greek shipping industry would help COSCO expand its shipping and logistics sectors around the world.

Nor were the terms of the lease agreement necessarily final. If Greece's economic condition continued to deteriorate, COSCO could simply renegotiate to reduce its annual lease fee. This, it turned out, was precisely what happened.

The Botched Renegotiation

Four days after the lease agreement went into effect, PASOK won the Greek general election. George Papandreou became the prime minister. Louka Katseli, the new minister of shipping, complained that the lease agreement was a "hot potato" from the previous government and said that PASOK had no responsibility to honor it. Unfortunately for Katseli, the agreement had already taken legal effect, and China was such an important potential partner that Greece could not afford to renege. Instead, Katseli tried to thread the needle by renegotiating only the terms that had most aggravated the unions. It was in COSCO's interest to resolve the labor problem, she argued. The workers had been striking for most of the past year, pushing the port's finances from bad to worse. Katseli was the only Greek government official to use the striking workers as leverage to extract better terms from COSCO. Unfortunately for Greece, Katseli was removed in a Cabinet reshuffle before her efforts could bear fruit.

PASOK wanted to close the book on the COSCO affair, which it saw as a political lose-lose. In December 2009, the government appointed new leadership at PPA and ordered it to renegotiate as quickly as possible. Working under time pressure and with minimal leverage, PPA did an admirable job of balancing COSCO's interests with those of the port workers. COSCO had already consented to two of the workers' demands. First, PPA would have representation on the board of directors of the COSCO-controlled holding company that would lease Piers II and III. Second, port administrators would make an effort to hire local residents.[30] The Greeks extracted one more concession: that the handover of Pier II's operations to COSCO would happen in stages over the first half of 2010, rather than all at once. It was not clear whether these commitments would be binding, but they gave PASOK enough political cover to declare the issue closed.[31] COSCO was happy that the labor issue was resolved.

The new deal achieved the appearance of consensus by paying off the port employees. These men and women were already well compensated. In a good year, they could make as much as €76,000, more than four times the national median income. To quiet the unions, the PPA—still backed by Greek taxpayers—agreed to cough up additional funds.[32] Unions also won a promise that wages at Pier I, the part of the port that COSCO had not leased, would remain at the same high levels. Anastasia Frantzeskaki, a member of the union's board of directors, dismissed these figures to me as "an exercise in how to lie with statistics."[33] In her account, popular media reports were heavily biased toward privatization, and selected baseline years in the early 2000s when the port was operating at full capacity and double-overtime shifts were the norm. Whatever the true figures, the fact remained that payroll had accounted for three-quarters of PPA's operational expenses in 2007. For the Greek government, the price of quieting unions' opposition was further strain on PPA's balance sheet.

More importantly, the renegotiated deal intensified the conflict of interest between COSCO and the Greek government. Under the original operational lease agreement, COSCO and PPA were partners. COSCO paid PPA an annual fee to run Piers II and III for thirty-five years and committed to finishing the construction of Pier III. In return, the Greek state would get a share of profits. But in another sense, COSCO and PPA were competitors, because PPA continued to operate Pier I. Under the new agreement, by agreeing to subsidize higher wages for the Pier I workers, the Greek government had put the state-owned PPA at an even greater competitive disadvantage. A year later, COSCO's services were 40 percent cheaper than PPA's, only a few hundred yards away.

This had very important implications for the future privatization of Piraeus. If the original lease agreement had gotten COSCO's foot in the door, the revised agreement effectively allowed COSCO to walk through the doorway and lock the door behind it. The new lease terms were such that no company other than COSCO would want to buy an equity stake in PPA (fig. 7.1). By late 2010, it was therefore all but guaranteed that China would have a long-term presence at Piraeus Port. The only questions were when—and at what price—COSCO would make a bid for full control.

FIGURE 7.1: COSCO headquarters at Piraeus Port, November 2018. Photograph by the author.

Doubling Down

By early 2010, Greece's public finances were so strained that the government had no leverage left. In January the EU condemned Greece for falsifying statistics about government finances. In February the government introduced harsh austerity measures, including pay cuts for public employees and across-the-board tax increases. PPA continued to post losses. So COSCO struck another agreement with the Greek government. COSCO would channel 300,000 containers a year to the (uncompetitive and state-run) Pier I and hire only Greek workers to operate Pier II. In return, the Greek government would lock in COSCO's tax concessions—which had come under scrutiny by European regulators—for the long run.[34] This agreement came at the peak of Greece's first fiscal crisis. In April, unable to meet its debt obligations, the Greek government accepted a €110 billion bailout from the troika, subject to painful conditions that included austerity, structural reforms, and privatization of state assets. The Greek people were desperate and humiliated.

Against the backdrop of the economic crisis, China and Greece redoubled their efforts to improve relations. Two weeks after Greece signed the first bailout agreement, COSCO's chairman, Wei Jiafu, paid a visit to Athens. In private discussions, Wei insisted that the Greek government owed COSCO €9 million in tax rebates. In public, by contrast, Wei was on a pure charm offensive. He gave interviews on Greek television and appealed directly to the Greek people, actions that were highly unusual for a Chinese executive, particularly one from an SOE. "The Chinese people respect Greek culture," Wei said. "Greece has a long and great ancient history, like China. We have many cultural characteristics in common. Educated Chinese people understand the *Iliad*."[35]

Wei's thirst for the spotlight, ebullient praise of Greek culture, and profile as an enthusiastic potential investor turned him into a minor celebrity. "In China, they say that somebody does not become a man unless he goes to the Army," Wei told a journalist on another trip to Athens that July. "I paraphrase this and say: somebody does not become a good shipowner unless he is born Greek."[36] Wei visited again in October, accompanied by Wen Jiabao, the Chinese premier. Touring the Acropolis, Wen promised that China would do everything possible to facilitate the return of the Parthenon marbles from the British Museum to Athens.

China's attempts to curry favor were transparent appeals to the pride of a wounded nation. Still, many Greeks believed—quite reasonably— that China would not be making such an effort if it were not serious about forming a lasting partnership.[37] Chinese officials dropped hints that they would buy billions of euros of Greek debt, although they never ultimately followed through. In June, the two countries signed fourteen new agreements, including several deals directly with Greece's largest shipbuilders. Wei himself repeatedly hinted that Greece could attract much more Chinese investment in the future. "From a strategic point of view, the port is not enough . . . We need a trade center," he said. "We have a saying in China: 'Construct the eagle's nest, and the eagle will come.' We have constructed such a nest in your country to attract such Chinese eagles. This is our contribution to you."[38]

Warming Up to China

Greek public opinion rapidly warmed toward China. The Greek press called Chinese investments a "sailboard for Greek economy," a "breath of investment," and "manna from heaven." They quoted Nikolaos Makarezos, the general who led the military junta in the 1970s, as saying: "If we sold one olive tree to every Chinese person, we could solve Greece's economic problem." The risk, critics retorted, was that the Chinese will "spit their pits on us."[39] An opinion poll from March 2011 found that 26 percent of Greeks named China as the "friendliest country toward Greece," second to Russia with 48 percent. The United States came in third, with 13 percent. Only 4 percent named Germany. The previous year, France had come in first place. Respondents also broadly approved of COSCO's involvement at Piraeus: 53 percent supported it, and only 29 percent were opposed.[40]

By 2010, three years before OBOR was announced, it was clear that China had taken a special interest in Greece. The repeated state visits signaled a level of interest incomparably greater than a decade before, when China and Greece had had no political relationship to speak of, and far out of proportion to Greece's neighbors. Not only did COSCO have a longer-term plan to turn Piraeus into China's gateway to Europe, the Chinese party-state stood behind Wei and his vision. COSCO began to drop hints about possible investments outside its traditional shipping business. It signed collaboration agreements with the national airport. It announced plans to submit a proposal to connect Piraeus to the national rail network by building an international logistics center at Thriasio at the cost of €150 million. COSCO's leaders spoke of turning Piraeus into a rival to Rotterdam—the largest port in Europe.

Mainstream Greek politicians were thrilled at the prospect. Syriza criticized COSCO's "monopoly" power, but the party was still largely irrelevant in parliament. Even Thodoris Dritsas, a Syriza politician from Piraeus who later served as minister of shipping, admitted to me that "a bankrupt country had no choice but to listen with open ears" when China declared an interest in massive investments.[41] The political moderates who led the Greek government at the time were even more enthusiastic. "The Chinese want a gateway into Europe," said Theodoros Pangalos, then deputy prime minister. "They are not like these Wall Street fucks, pushing financial investments on paper. The Chinese deal in real things, in merchandise."[42]

Observers from other EU countries were equally unconcerned about COSCO's interest in Greece. "The danger that COSCO will behave like some of the Chinese mining and oil companies in Africa is pretty remote," said Katinka Barysch, deputy director of the Centre for European Reform. "Greece is a member of the EU, so it has a much more solid legal framework. There are clear constraints about what foreign investors can and cannot do in our markets." The risk, rather, was that COSCO would "invest too quickly in trophy assets and then manage them badly." In any case, she pointed out, if not from China, "where else would the money come from?"[43]

Growing Desperation

Over the course of 2011, the Greek government came under intense pressure from all sides to privatize state-owned companies. In March, in exchange for a loan extension, the troika demanded that Greece privatize €50 billion of state-owned assets. The Piraeus Port was an obvious candidate. The port's financial situation was even more dire than reported, because COSCO was also discreetly pressing to renegotiate its lease terms with PPA in a way that would further depress government revenues. Not only was COSCO demanding a mounting pile of tax rebates, it also wanted to reduce the lease price for Piers II and III on the grounds that Greek economic growth had slowed since the original agreement was signed.

China used pressure tactics to push Greece back to the negotiating table. When PPA tried to partner with the French shipping conglomerate MSC to improve the competitiveness of Pier I, COSCO threatened to sue.[44] COSCO also threatened not to invest in the rail logistics site at Thriasio unless the Greeks met their demands.[45] The writing was on the wall: Greece had no alternatives to partnership with China. In April, a delegation of Greek business and government officials visited Wei and Wen in Beijing. The following month, COSCO and the PPA resolved their main disagreements over the lease contract. The Greek government announced that it would sell some of its shares in Piraeus port. Without publicly asking for privatization, COSCO had forced the Greek government's hand.

From the beginning of the negotiations, it was clear that COSCO was going to win an extremely favorable deal. According to Dritsas, who later served as shipping minister, "all the European institutions knew it."[46] Stripped of its profitable assets, the PPA had lost most of its value. It was now worth less than what COSCO had paid for its thirty-five-year operational lease.[47] The PASOK government threw in three smaller regional ports to sweeten the deal.[48] PPA's chairman, who had strongly supported the lease agreement, condemned the government's "failed" and "Thatcherite" proposal to do an equity sale. The dockworkers' and foremen's unions pledged to "fight the mother of all battles" to stop the privatization in its tracks.[49] But none of this mattered to the Europeans. They had dropped their opposition to China taking over Piraeus when the Greek bailout had put their own money on the line.

The Greek political establishment buckled under renewed pressure from creditors. In spring 2011, thousands of Greeks of all ideological stripes began to gather nightly in front of the parliament building in Athens's Syntagma Square. The so-called Indignants waved flags and took turns speaking from a makeshift podium. At its peak, the crowd was estimated to exceed 100,000 people. "It might not have been democracy at work, since no binding decisions were possible," recalls Yanis Varoufakis, the bombastic leftist economist who later served as finance minister. "But at least it was a huge *agora* vibrating with possibility, in sharp contrast to what went on in the Parliament House nearby, site of our national humiliation and submission to a great depression."[50] In June, the troika demanded that the Greek legislature pass tough labor reforms. For the first time, the protests began to turn violent. The police broke them up with teargas, water cannons, and smoke grenades. "Walls and pavements were blackened by the smoke," Varoufakis writes, "and the whole city smelled of chemicals for weeks."

Varoufakis argues that the labor reforms were "the rites of [Prime Minister] Papandreou's departure"—one "last humiliation before the rug was finally pulled from under his feet by the second bailout."[51] In November 2011, in a botched attempt to project strength, Papandreou threatened to call a national referendum on the debt restructuring deal the troika had proposed. The announcement stirred up panic in the financial markets and European capitals, since a negative result could clear the way for Grexit. Papandreou's allies deserted him, and within days he canceled the referendum and resigned. The new caretaker government caved to the troika's demands and granted some of the modifications to the Piraeus lease agreement that COSCO had requested.[52]

During this period of political turmoil in Greece, COSCO and the Chinese government drifted into the background. They made no new public demands of Greece. Every two months or so, another Chinese trade delegation would make news with vague promises of investment deals. Behind the scenes, representatives from COSCO and the Chinese government hedged by quietly courting all the major political parties in Greece. As Greece's economy slid and its humiliated population grew more bitter toward the troika, the facts on the ground were changing in China's favor. COSCO bided its time.

Return of the Right

In June 2012, new elections brought New Democracy back to power. The center-right Antonis Samaras became prime minister. Samaras's top priorities were to stabilize the Greek economy, impose fiscal discipline, and speed up privatizations. In its first year, the Samaras government passed a tax reform package and laid off tens of thousands of public employees. Over a longer time horizon, the reforms were probably necessary to lay the foundations for future growth, but they did little in the short term to pull the economy out of its tailspin. A year into the new government, Greece became the first developed economy in history to be reclassified by ratings agencies as an emerging market.[53] Per capita GDP did not bottom out for another two years, at which point it had fallen 26 percent since the beginning of the crisis. Unemployment hovered above 28 percent. Measured in several ways, Greece's economic crisis was deeper and longer by far than the Great Depression in the United States.

Samaras focused on improving relations with China, just as his party had done in the mid-2000s before the crisis. The previous center-left PASOK government had paid lip service to workers' demands and shown some willingness to string China along. No longer. Less than a month after Samaras took power in June 2012, newspapers reported that his government wanted to speed up the port's privatization. The government considered leasing agreements for Pier I along the lines of Piers II and III. It also considered a full-on equity sale.[54] Whichever it chose, it was clear to all that the Greek state wanted COSCO to take a larger role at the Piraeus Port. Samaras's new finance minister was reported as saying that "we hope to see more successful investments, such as COSCO's."[55]

Samaras's corporate backers had other, self-interested reasons to push for privatization. Greece's most prominent businessmen, including media and shipping mogul Aristeidis Alafouzos and the Constantakopoulos family, were very exposed to the Chinese market and stood to gain from reforms that would lower their operating costs at Piraeus port. The chair of the International Shippers Association praised COSCO's contributions in extravagant terms. "Since the first moment that [COSCO] took over" the Piraeus terminals, he said, "it changed our mentality concerning costumer care and increased productivity."[56] COSCO had passed its lower labor costs on down the chain, translating into higher profits for the shippers. Multiple reliable sources confirmed to me that Greece's leading shipping families leaned on the leading newspapers and TV stations to downplay the dock workers' concerns and highlight the benefits of trade with China.

In the end, the Greek people's sense of betrayal by the West was the most important factor in opening the door to COSCO. Given the nearly revolutionary mood in Greek politics in 2012, the left's opposition to COSCO was far less ferocious than it might have been. "If COSCO [were] an American company," one commentator pointed out, "the blaze from the star-spangled banners that would be burnt in Piraeus and the screams of 'ruthless imperialists' would reach Shanghai and beyond." Why was the Greek reaction to COSCO so muted, the commentator asked? Perhaps because "Chinese people are like us, because they develop as Greeks do: gluttonously, unequally, and in a statist way."[57] This cultural argument is intriguing, but the political argument is more persuasive. Why did Greek politicians prefer to privatize Piraeus in what was essentially a direct sale to COSCO, rather than run the risk of another European buyer winning? The toxic politics of debt negotiations with Europeans had left China as the only politically acceptable partner.

Secret Talks

As the prospect of a new tender came into view, the Chinese again dialed up their shows of friendship. In November 2012, the Greek vice minister of foreign affairs met with his Chinese counterpart and COSCO's leadership team in Beijing. At the meeting, Wei said that COSCO would like to invest elsewhere in Greece, including the depressed energy and transport sectors. The Greek vice minister was excited, telling a journalist that "the Chinese people believe in Greece's recovery."[58] Wei also spoke of his gratitude for all of the times that Greece helped China in the past, including sharing its knowhow in advance of the 2008 Beijing Olympics. Of course, Wei's statements were a transparent example of the Chinese concept of giving face. No one who watched the opening ceremonies of the Beijing Olympics, which set a new standard for extravagance, would think that they had learned a thing from the Greeks.

In 2013, with the prospect of privatization clearly in sight, China dangled the prospects of massive investments in a range of sectors. The party mouthpiece *China Daily* reported that COSCO was willing to pay $1 billion to acquire PPA.[59] (In the end, it paid little more than a third of that.) In March 2013, COSCO signed an agreement with consumer electronics manufacturer Hewlett-Packard and the Greek rail network to assemble products at the port industrial zone and transport the cargo by rail to warehouses in the Czech Republic. COSCO also announced plans to develop the western side of Pier III and massively increase its warehouse capacity at the port.[60] The Samaras government scrambled to accommodate COSCO's indications of interest. To support the Hewlett-Packard deal—and in the hopes that COSCO would put in a bid for the rail network—it authorized new tax exemptions that would effectively turn Piraeus into a backdoor for Chinese products entering the European market.[61]

The timing of these moves strongly suggests that the Samaras government, COSCO, and the Chinese government were secretly coordinating to make sure the privatization went smoothly. In April 2013, COSCO finally officially declared its interest in purchasing all of PPA's shares. Four days later, a Shenzhen-based company expressed interest in buying all the shares in the Athens national airport.[62] That summer, COSCO and Greek government officials exchanged visits in advance of a big announcement. In May 2013, Wei received Samaras in the Diaoyutai State Guest House in Beijing. The delegations discussed the prospects of COSCO managing the Piraeus Port, and Chinese Premier Li Keqiang expressed interest in airports and other seaports in Greece. The Greek government signed an agreement with Chinese consumer electronics producers Huawei and ZTE to set up their Europe transshipment hubs in Piraeus. The Hellenic Republic Asset Development Fund (TAIPED), the independent agency set up by the troika to oversee Greek privatizations, also signed a cooperation agreement with the China Development Bank.[63] The process was neither transparent nor competitive.

The announcement finally came on June 26, 2013, when Wei was in Athens yet again to attend the opening ceremony for COSCO's renovated Pier III. At the event, Samaras awarded Wei the Grand Cross, Greece's highest honor. In the afternoon, TAIPED announced a plan to sell the government's equity stake in the PPA. Port employees across Greece went on strike again. Syriza crowed that privatization would turn Greece into a "colony of our creditors."[64] But the government was pressing ahead to resolve final issues. It was not an accident that these events occurred on the same day and followed Samaras's trip to China. The entire thing was being coordinated in private between COSCO and the Greek and Chinese governments.

"Let COSCO Negotiate with Itself"

The government's coalition partners were divided about how to proceed, so the troika seized control of the privatization drive. New Democracy favored an equity sale; PASOK wanted a concession agreement on the model of Piers II and III. At this point, the Greek state owned 75 percent of PPA. TAIPED's only objective was to bring in €450 million as quickly as possible.[65] In February, the government announced plans to auction off 67 percent of PPA's total equity. "We can't wait anymore," the TAIPED spokesperson said. "The privatization of the ports is high on the government's agenda. If COSCO is the [only] bidder, let it negotiate with itself."[66]

At this point COSCO was clearly the only politically and financially viable candidate to buy out PPA. In August 2013, COSCO and PPA resolved their more recent dispute. COSCO would build an oil terminal for Pier I, nearly double the warehouse capacity on the western side of Pier III, and upgrade gantries and other machinery across the port. In return, Greece would lower the annual lease fee even further. These investments disproportionately benefited the parts of the port that COSCO already controlled, but they chipped away at PPA's last remaining source of revenue—the lease payments from COSCO. The state-controlled Pier I had become a hopeless loss-maker, posting more than €13 million in losses before taxes in 2013.[67] COSCO was a lock to win.

Five other investment groups submitted bids, but the Greeks made it clear from the beginning that COSCO was the favorite. As long as COSCO had created reasonable legal doubt about the size of its annual lease payments, outside investors could not properly appraise the value of PPA's equity. Meanwhile, COSCO's track record of improvements at the port spoke for themselves. Under their management, container handling at Piraeus had increased by 26 percent that year, turning Piraeus into the eighth-largest port in Europe. In June, China's new premier, Li Keqiang, visited Athens (fig. 7.2). Samaras took him on a personal tour of Piraeus. Before he departed, Li signed nineteen agreements worth $6.4 billion, most of them in the shipping sector. He also promised (falsely) that China would invest once the Greek government issued new bonds.[68]

PASOK and Syriza came out strongly against the equity sale proposal. "Substituting a state monopoly with a private monopoly is unacceptable," the president of PASOK said.[69] The unions took up their fight with renewed ferocity. The leader of the largest union claimed that COSCO's growth was "based on the blood and sweat of the employees" and exhorted the prime minister to "bring an end to COSCO's chain gang."[70] The unions demanded an end to sixteen-hour shifts and asked for overtime pay for weekends and holidays. Workers blocked the entrance to COSCO's Container Terminal. The unions sued, claiming that the latest version of the equity sale was invalid because COSCO's plan to expand

FIGURE 7.2: Chinese Premier Li Keqiang gestures at a map during a visit to Piraeus, June 20, 2014. Courtesy of Reuters/Louisa Gouliamaki/Pool.

Pier III had not passed a new public tender process or environmental impact assessment.[71] After gaining seats in local elections, Syriza representatives gave the unions their full backing. Party members pledged in parliament that Syriza would "defend with all the democratic means that it possesses" the "public nature and the social orientation of the Port of Piraeus."[72]

TAIPED and the New Democracy government plowed ahead anyway. When the tender wrapped up in April, six companies had submitted bids for the equity stake in the port.[73] COSCO's offer was the only one the Greek state took seriously. The government spent the second half of 2014 haggling with COSCO over the details. A court modified certain aspects of the agreement, and the two sides had to negotiate a workaround.[74] Parliament finally ratified the deal just before Christmas.

Greece on the Precipice

Days later, the government called a snap election, which Syriza won in a stunning upset. In January 2015, Alexis Tsipras became prime minister and Varoufakis, the scholar who had risen to prominence in the Syntagma Square protests, became finance minister. During the campaign, Tsipras had promised his constituents on Twitter that he would put the COSCO deal "back on the table" if elected.[75] Before he was sworn in, the incoming shipping minister, Dritsas, announced that he planned to walk away from negotiations on the equity sale.[76] Chinese ministries of trade and foreign affairs released statements of concern at these comments, claiming that they had first heard the news from press releases. Once again, a new Greek government had inherited a "hot potato" deal from its predecessor.

The Syriza leadership was divided about whether to confront the Chinese publicly. Dritsas and the rest of the leftist faction wanted to block the equity sale. In contrast, Varoufakis fully supported COSCO's involvement at Piraeus. In public, he praised COSCO's "very positive" contribution and even visited the port to meet with COSCO executives. On February 12 Tsipras received a tongue-lashing in a phone call with the Chinese premier.[77] In March, Tsipras's deputy, Yannis Dragasakis, visited China and was quoted in the state press saying that the equity sale could go ahead as planned despite the "small delay." Asked to comment on Dragasakis's statements, Dritsas refused to confirm them.[78] Syriza had achieved national appeal partly because of its absolutist position on privatization, but the circumstances it had inherited put it in a bind. It took more than two months for the government to clarify its position. If China had not worked in advance to frame Piraeus as a test of Greece's commitment to the budding bilateral relationship, the Syriza hardliners likely would have succeeded in scuttling the equity sale.

Instead, Tsipras caved to China and allowed the equity sale to proceed. Multiple sources I interviewed believed that this had been Tsipras's intention all along. In April 2015, the press reported that the government would proceed with the sale of a controlling interest (51 percent) of PPA's equity. After five years, the winner of the tender would have the option to acquire an additional 16 percent stake, bringing the winner's total stake to 67 percent. The only condition attached to the option was that the buyer would have to make at least €300 million of new investments in the port.[79] Three bidders from the previous tender were specifically invited to participate in the new bidding process. COSCO, of course, was one of them.[80] Meanwhile, Syriza representatives made half-hearted attempts to spin their capitulation to their voters. They insisted on calling the deal a "concession agreement" rather than a "sale," denied the obvious rifts within their own leadership, and suggested that there would be no substantial change from COSCO's existing lease agreement. These claims were absurd. The entire point of the agreement was to allow Greece to liquidate its equity in the port.[81]

Meanwhile, Grexit once again had become frighteningly likely. Tsipras calculated that only the prospect of mutual economic destruction could pressure the troika to moderate its demands. On June 27, in a show of resolve, he announced a snap referendum on the terms of the new bailout agreement. The market panicked, and the Finance Ministry imposed capital controls. Two days later, Greece missed a payment to the IMF, putting the country in technical default. The Greek people voted overwhelmingly to reject the bailout terms, a surprisingly emphatic show of support for Tsipras that allowed the country to save face. But it made little difference in the substance of the negotiations, as Tsipras had already caved to the troika's core demands. The following week, the Greek parliament approved an €86 billion bailout package that was essentially identical to the one voters had just rejected.

Once the bailout issue was resolved, Syriza's antiprivatization crusaders tried again to delay or scuttle the tender. On September 28, one month before the bidding deadline, Dritsas, now the shipping minister, tried to reclaim control of the tender from the privatization board. He argued that residents of Piraeus, which happened to be his home constituency, had not been offered public hearings to consult on the privatization. COSCO fired back that if the Greek government were acting in good faith, it should have held hearings in April, when it decided to proceed with the equity sale. Dritsas managed to push back the tender deadline by three months, but he failed to stop it altogether. Tsipras removed him in the next Cabinet reshuffle. The government had no choice but to proceed—it needed the cash to meet its privatization commitments under the terms of the third bailout.

When the tender finally closed, COSCO was revealed to be the only bidder.[82] The Chinese firm had been allowed to negotiate with itself, just as the privatization board had promised. Greece had done itself no favors by delaying the tender. Now it needed cash more than ever and had no contingency plan to raise the money elsewhere. COSCO submitted an embarrassingly low bid. Outside estimates of PPA's entire market capitalization were as high as €700 million.[83] At the urging of the privatization board, COSCO submitted a revised bid, though it is not clear whether this included any new concessions. COSCO offered to pay €368.5 million for the 67 percent stake in the port—€280 million up front, and the rest to acquire the remaining 16 percent stake in five years' time. It was a paltry offer, but a desperate Greece accepted.

Making Peace with the Terms

After the deal was announced, Greek press reports argued that the government had sold its stake for far less than fair market value. COSCO had used creative arithmetic to inflate the headline figures of its promised investments in the port.[84] The price was pitiably low: that same year, COSCO had paid nearly three times as much to acquire the Turkish port of Kumport, which was a third the size of Piraeus.[85] In any case, the entire context of the deal was humiliating. The Greek people would never see the money, since all €280 million that COSCO would pay upfront would go directly toward Greece's debt repayment bill.

Yet the Greek people did not blame China for taking advantage of the country's weak position. In fact, a poll of Piraeus residents conducted two months after the equity sale found that 57 percent of respondents approved of COSCO.[86] Three out of four respondents blamed their own government for fumbling the privatization process. Respondents were hesitant about privatization in general, but they were optimistic about what COSCO in particular could contribute. Sixty-nine percent expected COSCO to add new infrastructure after the takeover. Substantial majorities also expected that new jobs would be created in Piraeus, that port services and work conditions would improve, and that local small businesses would benefit.

COSCO had sidestepped the politically charged domestic politics of the Greek financial crisis. It was able to do so because its involvement in Piraeus did not fit the narrative of an outside power stripping Greece of its sovereignty, as the troika's bailouts had done. COSCO had expanded the port's footprint, replaced old equipment, and brought in new business. Chinese officials had presented their country as a friend to Greece, willing to lend a hand to help meet the troika's demands. As Dritsas said three months after the sale: the Greek government could have gotten more concessions from COSCO if "pressure created by the circumstances" had not "led to choices that were out of our control."[87] Having presented itself as a sympathetic friend, China escaped the blame for making those circumstances worse.

The Second Botched Renegotiation

Just before the Greek government transferred its shares to COSCO, Syriza's radical wing made a desperate, last-ditch effort to undermine the privatization. Using fast-track procedures, the legislature passed new measures that would allow PPA employees to transfer to other state-run companies. The bill also tried to lock in pro-union employment regulations so that COSCO could not amend them and tried to increase PPA's annual payment to the Greek state.[88] These changes would undermine the contract the government had just signed, and they rested on weak legal justifications. COSCO was understandably furious. Leading Chinese politicians called Tsipras and pressured him "in the strongest possible way" to back down, Dritsas recalls.

Tsipras folded under the Chinese pressure. At his insistence, parliament hurriedly passed a new bill annulling the previous law.[89] The entire affair was an embarrassment for Tsipras and his government. One former Syriza member of parliament, Panagiotis Lafazanis, declared that "the Chinese have humiliated Greek democracy."[90] The leader of the far-right party Golden Dawn asked whether Syriza was "proud of selling-off the country's first port."[91] Once again, Greece's attempt to renegotiate with China had backfired: China had proven its ability to influence Greece, and Tsipras had no one but himself to blame.

Greece's perfidy gave COSCO executives and Chinese officials an excuse to break most of the verbal promises they had made during negotiations. In July 2016, COSCO announced that it would use the Macedonian rail network because of its frustration with Greece's railway strikes.[92] COSCO had also pledged to use the existing Greek infrastructure at Elefsina for shipbuilding and repairs. But after the Greeks tried to meddle with the contract, COSCO announced that it would bring in its own 300,000-ton floating dock and run the operations itself.[93] China never did persuade the British to return the Parthenon marbles, nor did they make large purchases of Greek sovereign debt. As one well-connected Greek commentator later put it to me: "with the Chinese, if it's not on paper, it doesn't exist."

Conclusions

Behind all the twists and turns of the politics and negotiations, the underlying story of the case is one of COSCO transforming Piraeus for the better. In 2008, the port moved fewer than 434,000 containers; in 2018 it moved 4.9 million. The port is increasingly interconnected with a growing Chinese-run logistics network in Eastern Europe, including railways in Montenegro and a transshipment center in the Czech Republic. It has made a big positive contribution to COSCO's bottom line, now account-ing for almost a quarter of the company's global turnover. It continues to grow, with profits and transshipment volume increasing every year. Even China skeptics grudgingly acknowledge that Piraeus was a win-win. In 2017, the US ambassador to Greece said that "the rise of Piraeus in global rankings" was "partly due to the fact that Chinese have brought technol-ogy, a disciplined approach to employment relations, and have made the port function efficiently."[94] The expanded passenger terminal is an entry point for ever-larger numbers of Chinese tourists. Most important, every major Greek political party has been reconciled. The labor unions that oppose China are now all alone.

Chinese media and senior officials frequently point to Piraeus as an example of a successful OBOR project. One cartoon in the party mouth-piece *Global Times* even depicted OBOR as a watering can and Greece as a tender flower.[95] Yet these claims are based on a revisionist narrative of how the port came to be privatized. When Xi announced OBOR in 2013, COSCO was already three years into its operational lease on the Piraeus port and had already renegotiated the lease terms so that the Greek-run Pier I would be unattractive to other commercial buyers. Meanwhile, China was looking to hedge its exposure to political risk in Greece, since the politics of the debt crisis were becoming increasingly toxic. Through a series of renegotiations with successive Greek govern-ments, COSCO restructured the lease agreement to reduce its annual li-abilities and lock in its long-term tax exemptions. These would remain valuable no matter what happened to the Greek economy, since the main purpose of the Piraeus port was to be a gateway for Chinese products to enter the European market as cheaply and efficiently as possible.

It was Greek domestic politics that cleared the way for COSCO to take over Piraeus. When COSCO first identified Piraeus as a potential gateway to Europe in the mid-2000s, Greece's powerful shipping indus-try pressured its government to invite COSCO in. The New Democracy party saw COSCO as a vehicle to achieve the party's long-standing goals of privatizing state assets and confronting the unions. From COSCO's point of view, Greece was an attractive partner because its governments were weak and short-lived. First, New Democracy offered long-term tax exemp-tions and political support in taking on the unions. When the center-left

PASOK took power, Athens took on the cost of paying off the striking dock workers. When New Democracy returned, COSCO won new tax concessions as it dangled further investments. As Greece's sovereign debt crisis grew more acute, and the voting public increasingly radicalized, Greek politicians wanted a respectful and reliable partner at Piraeus—a role that China was all too happy to play.

Greek observers think about the Piraeus case from the perspective of their tumultuous recent history—just another subplot in the country's complex domestic politics. They note that the immediate catalyst for privatization was pressure from Greece's creditors, not COSCO. The final terms of the deal favored COSCO because Greece was negotiating from a position of weakness: an urgent need for capital, a series of weak governments, and a legacy operational lease deal that made Piraeus unattractive to other buyers. Chinese carrots and sticks helped move the process along. Senior Chinese officials hinted many times that China would buy Greek debt and revamp the Greek railway network, unsubstantiated promises that most Greeks were wrong to take seriously. Yet every Greek official I spoke to, including affiliates of all three major parties, described the Piraeus case as a *Greek* political issue, in which China had emerged as a convenient partner. Like in Sri Lanka and Tanzania, most of them laughed off my questions about whether China had used pressure tactics to get its way. With only one exception, the Greeks I interviewed blamed the country's desperate financial situation for any flaws in the agreement.

Before the financial crisis, only one major political party in Greece was pro-China; today, all of them are. Most surprising has been the transformation of far-left Syriza. Back in 2008, no Greek politician opposed COSCO's lease agreement more prominently than did Alexis Tsipras. Seven years later, as prime minister, Tsipras not only oversaw the equity sale of the port, he positioned himself as one of China's closest partners in the West. In 2016, Tsipras blocked EU resolutions to condemn Chinese human rights violations and territorial grabs in the South China Sea. From Beijing's perspective, Piraeus is a model for political relationships where client states built through OBOR can pay clear geopolitical dividends. In November 2019, Xi himself visited Piraeus. Standing next to the new Greek prime minister, Kyriakos Mitsotakis, he announced yet another ambitious $150 million expansion plan, much to the dismay of the French, Germans, and Dutch (fig. 7.3).

FIGURE 7.3: Chinese President Xi Jinping and Greek Prime Minister Kyriakos Mitsotakis tour COSCO container terminal, in Piraeus, November 11, 2019. Courtesy of Reuters/Orestis Panagiotou/Pool.

Greece will become an even more valuable partner for China in the 2020s. Chinese industrial policy goes far beyond the well-known "Made in China 2025" production targets for high-tech goods.[96] From cars to wind turbines, from commercial jets to industrial equipment, China aims to supplant the industrial economies of Northern and Western Europe as the world's dominant manufacturer of high-end products. China is actively preparing for this emerging era of industrial competition by locking in its relationships with Southern and Eastern European countries. Belatedly, the French, Germans, and Dutch are coming to recognize the scope of the China challenge. "Seen from Beijing," German Chancellor Angela Merkel said in 2017, "Europe is an Asian peninsula."[97]

It may be too late for Europe to change direction. In February 2017, when Germany, France, and Italy sent a joint letter to the European Commission complaining about the Made in China 2025 initiative, Beijing's allies in Greece, Hungary, and Portugal blocked the commission from taking action. No EU-wide investment screening mechanism was set up until April 2019, and Chinese money still finds its way in. The wealthy and advanced economies of Northern and Western Europe are undoubtedly growing fearful of Chinese power. Yet the countries of the periphery and the European companies that depend on the Chinese market continue to lobby on Beijing's behalf to preserve the status quo. The longer it takes Europe to settle on a strategy, the harder it will be to drive the eagle from its nest.

CHAPTER 8

OBOR Shapes Four Regions

This book so far has examined OBOR on two levels. On a macro level, OBOR's strategic value for China goes far beyond the infrastructure itself. OBOR gives China political influence in recipient countries and extends Xi Jinping's personal control over the domestic economy. Both of these are more strategically important than the economic benefits that may accrue to China from new infrastructure "connectivity." On a micro level, recipient countries experience OBOR in a multitude of ways. How they perceive and interact with OBOR has far more to do with their domestic and regional politics than with variations in China's behavior or strategic objectives. In Sri Lanka, Tanzania, and Greece, China's port development projects succeeded or failed, were completed or abandoned, depending on power shifts between local political factions over the course of multiple rounds of negotiation. Most commentary inside and outside of China still describes OBOR as a coordinated and orderly strategic master plan. The last three chapters have shown that this diagnosis misses the point. OBOR is neither coordinated nor orderly.

Yet Chinese overseas construction projects often have profound strategic implications for the countries that host them and their neighbors. This chapter takes a higher-level look at how OBOR is reshaping global geopolitics. It focuses on China's use of investments and OBOR-branded political exercises in four countries—Russia, Malaysia, Pakistan, and Iran—and discusses how these are influencing the surrounding regions—Central Asia, Southeast Asia, South Asia, and the Middle East, respectively. As chapters 5–7 have shown, China tends to use similar negotiating tactics everywhere, but recipient countries experience OBOR very differently. Overall, OBOR has been a net positive for China's national interests in all four regions discussed in this chapter. This is partly because in each region, US policy has opened up strategic space for China to take on a more active role.

The point of this chapter is not be comprehensive but to show how the case study approach can also be useful at a broader level of analysis. Every OBOR country and project is unique. Yet it is equally important to look through the other end of the telescope. Thinking about how OBOR functions from the inside out and the outside in is useful for quickly grasping the core dynamics of a new case. It is also an essential intellectual exercise to make sure that big-picture conclusions follow from facts.

Central Asia

In Central Asia, OBOR has failed to live up to the hype. Russia has quietly resisted any significant OBOR projects in own borders outside the oil and gas sector. It has allowed a few Chinese trans-Eurasian connectivity projects to go ahead, but slowly and at a far smaller scale than Chinese propaganda suggests. Meanwhile, Moscow has strengthened its security ties with all of the Central Asian states, notably Tajikistan and Afghanistan, to counterbalance the rapid growth of Chinese economic influence.[1] Vladimir Putin's "join and co-opt" strategy has not stressed Sino–Russian relations. In fact, it is largely compatible with China's interests in the region. Beijing does not want the sole responsibility of guaranteeing security in Central Asia. OBOR has helped it acquire political influence there at a relatively low cost. This frees up Chinese attention and capital for other regions, particularly Southeast Asia and Europe, where the geopolitical stakes and potential returns on investment are higher.

Outside of China, Russia (map 8.1) is OBOR's most important geopolitical booster. Putin first embraced OBOR after relations with the West soured in 2014, to show that it had strategic options. Since 2015, his rhetoric has evolved from warm to effusive. In May 2017, he delivered opening remarks at the first Belt and Road Forum in Beijing. Praising Xi's "creative approach," Putin offered unconditional support for the New Silk

MAP 8.1: Map of Russia, courtesy of Scott Walker.

Road concept. "We welcome China's One Belt One Road initiative," he said.[2] "The greater Eurasia is not an abstract geopolitical arrangement but, without exaggeration, a truly civilization-wide project." Putin was photographed smiling broadly as he shook Xi's hand. When the twenty-nine visiting heads of state proceeded down the red carpet, Putin and Xi walked side by side at the front of the pack.

That a Russian president should smile on a Chinese attempt to project influence in Central Asia is a historical puzzle in need of explanation. Since the early nineteenth century, Russia and China have competed for dominance over Central Asia. China still blames Russia for pressuring it to cede more than 200,000 square miles of Manchurian territory in the 1858 Treaty of Aigun and for occupying the western province of Xinjiang in the early twentieth century. In the twilight of the czarist period, Moscow built the Trans-Siberian Railway in a bid to turn itself into an Asian power. The rail line from Moscow to Vladivostok was completed in 1916. During the Cold War, enmity between Russia and China became so toxic that Moscow discreetly asked Washington if it would remain neutral in the event of a preemptive nuclear attack on China. (Washington refused.)[3] Relations between China and Russia have improved immeasurably since the 1980s, but a legacy of distrust persists. Xi has explicitly instructed his chief lieutenants to study the mistakes of the Communist Party of the Soviet Union, so that the Chinese Communist Party should never repeat them.[4]

In 1991, the break-up of the Soviet Union left Russia down but not out. The largest state industries were auctioned, producing a class of oligarchs overnight. Within six years, Russia had defaulted on its international debts. The country found itself encroached on from every side. Former Soviet satellite states in Eastern Europe and the Baltic lined up to join NATO and the European Union. China resolved its territorial disputes with the new Central Asian republics and continued its economic miracle. Moscow still had nuclear weapons and a seat on the UN Security Council, but when it worked to improve ties with China in the 1990s, it did so from a position of weakness.

Russia and China clearly had common interests. The question for Moscow was how to maximize cooperation while containing areas of potential conflict. In the 1990s, Russia and China signed three joint statements and announced a "strategic partnership" to "adjust the balance of world power" and "offset the influence of the United States." But Russia was also concerned about the long-term implications of China's rise. It helped form the Shanghai Cooperation Organization, the first transnational body for Central Asia, partly because such an institution could contain China's revanchist tendencies.

Under Putin, Russia rode the global oil boom to an economic revival in the 2000s, but its economy remained puny and undiversified. Putin pushed for the creation of a Eurasian Economic Union (EAEU) to integrate Russia's smaller neighbors into a single market. This structure would be Russian-dominated and implicitly opposed to the European Union. The EAEU concept was based on shaky foundations. Russia is a petro-economy with few globally competitive industries. The Chinese provinces of Zhejiang and Guangdong each have a larger GDP than all of Russia. Understandably, when Xi began to tout OBOR in 2013, Putin's first reaction was skepticism and suspicion.

After Xi announced OBOR, one senior Russian official captured the prevailing mood: this Chinese plan was "just another attempt to steal Central Asia from us."[5] Russian analysts were concerned that OBOR could smother the EAEU customs union by offering member states more favorable trading terms. They feared that China would turn to Central Asian states for energy contracts and build new transcontinental rail links that would redirect traffic from the Trans-Siberian Railway.[6] According to Alexander Gabuev, who conducted a remarkable series of interviews with senior officials in this period, the Russian security services and intelligence agencies (the Security Council, Federal Security Service, and External Intelligence Service) were the most extreme in their opposition to OBOR.[7] These agencies had worked for years to block Chinese attempts to convert the Shanghai Cooperation Organization into a trade union and development bank. In their eyes, a large Chinese-led investment program in Central Asia would surely come at Russia's expense.

Russian skepticism and fear were potentially serious problems for Xi. China could not claim to be restoring the ancient Silk Road without the appearance of enthusiastic Russian buy-in. Fortunately for China, other arms of the Russian state were less concerned about OBOR. The officials Gabuev interviewed in Russia's Government Office, Ministry of Economic Development, and Ministry of Finance were far more likely than their military counterparts to take China's promises of foreign investment at face value. Essentially, OBOR had divided the Russian state. On balance, Russia's OBOR skeptics outnumbered its supporters. The question for China was how to make sure the pro-China Russian elites won the internal argument.

The United States solved Xi's problem for him. In the wake of the 2014 Ukraine crisis, the United States and the EU imposed three rounds of crippling sanctions against the Russian energy, finance, and defense sectors. With the ruble and the Russian economy in free-fall, China seemed a more attractive partner than before. The souring of relations with the West gave Putin domestic reasons to perform a strategic "pivot to the East."

By the time Putin returned from a successful trip to Shanghai in May 2014, the Russian state had coalesced around a plan to respond to OBOR: Moscow would join and try to coopt it. In public, Russia would praise China's involvement and deny any suggestions that it would come at the expense of Russian influence in Central Asia. By framing Russian participation as a "linking up" of the EAEU scheme and OBOR, Putin could plausibly claim that he was joining as an equal, not a junior partner. Meanwhile, Russia would maintain strict limits on Chinese megaprojects. No Chinese firm could be allowed to take a majority share in any Russian strategic infrastructure. Russia would use its position from "inside" OBOR to manage the geopolitical threat of Chinese expansion in Central Asia.[8]

In early 2015, Russian and Chinese negotiators hurriedly hammered out language acceptable to both sides. The staffing patterns quickly made clear that Russia's "China doves" had taken the lead. In March, Russian First Deputy Prime Minister Igor Shuvalov, a long-standing advocate of closer ties with Beijing, praised OBOR in remarks at the Boao Economic Forum.[9] Russia and China formed two bilateral commissions, chaired by Deputy Prime Ministers Dmitry Rogozin and Arkady Dvorkovich and equally high-ranking Chinese officials. The Valdai Discussion Club, a prominent foreign policy think tank, supported the détente with China and contributed extensive policy analysis.[10] Russian oligarchs with stakes in infrastructure and rail who stood to gain from Chinese investment pressed hard for a deal. During Xi's trip to Moscow that May, the Russian and Chinese governments released a bilateral declaration pledging to "link up" OBOR and the EAEU.

On closer inspection, it is clear that the two sides agreed to disagree on what "linking up" actually meant. The official Russian view was that the EAEU would remain an implicitly Russian-led bloc, and that China had promised to partner with it. China by contrast interpreted "linking up" as a bilateral agreement to promote OBOR in Russia.[11] Since Xi and Putin announced the joint statement in 2015, Beijing has continued to negotiate with EAEU members individually, not as a group. The Russian government has continued to resist OBOR investments in its borders, even though US and EU sanctions have made Chinese investment far more attractive in pure economic terms. As of this writing, there are only two major OBOR-related projects active in Russia. The first is the planned Moscow–Kazan high-speed rail link, which has been mired in delays. The second is the liquefied natural gas plant at Yamal in the Russian far north, which Chinese ships are not allowed to access without Russian naval escorts.

From the beginning, the Moscow–Kazan high-speed rail proposal has been a domestic Russian political issue, more about power and patronage than transportation policy. Before 2011, the only high-speed rail scheme under consideration was one to link Moscow and St. Petersburg, a pet project of Denis Muratov, an executive at Russian Railways. A 2011 report found Muratov's project to be unviable.[12] In August 2013, a month before Xi announced the launch of OBOR, the new leader of Russian Railways, Alexander Misharin, announced that another line from Moscow to Kazan would go ahead instead. Misharin had his own reasons for backing the new scheme: it would be the first step toward linking his hometown of Yekaterinburg to the capital.[13]

China billed the Moscow–Kazan line as the crowning achievement of OBOR in Russia, but the more interest China showed, the less enthused Putin seemed to become. Misharin had originally claimed that the project had Putin's full support. Under the initial scheme, the Russian government would fund 70 percent of the project, with the rest coming from the private sector. When China Railway International Group offered $6 billion in debt financing to take the minority stake in the project, the Russian and Chinese governments leaked conflicting information about the terms.[14] Meanwhile, Russian authorities actively solicited bids from Western firms such as Siemens to counter the Chinese.[15] The planned completion date has been pushed back by a decade—to 2028.

Announcements and fanfare have run far ahead of the reality.[16] Just like in Sri Lanka, Tanzania, and Greece, the most important factor affecting the project's implementation has been Russia's opaque domestic politics—not China's strategic plans for transcontinental connectivity. If anything, China's interest has hurt the project's chances of ever being completed. Putin, it seems, would rather have a white elephant railway owned by the Russian state than a successful line owned or run by the Chinese.

Russia and China have cooperated more effectively in the energy sector and in the Arctic, where domestic politics are less of an obstacle. The $27 billion liquefied natural gas plant on the Yamal Peninsula, on Russia's Arctic coast, has been a major success. Russia's Novatek holds a majority stake. The rest is held by Chinese and French firms.[17] Elements of the Chinese party-state clearly see Yamal as a step toward further energy cooperation in the Arctic. China already regards itself as a "near-Arctic state" with vested interests in the region. In January 2018, the State Council released its first white paper on the region, in which it called for "jointly build[ing] a 'Polar Silk Road.'"[18] The two countries are building their own satellite navigation systems—GLONASS and BeiDou—to serve as alternatives to US-run GPS, and Moscow and Beijing are cooperating to make these systems interoperable.[19]

Nevertheless, claims that "Putin and Xi are dreaming of a Polar Silk Road" are premature.[20] Russia has an economic interest in selling more energy to China, but it has an equally clear interest in preventing China from gaining an independent foothold in the Arctic that might one day threaten the offshore fields in Russia's territorial waters. Putin has prioritized the expansion of the Russian navy's northern fleet at Murmansk, ordering the construction of five new icebreakers.[21] These new capabilities will help Russian power projection against US and NATO pressure—but they are also an insurance policy against the threat of Chinese naval encirclement. When the first Chinese merchant vessel followed the polar route to Europe in 2018, the Russians sent naval vessels alongside it, much to Beijing's irritation.

In Central Asia, Russia has successfully contained OBOR's advance even though it cannot match China's investments. Most Central Asian republics have large Russian and Russian-speaking populations, a vestige of Soviet policy that continues to pay political dividends to Moscow. Ethnic and family ties create different types of dependency. For example,

Tajikistan's economy is the most dependent in the world on remittances, most of which come from Tajiks working in Russia. Moscow has secured leases for uranium mines and inked nuclear cooperation agreements with countries from Kazakhstan to Belarus in a bid to counter Chinese influence.[22] Many of these countries do not need to be convinced that China is now a dominant regional power that must be balanced against. The well-publicized system of concentration camps in western China has undermined OBOR's soft power benefits. In addition to Uyghur Muslims, China has targeted ethnic Kazakhs and Kyrgyz in its own borders, sparking outrage across Central Asia.

Finally, China's promises of a New Silk Road of trans-Eurasian rail links to Europe have not materialized, whether because of Russian opposition or a lack of urgency on the Chinese side. Contrary to Chinese OBOR propaganda, less than 5 percent of Chinese exports to Europe are transported by rail, and most transcontinental trains run big losses and pull many empty cars.[23] Moscow has every incentive to preserve this status quo. If China builds a truly functional rail line through Central Asia, it would divert traffic from the Trans-Siberian Railway, severing the economic lifeline of the Russian Far East.

Since 2013, a large body of Western analysis has portrayed OBOR essentially as a Chinese scheme to dominate the geopolitics of the Eurasian continent.[24] These arguments stem in one way or another from the work of Halford Mackinder, a geopolitical theorist. Mackinder called the Eurasian landmass the "geographical pivot of history." In 1919, Mackinder wrote that "who rules the World Island [Eurasia] commands the World."[25] In their own media and in editorials in foreign outlets such as the *Financial Times*, Chinese leaders have repeatedly and categorically denied that OBOR is a hegemonic geostrategy inspired by Mackinder.[26] Graham Allison and many other leading Western commentators disagree. Allison argues in *Destined for War* that through OBOR, "Mackinder's vision may even come to overshadow [Alfred Thayer] Mahan's thesis about the centrality of sea power that has so dominated the minds of strategists for more than a century."[27]

The Russia case shows that Allison is wrong: OBOR is not a Mackinderian strategy. Despite the fanfare, OBOR has not fundamentally changed the existing balance of power in Central Asia. Chinese influence has increased, thanks mainly to purchases of fuel and other commodities.

FIGURE 8.1: Russian President Vladimir Putin speaks during a news conference at the Second Belt and Road Forum for International Cooperation in Beijing, April 27, 2019. Courtesy of Reuters/Sergei Ilnitsky/Pool.

The fact that China has maintained productive relations with Kazakhstan while putting ethnic Kazakhs into internment camps illustrates that OBOR has at least some political value. Yet OBOR has not disrupted the balance of power in Central Asian security, and both Russia and China seem happy with this compromise (fig. 8.1). One study found that China has not invested in a single one of the forty proposed projects that would "support transport connectivity between Western China and Europe through EAEU states."[28] OBOR has increased Chinese influence on the margin, but it has brought about no geopolitical transformation in Russia's backyard.

South China Sea

In Southeast Asia, domestic and regional politics leave no alternative to accepting Chinese investments and acceding to OBOR. Malaysia—the state in the region that has put up the strongest resistance—is the exception that proves the rule. When former Prime Minister Mahathir Mohamad came to power in 2018, he ostentatiously froze all Chinese projects. In particular, he vowed to renegotiate the country's flagship OBOR scheme, China Communications Construction Company's $16 billion East Coast Rail Link (ECRL). In April 2019, Mahathir proudly announced that he had negotiated the price of the ECRL down by $5 billion, a savings of 30 percent. But this renegotiation was a bait and switch, a political performance for a domestic audience. It did not demonstrate that China had planned to exploit Malaysia under the original terms of the deal, and it certainly did not signal a substantial shift of China–Malaysia relations. As Mahathir freely admitted, Malaysia (map 8.2) has no interest in pivoting geopolitically back toward the United States. In fact, Malaysia is more pro-OBOR today than ever before.

Most Southeast Asian countries face a similar dilemma. Many member states of the Association of Southeast Asian Nations (ASEAN) fear China—its massive and concentrated economic power, its influence operations in regional politics, and its island-building activities in the South China Sea. But China has split the eleven-member bloc by courting its poorest members, turning Cambodia and Laos into de facto vassal states.

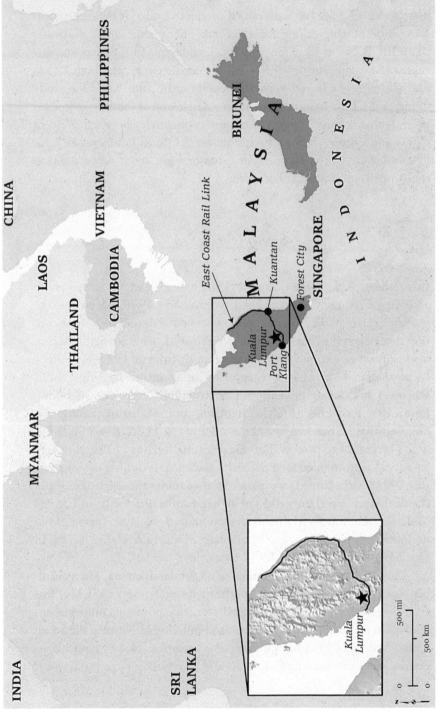

MAP 8.2: Map of Malaysia, courtesy of Scott Walker.

By basing diplomatic relations on trade and investment, OBOR has given China a new tool to divide Southeast Asian countries from each other, leaving the region incapable of collectively resisting China's advances.

On a state visit to Beijing in August 2018, as the press stood by, the newly elected Mahathir brashly accused his hosts of practicing "a new version of colonialism."[29] It was a stunning public rebuke. Three months before, the ninety-three-year old Mahathir had returned from retirement and toppled his former protégé, Najib Razak, in an extraordinary electoral upset. During Mahathir's previous tenure in power, from 1981 to 2003, he aggressively sought friendlier relations with China. Now he was back, provocative and plainspoken, threatening to cancel over $20 billion worth of OBOR contracts in the name of national sovereignty. "We don't want a situation like Sri Lanka," Mahathir's new finance minister, Lim Guan Eng explained, "where they couldn't pay and the Chinese ended up taking over the project." Chinese government agencies raced to contain the damage, issuing dozens of statements defending Malaysia's OBOR projects as "win-win" ventures.

Within months, Mahathir's stunt had blown over and China–Malaysia relations were once again on solid ground. Although some investments were still delayed, Mahathir made clear that he was seeking "renegotiation," not sweeping cancellation. His public show of resistance—followed by quiet acquiescence—is reminiscent of Maithripala Sirisena in Sri Lanka and Alexis Tsipras in Greece. The difference is that, in an era of US retrenchment, there is no other regional power in Southeast Asia strong enough to balance against China. OBOR has therefore become a brand for China's emerging regional hegemony.

China and the Malay kingdoms have had contact for centuries. Ming dynasty records show the first sultan of Malacca, Iskandar Shah, paid four tributary visits to the imperial court of the Yongle emperor between 1405 and 1411.[30] Around this time, a first wave of Chinese laborers began to migrate to Southeast Asia, forming a hybrid culture known as the Peranakan. In the late nineteenth century, Britain extended its influence over peninsular Malaya, which it named the Straits Settlements. Through the 1930s, a second wave of laborers migrated from China's southern coast to work on the British rubber plantations and tin mines. Their descendants in present-day Malaysia have preserved their potpourri of dialects—the Fujianese dialects Hokkien and Hakka, as well as Cantonese. In the first years of the twentieth century, when Sun Yat-sen traveled the world to raise funds for his revolutionary movement in China, he found his warmest reception in the ethnic Chinese enclaves of Malaya and present-day Singapore.

Since the end of the Cold War, Malaysian leaders have hedged by seeking closer ties with China while pressing hard for regional integration. In 1974, Malaysia was among the first Southeast Asian states to recognize the People's Republic of China.[31] In the 1980s and 1990s, Mahathir pursued an independent foreign policy, embraced Malaysia's Muslim roots, and actively pressed for free trade and regional integration. Mahathir ruled as a nationalist. He promised a "a new and peaceful revolution" through market reforms and delivered rapid economic growth by attracting foreign investment and developing the oil sector.[32] In foreign policy, Mahathir spoke his mind while seeking closer relations with all sides. In the late 1990s, he reversed his public criticism of China's territorial claims in the South China Sea and agreed in principle to resolve the dispute bilaterally.[33] China and Malaysia signed a mutual defense agreement in 2005. Mahathir often criticized US foreign policy, too—he once called the Iraq war a "campaign to dominate non-white nations."[34] But this did not stop him from deepening Malaysia's security relationship with Washington, which since 1945 has been the dominant power in Southeast Asia.

Mahathir envisioned a prosperous and independent Malaysia. The country's most valuable strategic resource is its geographic position astride the Straits of Malacca, a strategic chokepoint. Every day, a quarter of the world's traded goods and 17 percent of the global oil supply pass through the 550-mile channel between peninsular Malaysia and the Indonesian island of Borneo. Moving west to east, ships pass Penang and Malacca and finally Singapore, an island off the southern coast. The British recognized the strategic value of the straits in the nineteenth century and built a garrison on Fort Canning overlooking Singapore harbor. The fall of Singapore to the Japanese in 1942 was a devastating blow to the Allied forces, cutting their supply lines between the Indian Ocean and the Pacific. No wonder Malaysia is keenly interested in heading off the risk of great power conflict. Not only would the trade-dependent economy suffer terribly from a blockade, but the country's military is too weak to repel a foreign occupation.[35] Malaysia's commitment to free trade and regional stability is not merely ideological—it is existential. As Mahathir put it in 2018, in an atypical understatement: "We prefer if there are no warships around Malaysia."[36]

After Malaysia, no country is more vulnerable to a blockade of the Malacca Straits than China. Nearly all of China's oil imports from Africa and the Middle East pass through the straits. For decades, the largest and most modern ports have been located in Singapore, which has the added advantage of a world-class financial industry. But Singapore also hosts a permanent US Navy presence. Because of this strategic vulnerability, what Chinese analysts call the "Malacca dilemma" (马六甲 困境), Beijing sees a strong security interest in improving relations and deepening economic interdependence with Malaysia and Singapore.

China's strategy has two prongs. First, the People's Liberation Army Navy is building up a presence in the South China Sea, on the Pacific side of the straits. China wants to be able to impose its own blockade against Japan and South Korea by obstructing navigation through the South China Sea. Second, China is keen to prevent these activities from pushing Malaysia into the arms of the Americans or into some other regional anti-China security bloc. If China controls its own ports and logistics infrastructure along the straits, it will have more economic leverage when it negotiates bilaterally with Malaysia and Singapore. OBOR investments throughout the region are already pulling poorer states such as Myanmar, Cambodia, Laos, and possibly Thailand into structural dependence on Chinese largesse. (Former Australian Foreign Minister Gareth Evans has derisively referred to Cambodia and Laos as "wholly owned subsidiaries of China.")[37] In a crisis, China would exploit these fissures to prevent Southeast Asia from speaking with one voice. In 2016, the two countries blocked an ASEAN resolution condemning Chinese island-building in the South China Sea—just as Greece and Hungary did in the European Union the following year.

When Xi announced the Maritime Silk Road in Indonesia in October 2013, Southeast Asian nations responded positively. They had two main reasons for optimism. First, over the previous two decades, the region had built up elaborate industrial supply chains. For uncommonly trade-dependent economies, more Chinese investment in the logistics sector could be nothing but good news. Second, most Southeast Asian observers thought that OBOR was inevitable in some form or other. Given

Chinese firms' extensive trade with the region, the Chinese government would eventually seek to build its own network of logistics hubs. For the new Chinese leader to frame this development using the rhetoric of globalization and economic openness seemed to be a hopeful sign. In the 2014 Pew Global Attitudes survey, 74 percent of Malaysians reported a positive opinion of China, the third highest figure in the world.[38] Less than seven months after Xi announced OBOR, Malaysia signed a communiqué to join it.

True to Xi's promise, a wave of Chinese investment flooded into Southeast Asia. What proportion of these funds were formally part of OBOR or centrally guided by the Chinese government remains an open question. The lion's share went to projects and companies in real estate, retail, and business services that had only the most tenuous connection to OBOR's supposed "connectivity" goals. Yet the cumulative data speak for themselves: in 2015, Malaysia was the twentieth-largest recipient of China's foreign direct investment. Two years later, it had risen to fourth place.[39]

Chief among China's infrastructure capital investments were port and rail projects. China Communications Construction Company won a $13 billion bid—without a public tender—to construct a 688-kilometer "East Coast Rail Line" between Port Klang on the Malacca Straits and Pengkalan Kubor in the northeast of the peninsula. The line was to be owned and operated by the domestic firm Malaysia Rail Link.[40] On the straits, the $10 billion Melaka Gateway Project consisted of three man-made islands and a cruise ship terminal.[41] China Railway Group began work on a $2.9 billion port and bunkering facility at Kuala Linggi, hoping to attract some lucrative oil bunkering business from Singapore. Another Chinese state-owned firm paid $900 million for a 40 percent stake and thirty-year operational concession at the Malaysian port of Kuantan.

China won so many contracts partly because Malaysia's state governments and business elites were even more keen to do business than was the national government. Seven of Malaysia's states have sultans, each of whom has a large fortune and influences local politics. The sultan of Johor, the Malaysian state just across the causeway from Singapore, was particularly enthusiastic about Chinese investment. What Shenzhen was to Hong Kong, the sultan argued, Johor should be to Singapore. The sultan made $1.1 billion on the Tanjung Puteri development alone, in a joint venture with a Chinese firm.[42] A consortium he led was a major investor in the $100 billion Forest City real estate scheme, the largest Chinese investment project in the country. (The sultan liked to claim that the project was originally his idea, and the Chinese did not correct him.[43]) In the 2018 general election, the sultan took sides, defending himself and condemning Mahathir for "playing the politics of fear and race" with his critique of Chinese investments. The sultan of Selangor, who had also built up extensive business ties with the Chinese, joined the sultan of Johor in supporting Najib Razak, the pro-China candidate in the race. When Mahathir criticized OBOR on the campaign trail, the sultan of Selangor denounced him as "an angry man who will burn the whole country with his anger."[44]

Mahathir's portrayal of Chinese investment as a potential threat to Malaysian national identity struck a chord with the voting public. On the campaign trail, Mahathir drew a connection between the rise of foreign influence and the increasingly unpopular prime minister Najib, who was known to have been cozy with the corporate elite and had been found guilty of pilfering billions of dollars from the state investment fund. Even in Malaysia, an uncommonly open economy, there was an emerging sense that China had amassed so much influence that national sovereignty was in jeopardy. Chinese money visibly touched nearly every sector of the Malaysian economy. In 2017, a Chinese state-owned firm had bought a controlling stake in Proton, the Malaysian "national champion" automaker that Mahathir had painstakingly built up in the 1990s. Mahathir's public comments foreshadowed the anti-China rhetoric that he used successfully on the campaign trail the following year. "As I slip into my final years, or months, or days," he said, "I will watch as our beloved country is sold to foreigners to settle the trillion ringgits that we owe. We will have to sell more and more of our country. I am a sissy. I cry even if Malaysians are dry-eyed. My child is lost. And soon my country."[45]

After winning the 2018 election on a nationalist platform, Mahathir made a big show of standing up to Beijing (fig. 8.2). His supposed success in negotiating down the cost of the ECRL by 30 percent drew international headlines. Yet the bulk of the cost savings came not from driving down the profit margin of the Chinese contractor but from a "comprehensive value engineering exercise." This was the Malaysian government's euphemism for a rerouting that made the rail line less ambitious and less

FIGURE 8.2: Malaysian Prime Minister Mahathir Mohamad with Chinese Premier Li Keqiang in Beijing as he prepares to renegotiate OBOR projects, August 20, 2018. Courtesy of Reuters/Jason Lee.

functional. The ECRL's revised route is forty-eight kilometers shorter, eliminates three of the largest stations, and moves several other stations to less central locations in their respective cities. Perhaps most significant, to save money on tunnel excavation, the line has been rerouted so that it no longer passes through the capital of Kuala Lumpur.[46] In other words, the "cost savings" turned the project into a white elephant. As in Sri Lanka and Greece, Malaysia's threat to cancel the project for good was never truly credible. As the ECRL website admits, "the cost of termination" as opposed to renegotiation "is estimated at [$4 billion] with nothing to show on the ground."[47]

In short, the ECRL renegotiation was not a meaningful realignment of relations with China, nor was it a brilliant show of Mahathir's negotiating prowess. Rather, it was the best Malaysia could do to save face. Just months after his controversial statements in Beijing, Mahathir walked back his comments about a "new version of colonialism," claiming that they were "not at all" directed at Chinese lending practices. He signed a communiqué affirming Malaysia's membership in OBOR and lavished praise on the initiative at the Belt and Road Forum the following year. When the United States began a campaign to pressure its trading partners not to allow Huawei to build 5G telecom infrastructure, Mahathir provocatively pledged to use Huawei products "as much as possible." "Yes, there may be some spying," Mahathir said. "But what is there to spy [on] exactly in Malaysia? We are an open book."[48]

Mahathir's candid remarks on China's rise are devastating retorts to the narrative that there is a mounting "backlash" against OBOR in recipient countries. When an interviewer from the *South China Morning Post* asked him explicitly about the charge that China practices "debt-trap diplomacy," Mahathir admitted that "China has the power derived from its very good growth, in terms of its economy. So they want to use that power to enlarge their influence."[49] Yet he cautioned that this was a "natural reaction" to rising levels of prosperity in China. "We have had China as a neighbor for 2,000 years," he said. "We were never conquered by them. But the Europeans came in 1509—[and] in two years, they conquered Malaysia. So the attitudes of different countries are different. China's attitude of course is to gain as much influence as possible. But so far China doesn't seem to want to build an empire, so we will remain free people." "If you were forced to take sides," the interviewer pressed, "if you had to make a choice—China or the US?" Mahathir's response was matter-of-fact. "Well, it depends on how they behave," he said. "Currently the US is very unpredictable as to the things they do. At this moment, we have to accept that China is close to us—and it is a huge market. We want to benefit from China's growing wealth. So, at this moment, economically, we would prefer China."

Today, other Southeast Asian countries find themselves in similar positions. On the level of individual projects, sufficiently motivated leaders can extract symbolic concessions from China if they push long and hard enough. On a strategic level, however, they have little power to resist OBOR's expansion in the region. At the same time, Southeast Asian states are concerned about the rise of Chinese power, cautiously optimistic that Beijing does not seem to be interested in overt territorial expansion, and resigned to the reality that no country in Southeast Asia is powerful or economically diversified enough to take on China alone. "We have to deal with China whether we like it or not," Mahathir exhorted an audience in Tokyo the month after he took power. "We should deal with it as a group."[50] But OBOR's ability to get businesses, elites, and other domestic political actors on board with China makes this kind of collective bargaining impossible.

South Asia

In South Asia, OBOR's strategic goals are to improve relations with the buffer states that lie between China and India and deepen Chinese influence over Pakistan (map 8.3). China has not fully succeeded on either count, but neither has it failed. Thanks to OBOR, China's diplomatic relationships with Pakistan, Bangladesh, Nepal, Myanmar, and Afghanistan have all strengthened since Xi took power.[51] Fear of OBOR has activated the Indian government to reengage diplomatically with its neighborhood. Since 2017, the Narendra Modi government has joined the Donald Trump administration in a public diplomacy campaign to tar OBOR as "predatory." Indian pressure and generous development aid have persuaded the Himalayan kingdom of Bhutan to boycott OBOR and helped a pro-India government come to power in the Maldives. On balance, however, OBOR is tilting the strategic balance in the region toward China. Backed by money and diplomatic skill, Beijing is cultivating relationships with political parties and local stakeholders that New Delhi cannot match.

OBOR has had the deepest impact in Pakistan, China's closest regional ally. Pakistan is the only OBOR country that can boast its own branded master plan. The China–Pakistan Economic Corridor (CPEC) was once billed as a geopolitical masterstroke that would help China overcome the Malacca dilemma by building an overland shortcut directly to the Indian Ocean.[52] This was a pipe dream. China never planned to ship vast convoys of products through a circuitous Himalayan highway and nearly a thousand miles of ungoverned tribal territory. Sea freight is cheaper and more reliable—and always will be. As a result of these unrealistic expectations, sloppy implementation, and local corruption, CPEC has been costly for both sides, and the countries have taken a temporary step back. Pakistan has locked itself into a position of long-term fiscal dependence, and China now recognizes that it will probably lose a great

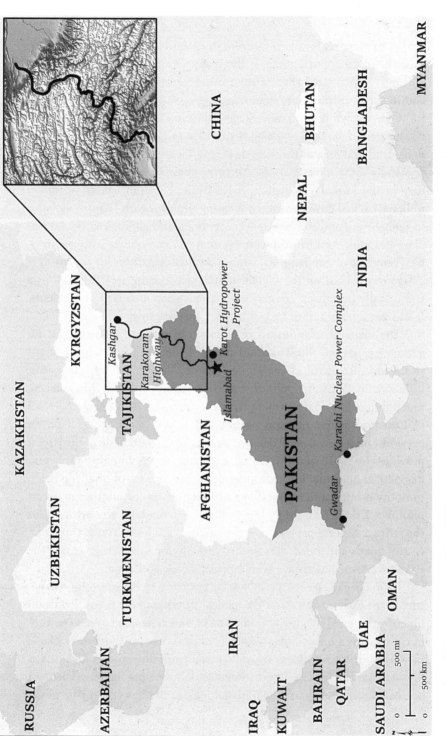

MAP 8.3: Map of Pakistan, courtesy of Scott Walker.

deal of money. Yet CPEC is far from dead, and to call it a debt trap is to miss the more important story. The major factions in Pakistani politics willingly reorganized themselves around Chinese patronage, and they continue to cultivate close ties to Beijing.

China is willing to pay to keep Pakistan stable and loyal. Pakistan was created in 1947 out of a bloody partition of British India that left millions dead and tens of millions displaced. Seven decades later, Pakistan and India remain bitter rivals. All three countries claim disputed territory in the Himalayan region of Kashmir. Pakistan has an unstable, military-backed government, an ongoing problem with Islamist violence in Balochistan and the North-West Frontier, and approximately 150 nuclear weapons. As a Muslim country that shares a border with the troubled province of Xinjiang, Pakistan is a valuable partner for Beijing as it cracks down hard on the Uyghurs. In short, Beijing sees Pakistan as a strategically important country with deeply rooted structural problems. It will pay a premium to keep it in the Chinese camp.

The bilateral relationship is unbalanced because Pakistan has no alternative patron. The Pakistani public is deeply antagonistic toward India and distrustful of the United States. The Arab Gulf states want influence in Pakistani politics, but they are not interested in offering much more aid and investment than they already have. For decades, all of Pakistan's major political parties and balkanized provincial power networks have by necessity oriented themselves toward China. The largest provinces of Sindh and Punjab are each run by a dominant family and its political machine. In the frontier provinces, dozens of smaller parties, minority groups, and regional factions align with one another to access resources from Islamabad. The military, particularly the army, pulls the strings. Since independence, the military has orchestrated three successful coups and ruled the country directly for thirty-three years. The Pakistani Army has always been especially close to China.

China began to express interest in investing in Pakistani infrastructure in the early 2000s. After the nuclear disputes of the 1990s, Pakistani officials had noted that the port of Karachi, which handled over 80 percent of the country's international trade, would be easy for India to blockade in a crisis. The government commissioned feasibility studies for ports at Gwadar and Bin Qasim. International lenders were not interested because both are located in sparsely populated regions in the western part of the country, where Balochi and Sindhi insurgent movements are powerful and the central government's writ barely runs. In 2001, Chinese Premier Zhu Rongji visited Pakistan and promised that the Chinese would build not only the Gwadar port but also a coastal highway to connect it to the population centers in the east. Since then, China's development plan for Gwadar has expanded to include an international airport, a hospital, and other infrastructure.

Gwadar has much in common with Hambantota. For China, the location made some strategic sense. The Pakistanis paid a high interest rate to compensate for the high credit risk, and the process of building the port promised to create opportunities to deepen the bilateral political relationship. For its part, Islamabad was thrilled it had found a funder. China Overseas Ports Holding, a state-owned enterprise, took over Gwadar port on a forty-year concession in May 2013, five months before OBOR was first launched. On November 11, 2015, Pakistan handed over the land rights to 692 acres of land on a forty-three-year lease.[53] The port is growing now, but the profits are wildly lopsided. According to a report commissioned by the Pakistani Senate, China receives 91 percent of the port's revenue for the duration of the concession, and Pakistan gets only 9 percent.[54] Just as in Hambantota, Bagamoyo, and Piraeus, the Chinese firm was allowed to negotiate with itself. Under Article II of the CPEC Framework Agreement, only Chinese firms are allowed to bid for CPEC projects.[55]

Just as in Sri Lanka, once the Gwadar port had gained traction, the Chinese and Pakistani governments signed a secret agreement to link the port into a national infrastructure framework: the "Long Term Plan." The planning process for this was led by the China Development Bank and agreed on by the two governments in December 2015. Pakistan's opposition parties, provincial or local governments, business leaders, and civil society groups were not consulted. The "Long Term Plan" became public only when Pakistani newspaper *Dawn* leaked it in 2017.[56] The document showed that China was much more deeply involved in Pakistan—and stood to profit far more on a project level—than the government had previously let on.

The CPEC "Long Term Plan" was madly ambitious—the largest package of Chinese infrastructure investments anywhere in the world.[57] CPEC would stretch from Gwadar on the Indian Ocean coast to the

Karakoram Highway, which winds its way to the Chinese border between snow-capped Himalayan peaks. It also went far beyond transportation infrastructure, encompassing coal-fired power plants and power distribution networks, twenty-nine Special Economic Zones, urban renewal projects, agriculture, and even a metro rail line in Karachi. China has committed over $62 billion to CPEC, of which it has spent $22 billion as of September 2018.[58]

CPEC was so economically damaging to Pakistan mainly because local politicians rushed its implementation for self-interested reasons. The developmental logic of the plan would have made sense only if the new infrastructure had substantially boosted labor productivity, thus lifting the country's long-term potential growth rate. But the Pakistani politicians and business interests that benefited from CPEC projects used them instead as a short-term economic stimulus funded by dollar-denominated debt. As long as Chinese capital inflows poured in, Pakistan's real annual growth rate soared above 6 percent, far above any plausibly sustainable level. When the flow of CPEC funds into the country slowed in 2018, Pakistan's economy fell into a deep recession.

CPEC also pushed Pakistan into the current account crisis that resulted in the collapse of the rupee. After CPEC was announced in 2013, Pakistan massively increased its imports of Chinese capital equipment and construction materials. By the 2018 fiscal year, Pakistan's trade deficit with China had surpassed $10 billion, an increase of over 400 percent in less than five years. This blew up the current account deficit, and the economy did not have enough money to pay for all the Chinese imports. Pakistan's central bank spent its reserves trying to prop up the rupee at its pegged value. In 2018, the peg broke. With its reserves spent, the central bank had no choice but to let the rupee fall to its true market value. The government was able to smooth out the devaluation by persuading China, Saudi Arabia, and the United Arab Emirates to offer a series of small bailouts. (It is not known what Pakistan promised to secure these funds. Many believe it was long-term land concessions or even secret nuclear deals.) Eventually, China recognized that Pakistan was spending the money not to fix its structural problems but to keep the rupee from falling further. Because Pakistan's loans from China are denominated in dollars or renminbi, the long-term effective cost of its debt load is now more than 40 percent higher than it expected when it borrowed the money. It is now a question of when, not if, Pakistan will have to restructure its debt to China, just as Sri Lanka did.[59]

The tax incentives and sovereign guarantees that Pakistan has quietly conceded will also damage the country's long-term finances in less visible ways. S. Akbar Zaidi has uncovered contracts that give Chinese-built power plants lifetime waivers on corporate taxes.[60] The Pakistani government has made sovereign guarantees to some Chinese power producers to meet 22 percent of their liabilities—whether or not they are profitable. Chinese enterprises entering Pakistani agriculture "will be offered extraordinary levels of assistance from the Chinese government," including "free capital and loans," from the China Development Bank. The Pakistani government has not made public any analysis of how these tax concessions will affect national finances, let alone how the impact of these new incentives will affect the economy. They may be harder for Pakistan to restructure than the national debt.

It was not just the politicians to blame: Pakistan's powerful military also used CPEC deals with China to enrich itself and tighten its grip on the country's politics and economy.[61] From 2013 through the election in August 2018, the military battled with Prime Minister Nawaz Sharif and his powerful family. Sharif was also inclined toward China, and the two sides laid aside their differences in supporting CPEC. In fact, the early years of CPEC were marked by intense secrecy and corruption precisely because the Chinese were playing Sharif's faction and the military leadership off of each other. What little opposition CPEC faced came from outside Islamabad—power brokers in the provinces who feared that the centralized planning process would deny them a cut of the spoils. In 2018, with the support of the military and the tacit assent of the Chinese, Sharif was ousted in a corruption scandal.

In the next elections, Imran Khan came to power on a populist platform similar to Mahathir's in Malaysia. Also like Mahathir, Khan was an outsider. He pledged to investigate and reexamine CPEC projects under the guise of auditing his predecessor's corrupt and wasteful spending. Before the economic crisis hit, his main complaint was not that the debt load was unsustainable but that CPEC was unfair to Pakistani firms. "Chinese companies received tax breaks" that gave them an "undue advantage," he said. "One of the things we're looking at because it's not fair that Pakistan companies should be disadvantaged."[62] Khan entered government with a sincere desire to shine light on CPEC projects, though he never contemplated pulling out of CPEC entirely.

But pressure from the military and the disastrous state of the economy made it impossible for Khan to challenge Beijing after he took office. Less than three months after Khan took power, the *Financial Times* published a dramatic front-page report, headlined "Pakistan Rethinks Its Role in Xi's Belt and Road Plan."[63] The story followed a visit to Islamabad by Wang Yi, the Chinese foreign minister. Citing sources at the highest level of the Pakistani government, including the new finance and commerce ministers, the article reported that Khan planned to "review or renegotiate agreements" with China, which he considered "unfair and financially onerous." One close associate of Khan said that CPEC might be put on hold. Still reeling from Mahathir's visit to Beijing, the Chinese government raced to repair the diplomatic damage. Pakistani's army chief made an emergency visit to Beijing.[64] Despite the public evidence that CPEC's terms have been wildly unfavorable to Pakistan, Khan has continued to signal that the country's primary loyalty remains to China (fig. 8.3).

Pakistan's leading opponents of CPEC have also framed their opposition in terms of costs and benefits for local communities, not hostility to China itself. For example, Senator Azam Moosa Khel argued that "CPEC will not be successful" because "the people of Balochistan have not gained anything."[65] A few intellectuals and scholars on the national level lambasted CPEC as misuse of public funds.[66] Yet no major voices dispute that Pakistan's economic future depends on partnership with China. In March 2019, the two countries established a CPEC Political Parties Joint Consultation Mechanism, which brings representatives from all of Pakistan's political parties and provincial factions to China for closed-door negotiations with the Chinese Communist Party.[67]

Much like Mahathir, Khan entered office determined to reorient his country's engagement with OBOR. He had the misfortune to inherit a succession of crises that put his reform plans on the back burner. In particular, the current account crisis that CPEC had brought about forced him to travel to China multiple times, hat in hand, during his first year in office. Now, rather than holding Beijing to account, Khan has resigned himself to doubling down. In October 2019, Islamabad set up a

FIGURE 8.3: Pakistani Prime Minister Imran Khan speaks at the opening ceremony for the Second Belt and Road Forum in Beijing, behind replica Long March series Chinese rockets, in Beijing, China, April 26, 2019. Courtesy of Reuters/Jason Lee.

new agency to "eliminate bureaucratic hurdles" to CPEC implementation and "accelerate the pace" once again.[68]

The Middle East

In the Middle East, China has quietly capitalized on US disengagement by using OBOR to deepen its political relationships. Since 2010, China has supplanted the United States as the largest buyer of Middle Eastern energy. It is now the largest or second-largest trading partner of every major country in the region. Iran, Iraq, Egypt, Qatar, the United Arab Emirates, Saudi Arabia, and Turkey have all signed memoranda of understanding expressing approval for the OBOR concept and committing (in vague language) to partnering with it. The UAE is "willing to continue to actively participate in OBOR cooperation," *Xinhua* reported after Xi's visit to Abu Dhabi in 2018.[69] "The Iraqi side is willing to deepen pragmatic cooperation in various fields within the OBOR framework," it wrote, cryptically, after Xi's trip to Baghdad in 2018.[70] Even Israel, the closest US ally in the region, has angered Washington by accepting a bid from a Shanghai-based construction group to modernize and take a twenty-five-year operational lease on the port of Haifa. Yet China has tried to keep its diplomatic engagement in the Middle East out of the headlines. It has also kept its infrastructure and construction footprint in the region as light as possible. A curiously large share of Middle Eastern countries' OBOR agreements have never been released in full—in English, Chinese, or the local language. This indicates Beijing's intense fear of getting pulled into the region's national rivalries and sectarian conflicts.

Across the Middle East, OBOR has been most useful for Beijing in improving relations with Iran (map 8.4), which sees China as a likeminded critic of the US-led international order. Iranian views on China fall into two major camps. The moderately pro-China "reformist" faction wants to improve relations with both East and West. The "hardline" anti-American faction wants to bet the farm on the relationship with Beijing. The US withdrawal from the 2015 nuclear deal has empowered the hardline pro-China faction. Beijing is working hard to deepen ties, including illicitly buying Iranian oil in defiance of US sanctions.

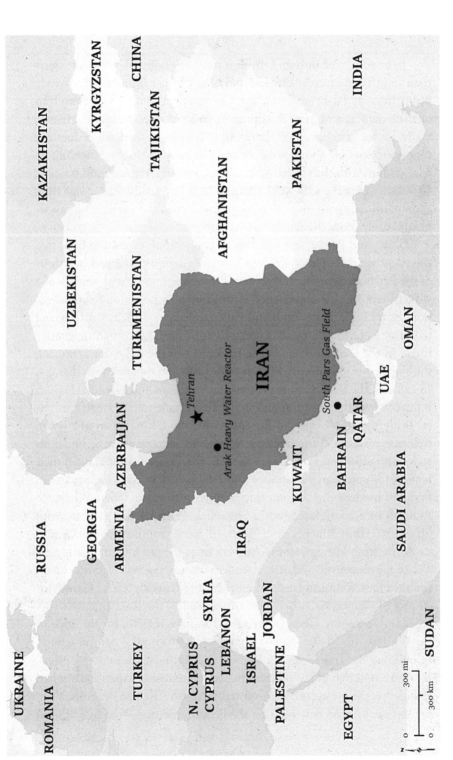

MAP 8.4: Map of Iran, courtesy of Scott Walker.

To be sure, even in Iran, OBOR is more of a political brand for China than an infrastructure investment initiative. China has promised relatively little capital and delivered even less. Chinese firms pulled back from Iran of their own accord after Washington targeted telecom giants Huawei and ZTE for doing business there. All this suggests that China does not care quite enough about partnership with Iran to risk endangering its relationships with the United States, Israel, and the Arabian Gulf states. It also shows how the OBOR slogan can be a powerful tool for signaling and coordinating political alignment, even when the underlying investments barely move the needle in macroeconomic terms.

China and Persia have a history of cooperation extending back two thousand years. Explorer Zhang Qian (see chapter 3) stopped just short of the Parthian domains and returned from his journey with reports of a western empire that approached China's own in power and sophistication. In 115 BCE, Han Wudi and Parthian Emperor Mehrdad II agreed to jointly fight the Xiongnu, a nomadic tribe posing a recurring security threat in the Central Asian borderlands.[71] Over the following centuries, the empires steadily deepened their trade links and diplomatic exchanges. In 224 CE, the Sassanians overthrew the Parthians and extended Persian influence over the most important Silk Road trade routes. Persian travelers bringing Buddhism and Zoroastrianism to China received a warm welcome from the Tang dynasty. When the Sassanians came under attack during the Arab conquest in 661 CE, the Tang emperor granted their request for emergency assistance and established an Area Command of Persia in modern-day Afghanistan. Chinese assistance failed to halt the Arab advance, so the last Sassanian monarch, Peroz III, fled to China with his retinue. The Chinese city of Xi'an still has a prominent monument to its Zoroastrian history just blocks away from the old imperial palace.[72]

In the nineteenth and early twentieth centuries, a new common threat emerged for China and Persia: the British and Russian "Great Game" for control of Central Asia. Between 1803 and 1828, the Russian empire occupied modern-day Georgia, Armenia, and Azerbaijan, on the edge of Persia's domain.[73] Later, Russia dominated its Central Asian hinterland by building the Trans-Caspian Railway and setting up military garrisons. By the second half of the nineteenth century, Russian expansionism had emerged as the greatest threat to Britain's South Asian possessions. Viceroy George Curzon believed that the Persian question—the urgent need to turn Persia into a pliable buffer state between India and Russia—was a critical interest for Britain. In 1872, Curzon negotiated the Reuter concession with the Persian shah, an agreement more humiliating than any unequal treaty Britain forced on China after the Opium Wars.

Britain and Russia continued to threaten Iran and China in the twentieth century. From 1908 onward, the Anglo-Persian Oil Company (later renamed British Petroleum) monopolized Iranian energy production for imperial use. In 1941, after the German invasion of the Soviet Union, the British and Soviets jointly invaded Iran to secure its oil fields and rail lines against Axis attack. In 1953, Iranian Prime Minister Mohammad Mosaddegh tried to nationalize the Anglo-Persian Oil Company, so the British and Americans overthrew him. China was sympathetic to Tehran's position. When Mohammad Reza Pahlavi allied with the United States in 1959, Beijing blamed US "hegemonism" for forcing his hand.[74] A decade later, the Sino–Soviet split created a new shared interest for China and Iran: containing the spread of Soviet influence in India, Central Asia, and Iraq. Beijing and Tehran established diplomatic relations in 1971. In the following two decades, they used their relationship with one another as leverage to extract aid and arms sales from the United States.[75]

After the shah was deposed in the 1979 Islamic Revolution, China actively began to play up the two countries' shared history of colonial humiliation. China had badly misplayed its hand by continuing to back the shah even after he had fled the country.[76] With the new ayatollah proclaiming a foreign policy of "neither West nor East," and the prospect that the Soviets would seize the advantage, Beijing feared it had lost its most important partner in the Middle East. Chinese Premier Hua Guofeng visited Tehran to apologize—abjectly—for failing to support the revolution.[77] Thereafter, China increased the frequency of state visits to Iran and directed its diplomats to play up the countries' common anticolonial identity. China showed goodwill to the Islamic Republic by covertly selling it weapons systems. By 1987, just before the end of the Iran-Iraq War, 70 percent of Tehran's arms supplies came from either China or North Korea.[78] China's efforts to reconstitute the relationship with Iran had succeeded. The driver of détente was common geopolitical interest, lubricated by a revisionist account of the countries' long history of partnership. "Factual accuracy," Garver observes wryly, was "not the crux."[79]

China and Iran dramatically expanded their relations in the late 1990s and early 2000s. In January 2002, US President George W. Bush named Iran as part of the "Axis of Evil." Three years later, hardliner President Mahmoud Ahmadinejad came to power arguing that Iran should "look east" to seek new export markets in East Asia. Iran dramatically expanded its oil exports to Taiwan, South Korea, and Japan, but China was the most important market. Beijing supported Tehran's attempts to build "civilian" nuclear capacity in the 2000s, over the objections of the United States. In that decade, China replaced South Korea as Iran's leading source of consumer goods and as the largest buyer of Iranian oil.

Today, all of Iran's major political factions are pro-China, particularly the so-called hardliner grouping. The question of factions in Iranian politics is hotly debated. However, it is fair to say that Ayatollah Khameini and the clerical bureaucracy that he controls are hardline in the sense that they believe the West to be inherently untrustworthy. Iran's clerical and parliamentary system operate in parallel, and the ayatollah exercises a de facto veto over the president's policy decisions through his control of the Guardian Council. Almost as powerful as the ayatollah is the Islamic Revolutionary Guard Corps (IRGC), a military-industrial conglomerate that controls all major sectors of the economy, as well as Iran's missile and nuclear programs. The IRGC strongly opposes détente and trade with the West, arguing that Iranian national strategy should focus on improving ties to China and, to a lesser extent, Russia.[80] The IRGC has a great deal to gain from OBOR investments in strategic sectors and from a broader expansion in bilateral trade with China.

Some observers distinguish a "neoconservative" faction associated with former president Ahmadinejad: this faction is more anti-Western than it is pro-China. With representation in both the military and clerical bureaucracy, the neoconservatives advocate more populist economic policy and promise to export the fruits of the revolution.[81] They seek strategic flexibility and support expanding economic ties with all of the major Asian countries. During Ahmadinejad's presidency (2005–2013), Iran greatly expanded its oil exports to Japan, Korea, Taiwan, and Southeast Asia while it pursued a nuclear weapons program.[82] In the five years after Ahmadinejad took power, all three Chinese major state energy companies signed contracts to explore and drill for oil in Iran. China committed to downstream production as well, including refineries at Hormuz and Abadan.[83] Ahmadinejad's "look east" policy was prescient. When the Barack Obama administration imposed crippling sanctions on Iran over its nuclear program, trade with Asia offered crucial breathing room.

Iran's reformist or moderate faction also supports closer relations with China, but only in the context of a broader strategy to reintegrate into the international system. This faction is most closely associated with former President Mohammad Khatami, and to a lesser extent the current president, Hassan Rouhani (fig. 8.4). The reformists believe that Chinese foreign policy is more realistic than ideological. They fear that Beijing will abandon Iran if Washington makes the cost of doing business with Iran outweigh the benefits. China voted "yes" on all four US-backed UN Security Council resolutions to tighten sanctions on Iran. To the Iranian reformists, this proves that China cares more about preserving its relationship with Washington than it cares about Tehran. The rational choice is to hedge by engaging both sides.[84]

Washington's actions have made it possible for China to thread this needle, putting economic pressure on Iran while retaining its special relationship. During the Iran nuclear negotiations, Chinese diplomats repeatedly urged Iran to compromise.[85] When Foreign Minister Wang Yi visited Tehran in February 2015 to pitch OBOR to Rouhani, he spoke of the potential for vast Chinese investment in Iranian infrastructure, but warned that "the reality [is] that resolution of the nuclear issue is a precondition."[86] After China helped get Iran to agree to the deal later that year, Xi visited again and announced several joint projects in the energy, transportation, port, and rail sectors, plus a memorandum of understanding marking Iran's accession to OBOR. Thus, when Iran's disputes with the West posed larger geopolitical headaches, China held out the prospect of OBOR membership to motivate Iran to compromise. After the nuclear deal was signed, China used OBOR to help keep Iran from drifting back into the Western camp.

More than investments, the OBOR brand has been a critically important political tool for Iran and China to signal their continued desire for partnership. In 2018, the Trump administration withdrew from the Iran nuclear deal and began to pressure European countries and Iran's other largest trading partners to restrict their trade with the country. Soon after, French oil company Total withdrew from Phase II of its multibillion-dollar project to develop the South Pars oil field, citing political risks.

FIGURE 8.4: Iranian President Hassan Rouhani and Chinese President Xi Jinping review an honor guard during a welcome ceremony at the Xijiao State Guest House in Shanghai, May 22, 2014. Courtesy of Reuters/Kenzaburo Fukuhara/Pool.

China's state-owned China National Petroleum Corporation (CNPC) bought a controlling position in a deal that Iranian politicians proudly linked to OBOR. China moved forward with a plan to build a high-speed rail line from Tehran to Mashhad, also under the OBOR umbrella. Chinese media boast of a "Chinese-led initiative to redesign Iranian heavy water reactor in Arak . . . aimed at minimizing its plutonium production."[87]

In 2019, China began to pull back from Iran, seeming to confirm the reformists' fears that it would never be a reliable patron. In defiance of US sanctions, China continued to buy several hundred thousand barrels a day of black-market Iranian oil. But Chinese firms vulnerable to US retaliation began to plot their retreat. In March, Huawei laid off most of its 250 employees in Iran. So did Lenovo, the electronics manufacturer. In October 2019, CNPC announced that it would pull out of the South Pars phase II development. The bank that had facilitated the CNPC's involvement had come under the gun of US sanctions, and the corporate leadership was no longer willing to risk losing its access to the dollar financial system.[88]

Amid this pullback, Iranian political elites have become more explicitly supportive of OBOR than ever before. "It is not as if [OBOR] is canceled if we don't participate," Asghar Fakhrieh Kashan, Iran's deputy transport minister, said in 2017. "There are . . . political advantages to Iran [joining], compared to Russia. [The Chinese] are highly interested in working with us." As Fakhrieh Kashan understands it, "the Chinese plan is designed in such a way that it will establish Chinese hegemony across half of the world." He clarifies that "Iran will put its own interests first," but notes that selective engagement with OBOR "will give us huge access to new markets."[89] The Trump administration's return to a maximum pressure strategy since 2018 has intensified Iran's desire to send friendly signals to China. In August 2019, Iranian Foreign Minister Mohammad Javad Zarif wrote in an editorial in the *Global Times* that Iran "strongly supports China's position on the so-called 'trade war' and regards the protectionist approach of the U.S. and its abandonment of rules-based trade concepts as being counterproductive, unreasonable, and destructive. Moreover, Iran has always strongly supported the 'One China Policy,' praised the achievements of 'one country, two systems' and rejected any interference in the internal affairs of China."[90]

The COVID-19 pandemic, which hit Iran early and hard, has pushed Tehran and Beijing closer together for similar reasons. Starting in February 2020, senior Chinese officials began to promote conspiracy theories designed to antagonize and vilify the United States. "It might be US army who brought the epidemic to Wuhan," Chinese Foreign Ministry spokesman Zhao Lijian tweeted on March 12, 2020. "Be transparent! Make public your data! US owe us an explanation!"[91] Within the next two weeks, China sent medical teams to support Iran's public health response, Iran's Supreme Leader Ayatollah Ali Khamenei echoed Zhao's comments that COVID-19 may have been a US bio-weapon, and the Chinese foreign minister called on Washington to lift its sanctions on the Iranian regime.[92]

Across the Middle East, China wishes to brand itself as a purely commercial partner with an active disinterest in regional rivalries. Of all the countries in the region, history and geopolitics seem to align China's interests most clearly with Iran—which, like Pakistan, has no alternative patrons. China is willing to welcome Iran into its sphere of influence only if the risk of backlash from Washington and other regional powers is relatively contained. China is now the largest buyer from every major oil-producing country in the region, and it grows more dependent on imported fossil fuels from this area with each passing year.[93] Beijing does not want its activities in the Middle East to trigger fear and anger in the United States. It has learned from Washington's misadventures in Iraq, Afghanistan, and Libya that military interventions are costly and complicated to wind down. In the end, China's current relationship with the Middle East is quite favorable: it reaps the commercial benefits of a stable regional order underwritten—at great expense—by the United States. The purpose of OBOR in the Middle East is to preserve this status quo.

Conclusions

In all four regions discussed in this chapter, US foreign policy has influenced recipient countries' decisions to join OBOR and seek investments from China. The United States imposed sanctions on Russia after the annexation of Crimea in February 2014. Within months, Russian diplomats were in Beijing to discuss "linking up" OBOR and the Russia-led EAEU. When the Trump administration withdrew from the Trans-Pacific Partnership in 2017, it left Malaysia with little leverage to renegotiate its OBOR-branded projects. US–Pakistan relations have been souring for a decade, but the Trump administration's 2018 decision to cancel $3 billion in annual aid drove relations to a new low. In one fell swoop, Trump weakened Islamabad's finances, antagonized the military, and confirmed the suspicions of many Pakistanis that their government had no choice but to continue with CPEC. Finally, the US withdrawal from the Iranian nuclear deal weakened the Rouhani government, which is relatively skeptical of Chinese influence, and empowered hardline factions such as the IRGC that profit from closer ties to China.

In none of these cases did the US president consider OBOR as a major factor in policymaking. Yet each decision had the effect of weakening the other country in the negotiation it would hold next: the one with Beijing.

CONCLUSION

How Should the West Respond?

This book has diagnosed OBOR as a profound challenge to the supremacy of the West. Now that the time has come to discuss prescriptions, "the West" itself becomes a problematic category. I have used the term throughout the book as a shorthand for the United States and the alliance structure and multinational institutions it controls. In truth, OBOR poses unique dangers and offers different opportunities to each Western country. For the United Kingdom, it might be strategically wise to establish some sort of relationship with OBOR before beginning trade negotiations with the European Union and the United States. On the other hand, for Australia, the potential rewards of access to the Chinese market might not be worth the price of handing Beijing new tools for covert political influence. There is far too little space here to discuss the trade-offs for each Western country individually. Instead, I focus on the strategic decision that Washington faces, and I use "the West" as a collective term for the United States and those of its international partners that see an overriding interest in maintaining US supremacy.

First, a quick review of the book's main empirical findings. Part I argues that OBOR was originally conceived not to launch a novel type of commercial project but to impose some conceptual order on a sprawling, existing collection of foreign investments. In the process, Xi Jinping and his advisers hoped, the new OBOR framework would help advance China's political interests in the countries where it does business by allowing Chinese companies to operate at the behest of the state. Part I also shows how in certain contexts the OBOR slogan functions like a brand

with multiple layers of meaning. On the surface, and when China artic-
ulates the brand to Western audiences, OBOR is a boilerplate slogan
about the virtues of cooperation and connectivity. On a deeper, plausibly deniable level, the Chinese government pitches OBOR as a project to
resurrect the imperial tributary system—a regional or even global order
in which weaker countries pay obeisance to Beijing and receive gifts and
political backing in return.

The tributary concept is also useful for understanding how OBOR
changes incentive structures for Chinese actors. Those who praise and promote Xi's favored brand are rewarded, for they indirectly signal their
loyalty to Xi himself. OBOR can also be seen as a tool of Chinese domestic governance or an extension of Xi's cult of personality. The program's
implementation has taken the form of a bottom-up campaign, driven not
so much by the central government as by lower-ranking companies and
institutional actors who seek to please the party leadership.

Part II discusses the experiences of recipient countries in comparative perspective. Over time, interaction with OBOR tends to pull these
countries into closer political alignment with China. In this light, OBOR
takes on yet another face: not so much an investment policy as an emerging pattern of interactions and negotiations between Chinese firms, the
Chinese state, and foreign actors. Two key themes stand out from the case
studies. First, recipient countries tend to see China through the lens of
their own history and regional position. When their politicians and business elites negotiate with China, they are almost always preoccupied by
short-term, local issues: an upcoming election, an economic downturn,
the need to be seen as standing strong against a regional rival. Second,
politicians from new factions or opposition parties frequently rise to power
after criticizing their predecessors for botching negotiations with China.
But China has mastered the art of the renegotiation, and recipient countries rarely hold out for long. This proves that there are political benefits
from engaging with OBOR that go beyond the profitability of the underlying projects.

The bottom line is that politicians, senior advisers, and businesspeople outside the developed world are *far* more enthusiastic about OBOR
than one might assume from reading the *New York Times* or reports from
Washington think tanks. They are excited to join a formalized political-
economic partnership with China not because Beijing has deceived them

or lured them into debt traps but because of genuine self-interest. Even when OBOR deals go badly, most politicians in recipient countries take responsibility for their own decisions rather than claiming that China coerced them. Hardly anyone who has been on the other side of the table from Chinese negotiators describes OBOR as the "predatory" scheme that many US officials insist it is.

When it comes to building infrastructure megaprojects, the United States and the multilateral lenders it supports simply cannot compete. Not only does China have money, expertise, and a track record of rapid results, it is also more willing to lend to nondemocratic governments and steamroll local and environmental opposition. The success of the infrastructure-driven development model inside China has given Beijing the confidence to take on ambitious, long-term projects that Western countries would consider too risky to do themselves.

As I write these words, many US foreign policy experts are indulging in a new round of wishful thinking. Three scholars at the Council on Foreign Relations recently argued that "China's COVID-19 response [has] all but halted the Belt and Road Initiative in its tracks," citing temporary delays in construction projects.[1] Daniel Russell, who ran Asia policy at the National Security Council and State Department during the Barack Obama administration, predicts that many countries will blame OBOR for the global spread of COVID-19 and lose "enthusiasm for the kind of connectivity and dependence that China promotes."[2] As Russell puts it, "accepting a degree of Chinese influence, along with funding and infrastructure, is one thing; accepting pathogens is quite another."

To the contrary, I expect that the COVID-19 pandemic will intensify and accelerate all of the trends described in this book. As in the Spanish flu of 1918–20, developing countries with weak public health systems are likely to suffer the worst of the human and economic consequences. The United States and even some European countries are restricting exports of medical supplies, forcing countries like Italy to beg China for masks, ventilators, and other life-saving protective equipment. The economic contraction resulting from the pandemic is hitting emerging markets particularly hard—busting budgets, breaking currency pegs, driving up inflation, and forcing many poor countries to renegotiate their debts, particularly those denominated in US dollars. Meanwhile, COVID-19 seems likely to push the United States and European countries into a mood of isolationism and retrenchment, much as the Spanish flu did a century ago.

China, having contained the virus at home, is intervening in the global response with unprecedented confidence and assertiveness. Chinese public health administrators have occasionally invoked the metaphor of a "health Silk Road" (健康丝绸之路) since 2017.[3] Now Xi Jinping has embraced that slogan—illustrating that Chinese medical aid will come with much fanfare and at a political price. In March 2020, as the COVID-19 pandemic spread, the Serbian government publicly pleaded with Beijing to send medical aid. When the shipment arrived, a progovernment tabloid posted an enormous billboard facing the National Assembly building in Belgrade. "Thank you, Big Brother Xi!" it read in Chinese and Serbo-Croatian captions.[4] In June 2020, Xi promised sweeping debt relief for African OBOR countries hit by COVID-19. It may be years before we understand the full significance of COVID-19 for the global balance of power. For now, this much is clear: China is mounting a renewed push to take the mantle of global leadership from the United States—and it is beginning to pressure other countries to take sides.

Where Is OBOR Going?

In China, OBOR's conceptual reach will continue to expand as long as companies and institutions see political incentives to associate themselves with it. On September 3, 2018, for example, the front page of the *People's Daily* mentioned OBOR twenty times and Xi's name forty-four times.[5] Universities have set up over a hundred think tanks and centers for the study of OBOR or "Xi Jinping Thought."[6] Chinese companies sponsor OBOR conferences on topics from kitchen appliances to cosmetics, from blockchain to beer. So do their foreign competitors, because they also want access to the Chinese market. Chinese state agencies continue to extend the OBOR brand to new domains—a digital Silk Road built on blockchain or a Silk Road in outer space. As Xi looks forward to a third term in power, he is unlikely to reduce pressure on the party's propaganda apparatus to sustain his cult of personality.

Chinese megaprojects are also advancing on the ground, even as Washington tries to push back. In 2018 the United States and some of its allies began to implement new screening procedures to monitor Chinese investment into strategic infrastructure. One emerging domain of competition is over Huawei, a secretive firm with ties to the People's Liberation Army and a global leader in 5G mobile telecommunications technology. Huawei has a track record of spying: when China funded the construction of a new headquarters for the African Union, Huawei installed a cyber backdoor in the building's IT systems.[7] Even so, Huawei is the telecom of choice for most African countries. It is now expanding into Latin America and the Caribbean. Even though backdoor access to the world's 5G networks could potentially give China the ultimate surveillance tool, close US allies such as the United Kingdom and Germany have refused to push out Huawei altogether.

One reason so many countries associate with OBOR is that "member" status does not carry any specific responsibilities. OBOR itself has multiple dimensions—physical, political, institutional, and symbolic—and there are many tiers of membership. The only requirement is to sign a memorandum committing to the abstract values of win-win, mutual cooperation, and so forth. Each OBOR "member state" has wide latitude to define what its involvement means, while reaping the political benefits of alignment with China. If Chinese publications with prominent ties to the Communist Party cite conflicting information about which countries and projects are "in" or "out" of OBOR, it is because even they recognize that OBOR membership was never intended to be a precise label. The lower the bar for membership, the more countries will join—and the more weight the brand will carry. For now, OBOR (or #OBOR, as we might call it) is not yet an alliance or bloc of states in the traditional sense. The main strategic advantage that China derives from it is the set of political relationships it has built with foreign politicians and political parties and the intangible status benefit of showing how many countries want Beijing as a partner.

However, it is easy to see how OBOR in the future could broaden and deepen into a China-led trading bloc. On the most obvious level, China needs to manage its slow but inevitable decoupling from the US consumer market, as both major US political parties move toward protectionism. When Xi speaks of "greening" OBOR, he refers to China's industrial strategy to move up the value chain by exporting high-tech products like electric vehicles, power grid infrastructure, and generators for wind, solar, hydroelectric, and nuclear power. Through investments in lithium and cobalt mines in Chile, Bolivia, and the Democratic Republic of Congo, China has already secured its supplies of the critical and scarce minerals needed to make high-powered batteries. China will also need to secure consumer markets in which to sell these finished goods. If the US market is no longer open, an integrated OBOR market could be an alternative.

The smart or digital branch of OBOR could also be a vehicle for China to internationalize its tech and financial giants. Many countries—including some democracies—are tempted by Chinese facial recognition technologies and Big Data software for surveillance and social control. Alibaba, the Chinese equivalent of Amazon, is competing fiercely with Amazon in the developing world, building data centers and offering subsidized cloud computing services to governments and businesses. Even more important, the Chinese mobile payment services WeChat Pay and AliPay could internationalize the use of China's currency and collect vast quantities of data by offering zero-fee financial services to people in low-income countries. Western competitors such as PayPal currently lag far behind. Finance, tech, telecoms, and energy—in some OBOR countries, Chinese firms could soon control them all.

High-tech investments will be key to transforming OBOR from a loose collection of associated countries into a tighter-knit bloc with shared geopolitical interests. In outer space and cyberspace, Chinese infrastructure built out under the banner of OBOR will dramatically improve the Chinese military's capabilities in C4ISR—the full suite of command, control, communications, computers, intelligence, surveillance, and reconnaissance.[8] Wherever Huawei controls undersea cables or 5G infrastructure, Chinese intelligence agencies will potentially be able to access and manipulate flows of data. As China builds its capabilities and grows its international presence, it will become a desirable security and intelligence-sharing partner for many countries. It will also become a key merchant of arms, intelligence, and security technology to states that do not get along with the United States, and a power broker in the regions discussed in this book. As Europe has discovered with Google and Facebook, once a technology platform achieves scale in a country, it becomes extraordinarily hard to dislodge.

Could OBOR die out as Chinese economic growth slows? Maybe, but probably not. China's average annual GDP growth rate has already fallen by half since its heyday in the early 2000s, but it is still growing more than twice as fast as that of the United States and approximately five times as fast as Japan and the Eurozone. Because of the astonishing growth rate, China's total outbound flows of capital can still grow over the longer term, even as they become a smaller share of total GDP. Consider these figures to illustrate the point. In 2018, China's total stock of foreign direct investments abroad, including every OBOR project on Earth, was worth only 14 percent of Chinese GDP—far below the average for members of the Organisation for Economic Co-operation and Development. In the same year, the United States's foreign direct investment stock was worth 31 percent of its GDP. Japan's was 32 percent.[9] Simply put, most wealthy and developed economies have huge amounts of wealth tied up in investments abroad. As China grows wealthier and more developed, we should expect it to converge toward the global average. Indeed, the more China's growth rate slows, the more relentless Beijing will likely become in stealing foreign intellectual property, subsidizing high-tech industries, and prying open new markets.

OBOR is also increasingly linked with something even more important to Chinese leaders than the growth rate: the defense of the nation. OBOR infrastructure promises to help the People's Liberation Army and Navy operate further from the homeland, even without dedicated military bases. The US military has been tracking Chinese port-building in the Indian Ocean for almost two decades. As early as 2004, consulting firm Booz Allen Hamilton postulated that China was building a "string of pearls" from the South China Sea into the Indian Ocean—a series of ports encircling the Indian subcontinent.[10] After years of intense study, US military analysts have concluded that these ports are not well suited to conversion into conventional naval bases, and their designs as commercial ports make them vulnerable to missile strikes.[11] Still, in peacetime these sites will be valuable "dual-use" facilities that enable Chinese naval vessels to conduct longer and more frequent missions in the far seas.[12]

It is also inevitable that China's bilateral relationships with many OBOR countries will eventually expand into the security realm. In Cambodia, for example, Beijing has begun work on a new naval base.[13] Recent research has found that private Chinese security companies are active in more OBOR countries than was previously believed.[14] The Chinese People's Armed Police have personnel stationed in Central Asia, collaborating with local authorities to monitor the borders of Xinjiang province. Pakistan has promised to dedicate between 10,000 and 12,000 security personnel to protect Chinese projects. Even if China does not want to defend these foreign holdings, it may have no choice if circumstances put its personnel at risk.

China is actively readying its population for a new era in which Beijing routinely needs to deploy its security forces abroad. Chinese studios have released several blockbuster films about security crises in OBOR countries. The most famous example is the Rambo-style *Wolf Warrior 2* (战狼2), which became the highest-grossing Chinese film of all time on its release in 2017. The movie follows Leng Feng, an elite Chinese special forces agent, whose team deploys in an unnamed African country to save a group of Chinese aid workers who have been taken hostage. The hapless Americans offer no help, and Leng saves the day. The film ends with the words: "Don't give up if you run into danger abroad. Please remember, a strong motherland will always have your back!"[15]

Three Imperfect Options

The United States and its allies have no silver bullet for responding to OBOR, but they do have a measure of choice. They can shift to a much more assertive containment strategy. They can hedge, criticizing OBOR and pushing back selectively, without mobilizing vast resources to respond to it. Or they can join OBOR and try to shape it from within. Each option has trade-offs.

The first and most aggressive option is to contain and undermine. If a Cold War–style dynamic between the United States and China is inevitable, the West should press its advantage while time is still on its side. Drawing on the Cold War strategy of "containment," which eventually brought about the collapse of global communism, the West should expose China's attempts to infiltrate other countries' political systems and systematically work to prevent China from internationalizing its tech sector. It should sharply restrict high-tech exports to China with the aim of slowing its economic growth and build a digital iron curtain to pull wavering countries out of China's sphere of technological influence. It should expand arms sales to countries in China's neighborhood, offer technology transfers and favorable trade deals to OBOR countries on the brink, and eventually form an explicitly anti-OBOR coalition. This may seem like the grim and fatalistic logic of Cold War II, but aggressive and timely action may be the only way to stop OBOR and prevent China from locking its trading partners into an authoritarian, neotributary model.

Of course, a Cold War–style response to OBOR will not succeed everywhere. China will still have a sphere of influence in Asia, Africa, and possibly Europe. Just as in the Cold War, when much of the developing world formed a nonaligned bloc, many countries today that currently lean toward the West, including treaty allies in Asia and Europe, may resist choosing sides or even explore realigning with China. The United States would therefore be left with an economy increasingly insulated from direct Chinese competition, but with a smaller circle of friends and partners than it currently enjoys. OBOR could expand aggressively into Latin America, particularly if future US presidents are as unpopular there as Donald Trump has been. It has already begun to do so: since 2017, fifteen countries in the Western Hemisphere have signed some form of OBOR memorandum of understanding, and China is investing massively in many others, including close US partners such as Brazil and Argentina.[16] The Cold War analogy reminds us that this is a frightening prospect. The closest the United States and the Soviet Union ever came to nuclear war was after the Soviets refused to withdraw nuclear missiles from Cuba. Not only will an aggressive anti-OBOR strategy probably fail to shut China out of the Western hemisphere, it will slightly increase the chance of an accident or chain of mistakes that turns Cold War II into a "hot war" with China.

A second option is to continue the status quo policy—resist OBOR in a selective rather than absolutist way, with the goal of retaining strategic flexibility. If China experiences a financial crisis or popular uprising against party rule, OBOR could flame out of its own accord, and it may not be necessary to mount a global effort to hold it back. On the other hand, if China's economy continues to grow faster than the rest of the world's, Xi will cement his authority at home, OBOR will continue to expand abroad, and the West must be prepared to compete with an emboldened and wealthier adversary. A hedging strategy prepares for both possibilities at the same time. Under this approach, Western countries could criticize OBOR in broad terms without actively attacking it or making ultimatums to small countries. They could block Chinese investment in strategic sectors, such as telecommunications, avionics, and biotechnology, and push back with full force if China militarizes its overseas projects. Above all, the United States, Europe, and Japan could quietly pressure their close neighbors, allies, and trading partners not to join OBOR, outbidding Chinese offers when necessary. The name of the game is to pick battles, prioritizing countries and sectors connected to higher-ranking national interests.

A hedging strategy has the advantage of flexibility and lower costs, but it will not be easy to execute. Xi and his military advisers might mistake it for a contain and undermine strategy, weakly implemented. Hedging could therefore elevate the risk of war with China for the same reason that a contain and undermine strategy would, while giving OBOR more time and space to keep expanding.

A third option is for the United States and its partners to join OBOR and coopt it before China can turn it into a geopolitical bloc. Endorsing OBOR in its current form would undoubtedly be a huge symbolic concession. It would be read abroad as a sign of American weakness and represent a 180-degree shift in US policy. But it would win a substantive victory by forcing OBOR to become truly multilateral and limiting China's ability to use it as a neotributary system. Western countries could claim that they are "contributing to OBOR" by strengthening democratic institutions and standing for human rights; by expanding access to public health, education, clean water, and agricultural technology; by investing in high-speed internet infrastructure for disconnected populations; and by reassuring the world that the United States will continue to guarantee freedom of navigation in international waters and airspace.

The logic of joining and coopting OBOR draws on the findings of this book about Xi's preoccupation with domestic control. As Vladimir Putin has discovered, praising OBOR placated Xi and induced him to keep OBOR relatively unthreatening to Russian interests. Similarly, if the United States joins, it could use its new status as an OBOR member state to push from within for more multilateral projects and greater transparency in contract terms. The goal would be to give recipient countries more leverage when they negotiate with China. Just as Russia has embraced OBOR tightly while keeping China out of its critical infrastructure and parrying Beijing's designs on Central Asia, Western countries could join OBOR and still block Chinese investments that threaten their national interests, such as Huawei projects in North America. Furthermore, by "giving face" to Xi, the United States could indicate that it is willing to compromise and make space for China on the world stage as long as China's international activities are productive and transparent. This would open the door for cooperation with China on other urgent issues, from climate change to nuclear nonproliferation.

All three options entail risks and painful trade-offs. On one hand, any formal engagement with OBOR shows weakness. On the other hand, any attempt to prevent OBOR from becoming a security bloc could be self-fulfilling. A hedging strategy could be the best of both worlds, or it could be the worst of both if it visibly fails. What all three options have in common is that they take OBOR seriously as a long-term potential threat. Though OBOR's international implementation has thus far been halting and rather poorly coordinated, the concept is predicated on a fundamentally revisionist approach to the liberal international order.

Whatever path we choose, it is important to remember that all strategic choices have unintended consequences. The harder Washington tries to cut off Beijing's access to critical technologies, the more pressure China will feel to lock in its supplies of commodities and secure new markets for its exports, and the more sensible the strategic logic of the "new tributary system" will look. The higher the trade barriers Western countries erect to keep out Chinese high-tech products, the more reason China will have to offer those products on favorable terms to OBOR countries—while boasting that it is helping reduce global carbon emissions. The more aggressively Washington leans on other countries to choose sides, the greater the risk that some of its traditional allies will fall on China's side of the fence.

Putting Pride Aside

The best option—for the United States, at least—is to make a show of joining OBOR and then work to shape it from within. OBOR does not yet threaten the vital national interests of any Western country. By contrast, overreacting to OBOR could force the United States and China down a dangerous path of strategic escalation that ultimately threatens every country's vital interests. There is also no guarantee that the West could stop OBOR's expansion even if it tried. The risk of failure would be perilously high—other countries would see the United States as a vindictive declining power, unable to accept China's inexorable rise and incapable of stopping it. The alliances that undergird the international system would weaken. China, convinced that the United States will never accept it as an equal, would begin to question whether a "peaceful rise" is possible.

By contrast, China will struggle to turn OBOR into a true geopolitical bloc as long as the United States is part of it. Beijing could not deny a public request from Washington to join without undermining its own claim that OBOR is peaceful, apolitical, and open to all. Once Washington is nominally affiliated with OBOR, it could—with justification—demand more financial and legal transparency about how China proposes, finances, and administers OBOR projects. When other OBOR countries consider offers for Chinese megadeals, Washington could offer public and private advice and assistance to vet the projects and ensure that the terms are sound and meet best practices and international standards. The active presence of the United States in negotiations over OBOR projects would empower recipient countries to bargain harder with China. It would also give China stronger incentives not to get caught using debt as a tool of political control. If Chinese-built overseas infrastructure is interconnected with US-built infrastructure, it will be harder for China to militarize. Washington could pull out of OBOR at any time if it needed to call attention to Chinese bad behavior.

Joining and coopting OBOR is the simplest option to execute, with the fewest moving parts. To begin, the United States would announce its intention to join by sending top-level officials to speak at the Belt and Road Forum in Beijing. The US government would then need to seek tens of billions of dollars of funding from Congress to bulk up its own foreign aid and investment programs, coordinating closely with allies and private firms. As part of the join and coopt strategy, the United States would need to continue modernizing its military, particularly its cyber and intelligence capabilities, and focus on revitalizing existing alliances and partnerships.

If this recommendation seems creative and unorthodox, perhaps it is because US political culture is just as status-conscious as China's. Political scientist Jonathan Renshon has shown that rising powers that have gone to war throughout history have disproportionately been those that suffer from "status deficits."[17] That is, they conclude that established powers will never accept them as peers in the international system, and they must therefore fight to earn their place. For a variety of reasons, China is a great power uncommonly concerned with its status and reputation. But so is the United States. Not since Franklin Roosevelt met with Winston Churchill have US foreign policymakers acknowledged that another country could be a peer, sharing global leadership. As China grows more wealthy and powerful, the West should not hesitate to draw clear red lines where it sees its vital interests are at stake. But it must also recognize that Chinese power has already met the world, and most other countries have given it a rather warm welcome. China is not an interloper in the global system that can be sidelined or boxed in. Is a long-term rival that needs to be managed and outcompeted.

A Final Word

The choices that OBOR has forced on the rest of the world are about security and economics, but they are also about identity and ideas—a contest to define the emerging international order. For the past seventy years, the United States has been the world's most powerful brand. The US brand is composed of many others: blue jeans and rock and roll, Coca-Cola and Apple, capitalism and freedom, Harvard and Hollywood. On the world stage, the United States has claimed to stand for prosperity and innovation, trade and democracy, moral leadership and human rights. US foreign policy has often fallen short of these aspirations and has drawn its share of dissidents and critics. But the brand has kept its allure because its appeal is inclusive and universal. From the Marshall Plan to Desert Storm, the United States was, in Victoria de Grazia's brilliant phrase, the world's only "irresistible empire."

Today, America's image is tarnished. OBOR is a shiny new Chinese competitor that has copied many of the American brand's most attractive elements. Donald Trump and Xi Jinping are both concerned with branding. They use similar slogans, steeped in nostalgia for lost glory: the "Great Rejuvenation of the Chinese People" and "Make America Great Again." But it is the American brand that has a problem in the global marketplace. Beijing promises "win-win"; Washington speaks about "America first." China emphasizes communication and cooperation; the United States seems increasingly isolated and retrenched. In the emerging global contest with China, criticizing OBOR is not a strategy. Neither is the vain hope that the United States can beat China at its own game, matching a port for a port and a road for a road. However the United States chooses to respond to OBOR, it must start by looking beyond its own divided politics to articulate an open and inclusive national brand: a packaged vision that the world will want to buy.

APPENDIX A

Official List of OBOR Countries

This book has argued that "membership" in OBOR is a deliberately fuzzy concept. According to the Data section of the Belt and Road Portal, the official website for OBOR administered by the Chinese State Council, OBOR has sixty-three affiliate countries. This list has not been updated since 2018, if not earlier. It includes some countries, such as India, that have actively repudiated OBOR as a security risk. It neglects dozens more that have signed memoranda of understanding of various kinds expressing support for OBOR. It is not ordered alphabetically, and there is no chronological or geographic logic for clustering the countries by group.

The following is the full list of member countries, in the order that they appear on the website's drop-down menu, as of January 30, 2020:

1. Albania
2. Afghanistan
3. United Arab Emirates
4. Oman
5. Azerbaijan
6. Egypt
7. Estonia
8. Pakistan
9. Bahrain
10. Belarus
11. Bulgaria
12. Bosnia and Herzegovina
13. Poland
14. Bhutan
15. East Timor
16. Russia
17. Philippines
18. Georgia
19. Kazakhstan
20. Montenegro
21. Kyrgyzstan
22. Cambodia

23. Czech Republic
24. Qatar
25. Kuwait
26. Croatia
27. Latvia
28. Laos
29. Lebanon
30. Lithuania
31. Romania
32. Maldives
33. Malaysia
34. Macedonia
35. Mongolia
36. Bangladesh
37. Myanmar
38. Moldova
39. Nepal
40. Serbia
41. Saudi Arabia
42. Sri Lanka
43. Slovakia
44. Slovenia
45. Tajikistan
46. Thailand
47. Turkey
48. Turkmenistan
49. Brunei
50. Ukraine
51. Uzbekistan
52. Singapore
53. Hungary
54. Syria
55. Armenia
56. Yemen
57. Iraq
58. Iran
59. Israel
60. India
61. Indonesia
62. Jordan
63. Vietnam

APPENDIX B

Measuring OBOR's Size: Figures and Methodologies

Several prominent think tanks have set up databases of China's overseas investments. Among the most respected and frequently cited are: the Mercator Institute for China Studies; the Johns Hopkins University China Africa Research Initiative; the Center for Strategic and International Studies' Reconnecting Asia Project; and the American Enterprise Institute's China Global Investment Tracker.

These projects use partially overlapping methodologies for collecting and classifying data. As a result, they arrive at wildly inconsistent estimates of how many countries and projects fall under OBOR's ambit—not to mention how much money China has spent on them. Below is a summary of their methodology and findings as of January 30, 2020.

Table A.1

The Four Major OBOR Data Sets Use Different Criteria and Arrive at Different Figures

	Mercator Institute for China Studies	Johns Hopkins University China Africa Research Initiative	Center for Strategic and International Studies' Reconnecting Asia Project	American Enterprise Institute's China Global Investment Tracker
Geographic scope	Asia (including Middle East and Indonesia) and the Arctic, but excluding Japan), Africa, Europe, Australia	Africa	Asia (including Middle East, Indonesia, and Japan), Europe	Global
Number of OBOR projects identified	1,500 projects	N/A	373 projects	420 investments and 935 construction contracts
Total Chinese funds invested	N/A	$258.2 billion (gross annual revenues of Chinese companies' construction projects in Africa: (2013–2017); $457.4 billion (2000–2017)	N/A	$730 billion through December 2019 ($451.1 billion of construction, $278.9 billion of investment)
Distinguishes OBOR/non-OBOR?	Yes. Defines as "all projects that further [OBOR] policy goals—regardless of how they are marketed"	No. Aims to include all Chinese investment in Africa	Yes.	Yes. No stated criteria, but designates some projects after October 2013 as OBOR. Also includes countries not typically thought to be OBOR participants, including Bolivia and Trinidad and Tobago

Types of investment included	N/A	Loans, foreign direct investment, agricultural investments, and contracts	N/A	Investments, construction projects, troubled transactions
Categories	4 (railroads, gas pipelines, oil pipelines, ports)	27, including "unallocated"	7 (roads, railways, seaports, intermodal facilities, power plants, pipeline, transmission)	14 (agriculture, chemicals, energy, entertainment, finance, health, logistics, metals, other, real estate, technology, tourism, transport, and utilities); 21 subcategories
Sources	Chinese and international official sources, industry associations, companies and media.	Recipient governments, private firms, local and international press reports, in-country contacts, field visits, open and proprietary online sources, Chinese contractors, subcontractors and suppliers, public company filings, and bond prospectuses	Open source primary data in multiple languages from national government agencies of host countries, regional development banks, project contracts, and partner organizations including GlobalData	Unspecified
Minimum project size	$25 million	No stated minimum	No stated minimum	$100 million
Date range	Unspecified	2000–2017	2006–2019	2005–2019

Sources: Mercator Institute of China Studies, "Database and Project Design"; Brautigam and Hwang, "China-Africa Loan Database Research Guidebook"; Reconnecting Asia, "Methodology"; and American Enterprise Institute, "China Global Investment Tracker."

APPENDIX C

Selected Reading

The readings are organized into the following categories:

- Introductions to China for general audiences
- Chinese Communist Party propaganda and "thought work"
- OBOR and Chinese military strategy
- OBOR-related regional studies
- Pre-Xi discussion of the New Silk Road concept
- Selected Western perspectives on OBOR as a whole
- United States–China relations and the great power transition
- Unorthodox references to OBOR in Chinese sources

Introductions to China for General Audiences

Economy, Elizabeth. *The Third Revolution: Xi Jinping and the New Chinese State*. New York: Oxford University Press, 2018.

Fallows, James. *China Airborne*. New York: Vintage, 2013.

McGregor, Richard. *The Party: The Secret World of China's Communist Rulers*. New York: Harper Perennial, 2012.

Mitter, Rana. *Modern China: A Very Short Introduction*. Oxford: Oxford University Press, 2016.

Spence, Jonathan D. *The Search for Modern China*. New York: Norton, 2012.

Yu, Hua. *China in Ten Words*. Translated by Allan H. Barr. New York: Anchor, 2012.

Chinese Communist Party Propaganda and "Thought Work"

Brady, Anne-Marie. *Marketing Dictatorship: Propaganda and Thought Work in Contemporary China*. Lanham, MD: Rowman & Littlefield, 2007.

Brady, Anne-Marie. "China's Foreign Propaganda Machine." *Journal of Democracy* 26, no. 4 (2015): 51–59.

Cheng, Li. *The Power of Ideas: The Rising Influence of Thinkers and Think Tanks in China*. Singapore: World Scientific, 2017.

Holbig, Heike. "Ideology after the End of Ideology: China and the Quest for Autocratic Legitimation." *Democratization* 20, no. 1 (2013): 61–81.

Holbig, Heike. "Shifting Ideologics of Research Funding: The CPC's National Planning Office for Philosophy and Social Sciences." *Journal of Current Chinese Affairs* 43, no. 2 (2014): 13–32.

Ma, Damian, and Neil Thomas. "In Xi We Trust: How Propaganda Might Be Working in the New Era." *MacroPolo*, September 12, 2018. Accessed September 14, 2018.

Schoenhals, Michael. *Doing Things with Words in China*. Berkeley: University of Berkeley Press, 1992.

Yue, Qiwei. *Ru dang xu zhi* [What You Must Know to Join the Party]. Shanghai: Shanghai Renmin, 2003.

OBOR and Chinese Military Strategy

Dutton, Peter A., and Ryan D. Martinson, eds. *China's Evolving Surface Fleet*. Newport, RI: CMSI Red Books, 2017.

Erickson, Andrew S., and Austin M. Strange. *No Substitute for Experience: Chinese Antipiracy Operations in the Gulf of Aden*. Newport, RI: CMSI Red Books, 2013.

Fravel, M. T., and C. P. Twomey. "Projecting Strategy: The Myth of Chinese Counter-Intervention." *Washington Quarterly* 37, no. 4 (Winter 2015): 171–87.

Goldstein, Lyle J. *Meeting China Halfway: How to Defuse the Emerging US-China Rivalry*. Washington, DC: Georgetown University Press, 2015.

Pehrson, Christopher J. *String of Pearls: Meeting the Challenge of China's Rising Power across the Asian Littoral*. Asheville, NC: BiblioGov, July 2006.

Yung, Christopher D., et al. "Not an Idea We Have to Shun: Chinese Overseas Basing Requirements in the 21st Century." *China Strategic Perspectives* 7 (October 2014): 1–72.

OBOR-Related Regional Studies

Australia and New Zealand

Brady, Anne-Marie. "A Strategic Partnership: New Zealand-China Relations in the Xi Jinping Era and Beyond." In *Small States and the Changing Global Order: New Zealand Faces the Future*, edited by Anne-Marie Brady. New York: Springer, 2019, 127–44.

Brewster, David, and Rory Medcalf. "Cocos and Christmas Islands: Building Australia's Strategic Role in the Indian Ocean." *Journal of the Indian Ocean Region* 13, no. 2 (2017): 155–73.

Hamilton, Clive. *Silent Invasion: China's Influence in Australia*. Melbourne: Hardie Grant Books, 2018.

Medcalf, Rory. "Australia and China: Understanding the Reality Check." *Australian Journal of International Affairs* 73, no. 2 (2018): 1–10.

Medcalf, Rory. "Silent Invasion: The Question of Race." Lowy Institute, March 21, 2018. Accessed January 25, 2019. https://www.lowyinstitute.org/the-interpreter/silent-invasion-question-race.

Greece and Europe

Benner, Thorsten, et al. "Authoritarian Advance: Responding to China's Growing Political Influence in Europe." MERICS, February 2018.

Chang, Vincent K. L., and Frank N. Pieke. "Europe's Engagement with China: Shifting Chinese Views of the EU and the EU-China Relationship." *Asia Europe Journal* 16, no. 4 (December 2018): 317–31.

Hanemann, Thilo, and Mikko Huotari. "EU-China FDI: Working Towards Reciprocity in Investment Relations." MERICS, May 2018.

Tonchev, Plamen, and Polyxeni Davarinou. "Chinese Investment in Greece and the Big Picture of Sino-Greek Relations." Institute of International Economic Relations, December 2017.

Varoufakis, Yanis. *Adults in the Room: My Battle with Europe's Deep Establishment*. London: Vintage, 2018.

IRAN AND THE MIDDLE EAST

Ehteshami, Anoushiravan, Niv Horesh, and Ruike Xu. "Chinese-Iranian Mutual Strategic Perceptions." *China Journal* 79 (2018): 1–20.

Garver, John W. *China and Iran: Ancient Partners in a Post-Imperial World*. Seattle: University of Washington Press, 2006.

Garver, John. "China–Iran Relations: Cautious Friendship with America's Nemesis." *China Report* 49, no. 1 (2013): 69–88.

Hua, Liming. "Iran Nuclear Issue and China's Middle East Diplomacy." *Arab World Studies* 6 (2014): 4–16.

Reardon-Anderson, James, ed. *The Red Star & the Crescent: China and the Middle East*. New York: Oxford University Press, 2018.

LATIN AMERICA

Ferchen, Matt. "China's Belt and Road Initiative in Latin America and the Caribbean." International Institute for Strategic Studies (IISS), December 2018.

Ferchen, Matt. "China, Venezuela, and the Illusion of Debt-Trap Diplomacy." Asia Global Institute, August 16, 2018.

Swaine, Michael D. "Xi Jinping's Trip to Latin America." *China Leadership Monitor* 45 (September 5, 2014).

MALAYSIA AND SOUTHEAST ASIA

Allison, Graham, Robert Blackwill, and Ali Wyne. *Lee Kuan Yew: The Grand Master's Insights on China, the United States, and the World*. Cambridge, MA: MIT Press, 2013.

Erickson, Andrew S., and Austin Strange. "Pandora's Sandbox: China's Island-Building Strategy in the South China Sea." Foreign Affairs, July 13, 2014. https://www.foreignaffairs.com/articles/china/2014-07-13/pandoras-sandbox.

Hayton, Bill. "The Modern Creation of China's 'Historic Rights' Claim in the South China Sea." *Asian Affairs* 49, no. 3 (July 2018): 370–82.

Hayton, Bill. *The South China Sea: The Struggle for Power in Asia*. New Haven, CT: Yale University Press, 2014.

Kaplan, Robert D. *Asia's Cauldron: The South China Sea and the End of a Stable Pacific*. New York: Random House, 2014.

Studwell, Joe. *Asian Godfathers: Money and Power in Hong Kong and Southeast Asia*. New York: Grove, 2008.

Pakistan and South Asia

McCartney, Matthew and S. Akbar Zaidi, eds. *New Perspectives on Pakistan's Political Economy: State, Class and Social Change*. Cambridge: Cambridge University Press, 2019.

Small, Andrew. "The Backlash to Belt and Road: A South Asian Battle over Chinese Economic Power." *Foreign Affairs*, February 16, 2018.

Small, Andrew. *The China-Pakistan Axis: Asia's New Geopolitics*. New York: Oxford University Press, 2014.

Zaidi, S. Akbar. "A Road through Pakistan, and What This Means for India." Unpublished paper, September 7, 2018.

Polar Regions

Brady, Anne-Marie. *China as a Polar Great Power*. Washington, DC: Woodrow Wilson Center Press, 2017.

"China's Arctic Policy." State Council Information Office of the People's Republic of China. January 26, 2018.

Jakobson, Linda. "China Prepares for an Ice-Free Arctic." *SIPRI* no. 2 (March 2010).

Potter, Evan. "The Evolving Complementarity of Nation-Branding and Public Diplomacy: Projecting the Canada Brand through 'Weibo Diplomacy' in China." *Canadian Foreign Policy Journal* 24, no. 2 (2018): 1–15.

Russia and Central Asia

Dugin, Aleksandr. *Osnovy Geopolitiki: Geopoliticheskoye Budushcheye Rossii* [The Foundations of Geopolitics: The Geopolitical Future of Russia]. Moscow: Arktogeja, 1997.

Gabuev, Alexander. "Crouching Bear, Hidden Dragon: 'One Belt One Road' and Chinese-Russian Jostling for Power in Central Asia." *Journal of Contemporary East Asia Studies* 5, no. 2 (2016): 61–78.

Kassenova, Nagis. "More Politics than Substance: Three Years of Russian and Chinese Economic Cooperation in Central Asia." Foreign Policy Research Institute, October 24, 2018.

Lukin, Alexander. *The Bear Watches the Dragon: Russia's Perceptions of China and the Evolution of Russian-Chinese Relations Since the Eighteenth Century.* New York: Routledge, 2003.

Miller, Chris. *Putinomics: Power and Money in Resurgent Russia.* Chapel Hill: University of North Carolina Press, 2018.

Trenin, Dmitri. *Should We Fear Russia?* Cambridge: Polity, 2017.

Zuenko, Ivan. "Kak proidet kitajskiy Shelkoviy put I kto na nem zarabotaet" [Which Road Will the Chinese Silk Road Take and Who Will Win?]. Carnegie Moscow Center, April 21, 2016.

Zygar, Mikhail. *All the Kremlin's Men: Inside the Court of Vladimir Putin.* New York: Public Affairs, 2017.

Sri Lanka and the Indian Ocean

Bose, Sugata, and Ayesha Jalal. *Modern South Asia: History, Culture, Political Economy.* New York: Routledge, 2017.

Lerski, George J. "Sri Lanka Turns East." *Asian Affairs* 1 (1974): 184–96.

Menon, Shivshankar. *Choices: Inside the Making of India's Foreign Policy.* Washington, DC: Brookings Institution Press, 2016.

"Potential Disclosable Transaction Agreement in Relation to Hambantota Port, Sri Lanka." China Merchants Port Holdings Company Limited, July 25, 2017.

Sivaram, Karthik. "'Locked-In' to China: The Colombo Port City Project." Stanford Leadership Academy for Development, 2016.

Sivasundaram, Sujit. *Islanded: Britain, Sri Lanka, and the Bounds of an Indian Ocean Colony.* Chicago: University of Chicago Press, 2013.

Zhang, Hong. "Beyond 'Debt-Trap Diplomacy': The Dissemination of PRC State Capitalism." *China Brief* 19, no. 1 (January 2019).

Tanzania and Africa

Brautigam, Deborah. *The Dragon's Gift: The Real Story of China in Africa*. Oxford: Oxford University Press, 2009.

Dreher, Axel, et al. "Apples and Dragon Fruits: The Determinants of Aid and Other Forms of State Financing from China to Africa." *International Studies Quarterly* 62, no. 1 (March 2018): 182–94.

Lü, Youqing. "The Spread of Xi Jinping Diplomatic Thought in Tanzania" (Xi jinping waijiao sixiang zai tansangniya de chuanbo). *Sina*, December 4, 2017.

Sun, Irene Yuan. *The Next Factory of the World: How Chinese Investment Is Reshaping Africa*. Boston: Harvard Business Review Press, 2017.

Yan, Hairong, and Barry Sautman. "The Beginning of a World Empire? Contesting the Discourse of Chinese Copper Mining in Zambia." *Modern China* 39, no. 2 (January 2013): 131–64.

Pre-Xi Discussion of the New Silk Road Concept

Akayev, Askar. "Our Foreign Policy Doctrine Is the Great Silk Road." *Executive Intelligence Review* 26, no. 15 (1999): 49.

Burdman, Mark. "Kyrgyzstan President Promotes 'Renaissance of the Silk Road.'" *Executive Intelligence Review* 26, no. 38 (1999): 4.

Fu, Jing. "Rebuilding the Ancient Silk Road." *China Daily*, September 1, 2004.

Li, Xiguang. "New Silk Road Could Revitalize War-Torn Afghanistan." *Global Times*, June 6, 2011.

Lin, Justin. "Yi 'xin masa'er jihua' daidong quanqiu jingji fuxing" [Promote Global Economic Recovery through the 'New Marshall Plan'"]. *QQ*, October 22, 2012.

"Toward New Glory of Silk Road." *China Daily*, September 4, 2012.

Wang, Jisi. "'Marching Westwards': The Rebalancing of China's Geostrategy." *Global Times*, October 17, 2012.

Zhao, Minghao. "'March Westwards' and a New Look on China's Grand Strategy." *Mediterranean Quarterly* 26, no. 1 (2015): 97–116.

Selected Western Perspectives on
OBOR as a Whole

Arduino, Alessandro, and Xue Gong. *Securing the Belt and Road: Risk Assessment, Private Security and Special Insurances along the New Wave of Chinese Outbound Investments*. New York: Palgrave, 2018.

Blanchard, Jean-Marc F., and Colin Flint. "The Geopolitics of China's Maritime Silk Road Initiative." *Geopolitics* 22, no. 2 (2017): 223–45.

Cai, Peter. "Understanding China's Belt and Road Initiative." Lowy Institute for International Policy, March 2017.

Callahan, William A. "China's 'Asia Dream': The Belt and Road Initiative and the New Regional Order." *Asian Journal of Comparative Politics* 1, no. 3 (2016): 226–43.

Frankopan, Peter. *The New Silk Roads: The Present and Future of the World*. New York: Bloomsbury, 2018.

He, Baogang. "The Domestic Politics of the Belt and Road Initiative and its Implications." *Journal of Contemporary China* (2018): 1–16.

Johnson, Christopher K. "President Xi Jinping's 'Belt and Road' Initiative." Center for Strategic & International Studies, March 28, 2016.

Maçães, Bruno. *The Dawn of Eurasia: On the Trail of the New World Order*. New Haven, CT: Yale University Press, 2018.

Miller, Tom. *China's Asian Dream: Empire Building along the New Silk Road*. London: Zed Books, 2017.

Parker, Sam, and Gabrielle Chefitz. "Debtbook Diplomacy." Belfer Center for Science and International Affairs, Harvard Kennedy School, May 24, 2018.

Ratner, Ely. "Geostrategic and Military Drivers and Implications of the Belt and Road Initiative." Council on Foreign Relations, January 25, 2018.

Rolland, Nadège. "Beijing's Response to the Belt and Road Initiative's 'Pushback': A Story of Assessment and Adaptation." *Asian Affairs* 50, no. 2 (March 2019): 216–35.

Rolland, Nadège. *China's Eurasian Century? Political and Strategic Implications of the Belt and Road Initiative*. Seattle: NBR Books, 2017.

United States-China Relations and the Great Power Transition

Allison, Graham. *Destined for War: Can America and China Escape Thucydides's Trap?* New York: Houghton Mifflin Harcourt, 2017.

Beckley, Michael. "China's Century? Why America's Edge Will Endure." *International Security* 36, no. 3 (Winter 2011/12): 41–78.

Christensen, Thomas. *The China Challenge: Shaping the Choices of a Rising Power.* New York: Norton, 2015.

Mann, James. *About Face: A History of America's Curious Relationship with China, from Nixon to Clinton.* New York: Vintage, 2000.

Schweller, Randall, and Xiaoyu Pu. "After Unipolarity: China's Visions of International Order in an Era of U.S. Decline." *International Security* 36, no. 1 (Summer 2011): 41–72.

Swaine, Michael D. *America's Challenge: Engaging a Rising China in the Twenty-First Century.* Washington, DC: Carnegie Endowment for International Peace, 2011.

Unorthodox References to OBOR in Chinese Sources

Cheng Hui and Min Fang. "Shejian shang de 'yidaiyilu' gaibian shenghuo meishi pian" [A Bite of OBOR]. *Renmin Ribao*, May 22, 2015.

Li Yanzheng. "Gongxinbu: Zhichi rengong zhineng jishu zai 'yidaiyilu' yanxian guojia tuiguang" [Ministry of Industry and Information Technology: Supporting AI Technology to Promote in Countries along OBOR]. *Shanghai Securities News*, May 18, 2018.

Liu Yizhan, and Wenshuo Wang. "Zero Tolerance Toward Drugs: A Summary of China's In-Depth Promotion of the People's Anti-Drug War." Xinhua, June 26, 2017.

"Ofo chuangshiren Dai Wei: 'Yidaiyilu yinling gongxiang danche chengwei hai neiwai goutong qiaoliang" [Ofo Founder Dai Wei: 'OBOR' Turns Bike Sharing into a Communication Bridge between China and the World]. Belt and Road Portal, September 19, 2017.

"Qingdao Pijiu buju 'yidaiyilu' zhongguo pinpai shanyao Sili Lanka" [Tsingtao Brewery Strategically Deploys OBOR, Chinese Brand Shines in Sri Lanka]. *Nanfang Zhoumo*, October 21, 2016.

"Qingshaonian shijiao de 'yidaiyilu" [OBOR from the Perspective of Young People]. Yooknet, May 17, 2017.

"Shandong sheng chuju hangye 'yidaiyilu, lüse fazhan' funtan zai Xingfu zhen juxing" [Kitchenware Industry Holds 'OBOR Green Development' Forum in Xingfu Town, Shandong Province]. *KK News*, October 13, 2017.

Wang Yiwei. "'Yidaiyilu' de Zhongguo zhihui" [Chinese Wisdom on OBOR]. *Renmin Wang Lilun Pindao*, August 4, 2015.

Wang Yugang. "Le Ling: Taishan Tiyu: Jie li 'yidaiyilu' tuijin quanqiuhua buju" [Taishan Sports: Leveraging OBOR to Promote Strategic Deployment of Globalization]. *Qilu Wang*, May 25, 2018.

"Xiangying 'yidaiyilu' zhuyou jiudian jituan tisheng jingzheng shili" [Responding to OBOR, Sumitomo Hotel Group Enhances its Competitiveness]. Xinhua, May 15, 2017.

Yu Jiangwei. "Quan ming zhongwai keshang qi xianxue 'yidaiyilu' liantong guojia xuemai" [Thousands of Chinese and Foreign Businessmen Donate Blood, OBOR Connects the Blood of Nations]. *Fenghuang Wang Zhejiang*, July 15, 2017.

Zhang Boyu, Lipeng Wang, and Rui Xu. "'Yidaiyilu' Tulanduo geju lishi kaoku yu wenhua neihan yantao hui chenggong zhaokai" [OBOR Turandot Opera History Textual Research and Cultural Connotation Seminar Successfully Held]. Central Conservatory of Music, September 13, 2018.

"Zhongguo Yinhang: shenhua 'yidaiyilu' jinrong dadongmai jianshe zuo 'yidaiyilu' shouxuan yinhang" [Bank of China: Deepen the Construction of 'OBOR' Financial Artery to Become the Preferred OBOR Bank]. Bank of China, August 16, 2018.

APPENDIX D

Citations of Key Chinese Sources

Note to the Reader

Although it would have taken a prohibitive amount of space to list every URL cited in this book, a few sources are sufficiently central to the argument that they deserve special attention. Below are the full citations of the two main propaganda films discussed in chapter 3, the five redrawn Chinese maps, and the OBOR Outstanding Brand Contribution Trophy and OBOR branding awards ceremony discussed in chapter 4.

If any of the links below go dead, as is common on the Chinese Internet, cached versions of the pages may be available at archive.org.

Films

CCTV. "'Yidaiyilu' diyi ji gongtong mingyun" [One Belt One Road Part I: Common Destiny." YouTube, September 13, 2017. Accessed January 28, 2020. https://www.youtube.com/watch?v=MXzzbhEAwQw.

China Daily. "The Belt and Road Initiative and Globalization—Belt and Road Bedtime Stories Series." YouTube, May 10, 2017. Accessed March 2, 2018. https://www.youtube.com/watch?v=edzNYN4hZxo&list=PLIejz8bbgEwT- rJkWnG7x8BsmoGf G7Xns.

Maps

Fig. 2.1: Fu Jing. "Rebuilding the Ancient Silk Road." *China Daily*, September 1, 2004. Accessed January 28, 2020. http://www.chinadaily.com.cn/english/doc/2004-09/01 /content_370519.htm.

Fig. 4.2: *Guangming Daily* 光明日报. "Tongguan 'gaosulu' guanchuan sichouzhilu jingjidai 通 关'高速路'贯穿丝绸之路经济带" ["Highway" Runs through the Silk Road Economic Belt]. Last modified April 22, 2015.

Belt and Road Portal [一带一路网]. "Chronology of China's Belt and Road Initiative." June 25, 2016.https://eng.yidaiyilu.gov.cn/sljs/1080.htm.

Fig. 4.3: Hong Kong Trade Development Council 香港贸发局. "Jingjixuejia: 'yidaiyilu' lutongcaitong 經濟學家:「一帶一路」路通財通" [Economist: "One Belt One Road" Road Built and Money will Come]. Last modified December 15, 2015. Accessed December 14, 2017. http://hkmb.hktdc.com/tc/node/30148024.

Fig. 4.4: Sohu.com 搜狐网. "Zhitong yidaiyilu chuanyue bingfeng de beiji hangxian 直通一带 一路 穿越冰封的北极航线" [Along One Belt One Road Crossing the Arctic Route on Ice]. Last modified October 22, 2017. Accessed December 14, 2017. http:// www.sohu.com/a/199570607_182765.

Fig. 4.5: Changchun New Area Government 长春新区政务网. "Yidaiyilu linian dailaide jiyu 一带一路理念带来的机遇" [Opportunities Brought by Belt and Road]. Accessed December 14, 2017. http://www.ccxq.gov.cn/zhanluejiyu.aspx?id=231.

OBOR Outstanding Brand Contribution Trophy: Brand Alliance Network 品牌联盟网. "Zhong qi fazhan konggu jituan ronghuo 'yidaiyilu zhuoyue gongxian pinpai' jiang" [China Enterprise Development Holdings Group Wins "Belt and Road Initiative Outstanding Contribution Brand" Award]. January 4, 2019. Accessed January 28, 2020. http://zt.brandcn.com/2018ndrwdt/190104_429413.html.

Notes

Note to the Reader

1. For a funny and insightful take on the name change, see Shepard, "Beijing to the World."

2. For example, Office of the Secretary of Defense, "Annual Report to Congress."

Introduction

1. Joy-Perez and Scissors, "A Close Look."

2. The Marshall Plan cost $103 billion in 2014 dollars, though it was a larger percentage of global gross domestic product than OBOR. See Coy, "Afghanistan Has Cost."

3. On the Digital Silk Road, see "Full Text of President Xi's Speech." On the Silk Road in Outer Space, see "Jiakuai tuijin 'yidaiyilu' kongjian xinxi zoulang." Related discussion can be found in "China's BeiDou Navigation Satellite System" and "From Compass to BeiDou."

4. "Qianggang yuxiang baogao."

5. Burns, "Expanding Economic Connectivity."

6. On the same trip, Trump met with Japanese Prime Minister Shinzo Abe, where the two signed an MOU for the Overseas Private Investment Corporation to offer "United States-Japan infrastructure investment alternatives in the Indo-Pacific"—with the other alternative presumably OBOR. See Sevastopulo, "Trump Gives Glimpse" and White House, "President Donald J. Trump's Visit to Japan."

7. "U.S. Elevated Its Ties with India."

8. Abi-Habib, "How China Got Sri Lanka."

9. For the original take on this, see Parker and Chefitz, "Debtbook Diplomacy." They draw on my unpublished Sri Lanka data but arrive at different conclusions, with an approach based theoretically on a combination of Hirschman and neorealist international relations theory. See also Mearsheimer, "Can China Rise Peacefully?"

10. See, for example, White House Office of Trade and Manufacturing Policy, "How China's Economic Aggression."

11. Bolton, "Trump Administration's New Africa Strategy."

12. Department of Defense, "Summary of the National Defense Strategy of the United States of America: Sharpening the American Military's Competitive Edge," 2018.

13. White House National Security Council (@WHNSC), Twitter, March 9, 2019.

14. "Connectivity initiatives must follow principles of financial responsibility to avoid projects that would create unsustainable debt burden for communities," India's statement read, and "must be pursued in a manner that respects sovereignty and territorial integrity." See Bagchi, "India Slams China's."

15. Hankwon Kim, interview with the author, Seoul, August 9, 2018.

16. Lu, "'Pro-China' Boris Johnson."

1. What Is OBOR?

1. The question of references to the tributary system in OBOR propaganda, discussed in chapter 3, is sure to spark vigorous scholarly debate. I fall on the side of Brantly Womack, Howard French, and Henry Kissinger, who believe the concept is still relevant—as long as it is loosely interpreted—to China's foreign policy toward small states on its periphery. Since the OBOR propaganda discussed in chapter 3 seems designed to activate Chinese viewers' pride in this aspect of imperial history, collective beliefs about the historic tributary system take on a reality of their own, regardless of the underlying facts. Wang Gungwu, Warren Cohen, and David Kang offer useful historical perspective, noting that actual tributary system—if such a concept can be usefully said to have ever existed—varied enormously from counterparty to counterparty and dynasty to dynasty. See Womack, "Asymmetry and China's Tributary System"; French, *Everything Under the Heavens*; Kissinger, *On China*; Wang, "Ming Foreign Relations"; Cohen, *East Asia at the Center*; Kang, *East Asia before the West*; and Fairbank, *Chinese World Order*.

2. Rithmire, "Varieties of Outward Chinese Capital."

3. As Stephen Walt has argued, theory and history suggest that "a large aid relationship is more often the result of alignment than a cause of it." Why? Because "economic assistance is offered and accepted only when both parties feel it is in their interest to do so." See Walt, "Alliance Formation," 28.

4. The case studies in this book contribute to an extensive literature on the behavior of small states, a loose category that describes states too weak to influence regional or global order meaningfully on their own. In short, I follow Robert Kaufman, Michael Barnett, Jack Levy, and Steven David in arguing that domestic politics is the best explanatory variable for precisely when and how small states adjust their alignment with OBOR. But I recognize that domestic political explanations for alignment are often compatible with realist explanations. In the day-to-day practice of foreign policy, when the "national interest" is obvious, domestic special interests are usually not strong enough to override it. Yet the national interest is not always intuitively obvious, since threat perception is subjective and contestable. What are small states' options in the face of threat? The main strategies discussed in the literature are bargaining and bandwagon-

ing. Stephen Walt and Stephen Van Evera argue that the best and most common choice is to "balance" against the primary threat. There are two kinds of balancing: building up internal capabilities (internal balancing) or joining with other states against the threat (external balancing). Joining OBOR could serve both goals. For example, if Sri Lanka perceives India as the primary threat and China as a secondary threat, its leaders can argue that a (self-interested) megaport deal serves the national interest by cultivating a faraway patron and kick-starting an economic boom. Contra Walt, Randall Schweller, David Kang, and others argue that states usually "bandwagon," or align with the source of threat. States might do this to keep from being attacked, to share in the spoils of victory, or both. Of course, the decision to join OBOR can also seen be a form of bandwagoning. Bargaining and bandwagoning are not by themselves useful frameworks for predicting OBOR alignment without reference to domestic political context. Nor do the theoretical extremes of these approaches, which may make sense in wartime, map clearly onto more subtle policy choices in a globalized economy in peace. Singapore, for example, may benefit from the global system becoming more multilateral, and therefore balance away from the United States in the context of international institutions, but see China as a larger threat to regional security, and therefore bandwagon with the United States by deepening defense ties. Scholars have proposed a range of theories classifying these shades of gray. These include "soft balancing" (Robert Pape), "hedging" (Evan Medeiros), or "engagement" (Denny Roy). The cases in this book are studies of countries balancing or bandwagoning for profit in a hedged context. Arguably, the decision to accept an OBOR-branded megaproject or sign a memorandum of understanding joining OBOR is always a low-commitment form of engagement—and not itself a declaration of alliance. However, insofar as OBOR enables China to deepen its influence over domestic political institutions, OBOR may induce its member states to align with China in more formal and less hedged ways in the future. On domestic drivers, see Kaufman, "To Balance or to Bandwagon?"; Barnett and Levy, "Domestic Sources"; David, *Choosing Sides*; David, "Explaining Third World Alignment"; Walt, *Origins of Alliance*; Evera, "The Cult of the Offensive"; Pape, "Soft Balancing"; Medeiros, "Strategic Hedging"; and Roy, "Southeast Asia and China."

5. My case studies are based on the theoretical assumption that states are not Waltzian "rational" actors. Rather, states' actions are usually compromises negotiated by lower-level players, such as politicians, political parties, labor unions, and business groups. Negotiations for OBOR projects are therefore two-level games. The chief negotiators on the Chinese and recipient country sides each identify win-sets that will satisfy a critical mass of domestic constituencies. Then they seek to achieve one of these outcomes in negotiating with the other country. An outcome that strengthens the incumbent government in the next election or satisfies a powerful interest group is therefore usually acceptable, even if it entails taking on debt or credit risk that is arguably not in the long-term national interest. See Waltz, *Theory of International Politics*; Putnam, "Diplomacy and Domestic Politics."

6. Hans Tuch's classic text defines public diplomacy as "a government's process of communicating with foreign publics in an attempt to bring about understanding for its nation's ideas and ideals, its institutions and culture, as well as its national goals and current policies" (Tuch, *Communicating with the World*, 3). Joseph Nye's concept of soft

power is different: "the ability to affect others to obtain the outcomes one wants through attraction rather than coercion or payment" (Nye, "Public Diplomacy and Soft Power," 94). Soft power is therefore a resource, and public diplomacy is the policy means of deploying that resource. While public diplomacy plays a role in many OBOR cases, particularly the Piraeus case in chapter 6, Tuch's definition does not correspond perfectly to my characterization of the OBOR campaign as a competitive bottom-up affair. Nor does it capture the use of OBOR as a signaling mechanism or code for officials who want to indicate submissiveness to China's approach without saying so explicitly.

7. For example, Pomfret, "China Debt Traps."

8. Fallon, "New Silk Road."

9. Blackwill and Tellis, *Revising U.S. Grand Strategy.*

10. For example, Feng, "Belt and Road Helps China."

11. For example, Balding, "Why Democracies Are Turning."

12. Wang, "Offensive for Defensive."

13. For two best-selling examples, see Frankopan, *New Silk Roads*; Maçães, *The Dawn of Eurasia.* Frankopan is an Oxford professor. Maçães is Portugal's former minister for Europe.

14. Blackwill and Tellis, *Revising U.S. Grand Strategy.*

15. Phillips, "The $900 BN Question."

16. Perlez and Huang, "Behind China's $1 Trillion Plan."

17. Baculinao, "Belt and Road Initiative."

18. Huang, "Who Picks Up the Trillion-Dollar Tab."

19. Balding, "Can China Afford Its Belt and Road?" The $8 trillion figure is presumably drawn from the Asia Development Bank's assessment of the continent's infrastructure deficit, but it assumes (with no evidence) that China has promised to pick up the entire tab. See Ryall, "Japan Commits."

20. Hillman, "Statement on China's Belt and Road Initiative." To be fair, Hillman has done some of the most sophisticated work on the challenges of measuring OBOR. Yet his testimony shows that even experts describe OBOR with eye-popping headline figures to attract attention, even if they know the figures are misleading. See also Hillman, "How Big Is China's Belt and Road?"

21. Wu and Wang, "Central Bank Chief."

22. "China Focus: Belt and Road Development on High-Quality Path."

23. American Enterprise Institute, "China Global Investment Tracker."

24. The popular press routinely conflates OBOR with Chinese foreign policy more generally. Authors with academic and policy backgrounds tend to be more circumscribed in their judgments, but not always. See, for example, Djankov and Miner, "China's Belt and Road Initiative."

25. Horn, Reinhart, and Trebesch, "China's Overseas Lending."

26. Bandiera and Tsiropoulos, "A Framework to Assess Debt Sustainability."

27. Longer-term debt dynamics will depend on global interest rates and the impact of OBOR infrastructure projects on GDP growth in recipient countries. See Hurley, Morris, and Portelance, "Examining the Debt Sustainability Implications."

28. Kratz, Feng, and Wright, "New Data on the 'Debt Trap' Question."

29. Trebesch, Papaioannou, and Das, "Sovereign Debt Restructurings."

30. This understanding of OBOR as a multiplayer game echoes recent trends in Cold War historiography. Drawing—very belatedly—on a wider range of Third World archives, historians have discovered that countries once thought "peripheral" to global politics shaped US and Soviet behavior far more than was previously appreciated. See, for example, Westad, *Global Cold War*.

31. There are far too many articles on the OBOR backlash to list here. For a sample of this press coverage from over a dozen countries, see Smith, "China's Belt and Road Initiative." For a more general theory of the case, see Balding, "Why Democracies Are Turning."

32. The cases in this book partly resemble analytic narratives in that they supplement historical narrative with systematic analysis of how the major actors read each other's motives and how these calculations affect their behavior. See Bates et al., *Analytic Narratives*.

33. Many social scientists are skeptical of "small-*n*" qualitative case study methods because the researcher can easily cherry-pick cases that demonstrate predetermined conclusions. For a study of this size, it is therefore good practice to use John Stuart Mill's method of difference. Mill argues that the ideal set of case studies is alike in all respects— that is, "controls" for as many potential confounding variables as possible—but covers the full range of outcomes to be explained (the "dependent variable"). Chapters 5–7 contain extensive discussion of the similarities and differences between the Hambantota, Bagamoyo, and Piraeus cases. For more on Mill and other logics of case study selection, see Bennett and Elman, "Case Study Methods." The authoritative text on the potential pitfalls of qualitative case study methods and techniques for avoiding them is King, Keohane, and Verba, *Designing Social Inquiry*.

2. Origins

1. "President Xi Jinping Delivers Important Speech."

2. In Chinese: "我提出" 一带一路" 倡议. See these two speeches, among others: "Full Text: Xi Jinping's Keynote Speech" and "Keynote Speech by H.E. Xi Jinping."

3. Emphasis added. Song, "What Is 'Belt and Road Initiative'?"

4. Literally: "Our Party must always represent the development trend of China's advanced productive forces, the orientation of China's advanced culture and the fundamental interests of the overwhelming majority of the Chinese people." See "Full Text of Jiang Zemin's Report."

5. Wang has been dubbed "China's Kissinger" and the "architect of OBOR," although his precise procedural responsibilities are unclear. When OBOR first encountered criticism from former senior party officials in 2018, Wang was not seen in public for several months, leading some commentators to speculate that Xi had made him a scapegoat. Yet the crisis passed. Wang returned, and Xi has continued to promote the OBOR brand. See Cheng, "Wang Huning."

6. In Chinese: "我们党提出," or literally "our party proposes." See, for example, "Qieshi zuohao goujian shehui zhuyi."

7. Chin's study of Richthofen and Hedin is a thoroughly enjoyable read. See Chin, "Invention of the Silk Road."

8. Richthofen, *Baron Richthofen's Letters*, 151–52.

9. For more of his writings on the subject, see Richthofen, "Ancient Silk-Traders' Route," 13, quoted in Chin, "Invention of the Silk Road," 199.

10. For more on his travels, see Hedin and Bergman, *History of the Expedition*, 2:173–75, 3:118, 125, 154; and Steinmetz, *Devil's Handwriting*, quoted in Chin, "Invention of the Silk Road," 208.

11. Hedin, *Silk Road*, 223–34.

12. "Sichouzhilu," 6.

13. International Crisis Group, "Central Asia."

14. International Crisis Group, "Central Asia."

15. Shanghai Cooperation Organization, *Charter*.

16. The Chinese had used the Silk Road metaphor as a sign of friendship before, including on Premier Li Peng's April 1994 tour of Central Asia. However, references at that time were strictly metaphorical. As the *People's Daily* put it, "If the purpose of Premier Li Peng's trip to Central Asia is the promotion of good-neighborliness, friendship and the development of mutually beneficial cooperation, then the 'Silk Road' contains all of those implications." See Zhou et al., "Gongtong de qinghuai," 6.

17. "Geng haode shishi zouchuqu zhanlüe."

18. "Jiang Zemin zhuxi tong tukumansitan."

19. The best review of the Going Out policy in Central Asia can be found in Economy and Levy, *By All Means Necessary*.

20. "China Product Import Product Share."

21. Chinese commentators blamed the delays on Central Asians' unwillingness to adopt the Chinese railway gauge standard.

22. "Direct Rail Link Speeds up Europe-China Cargo Trip."

23. Kynge et al., "How China Rules the Waves."

24. "Zhongguo minhang zongju fujuzhang."

25. "Wulumuqi jianqi guoji shangmao datongdao."

26. The term reemerged after OBOR was announced, in different contexts. See "Jianshe wanli 'kongzhong xinsilu'"; and "'Shuang shuniu' jia qi kongzhong 'xinsilu'." For a fascinating study of the contest over airspace between the PLA Air Force and China's civil aviation bureaucracy, see Fallows, *China Airborne*.

27. Gamache, Hammer, and Jones, "China's Trade and Investment Relationship."

28. Kinfe, *China Comes to Africa*, 189.

29. Bräutigam, *The Dragon's Gift*.

30. Murdoch, "Thailand's Kra Canal Plan."

31. Leaked accounts claimed that the government of Myanmar would have received a 15 percent stake in the scheme, worth about $18 billion over fifty years. Under the original, secret deal, most of these proceeds would likely have been carved up as spoils for military figures and bureaucrats. "Controversy over Dam."

32. "China's Stimulus Package"; Plafker, "A Year Later."

33. Clinton, "Remarks on India and the United States."

34. Clinton, "Remarks at the New Silk Road Ministerial Meeting."

35. Shen, "One Road for Many Itineraries."

36. Kucera, "Clinton's Dubious Plan."

37. Clinton, "America's Pacific Century."

38. "Lin Yifu: yi 'xin maxie'er jihua.'"

39. Xu had completed his bureaucratic career as deputy chief of State Administration of Taxation in 2007 and continues to serve as a member of the Chinese People's Political Consultative Congress.

40. "Zhengxie weiyuan xianji chukou."

41. "Xu Shanda."

42. "Di 25 ke liangji shijie de xingcheng."

43. Brainard, "The Lessons of the Marshall Plan."

44. In Chinese: 一带一路绝非中国版"马歇尔计划." See Wang, "'Yidaiyilu' juefei zhongguoban."

45. Note that the Chinese phrasing of "new 'Silk Road'" (新的"丝绸之路") differs subtly from the more concise term that would emerge under Xi: "New Silk Road" (新丝绸之路). See China "Wen Jiabao 17 ri qianwang."

46. Wen, "Zaichuang sichouzhilu xin huihuang."

47. Wang, "'Xijin.'"

48. The anticipated imminent US withdrawal from Afghanistan was an important background narrative that underlay much of this debate. The month before Wang Jisi published his "March Westwards" essay, Zhou Yongkang visited Kabul in the first visit by a Politburo Standing Committee member since 1966. There he had signed memoranda of understanding on security and commerce, including agreements for the "training, funding and equipping" of the Afghan police.

49. "'Xiangxi kaifang.'"

50. Specifically, "国际形势复杂多变, 大国博弈日益激烈, 中国"西进"之路绝非坦途. 中国当务之急不是大踏步地"进去," 而是认清形势, 研判战略风险并妥谋规避之策, 把握好"西进"的度". See "'Xijin' xu fangfan sanda zhanlüe fengxian."

51. Xu, "Speech by Chinese President Xi Jinping."

3. Emperor Xi

1. China Daily, "Belt and Road Bedtime Stories: Episode One."

2. Anne-Marie Brady has done the best work on China's propaganda system. Her take on CCP propaganda for foreigners is a good place to start. See Brady, "China's Foreign Propaganda Machine," 51–59. It is interesting to read this article, published after Xi took power, alongside the corresponding chapter on the topic in Brady's 2009 book, *Marketing Dictatorship*, which I cite in more detail in chapter 4. See Brady, *Marketing Dictatorship*, 151–74. For a concise survey of the Chinese government's embrace of Joseph Nye's "soft power" concept under Hu Jintao, see Edney, "Soft Power and the Chinese Propaganda System." Apart from these works, CCP foreign-directed propaganda (also known as exoprop) has received too little scholarly attention.

3. The best study of historical revisionism and its role in legitimating the CCP is Wang, *Never Forget National Humiliation*.

4. A classic study on this topic is Schoenhals, *Doing Things with Words*.

5. Li and Xia, "Roles and Performance."

6. For one perspective from a mid-level party secretary in Hainan province, see Kong, "'Yidaiyilu' xuanchuan zhong de ba xiang zhuyi."

7. This chapter is inspired by the work of Peter Hays Gries, Jonathan Unger, and Geremie Barmé (in Unger's edited volume), who unpack revisionist historical narratives in official and unofficial Chinese texts and explain how they advance the interests of the party-state in various ways. Unger explicitly states the subtext of the English-language scholarship when he writes: "When the ship of state under [Deng Xiaoping's] helmsmanship cast off from its prior ideological moorings, [Chinese] historians were aboard as ever-obedient oarsmen, awaiting orders" (Unger, "Using the Past to Serve the Present," 6). Most critical studies of CCP historiography are more circumspect about criticizing the politicization of history in China, but not much—particularly Arthur Waldron's work on the reversal in official history of the Sino-Japanese War in the 1980s. James Harrison's classic study surveys how the party in the early years of the People's Republic rewrote Chinese history as a saga of class struggle. John Garver has the best take on the "patriotic education" campaigns to reestablish party control over history after the Tiananmen crisis of 1989. Rana Mitter and Kirk Denton have shown how the party uses museums to teach its version of history. Their work is useful for understanding the large number of Silk Road–themed museums that are now sprouting up around China. There is little good scholarship about the Chinese historiography of the Silk Road, Han Wudi, and Zhang Qian. However, Dieter Kuhn and Helga Stahl's edited collection is a good survey of how ideas of the role of antiquity have been contested throughout Chinese history. Peter Bol's essay in that collection, about the role of historiography in the Tang dynasty, is particularly good. As Bol puts it: "Once a certain interpretation of antiquity—or once a particular value formation—came to be widely accepted antiquity ceased to be problematic. It had served its purpose; it became a rhetorical gesture rather than a vehicle for thought." See Gries, *China's New Nationalism*; Unger, *Using the Past to Serve the Present*; Waldron, "China's New Remembering"; Harrison, *Communists and Chinese Peasant Rebellions*; Garver, *China's Quest*; Mitter, "Behind the Scenes," 280; Denton, *Exhibiting the Past*; and Kuhn and Stahl, *Perceptions of Antiquity*.

8. See https://www.youtube.com/watch?v=_NtprkECCiU.

9. For the original Chinese-language version, see CCTV, "'Yidaiyilu' diyi ji gongtong mingyun." For a dubbed version in English with only minor changes in the narration, see China Global Television Network, "One Belt One Road Documentary: Episode One."

10. Hansen, *Silk Road*.

11. See, for example, "Yidaiyilu shang de mingzhu."

12. In China, secondary schooling is broken into middle school or junior secondary (*chuzhong*), corresponding to grades seven to nine or ages twelve to fifteen; and senior secondary or high school (*gaozhong*), representing grades ten to twelve or ages fifteen to eighteen. Technically, only middle school is legally mandatory for all students in China, but most young people go on to high school unless there is a compelling reason not to do so. The middle school textbooks cited in this chapter are written in story form, with vivid language and illustrations. The high school history textbooks fall into two categories: compulsory and elective. Since the national university entrance exam (*gaokao*) tests

political, economic, and cultural history, these subjects are mandatory for all high school students, so I draw mainly from these. Naturally, all of the high school textbooks are written in a more academic and abstract style than their middle school counterparts.

13. Plenty of interesting work has been done on the other political uses of history in Chinese textbooks. See Weatherley and Magee, "Using the Past to Legitimise the Present"; Tse, "Creating Good Citizens"; and Baranovitch, "Others No More."

14. Garver, *China's Quest*, 476–78.

15. In Chinese: 丝绸之路又是怎样形成的?

16. In Chinese: 运送丝绸的商路又是谁在什么时候开辟的?

17. According to the 2016 edition, "Eastern Han Emperor Mingdi sent troops to attack the Huns and dispatched Ban Chao as an envoy to the Western Regions. Ban Chao overcame difficulties and reestablished communication . . . and won the trust of the countries in the Western Regions." In Chinese: 班超客服重重困难, 使西域各国重新与汉朝建立联系. 他得到了西域各国的信任. Ministry of Education, *Zhongguo lishi* (2016), 65.

18. The key phrase here is 倍偿其价, suggesting that tributary powers enjoyed greater commercial benefits than the Chinese empire.

19. Ministry of Education and Ma, *Lishi di er ce bixiu*.

20. Ministry of Education and Ma, *Lishi di er ce bixiu*, 46.

21. Ministry of Education, *Zhongguo lishi* (2016), 65.

22. In Chinese: 祖国的大航海家.

23. Li, "Hongyang Zheng He jingshen"; Wu, "Zheng He jingshen ji qi dangdai yiyi"; and Yang, "Zoujin Zheng He."

24. Ministry of Education and Ma, *Lishi di er ce bixiu*, 139.

25. Yang, "Belt and Road Initiative Warmly Welcomed."

26. For a thoughtful and concise review of the debate around the "responsible great power" concept, see Deng, "China: The Post-Responsible Power."

27. "Chuanmei Chahuahui," "'Yidaiyilu' baodao zhong."

28. Baogang He has done the best work on the institutionalization of OBOR in China. His notes are a gold mine for Chinese-language sources. According to his conversations with high-level officials, the idea to change OBOR's English-language name originated from the Center for China and Globalization, a Beijing think tank known for favoring closer ties with the United States and Europe. See He, "Domestic Politics of the Belt and Road."

29. China Daily, "Belt and Road Bedtime Stories: Episode 1."

30. China Daily, "Belt and Road Bedtime Stories: Episode 2."

31. China Daily, "Belt and Road Bedtime Stories: Episode 2."

32. China Daily, "Belt and Road Bedtime Stories: Episode 4."

33. China Daily, "Belt and Road Bedtime Stories: Episode 5."

4. The Emperor's New Brand

1. Yu, "Qianming zhongwai keshang."

2. Ling, "Ammar's Silk Road Dream."

3. Holbig, "Ideology after the End of Ideology," 61.

4. Holbig, "Ideology after the End of Ideology," 64.

5. Pieke, *The Good Communist*, 16, 26–55. For a portrait of elite cadre training during the Jiang Zemin era, see Liu, "Rebirth and Secularization," 105–25.

6. Brady, *Marketing Dictatorship*, 9.

7. Ma and Thomas ("In Xi We Trust") have the most recent (and readable) account of the structure and funding of China's propaganda system. Elizabeth Perry's ("Cultural Governance in Contemporary China") take on the history of the Chinese propaganda system, which she calls "cultural governance" and interprets through a lens of "responsive authoritarianism," is also highly informative. David Shambaugh's essay ("China's Propaganda System") sets a gold standard for mapping the structure of the propaganda system and its intersection with China's factional politics starting in the mid-1980s, but it is somewhat dated.

8. Ma and Thomas, "In Xi We Trust."

9. "Vision and Actions."

10. Xu Zhong, a director-general at the People's Bank of China, has eloquently theorized why the interdepartmental process for writing policy guidances tends toward the rhetorical and away from specific instructions: "Most policy documents are drafted by commissioners from different departments. When they come together to exchange ideas on the draft and to sign the papers, they often discover that different departments have different opinions. The varied views might be a result of different ideas and experience, or due to a conflict of interest. Whatever the reason, it is hard to coordinate and reach agreement in a limited time, especially when the commissioners are not empowered to adjust their positions or make any compromise for their own department. Therefore controversial issues, which attract differences of opinion, are usually taken out of final policy documents. So in fact, what appear to be unified positions are actually the result of disagreements being removed . . . The same rules can have totally different effects when administrative departments have too much discretionary power." See Xu, "Why China's Reform Documents."

11. The *New York Times* continues to refer to OBOR as a "$1 trillion plan" in nearly all of its articles on the topic, even though no official Chinese source has confirmed the figure. See for example Mauk, "Can China Turn?"

12. The document lists five such "cooperation priorities," but "policy coordination" comes first, which in the conventional structure of Chinese government documents suggests that it is the most important. The other four priorities are "facilities connectivity, unimpeded trade, financial integration, and people-to-people bonds."

13. "Ministry of Culture's Action Plan," quoted in He, "The Domestic Politics of the Belt and Road," 180–95.

14. Xinhua, "China's New Scholarship," quoted in He, "The Domestic Politics of the Belt and Road."

15. Godement and Kratz, "'One Belt, One Road,'" 10, quoted in He, "The Domestic Politics of the Belt and Road."

16. "Liangan meiye jingying huiju fuzhou."

17. In Chinese: 国家级战略部署.

18. Xiang, "Ban yiliu pingan saishi zonglü." See, for example, "Shanyang xian meishujia xiehui" and "Yidaiyilu cong guanzhong dao caoyuan."

19. For Wal-Mart, see "Woerma yu guangdong zhengfu shenhua hezuo"; for Boeing, see Boeing (China) Communications Department, "Boyin xieshou zhongguo hangkong"; for Allianz, see Chen, "Anlian yidaiyilu youwang"; for Samsung, see Shi and Wang, "'Yidaiyilu' meiti hezuo luntan"; and for Microsoft, see "Weiruan zishen fuzongcai."

20. Pu, "Xiangying yidaiyilu zhuyou jiudian jituan."

21. "Xiecheng CEO sunjie jiji buju."

22. In Chinese: 做"一带一路"首选银行. See "Qingdao pijiu buju yidaiyilu."

23. "Zhongguo yihang shenhua yidaiyilu jinrong."

24. Cao, "Ofo chuangshiren daiwei yidaiyilu."

25. "Law Society of Hong Kong's Belt and Road Conference."

26. "Zhongqi fazhan konggu jituan."

27. In Chinese: 一带一路卓越贡献品牌奖.

28. "Xiaohua kong."

29. Liu, "Yearender."

30. See, for example, Liu, "Yearender."

31. In Chinese: 蓝色经济通道 and 近北极国家. See Meng, "Vision for Maritime Cooperation."

32. For more on the role of LSGs in Chinese foreign policymaking under Xi, see Jakobson and Manuel, "How are Foreign Policy Decisions?," 101.

33. For example, between 2008 and 2015, Sri Lanka's ratio of government debt to GDP declined slightly from 77 percent to 76 percent. During the same period, the debt of state-owned companies rose from 8 percent of GDP to 25 percent. This brought the total effective national debt load from 86 percent to 100 percent of GDP—a dangerous jump for an emerging market economy. See Federal Reserve Bank of St. Louis, "Credit to Government."

34. Kornai, Maskin, and Roland, "Understanding the Soft Budget Constraint."

35. Joy-Perez and Scissors, "A Close Look at OBOR."

5. Strategic Promiscuity

1. China Xinhua News (@XHNews), Twitter, December 10, 2017.

2. Parker and Chefitz, "Debtbook Diplomacy."

3. "Remarks by Vice President Pence."

4. "Remarks by Vice President Pence at the 2018 APEC CEO Summit."

5. Hewage, "China in South Asia."

6. Holt, *Buddha in the Crown*; Dreyer, *Zheng He*, 83–94, 155–62.

7. Interview with Asanga Gunawansa, Colombo, January 22, 2018.

8. "Godavaya Wreck."

9. Sivasundaram, *Islanded*, 50.

10. Lee, *Making a World*, 50.

11. Patnaik and Haldar, "Sino-Sri Lanka Economic Relations," 28–29.

12. Lerski, "Sri Lanka Turns East," 187.

13. Lerski, "Sri Lanka Turns East," 187.

14. India drew a different set of lessons: Sri Lanka was a strategic headache, a poorly managed neighbor that had allowed sectarianism to dilute its development potential. Retired Indian Maj. Gen. Dhruv Katoch recalled to me his own experience as a young officer fighting the Tamil Tigers in Sri Lanka: "I remember asking one of my [Sinhala] Sri Lankan colleagues whether he spoke Tamil. He responded that 'I don't speak the language of the dogs.' I was shocked to hear that. It made me realize what a precarious situation we Indian officers had been sent into." Katoch described his combat memories in Sri Lanka as the most jarring and intense of his career. "Afghanistan was nothing, *nothing* compared to that." But his recollections of Sri Lanka are tinged with admiration. "Even in 1989, when we were marching through these torn-up villages, an Indian could not fail to notice that every person seemed to have his own house and latrine, every village had its school." The Sri Lankans understood the concept that basic development can be shared. To Katoch, Sri Lanka is advantaged by culture, not just resources and geography. "I still believe that Sri Lanka could be a Singapore in ten years." But "reaching the next level will require good leadership that can tone down the communal tensions . . . Sri Lanka is rich in water, land, and tourist potential. It has everything the Good Lord can give a country—except maybe brains." Interview with Dhruv Katoch, New Delhi, January 15, 2018.

15. Mahr, "Sri Lanka to Start Tally."

16. "Mahinda Chintana."

17. "Mahinda Chintana."

18. Interview with Paikiasothy Saravanamuttu, Colombo, January 22, 2018.

19. Menon, *Choices,* 142–43; emphasis added.

20. Interview with Dhruv Katoch, New Delhi, January 15, 2018.

21. "Sri Lanka: Growing Clout."

22. Menon, *Choices,* 150–51.

23. Interview with Adm. Jayanath Colombage, Colombo, January 22, 2018.

24. The firms—Marshall Macklin Monogan and BFC Civil—withdrew after the Sri Lankan Southern Development Authority demanded additional equity. Ladduwahetty, "Hambantota Port Will Attract."

25. Ferdinando, "No Funds for H'tota Port."

26. Niyas, "Hambantota Port Project."

27. Jansz, "Seaport Study in Stormy Seas."

28. Perera, "Life in the Limbo Zone."

29. Interview with Paikiasothy Saravanamuttu.

30. "Joint Press Communiqué."

31. Soysa, "China's Silicon Sea Route."

32. The only two powerful oversight committees were the Committee on Public Enterprises and Committee on Public Accounts, which worked on bureaucratic corruption and other "low-hanging fruit" unrelated to the Rajapaksa family. Interview with Nishan de Mel, Colombo, January 23, 2018.

33. "WikiLeaks: Basil Is Corrupt."

34. In 2008, the Rajapaksas closed the National Procurement Agency and replaced it two years later with a Standing Cabinet Appointed Review Committee that was

widely believed to reflect their political preferences. See Sivaram, "'Locked-In' to China," 3.

35. "Sri Lankan Expert Says."

36. The choices were a fixed rate of 6.3 percent or the floating London Inter-bank Offered Rate rate, then at 5.5 percent. Sri Lanka chose the fixed rate to minimize interest rate risk.

37. I have not seen any documents that corroborate the *Xinhua* account, but multiple interviews I conducted in Sri Lanka suggest that it is correct.

38. In Chinese: 坚忍不拔. For a thought-provoking and partially overlapping explanation of China's strategic objectives in Sri Lanka, see Zhang, "Beyond 'Debt-Trap Diplomacy'."

39. Interview with Asanga Gunawansa, Colombo, January 22, 2018.

40. Compiled by the author from Parliament of Sri Lanka, *Sri Lanka Ports Authority Annual Reports, 2010–2015.*

41. Ports Minister Arjuna Ranatunga admitted this to multiple interviewers in 2016.

42. Construction was expected to take thirty-six months.

43. "Xi Calls for Closer."

44. "Xi Says China Regards Sri Lanka."

45. Intriguingly, reports at the time in the Sri Lankan English-language press overstated Sri Lanka's equity stake in the project. According to the *Sunday Times*, the Chinese joint venture would control only 53 percent of the project equity, and the SLPA 47 percent. But in a public disclosure of the Agreement on Key Terms, China Merchants clarified that the joint venture would control 64.98 percent of the equity and invest $391 million in the project company. The SLPA's equity stake would be only 35.02 percent. This distribution had major financial implications. The Agreement on Key Terms stated that SLPA had agreed to invest $212 million, in proportion to its (35 percent) equity stake, bringing the project's total capital to $601 million. See Wijedasa, "Hambantota Port Phase II" and "Potential Disclosable Transaction Agreement."

46. For example, the Sri Lankan government described the deal as a "Supply, Operate and Transfer" agreement. The Sri Lankans claimed that this was different from the "Build, Operate, and Transfer" structure commonly used for public–private partnerships, but did not clarify the distinction. China Merchants' disclosure does not describe how the SLPA planned to obtain its share of the funds, stating that "detailed terms and conditions" were "still being discussed."

47. The SLPA, for its part, would receive commercial rights to sixty-two hectares of the reclaimed land and supervisory authority over the sixty-three hectares of newly created public spaces. See Sivaram, "'Locked-In' to China," 8.

48. "Four of Seven Berths."

49. Abi-Habib, "How China Got Sri Lanka."

50. Chalmers and Miglani, "Insight: Indian Spy's Role Alleged."

51. Interview with Jayanath Colombage.

52. Interview with Jayanath Colombage.

53. Interview with Jayanath Colombage.

54. Macan-Markar, "Sri Lanka Attempts."

55. Wickramasinghe, "'I Am Not a Person.'"

56. The government justified the claim that it owned 50.7 percent of the port's equity by adding together its stake in HIPS—the main holding company—to equity in HIPS that it claimed to hold "indirectly" through its 15 percent minority stake in HIPG.

57. "CMPort Acquire Stakes of Hambantota Project."

58. Incorporating Gainpro in the British Virgin Islands provided several benefits to China Merchants, including minimal disclosure requirements; corporate governance laws that allow a director of a wholly owned subsidiary to act in the best interests of the parent company, even when that action is not in the best interests of the subsidiary; the right for parties to create their own voting majorities for approving corporate matters; and the right of the board of directors to manage the company without the need for shareholder involvement.

59. He, "Zhongguo zhu sililanka dashi."

60. Lu, "Zhongguo dui sililanka shexia zhaiwu xianjing."

61. Aneez, "Sri Lanka Presidential Nominee Rajapaksa."

62. Dong and Wang, "India Appears Threatened."

63. An Indian member of parliament made this argument to me in 2018. See also "Govt. Talking to India" and "Sri Lanka to Lease Mattala Airport."

64. "Sri Lanka Wins Record Foreign Investment."

65. Interview with Asanga Gunawansa.

66. Interview with Duminda Ariyasinghe, Colombo, January 23, 2018.

67. Vogel, *Deng Xiaoping.*

6. The Skeptical Bulldozer

1. When British explorer and journalist Henry Morton Stanley arrived in Africa in 1871 in search of his lost colleague, David Livingstone, he came by way of Bagamoyo. Perhaps unsurprisingly, there is no monument.

2. "African Countries Take Bold Step."

3. On the crackdown on civil society and free expression, see "Opposition Parties in Tanzania."

4. The Swahili-language media have always been careful and restrained in their coverage of the Bagamoyo project, particularly after Kikwete embraced it and Xi visited in 2013. Still, a few interesting articles are notable. In 2010, opposition leaders criticized the government's proposals to build several large projects, including the Bagamoyo port. After Kikwete left office, the space to criticize the project opened somewhat: in November 2015, *Mainichi* newspaper reported that local communities in Bagamoyo were complaining about likely environmental impact. In February 2017, the press reported that Tanzanian and Chinese officials were blaming each other for the delays. The press always reported statements from government officials insisting that the project would go ahead as scheduled. See "Wapinzani wapinga miradi"; Ngarabali, "Ujenzi wa bandari"; "Bandari Bagamoyo"; Msuya, "China, Tanzania zatofautiana"; Simtowe, "Ujenzi Bandari ya Bagamoyo." A variety of rumors about corruption in the Bagamoyo project can be found on Swahili-language blogs and social media, but I could not satisfactorily substantiate them.

5. Prominent Tanzanian journalists also faced death threats and assaults even before Magufuli took power in November 2015. See Greenslade, "Tanzanian Journalists." In 2017, prominent reporter Azory Gwanda was kidnapped from his home by a group of men and has not been seen again. When a delegation from the nonprofit Committee to Protect Journalists arrived to investigate, they reported that "at least 10 government agents showed up in their hotel room in Dar es Salaam. Claiming that [the committee representatives] did not have the appropriate visas, the agents took them to a secret location and interrogated them for several hours." See "One Year After Disappearance."

6. Kelemen, "Planning for Africa."

7. Yu, "China Development in Africa."

8. Under the deal, China committed to buying £5 million of goods annually. Tanzania could buy what it liked from China and receive the difference in cash.

9. Sued, "Tazara."

10. Interview with Joseph Simbakalia, Dar es Salaam, December 4, 2018.

11. Bräutigam, *Dragon's Gift*, 39.

12. From 1949 to 1971, Taiwan represented China on the UN Security Council. Bräutigam, *Dragon's Gift*, 34.

13. Pauley, "China Takes the Lead."

14. Zhou, "How a Chinese Investment Boom."

15. For a nicely written balance of history and reportage, see French, *China's Second Continent*.

16. Interview with Joseph Simbakalia.

17. Reports from the World Bank and US Chamber of Commerce found that inefficiencies at the Dar es Salaam port cost regional economies up to $2.6 billion each year. See also Tanzania Ports Authority, "Dar es Salaam."

18. The report recommended constructing two new container berths, a multistory parking garage, a cargo freight station, and a waterfront area.

19. The other locations were Mbegani, Mwanbani, and Tanga.

20. Honan, "Tanzania Dreams Big."

21. Lü, "Xi jinping waijiao sixiang." I am indebted to Ruofei Shen for his advice in preparing this translation.

22. "Tanzania's Big Results."

23. China Merchants Group, "History."

24. Mu, "Oman Pledges to Support."

25. "Uncertainty Hits Kikwete's."

26. "Tanzania Bagamoyo Port Construction."

27. Elinaza, "Home Port."

28. Athumani, "Master Plan for Bagamoyo."

29. "Bulldozer" is an English translation. Magufuli's Swahili nickname is *Tingatinga*.

30. International Monetary Fund, "Tanzania 2016 Article IV Consultation."

31. "Tanzania Government Confirms."

32. Wafula, "Tanzania Building Electric Rail."

33. Mirondo, "Govt. Halts Building of Bagamoyo Port."

34. "John Magufuli Is Bulldozing."

35. "Zhongguo jumin fu tansangniya," 48.

36. "Zhongguo jumin fu tansangniya," 48. See also Lü, "Tansangniya xin zongtong Magufuli de zhizheng fengge."

37. Lü, "Tanzania: The Belt and Road Initiative and China-Tanzania Relations."

38. "Fei meng fenghui ruqi kaimu."

39. Not his real name. I have anonymized him out of concern for his safety and privacy.

40. Interview with Zitto Kabwe, December 11, 2018.

41. "Tanzania's China-Backed."

42. Chaudhury, "Tanzania President Terms."

43. Ssebwami, "Magufuli Suspends Bagamoyo Port Construction."

44. Zheng, "China, Tanzania in Talks."

45. The five demands were (1) a reduction in the lease duration from ninety-nine years to thirty-three; (2) removal of the tax holiday clause; (3) a clause that China Merchants must pay market rates for water and electricity; (4) a requirement that China Merchants remain subject to government inspection and regulation by the Tanzanian government; and (5) a clause confirming that Tanzania may develop other ports in competition with Bagamoyo. In short, the ultimatum was a political stunt, not a serious offer.

46. Interview with Togolani Mavura, London, June 27, 2018.

47. Interviews with Uledi Abbas Musa and Faustine Kamuzora, Dar es Salaam, December 6 and 11, 2018.

48. Kairuki, "Message from the Ambassador."

49. Belt and Road Portal, "Data."

7. The Eagle's Nest

1. Thucydides, *History of the Peloponnesian War*, 3–4.

2. Interview with Plamen Tonchev, Athens, November 3, 2018.

3. de Quetteville, "China Brings the Good Times."

4. Edwards, *United Nations Participants*, 92.

5. "Greek Shipping Is Modernized."

6. Hatzidakis, "China's COSCO Eyes."

7. de Quetteville, "China Brings the Good Times."

8. China opened the market to other entrants in 1998.

9. "History."

10. The best survey of COSCO's history and its broader operations in Europe is Zheng and Smith, "New Voyages."

11. Nolan and Wang, "Beyond Privatization."

12. Brødsgaard, "Politics and Business Group."

13. Jiang's three-day visit in 2000 focused on trade relations and a tour of Greek monuments. This visit did not yield any particularly significant results. The Chinese press reported that the Greek prime minister would visit China later that year, but two years passed before the trip occurred. See "Greece Welcomes" and "Jiang Visits in Greece."

14. Technically, Li confirmed that Beijing would continue to support Cyprus's efforts to defend its national sovereignty and its territorial integrity. He also expressed China's

wish that the Cyprus dispute be resolved by the UN Security Council. In Greece, this was interpreted as a discreet gesture of support. Papadopoulos, "To Thema Itan Kai."

15. Papadopoulos, "To Thema Itan Kai." The meeting's agenda included the harmonization of trade regulations, tourism, student visas, double taxation of imports, construction of transit centers connected to Greek ports, and the possibility of Special Economic Zones to facilitate Chinese manufacturing and assembly in Greece.

16. Terzis, "I Simfonia Tou Karamanli."

17. The full quote is of interest: "From the actual point of view of the bilateral relations in recent years, the EU has clearly emphasized more than ever the safeguarding of its own economic interests. It has intentionally raised its bargaining threshold in trade negotiations and conducted frequent anti-dumping investigations into China's export products, setting various obstacles for China's economic development. In politics, they frequently use 'human rights' and 'religious freedom' to talk about things and find faults with China, which puts pressure on the Chinese government. This change reflects the complexity and tortuousness of the development of China-EU relations. China-EU relations have indeed entered into a period of adjustment and transition." See Zhao, "Zhongou guanxi."

18. "S&P: Pithanotero Senario."

19. "8 Stous 10 Ellines."

20. Law 2688, 1999 (Gov. 40 Á/ 1999).

21. "Concession Agreement." In 2008 the duration of the concession agreement was modified from forty to fifty years. With this modification the lease will end in 2052. See also "Annual Financial Report 2016."

22. "I Epomeni Mera."

23. Interview with George Xiradakis, Athens, November 5, 2018.

24. Interview with George Xiradakis.

25. "Syn: Episkepsi."

26. In "Paranomes kai Kataxristikes."

27. Papadiochou, "Kritiki Apo ton Papandreou."

28. Terzis, "I Symfonia tou Karamanli."

29. In "To DS tou OLP Enekrine."

30. "Syntoma: Gia Darki Eirini."

31. Pier I, which would be operated by the state, was still under construction.

32. Under the deal, the PPA agreed to pay €82 million to fund a voluntary retirement scheme, plus an additional €8 million to compensate for the lower wages COSCO was expected to pay. The center-right press mocked the deal. See Mpardounias, "O OLP Plironei 82 Ek."

33. Interview with Anastasia Frantzeskaki, Athens, November 5, 2018.

34. Litigation on the European level over the tax concessions was an ongoing side plot in this case. The main points were as follows. In November 2008, after the operational lease agreement was signed, the European Commission requested that the Greek government explain some of the tax exemptions in the agreement. When PASOK took power in 2009, COSCO privately lobbied the new government to guarantee that it would continue to honor these exemptions. Greece agreed to do so in February 2010. In October 2012, the European Commission requested further clarifications, charging that COSCO's

tax exemptions may have constituted unlawful "state aid." COSCO and Greece denied the charges, but the commission was not convinced. On March 23, 2015, the commission found Greece in violation of state aid rules on eight counts and ordered the government to recover the funds from COSCO—with interest. Greece appealed and lost its case in the European Court in December 2017. Still, most of COSCO's tax advantages survived the legal challenge. See Yfanti and Gelantalis, "Fernoun Pelateia"; Mpardounias, "Eksigiseis gia to Forologiko"; "Commission Decision 2015/1827"; and "Judgment of the General Court."

35. Papahelas, "O Piraias."

36. Morou, "Foniki Epidromi."

37. Interview with Thodoris Dritsas, Athens, November 5, 2018.

38. Faiola, "Greece Is Tapping." Wei's slogan "build a nest to attract the phoenix" (筑巢引凤) is about two decades old. For a thought-provoking essay about the metaphors used in the Chinese development lexicon, see "'Zhuchaoyinfeng' he 'yinfengzhuchao.'"

39. Kostopoulos et al., "To Kryfo Mnimonio."

40. Papastathopoulou, "COSCO kai Thriaseio"; Koronaiou, "Ksafnikos Erotas me to Yuan."

41. Interview with Thodoris Dritsas.

42. Alexander, "China's New Silk Road."

43. Alexander, "China's New Silk Road."

44. MSC had had a prior contract with PPA, which it terminated after COSCO signed the operational lease agreement in 2008. In 2011, COSCO argued that the lease agreement had transferred the MSC contract to COSCO.

45. The Thriasio tender was extended five times but attracted no other bidders. COSCO never ended up submitting a bid. See Kassimi, "Meso Thriaseiou."

46. Interview with Thodoris Dritsas.

47. News reports assessed the government's 75 percent stake at €275 to €358 million. See Kontogiannis, "OLP Kai COSCO," and Tsamopoulos, "OLP: Kleidi o Tropos."

48. The ports in question were Elefsina, Rafina, and Lavrio.

49. Papastathopoulou, "Tichodioktes Pou Prin."

50. Varoufakis, *Adults in the Room*, 42.

51. Varoufakis, *Adults in the Room*, 43.

52. For the full text of the agreement, see Law 4072 2012, Appendix XII. See also "Private Agreement."

53. "MSCI Announces the Results."

54. Mpellos, "Allagi Montelou."

55. "Stournaras: 'Tha Kanoume ta Panta.'"

56. Mpardounias, "Katalitiki I Eisodos."

57. Zikou, "O Epomenos Igetis?"

58. Zikou, "O Epomenos Igetis?"

59. "I COSCO Oregetai."

60. "I COSCO Oregetai."

61. On February 28, 2013, to facilitate the agreement between COSCO-Hewlett-Packard and TrainOSE, the Greek government introduced an amendment for the "facilitation of foreign companies that import products to Greece with the ultimate aim of

channeling those products to other countries." These products would be tax-exempt, but accountants would track the amount exempted through to the products' final destination. France and the Netherlands used similar policies. "Doro O FPA."

62. Foteinos, "Prosgeiosi Kinezon."

63. "Greek PM's Visit to China."

64. "Antridraseis gia to Taksidi."

65. "Antridraseis gia to Taksidi." The percentage of shares for sale—51 percent, 67 percent, or 74.5 percent—would reportedly depend on an appraisal of PPA's assets.

66. Foteinos, "Crash Test Gia."

67. Tsimplakis, "Megales Zimies Gia to Ependitiko."

68. Maltezou, "China Hints at Purchase."

69. Tsimplakis, "Pur Omathon Stin Kivernisi."

70. "Anaptiksi Basismeni Sto Aima."

71. "Kinitopoiiseis Ton Ergazomenon."

72. "I Kivernisi Ekchorei."

73. After the new tender was floated, the former CEO of PPA, Nick Anastasopoulos, told a reporter that the government would renegotiate its arrangement with PPA. Anastasopoulos noted that this was a deliberate "gap" in the invitation to tender: before the government proceeded to the bidding stage, it would modify its arrangement with PPA to ensure that ownership of the port would revert to the Greek state in 2052. The issue receded from view while the tender process proceeded. Meanwhile, Greece returned to the international bond market, and China did not buy bonds as it had promised.

74. The court made two changes to the contract. The renegotiated agreement had exempted COSCO from annual guaranteed consideration as long as GDP remained below its 2008 level (plus 2 percent). The court suggested first that annual payments should resume in 2021, and second that COSCO would have to make additional annual payments for the western side of Pier III. Li and Samaras met again in October. In November, COSCO and PPA announced a revised deal. COSCO would not make either payment recommended by the court. However, starting in 2021, COSCO would guarantee minimum levels of throughput.

75. "Apantiseis Ef'olis."

76. "Th. Dritsas."

77. "China Premier Asks Greek PM."

78. "G. Dragasakis: Entos Ebdomadon."

79. "TAIPED: 'Prasino Fos.'"

80. Before the bidding began, the government announced that it had renegotiated its master concession of the port to the PPA. Under the new agreement, PPA—and by extension, its future owner—would lease the port's facilities and land from the Greek state until 2052. The state would receive 3.5 percent of PPA's revenues, as opposed to 2 percent previously. The Greek state would maintain certain privileges, including regulating fees on cruise ships.

81. "Ouden Neoteron Apo Ton OLP."

82. The tender closed on December 22.

83. Tsimplakis, "Stous Kinezous." See also Tsimplakis, "Entono Paraskinio."

84. COSCO's investment projections factored in funds that the EU had already committed to help modernize the port, as well as dividends of PPA shares calculated based on unrealistic assumptions of future profits.

85. COSCO paid €813.62 million for a 64.5 percent stake in Kumport. See Kamilali, "Ti Sta Alitheia."

86. "Poli-limani."

87. "Th. Dritsas: 'I Piesi.'"

88. The bill would have increased PPA's annual payment to the Greek state from 2 percent of its revenues to 3.5 percent.

89. "Psifistike Sti Vouli."

90. "P Lafazanis: Skandalo Ton Skandalon."

91. "Sfirokopima tis Kivernisis."

92. "I COSCO Parakamptei."

93. This was the approach favored by the Greek shipping industry, if not by the unions. See Tsimplakis, "Stin Yperdeksameni Tis COSCO"; Kouroumplis, "Greek Government Has Offered."

94. "Efsima Apo Ton Amerikano Presvi."

95. Liu, "NYT Sees Chinese Investment."

96. Wübbeke et al., "Made in China 2025."

97. Beat et al., "Von Peking aus betrachtet ist Europa."

8. OBOR Shapes Four Regions

1. The best work on this topic is Van der Kley, "China's Security Activities."

2. "Belt and Road International Forum."

3. For a gripping account of this dispute drawing extensively from the diaries and notes of the key players, see Gerson, "The Sino-Soviet Border Conflict," 34–38.

4. Kennedy, "Xi Jinping's Opposition."

5. Gabuev, "Crouching Bear," 65.

6. Zuenko, "Kak proidet kitajskiy Shelkoviy."

7. Gabuev also argues that personal relations between the leaders was a factor in Putin's change of heart on OBOR: "In September 2013 when Xi announced [OBOR] this personal relationship wasn't deep, and thus the initial reaction in the Kremlin was suspicious." See Gabuev, "Crouching Bear," 67. I do not believe that the evidence supports this claim.

8. Gabuev, "Crouching Bear," 74, 76.

9. Shuvalov, "Rossiya gotova k sovmestnoy rabote."

10. Karaganov, "Toward the Great Ocean."

11. Gabuev, "Crouching Bear," 74. Some Chinese scholars argue for a different interpretation of the Chinese term 对接. Wu Zelin contends that all Asian countries' relationship to OBOR is encapsulated in the "linking up" model, because the term implies more respect for national sovereignty than the European model of development, which is based on integration. See Wu, "Tanxi ouya liangzhong butong," 68–71.

12. "RZD Proposes Fast Trains"; "Moscow–St. Petersburg High Speed Study."

13. "Russian High-Speed Takes Two Steps Back."

14. Lu and Mo, "China-Backed Rail Project."

15. Mackoki and Popescu, "China and Russia," 38.

16. Kassenova, "More Politics than Substance."

17. Novatek holds a controlling 50.1 percent stake. In 2016, CNPC acquired a 20 percent stake, with the OBOR policy bank Silk Road Fund taking an additional 9.9 percent. France's Total also owns 20 percent.

18. "China's Arctic Policy."

19. "China, Russia to Promote."

20. A very good book on China's polar ambitions is Brady, *China as a Polar Great Power*.

21. Staalesen, "More Nuclear Power."

22. Rosatom, Russia's state-owned nuclear company, acquired Uranium One in 2013 and has expanded its holdings in Kazakhstan. The Russian and Kazakh governments have jointly created the world's largest uranium bank and have discussed building a new reactor in Kazakhstan, though no progress has been made so far. See Pannier, "Putin Offers Russian Help."

23. Sun, "Zhong-ou ban lie ji paomo."

24. This includes frequently cited academic literature on OBOR as well as commentary in the popular press. See Blanchard and Flint, "Geopolitics of China's Maritime."

25. Mackinder, *Democratic Ideals and Reality*, 150. See also Mackinder, "Geographical Pivot."

26. Liu, "New Silk Road Is an Opportunity."

27. Allison, *Destined for War*, 125–26.

28. Gabuev, "Belt and Road to Where?"

29. Hornby, "Mahathir Mohamad Warns."

30. "Iskander Shah."

31. Lockman, "The 21st Century Maritime Silk Road," 3.

32. Liow, "Malaysia-China Relations," 674.

33. Liow, "Malaysia-China Relations," 672–91.

34. "Asia's Muslim Countries."

35. Indeed, the Singaporean army explicitly drills contingency scenarios for occupying and pacifying Malaysia.

36. "PM: Presence of Warships."

37. Quoted in Parker and Chefitz, "Debtbook Diplomacy."

38. My interviews with Singaporean sources and other Malaysia watchers suggest that this figure has declined significantly since 2017, but there are no hard data to demonstrate this. See "Global Indicators Database."

39. "China Going Global Investment Index 2017."

40. Zainul, "Business as Usual."

41. The Chinese firms PowerChina (via SinoHydro Limited), Shenzhen Yantian Port Group, and Rizhao Port Group are all involved in the construction.

42. "It Will Be Insane to Tell Investors."

43. "It Will Be Insane to Tell Investors."

44. Sukumaran, "Mahathir, the Malaysian Dictator."

45. "Dr M: My 'Child' Is Lost."

46. See "ECRL Key Facts."

47. "ECRL Key Facts."

48. "Mahathir Says Malaysia."

49. Jaipragas, "'Chinese By Nature.'"

50. Lies, "Malaysia Wants to Be Friendly."

51. Next to Pakistan, Bangladesh is the most strategically important country in this list. For a concise and informative presentation of the range of views in Dhaka, see "Belt and Road Initiative." For a biased but highly detailed policy paper on how Afghanistan thinks it can gain from partnering with OBOR, see Safi and Alizada, "Integrating Afghanistan."

52. See, for example, Brewster, "Silk Roads and Strings of Pearls." Similar claims were made about the Kyaukphyu port in Myanmar, which is just as unviable as a massive overland trade corridor.

53. Lee, "The Strategic Importance."

54. "Govt Asked to Review Accord."

55. Kiani, "Chinese Firms to Get Contracts."

56. Husain, "Exclusive: CPEC Master Plan Revealed."

57. CPEC was announced before OBOR, on May 22, 2013, but was quickly folded into OBOR and is touted by official Chinese sources as a model partnership in the OBOR framework.

58. Mustafa, "China Has Provided $5 BN Loan."

59. For a full breakdown of Pakistan's foreign obligations, including its sovereign and commercial debts to China, see "Pakistan: IMF Country Report."

60. Zaidi, "Has China Taken Over Pakistan?"

61. For an excellent journalistic account of Pakistan's civilian-military divide, see Hadid, "In Pakistan, Growing Concern." Since 2014, the military has rapidly extended its control over the economy via the Fauji Foundation and other commercial ventures. See Kay and Marlow, "Military Tightens Grip," and "Financial Highlights."

62. Anderlini et al., "Pakistan Rethinks Its Role," and Press Trust of India, "Pakistan Government Plans."

63. Anderlini et al., "Pakistan Rethinks Its Role."

64. Gupta, "Pakistan Confirms the Bugs."

65. Guramani, "Reservations Regarding CPEC."

66. "CPEC Mess."

67. Ali, "Pak Political Parties."

68. Awan, "Pakistan Establishes CPEC Authority."

69. "Xi Jinping Holds Talks."

70. "Xi Jinping Meets."

71. Garver, *China and Iran*, 23.

72. Dillon, *Encyclopedia of Chinese History*, 524.

73. Garver, *China and Iran*, 7.

74. Garver, *China and Iran*, 36.

75. Bilateral relations were otherwise minimal until the 1970s largely because the shah of Iran was a staunch anticommunist. Pahlavi spoke derisively of Chinese society under

Mao as "totalitarian" and "ant-like." A good survey of China's arms sales to Iran is Gill, "Chinese Arms Exports to Iran."

76. Garver notes, "The PRC found itself in 1979 and vis-a-vis the Islamic Republic of Iran in a situation very similar to that of the *United States* in 1949 vis-a-vis the PRC." Garver, *China and Iran*, 58.

77. Garver, *China and Iran*, 64.

78. Garver, *China and Iran*, 72.

79. Garver, *China and Iran*, 6.

80. The People's Liberation Army conducts joint exercises with the IRGC and has long been a major supplier of weapons and military technology. Rubin, "Iran: IRGC Training."

81. Ehteshami et al., "Chinese-Iranian Mutual"; Ehteshami, "Rise and Impact."

82. Soltaninejad, "Iran and Southeast Asia."

83. Mackenzie, "A Closer Look at China-Iran Relations," 5.

84. Garver, "China and the Iran Nuclear," 123–24 and 127.

85. In Chinese: 相向而行.

86. Garver, "China and the Iran Nuclear," 143.

87. Yang, "China Fully Committed."

88. Faucon, "China Pulls Out."

89. Erdbrink, "For China's Global Ambitions."

90. Zarif, "Shared Vision Binds."

91. Lijian Zhao (@zlj517), "2/2 CDC was caught on the spot. When did patient zero begin in US? How many people are infected? What are the names of the hospitals? It might be US army who brought the epidemic to Wuhan. Be transparent! Make public your data! US owe us an explanation!" Twitter, March 12, 2020.

92. "Iran Leader Refuses US Help."

93. In 2016, China bought 33 percent of Iran's exports and 30 percent of its imports. See "Iran."

Conclusion

1. Lancaster, Rubin, and Rapp-Hooper, "What the COVID-19 Pandemic May Mean."

2. Russell, "The Coronavirus Will Not Be Fatal."

3. Tan, "Gongtong dazao jiankang sichouzhilu."

4. Wen and Hinshaw, "China Asserts Claim."

5. "People's Daily Front Page."

6. Zhao, Zhang, and Ding, "Rang dang de qizhi."

7. "African Union Accuses China."

8. Chase, "Space and Cyberspace Components."

9. OECD, "FDI Stocks."

10. MacDonald, *Energy Futures in Asia*. For an example of an early US military perspective, see Pehrson, "String of Pearls."

11. Yung et al., "'Not an Idea We Have to Shun.'"

12. Xie, "Potential Dual Use."

13. Page, Lubold, and Taylor, "Deal for Naval Outpost."

14. Arduino, "China's Private Security Companies."

15. For a thoughtful discussion of *Wolf Warrior 2*, see Osnos, "Making China Great Again."

16. These countries include Antigua and Barbuda, Barbados, Bolivia, Chile, Costa Rica, Cuba, Dominican Republic, Ecuador, El Salvador, Guyana, Jamaica, Panama, Trinidad and Tobago, Venezuela, and Uruguay.

17. Renshon, *Fighting for Status.*

Bibliography

Nonattributed Sources

"8 Stous 10 Ellines: Ypiretis Ton Poliethnikon i Troika" [8 in 10 Greeks: Troika Serves Multinational Companies]. *Newsbomb*, November 15, 2012.

"African Union Accuses China of Hacking Headquarters." *Financial Times*, January 29, 2018.

"Ambassador Yang Youming Attends the Issuance Ceremony of Commemorative Stamps on the 50th Anniversary of China-Zambia Diplomatic Relations." Ministry of Foreign Affairs of the People's Republic of China, December 31, 2014.

"Anaptiksi Basismeni Sto Aima Ton Ergazomeon" [Growth Based on the Blood and Sweat of Employees]. *Efsyn*, July 18, 2014.

"Annual Financial Report 2016." Piraeus Port Authority, February 16, 2017.

"Antridraseis gia to Taksidi tou Prothipourgou stin Kina" [Reactions to the Prime Minister's Trip to China]. *Enet*, May 16, 2013.

"Apantiseis Ef'olis Tis Ylis Meso Diadiktuou Apo Ton Al. Tsipra" [Alexis Tsipras Responds on All Matters Online]. *Naftemporiki*, January 15, 2015.

"Asia's Muslim Countries Wrestle with Looming Iraq War." *Voice of America*, October 30, 2009.

"Bandari Bagamoyo hapana jenga 'airport'" [Build an Airport, not Bagamoyo Port]. *Mainichi*, March 16, 2016.

"Belt and Road Initiative: Perspective from Bangladesh." *Daily Star*, August 7, 2019.

"Belt and Road International Forum." Presidential Executive Office of Russia, May 14, 2017.

"Belt and Road Portal: Data." Belt and Road Portal. Accessed February 12, 2019.

"Building the Future: A Look at the Economic Potential of East Africa." U.S. Chamber of Commerce. October 14, 2016.

"China Focus: Belt and Road Development on High-Quality Path as Second Forum Closes." Xinhua, April 27, 2019.

"China Going Global Investment Index 2017." Economist Intelligence Unit. Accessed December 8, 2018.

"China Premier Asks Greek PM to Deepen Cooperation on Port." *Kathimerini*, February 12, 2015.

"China Product Import Product Share % Kazakhstan 2000–2010." World Bank, World Integrated Trade Solution. Accessed December 15, 2017.

"China, Russia to Promote Compatibility of BeiDou and GLONASS Navigation Systems." *Global Times*, September 2, 2019.

"China's Arctic Policy." State Council Information Office of the People's Republic of China. Accessed December 7, 2018.

"China's BeiDou Navigation Satellite System." State Council Information Office, June 16, 2016.

"China's Stimulus Package: A Breakdown of Spending." *Economic Observer*, March 7, 2009.

"Chuanmei Chahuahui" [Media Tea Party]. "'Yidaiyilu' baodao zhong zhexie leiqu qianwan buyao peng" [Don't Step into these Minefields in OBOR Reports]. WeChat post, April 17, 2017. Accessed on *Bianji*, November 20, 2019.

"CMPort Acquire Stakes of Hambantota Project." China Merchants Port Holdings Company, July 25, 2017.

"Commission Decision 2015/1827 on State aid SA 28876 (12/C) (ex CP 202/09) implemented by Greece for Piraeus Container Terminal SA & COSCO Pacific Limited." *Official Journal of the European Union*, March 23, 2015.

"Comprehensive Transport and Trade System Development Master Plan in the United Republic of Tanzania." Japan International Cooperation Agency, March 2014.

"Concession Agreement Regarding the Use and Operation of Certain Spaces and Assets in the Piraeus Port." Piraeus Port Authority S.A. Accessed February 25, 2019.

"Controversy over Dam Fuels Rare Public Outcry in Myanmar." *New York Times*, September 21, 2011.

"CPEC Mess: Chinese Company Building Gwadar Port Operating in Pakistan Illegally, Lawmakers Told." Zee Media Bureau, March 14, 2018.

"Dar-es-Salaam Port Improvement Programme (Preparatory Phase)." Department for International Development, 2015.

"Database and Project Design." Mercator Institute for China Studies. September 19, 2018.

"Di 25 ke liangji shijie de xingcheng" [Lesson 25: The Formation of Bipolar World]. In *Gaozhong lishi bixiuyi* [Senior High School History Compulsory I], 119. Beijing: Renmin Jiaoyu Chubanshe, 2007.

"Direct Rail Link Speeds up Europe-China Cargo Trip." *China Daily*, May 11, 2011.

"Doro O FPA Gia COSCO-HP Sto Limani" [VAT Given Away to COSCO-HP for Free]. *Enet*, February 28, 2013.

"Dr M: My 'Child' Is Lost." *The Star*, May 25, 2017.

"ECRL Key Facts." Malaysia Rail Link. Accessed October 30, 2019.

"Efsima Apo Ton Amerikano Presvi, Jeffrey Pait Gia Tis Idiotikopoiiseis" [American Ambassador Jeffrey Pait's Credit for Privatizations]. *Kathimerini*, July 14, 2017.

"Fei meng fenghui ruqi kaimu, tan zongtong magufuli zaici quexi" [African Union Summit Opens as Scheduled, Tanzanian President Magufuli Absent Again]. *Feizhou Huaqiao Zhoubao*, January 31, 2018.

"Financial Highlights." Fauji Foundation. Accessed January 7, 2019.

"From Compass to BeiDou: Chinese Wisdom Helps Navigate Belt & Road." Xinhua, November 19, 2018.

"Full Text of Jiang Zemin's Report at 16th Party Congress on Nov 8, 2002." Ministry of Foreign Affairs of the People's Republic of China, November 18, 2002.

"Full Text of President Xi's Speech at Opening of Belt and Road Forum." Xinhua, May 14, 2017.

"Full Text: Xi Jinping's Keynote Speech at the World Economic Forum." State Council Information Office, April 6, 2017.

"G. Dragasakis: Entos Ebdomadon I Oloklirosi Tis Idiotikopoiisis Tou OLP" [Dragasakis: PPA Privatization Weeks Away from Completion]. *Naftemporiki*, March 28, 2015.

"Geng haode shishi zouchuqu zhanlüe" [Better Implementing the 'Going Out' Strategy]. China Central Government Portal, March 15, 2006.

"Global Indicators Database." Pew Research Center's Global Attitudes Project. Accessed December 8, 2018.

"Godavaya Wreck (2000 Years Ago)." UNESCO. Accessed February 21, 2018.

"Govt Asked to Review Accord with China on Gwadar." *Dawn*, November 27, 2017.

"Govt. Talking to India on Mattala Int'l Airport." *Daily Mirror*, January 29, 2018.

"Greece Welcomes President Jiang's Visit: Ambassador." *People's Daily*, April 12, 2000.

"Greek PM's Visit to China Yields Results on First Day." *Kathimerini*, May 16, 2013.

"Greek Shipping Is Modernized to Remain a Global Leader and Expand Its Contribution to the Greek Economy." National Bank of Greece, May 11, 2006.

"History." China COSCO Shipping Corporation Limited. Accessed January 11, 2019.

"I COSCO Oregetai Kai to Upoloipo Limani" [COSCO Fancies the Rest of the Port Too]. *Enet*, January 18, 2013.

"I COSCO Parakamptei to Diktuo Tis TRAINOSE" [COSCO Skips TRAINOSE's Network]. *Naftemporiki*, July 18, 2016.

"I Epomeni Mera Gia Ton Piraia Einai . . . Tora" [The Next Day for Piraeus Is . . . Now]. *Naftemporiki*, April 11, 2016.

"I Kivernisi Ekchorei Stin COSCO Olo to Limani tou Piraia" [Government Concedes the Whole Port to COSCO]. *Efsyn*, July 24, 2014.

"Investment Opportunities in EPZ and SEZ - Tanzania," Export Processing Zones Authority (EPZA). Accessed March 14, 2019.

"Iran." MIT Observatory of Economic Complexity. Accessed December 11, 2018.

"Iran Leader Refuses US Help." Associated Press, March 22, 2020.

"Iskander Shah." National Library Board. Accessed December 7, 2018.

"It Will Be Insane to Tell Investors Not to Come to Johor." *New Straits Times*, March 22, 2015.

"Jiakuai tuijin 'yidaiyilu' kongjian xinxi zoulang" [Accelerate the Promotion of the "OBOR" Space Information Corridor]. National Development and Reform Commission, National Defense Science and Technology Bureau, October 22, 2016.

"Jiang Visits in Greece." *BBC News*, April 21, 2000.

"Jiang Zemin zhuxi tong tukumansitan zongtong niyazuofu huitan" [President Jiang Zemin Speaks with Turkmenistan President Niyazov]. Foreign Ministry of the People's Republic of China, November 17, 2000.

"Jianshe wanli 'kongzhong xinsilu' guohang yizhou lian kai liang tiao feizhou hangxian" [Erect a Multi-Thousand Mile "New Silk Road in the Sky": Air China Opens Two African Routes This Week]. Ministry of Foreign Affairs of the People's Republic of China, November 6, 2015.

"John Magufuli Is Bulldozing the Opposition and Wrecking the Economy." *The Economist*, October 19, 2017.

"Joint Press Communiqué of the Foreign Ministers of China and Sri Lanka." Consulate-General of the People's Republic of China in San Francisco, July 16, 2006.

"Judgment of the General Court of 13 December 2017—Greece v. Commission (Case T-314/15)." *Official Journal of the European Union*, December 13, 2017.

"Keynote Speech by H.E. Xi Jinping at the Opening Ceremony of the G20 Summit." Embassy of the People's Republic of China in Italy, September 7, 2016.

"Kinitopoiiseis Ton Ergazomenon Ston OLP Kata Tou Filikou Diakanonismou Me Tin COSCO" [PPA's Employees Mobilize against the Dispute Settlement Agreement with COSCO]. *Naftemporiki*, December 17, 2014.

"The Law Society of Hong Kong's Belt and Road Conference." Government of Hong Kong Special Administrative Region. Accessed February 6, 2019.

"Liangan meiye jingying huiju fuzhou, gonghua meiye fazhan xin qushi" [Cross-Strait Beauty Industry Elites Gather in Fuzhou, Discuss the New Trend in the Development of the Beauty Industry]. *Zhongguo Xinwen Wang Fujian*, August 13, 2017.

"Lin Yifu: yi 'xin maxie'er jihua daidong quanqiu jingji fuxing'" [Lin Yifu: Driving the Global Economic Renaissance with the "New Marshall Plan"]. *National Office for Philosophy and Social Sciences*, October 15, 2012.

"Mahathir Says Malaysia Will Use Huawei 'As Much as Possible.'" *Channel News Asia*, May 30, 2019.

"Mahinda Chintana: Vision for a New Sri Lanka. A Ten-Year Horizon Development Framework 2006–2016." Government of Sri Lanka, January 2005.

"Ministry of Culture's Action Plan for Belt and Road Cultural Development (2016–2020)." HKDTC Research. Accessed August 31, 2017.

"Moscow–St Petersburg High Speed Study to be Submitted Next Year." *Railway Gazette*, November 10, 2010.

"MSCI Announces the Results of Its Annual Market Classification Review." MSCI. Accessed February 9, 2019.

"One Year after Disappearance, CPJ Calls for Credible Investigation into Tanzanian Journalist Azory Gwanda's Fate." Committee to Protect Journalists, November 21, 2018.

"Opposition Parties in Tanzania Protest New Law: 'It Will Criminalise Politics.'" *Africa News*, December 11, 2018.

"Ouden Neoteron Apo Ton OLP" [Nothing New from PPA]. *Naftemporiki*, April 22, 2015.

"P Lafazanis: Skandalo Ton Skandalon" [P. Lafazanis: The Greatest Scandal]. *Naftemporiki*, June 30, 2016.

"Pakistan: IMF Country Report No. 19/212." International Monetary Fund, July 2019.

"Paranomes kai Kataxristikes Ekrine tis Kinitopoiiseis ston OLP to Efeteio Piraia" [Piraeus Court of Appeal Judges Mobilizations at PPA Illegal and Abusive]. *In*, April 9, 2008.

"People's Daily Front Page." *ChinaFile*. Accessed February 6, 2019.

"PM: Presence of Warships in Area Sending Wrong Signal." *The Star*, June 7, 2018. Quoted in Sam Parker and Gabrielle Chefitz. "Debtbook Diplomacy." Belfer Center for Science and International Affairs, Harvard Kennedy School, May 24, 2018.

"Poli-limani: Ti Leei O Peiraias Gia Mia Dyskoli Schesi" [City-Port: What Does Piraeus Say About a Difficult Relationship]. *Portnet*, February 14, 2016.

"Potential Disclosable Transaction Agreement in Relation to Hambantota Port, Sri Lanka." China Merchants Port Holdings Company Limited, July 25, 2017.

"President Xi Jinping Delivers Important Speech and Proposes to Build a Silk Road Economic Belt with Central Asian Countries." Ministry of Foreign Affairs of the People's Republic of China, September 7, 2013.

"Private Agreement on the Amendment of the Concession Agreement of 25/11/2008 for the Port Facilities at Piers II and III of the Piraeus Port Authority SA's Container Terminal." *Tax Heaven*, April 12, 2012.

"Psifistike Sti Vouli to Nomoschedio Gia Ton OLP" [The Parliament Ratifies the Bill for PPA]. *Newsbomb*, June 30, 2016.

"Qiangang yuxiang baogao: dangmei guanjianci wendu ceshi" [Qian Gang Language Report: Party Media Keyword Temperature Test]. *QQ*, February 23, 2017.

"Qieshi zuohao goujian shehui zhuyi hexie shehui gexiang gongzuo" [We Must Do a Good Job in All Aspects of Building a Harmonious Socialist Society]. Central People's Government of the People's Republic of China, October 11, 2006.

"Qingdao pijiu buju yidaiyilu zhongguo pinpai shanyao sililanka" [Tsingtao Brewery Strategically Deploys OBOR, Chinese Brand Shines in Sri Lanka]. *Nanfang Zhoumo*, October 21, 2016.

"Remarks by Vice President Pence at the 2018 APEC CEO Summit." White House, November 16, 2018. https://www.whitehouse.gov/briefings-statements/remarks-vice -president-pence-2018-apec-ceo-summit-port-moresby-papua-new-guinea/

"Remarks by Vice President Pence on the Administration's Policy Toward China." White House, October 4, 2018.

"Russian High-Speed Takes Two Steps Back, One Step Forward." *International Railway Journal.* September 25, 2013.
"RZD Proposes Fast Trains to Serve 2018 World Cup." *Railway Gazette,* June 30, 2010.

"S&P: Pithanotero Senario to Grexit Apo tin Paramoni sto Euro" [S&P: Grexit a More Likely Scenario Than Remaining in the Eurozone]. *Kathimerini,* July 6, 2015.
"Sfirokopima tis Kivernisis apo tin Antipolitefsi gia ton OLP" [The Opposition Moves Ruthlessly against the Government on PPA]. *Capital,* June 30, 2016.
"Shanyang xian meishujia xiehui yidaiyilu damei fengyang yang pinguo zuopinzhan kaimu" [Shanyang County Artists Association Opens "OBOR" Exhibition of Damei Fengyang and Yang Pinguo's Works]. *Jiankang Baodao Minsheng Zhougan,* December 28, 2018.
"'Shuang shuniu' jia qi kongzhong 'xinsilu'" ["Double Hub New Silk Road in the Sky" Set Up]. *Communist Party News (Henan Daily),* May 27, 2017.
"Sichouzhilu" [The Silk Road]. *Renmin Ribao,* July 24 1971, 6.
"'Sichouzhilou jingji dai' wei Zhongguo xibu fazhan tigong xin zenzhang dian" [Silk Road Economic Belt Provides a New Rising Point for China's Western Regions]. Xinhua, May 16, 2014.
"Sri Lanka: Growing Clout and Appeal of Non-Western Donors." Wikileaks. February 9, 2007.
"Sri Lanka to Lease Mattala Airport to India by August: Report." *Economy Next,* January 30, 2018.
"Sri Lanka Wins Record Foreign Investment in Oil Project." *Island,* March 21, 2019.
"Sri Lankan Expert Says Interest Rate of Chinese Loan for Port Project Appropriate." Xinhua, June 4, 2015.
"Stournaras: 'Tha Kanoume ta Panta gia tis Idiotikopoiiseis' Leei Pros Kineziki Efimerida" [Stournaras Tells a Chinese Newspaper: "We Will Do Whatever It Takes for Privatization"]. *Kathimerini,* September 25, 2012.
"Syn: Episkepsi Al. Tsipra Ston OLP" [Syn: Tsipras Visits PPA]. *Euro2day,* October 2, 2009.
"Syntoma: Gia Darki Eirini Sto Limani tou Piraia" [In Short: Toward Long-Lasting Peace at Piraeus' Port]. *Kathimerini,* December 3, 2009.

"TAIPED: 'Prasino Fos' Gia to 51% Tou OLP" [TAIPED: A Green Light for 51% of PPA]. *Naftemporiki,* May 13, 2015.
"Tansangniya zhu hua dashi: 'Yidaiyilu' wei geguo tigong gongtong fazhan jiyu" [Tanzanian Ambassador to China: "OBOR" Provides Common Development Opportunities for All Countries]. *Guoji Zaixian,* May 10, 2017.
"Tanzania." Freedom House Report, 2010.
"Tanzania 2016 Article IV Consultation." International Monetary Fund.
"Tanzania Bagamoyo Port Construction to Begin Ahead of Schedule." *Tanzania Invest,* August 28, 2014.
"Tanzania Government Confirms Construction Works of Bagamoyo Port and Special Economic Zone." *Tanzania Invest,* January 21, 2016.
"Tanzania's Big Results Now Initiative an Example of South-South Cooperation." *Africa Platform,* July 2013. Accessed May 1, 2018.

"Tanzania's China-Backed $10 Billion Port Plan Stalls over Terms: Official." Reuters, May 22, 2019.

"Th. Dritsas: 'I Piesi Ton Pragmaton Odigise Se Epiloges Pou Den Einai Dikes Mas Gia Ton OLP'" [Thodoris Dritsas: "The Pressure of Circumstances Led to Choices that Are Not Ours for PPA"]. *Naftemporiki*, April 10, 2016.

"Th. Dritsas: Tha Epixeirithei Epanadiapragmateusi Me Ti COSCO: 'Den Tha Prochorisei I Polisi Metochon Tou OLP Kai Tou OLTH'" [Th. Dritsas: We Will Attempt to Renegotiate with COSCO: Equity Sale of PPA and ThPA Ports Will Not Go Ahead]. *Naftemporiki*, January 28, 2015.

"The Ancient Silk-Traders Route across Central Asia." *Popular Science Monthly: Supplement 7–12* (1878): 381.

"To DS tou OLP Enekrine to Diagonismo Idiotikopoiisis tou Stathmou Emporevmatokivotion" [PPA Board of Directors Approves Competition to Privatize Container Terminal]. *In*, November 16, 2006.

"Uncertainty Hits Kikwete's $11 Billion 'Legacy' Project." *IPP Media*, 27 October 2016.

"United Republic of Tanzania: Staff Report for the 2016 Article IV Consultation," International Monetary Fund, June 28, 2016.

"US Elevated its Ties with India for Free, Open Indo-Pacific: Rex Tillerson." *Economic Times*, December 13, 2017.

"Vision and Actions on Jointly Building Silk Road Economic Belt and 21st-Century Maritime Silk Road." National Development and Reform Commission, March 2015.

"Wang Huning Speaks at the 26th National Higher Education Party Construction and Political Thought Work Meeting." CCTV, January 15, 2019.

"Wapinzani wapinga miradi mikubwa kujengwa kwa JK" [Opponents Oppose Major Projects Built by Jakaya Kikwete]. *Mainichi*, July 4, 2010.

"Weiruan zishen fuzongcai keji chuangxin zai yidaiyilu zhong qidao yinling he zhicheng zuoyong" [Senior Vice President of Microsoft: Technology Innovation Plays a Leading and Supporting Role in "OBOR"]. *Sohu*, March 19, 2017.

"Wen Jiabao 17 ri qianwang dibai longcheng maoyicheng yu huaqiao qinqie jiaoliu" [Premier Wen Jiabao Visited Longcheng Trade City in Dubai on the 17th, Conducted Cordial Exchanges with Overseas Chinese]. China Central Government Portal, January 18, 2012.

"WikiLeaks: Basil Is Corrupt, Limited Educated and Expelled from School." *Colombo Telegraph*, January 5, 2012. Accessed February 22, 2018.

"Woerma yu guangdong zhengfu shenhua hezuo weilai wunian yuji xinzeng sishi dian" [Wal-Mart and Guangdong Government Deepen Cooperation, Expected to Add 40 Stores in the Next 5 Years]. Wal-Mart China, April 20, 2017.

"Wulumuqi jianqi guoji shangmao datongdao" [Urumqi Builds a Wide Channel of International Commerce]. *Xinjiang Renmin Guangbo Diantai*, September 11, 2007.

"Xi Calls for Closer China-Sri Lanka Partnership." Xinhua, September 16, 2014.

"Xi Jinping Holds Talks with UAE Vice President and Prime Minister Muhammad and Crown Prince Abu Dhabi Muhammad" [Xi Jinping tong alianqiu fu zongtong jian zongli muhanmode, abu zha bi wangchu wuhanmode ju hang huitan]. Xinhua, July 20, 2018.

"Xi Jinping Meets with Iraqi Prime Minister Abdul-Mahdi" [Xi Jinping huijian yilake zongli abodulei maheidi]. *Xinhua*, September 23, 2019.

"'Xiangxi kaifang' xu waijiao quanju tongchou" ["March Westwards" and Overall Diplomatic Coordination]. *Huanqiu Shibao*, July 31, 2013.

"Xiaohua kong: Yidaiyilu xianmu, qu waiguo niu" [Joke Lover: OBOR Project, Marry a Foreign Chick]. *XHK*, n.d. Accessed January 31, 2019.

"Xiecheng CEO sunjie jiji buju yidaiyilu litui fupin lüyou" [Ctrip CEO Sun Jie Actively Deploys "OBOR" to Promote Poverty Alleviation]. *Sohu*, October 19, 2017.

"'Xijin' xu fangfan sanda zhanlüe fengxian" [Three Strategic Risks that Must Be Prevented in Marching Westwards]. *Huanqiu Shibao*, August 26, 2013.

"Xin sichouzhilu daxue lianmeng fabu ⟨Xi'an xuanyan⟩" [University Alliance of the New Silk Road Issues Xi'an Declaration]. *Xian Jiaotong Daxue Xinwen Wang*, May 22, 2015.

"Xu Shanda: zuohao zhongguoban 'maxie'er jihua'" [Xu Shanda: Making a Perfect Chinese "Marshall Plan"]. *Zhengquan Ribao*, March 12, 2010.

"Yidaiyilu cong guanzhong dao caoyuan e'erduosi tongchuan shuhua zuopin lianzhan kaizhan!" ["OBOR" from Guanzhong to the Grassland: Exhibition Opened for Erdos and Tongchuan Painting and Calligraphy Works!]. *TPNice*, December 21, 2018.

"Yidaiyilu shang de mingzhu: bileiaifu sigang" [Pearl on the Belt and Road: Piraeus Port]. *China Daily*, May 14, 2017.

"Zhengxie weiyuan xianji chukou, tichu zhongguo ban 'maxie'er jihua'" [CPPCC Member Offers a Plan on Exports to Propose a Chinese "Marshall Plan"]. *China News*, July 13, 2009.

"Zhongguo jumin fu tansangniya touzi shuishou zhinan" [Investment Tax Guide for Chinese residents in Tanzania State Administration of Taxation]. China State Taxation Administration. Accessed September 9, 2018.

"Zhongguo minhang zongju fujuzhang: kuo hangkong yunshu jia kongzhong zoulang" [Deputy Director General of Civil Aviation Administration of China: Expand Air Transport and Build Air Corridors]. *Xinjing Tianshang Wang*, August 27, 2004.

"Zhongguo yihang shenhua yidaiyilu jinrong dadongmai jianshe zuo yidaiyilu shouxuan yinhang" [Bank of China: Deepen the Construction of the "OBOR" Financial Artery; Become the Preferred OBOR Bank]. Bank of China, August 16, 2018.

"Zhongha qianshu gongtong jianshe 'sichouzhilu jingjing dai' hezuo wenjian" [China and Kazakhstan Sign Cooperation Agreement on Jointly Building the "Silk Road Economic Belt"]. *QQ*, December 14, 2014.

"Zhongqi fazhan konggu jituan ronghuo yidaiyilu zhuoyue gongxian pinpai jiang" [China Enterprise Development Holding Group Wins "One Belt and One Road Outstanding Contribution Brand" Award]. *Pinpai Lianmeng Wang*, January 4, 2019.

"'Zhuchaoyinfeng' he 'yinfengzhuchao'" ["Building a Nest to Attract the Phoenix" and "Leading the Phoenix to the Nest"]. *Dadi* 31. Accessed February 9, 2019.

Attributed Sources

Abi-Habib, Maria. "How China Got Sri Lanka to Cough Up a Port." *New York Times,* June 25, 2018.

Acheson, Dean. *Present at the Creation: My Years in the State Department.* New York: Norton, 1987.

Alden, Chris, and Cristina Alves. "History and Identity in the Construction of China's Africa Policy." *Review of African Political Economy* 35, no. 115 (2008): 43–58.

Alden, Chris, and Daniel Large. "On Becoming a Norms Maker: Chinese Foreign Policy, Norms Evolution and the Challenges of Security in Africa." *China Quarterly* 221 (2015): 123–42.

Alexander, Harriet. "China's New Silk Road Into Europe." *The Telegraph,* July 4, 2010.

Ali, Shafqat. "Pak Political Parties, China Adopt Declaration on BRI, CPEC." *The Nation,* March 20, 2019.

Allison, Graham. *Destined for War: Can America and China Escape Thucydides's Trap?* New York: Houghton Mifflin Harcourt, 2017.

American Enterprise Institute. "China Global Investment Tracker." Accessed November 6, 2019.

Andaya, Barbara Watson, and Leonard Y. Andaya. *A History of Malaysia.* London: Red Globe Press, 2017.

Anderlini, Jamil, Henny Sender, and Farhan Bokhari. "Pakistan Rethinks Its Role in Xi's Belt and Road Plan." *Financial Times,* September 9, 2018.

Aneez, Shihar. "Sri Lanka Presidential Nominee Rajapaksa Would Restore Relations with China: Adviser." Reuters, September 19, 2019.

Anyimadu, Adjoa. "Politics and Development in Tanzania: Shifting the Status Quo." Chatham House, March 18, 2016.

Anyimadu, Adjoa. "Tanzania Pipeline Deal Reflects Uganda's Practical and Strategic Concerns." Chatham House, May 4, 2016.

Anyimadu, Adjoa. "Tanzania: A Young Country at a Turning Point." Chatham House, July 14, 2015.

Anyimadu, Adjoa. "Tanzania's Elections Should Not Be a Political Hurdle to Development." Chatham House, October 19, 2015.

Arduino, Alessandro. "China's Private Security Companies: The Evolution of a New Security Actor." National Bureau of Asian Research 80, September 2019.

Athumani, Rose. "Master Plan for Bagamoyo Mega Project in the Offing." *Daily News,* February 17, 2017.

Awan, Zamir Ahmed. "Pakistan Establishes CPEC Authority." *China Daily,* October 9, 2019.

Baculinao, Eric. "Belt and Road Initiative: China Plans $1 Trillion New 'Silk Road'." *NBC News,* May 12, 2017.

Bagchi, Indrani. "India Slams China's One Belt One Road Initiative, Says it Violates Sovereignty." *Times of India,* May 14, 2017.

Balding, Christopher. "Can China Afford Its Belt and Road?" Bloomberg, May 17, 2017.

Balding, Christopher. "Why Democracies Are Turning against Belt and Road." *Foreign Affairs*, October 24, 2016.

Bandiera, Luca, and Vasileios Tsiropoulos. "A Framework to Assess Debt Sustainability and Fiscal Risks under the Belt and Road Initiative." World Bank Policy Research Working Paper 8891 (June 2019).

Baranovitch, Nimrod. "Others No More: The Changing Representation of Non-Han Peoples in Chinese History Textbooks, 1951–2003." *Journal of Asian Studies* 69, no. 1 (2010): 85–122.

Barnett, Michael N., and Jack S. Levy. "Domestic Sources of Alliances and Alignments: The Case of Egypt, 1962–73." *International Organization* 45, no. 3 (Summer 1991): 369–95.

Bates, Robert H., Avner Greif, Margaret Levi, Jean-Laurent Rosenthal, and Barry R. Weingast. *Analytic Narratives*. Princeton, NJ: Princeton University Press, 1998.

Beat, Balzli von, Miriam Meckel, and Gregor Peter Schmitz. "Von Peking aus betrachtet ist Europa eher eine asiatische Halbinsel. Das sehen wir natürlich anders" [From Beijing, Europe Is More of an Asian Peninsula. Of Course We See It Differently]. *WirtschaftsWoche*, June 29, 2017.

Beijing: People's Education Press, 2005. Ministry of Education. *Lishi di er ce bixiu: Putong gaozhong kecheng biaozhun shiyan jiaoke-shu* [History II Compulsory: Normal Senior Secondary School Curriculum Experimental Textbook, Volume 2 历史第二册: 普通高中课程标准实验教科书]. Beijing: People's Education Press, 2007.

Bengali, Kaiser. "China-Pakistan Economic Corridor: The Route Controversy." Chief Minister's Policy Reform Unit, Government of Balochistan, May 2015.

Bennett, Andrew, and Colin Elman. "Case Study Methods in the International Relations Subfield." *Comparative Political Studies* 40 no. 2 (February 2007): 170–95.

Blackwill, Robert D., and Ashley J. Tellis. *Revising U.S. Grand Strategy toward China*. New York: Council on Foreign Relations, 2015.

Blanchard, Jean-Marc F., and Colin Flint. "The Geopolitics of China's Maritime Silk Road Initiative." *Geopolitics* 22, no. 2 (2017): 223–45.

Blanchard, Jean-Marc, and Kun-Chin Lin. "Contemplating Chinese Foreign Policy: Approaches to the Use of Historical Analysis." *Pacific Focus* 28, no. 2 (August 2013): 145–69.

Boeing (China) Communications Department. "Boyin xieshou zhongguo hangkong huaban zhuli yidaiyily fazhan" [Boeing Joins Hands with Chinese Aviation Partners to Help Develop the "Belt and Road"]. *Minhang Ziyuan Wang*, June 25, 2015.

Bolt, Paul J., and Sharyl N. Cross. *China, Russia, and Twenty-First Century Global Geopolitics*. Oxford: Oxford University Press, 2018.

Bolton, John. "The Trump Administration's New Africa Strategy." Heritage Foundation, December 13, 2018.

Brady, Anne-Marie. *China as a Polar Great Power*. Washington, DC: Woodrow Wilson Center Press, 2017.

Brady, Anne-Marie. "China's Foreign Propaganda Machine." *Journal of Democracy* 26, no. 4 (2015): 51–59.

Brady, Anne-Marie, ed. *China's Thought Management*. Oxford: Routledge, 2012.

Brady, Anne-Marie. "Guiding Hand: The Role of the CCP Central Propaganda Department in the Current Era." *Westminster Papers in Communication & Culture* 3, no. 1 (March 2006): 58–77.

Brady, Anne-Marie. *Making the Foreign Serve China: Managing Foreigners in the People's Republic.* Lanham, MD: Rowman & Littlefield, 2003.

Brady, Anne-Marie. *Marketing Dictatorship: Propaganda and Thought Work in Contemporary China.* Lanham, MD: Rowman & Littlefield, 2007.

Brainard, Lael. "The Lessons of the Marshall Plan." Brookings, June 4, 2007.

Bräutigam, Deborah. "Aid 'With Chinese Characteristics': Chinese Foreign Aid and Development Finance Meet the OECD-DAC Aid Regime." *Journal of International Development* 23, no. 5 (2011): 752–64.

Bräutigam, Deborah. *Chinese Aid and African Development: Exporting Green Revolution.* New York: Palgrave, 1998.

Bräutigam, Deborah. *The Dragon's Gift: The Real Story of China in Africa.* New York: Oxford University Press, 2009.

Bräutigam, Deborah. *Will Africa Feed China?* New York: Oxford University Press, 2015.

Bräutigam, Deborah, and Kevin P. Gallagher. "Bartering Globalization: China's Commodity-Backed Finance in Africa and Latin America." *Global Policy* 5, no. 3 (2014): 346–52.

Bräutigam, Deborah, and Jyhjong Hwang. "China-Africa Loan Database Research Guidebook." SAIS China-Africa Research Initiative, 2016.

Brewster, David. *India's Ocean: The Story of India's Bid for Regional Leadership.* New York: Routledge, 2014.

Brewster, David. "Silk Roads and Strings of Pearls: The Strategic Geography of China's New Pathways in the Indian Ocean." *Geopolitics* 22, no. 2 (2017): 269–91.

Brødsgaard, Kjeld Erik. "Politics and Business Group Formation in China: The Party in Control?" *China Quarterly* 211 (2012): 624–48.

Burns, William. "Expanding Economic Connectivity in Central Asia." Speech, Asia Society, New York City, September 23, 2014.

Callahan, William. *China: The Pessoptimist Nation.* New York: Oxford University Press, 2012.

Cao, Jianing. "Ofo chuangshiren daiwei yidaiyilu yinling gongxiang danche chengwei haineiwai goutong qiaoliang ofo" [Ofo Founder Dai Wei: "One Belt, One Road" Turns Bike Sharing into a Bridge of Communication between China and the World]. Belt and Road Portal, September 19, 2017.

CCTV. "'Yidaiyilu' diyi ji gongtong mingyun" [The Belt and Road EP 1 Common Destiny | CCTV]. YouTube, September 13, 2017.

Chacko, Priya. *New Regional Geopolitics in the Indo-Pacific: Drivers, Dynamics and Consequences.* New York: Routledge, 2016.

Chaisse, Julien, and Jędrzej Górski. *The Belt and Road Initiative: Law, Economics, and Politics.* Leiden: Brill Nijhoff, 2018.

Chalmers, John, and Sanjeev Miglani. "Insight: Indian Spy's Role Alleged in Sri Lankan President's Election Defeat." Reuters, January 18, 2015.

Chase, Michael S. "The Space and Cyberspace Components of the Belt and Road Initiative." National Bureau of Asian Research 80, September 2019.

Chaudhuri, K. N. *Trade and Civilisation in the Indian Ocean: An Economic History from the Rise of Islam to 1750.* New York: Cambridge University Press, 1985.

Chaudhury, Dipanjan Roy. "Tanzania President Terms China's BRI Port Project Exploitative." *Economic Times*, July 6, 2019.

Chen, Tingting. "Anlian yidaiyilu youwang cuisheng 466 yi baofei" [Allianz: OBOR Expected to Generate 46.6 Billion Premiums]. *Zhongguo Zhengquan Wang*, August 29, 2017.

Cheng, Li. "Wang Huning." Brookings, n.d. Accessed December 29, 2018.

Cheng, Yu, Lilei Song, Lihe Huang, eds. *The Belt & Road Initiative in the Global Arena: Chinese and European Perspectives*. New York: Palgrave, 2018.

Chin, Tamara. "The Invention of the Silk Road, 1877." *Critical Inquiry* 40, no. 1 (Autumn 2013): 194–219.

China Global Television Network. "One Belt One Road Documentary Episode One: Common Fate." YouTube, November 10, 2016.

China Merchants Group. "History." Accessed May 1, 2018.

Chinese Communist Party. "Zhonggong zhongyang guanyu shenhua wenhua tizhi gaige tuidong shehuizhuyi wenhua ta fazhan da fanrong ruogan zhongda wenti de jueding" [Resolution of the CCP Central Committee on Various Important Questions Concerning the Deepening of Cultural System Reform and the Promotion of Development and Enrichment of Socialist Culture]. In *Zhongguo Gongchandang Di Shiqi Jie Zhongyang weiyuanhui di Liu Ci Quanti Huiyi Wenjian Huibian* [Compilation of Documents of the 6th Plenary Session of the 17 Central Committee of the CCP]. Beijing: Renmin Chubanshe, 2011, 11–50.

Choudhry, Shabir. *Economic Growth or a Debt Trap for Pakistan: CPEC Can Be a Mega Disaster for Pakistan*. Bloomington, IN: Author House, 2018.

Christiansen, Thomas, and Richard Maher. "The Rise of China: Challenges and Opportunities for the European Union." *Asia Europe Journal* 15, no. 2 (June 2017): 121–31.

Chu, Daye. "Both Iran, Pakistan Stand to Benefit from One Belt, One Road." *Global Times*, February 21, 2016.

Clinton, Hillary Rodham. "America's Pacific Century." *Foreign Policy*, October 11, 2011.

Clinton, Hillary Rodham. "Remarks at the New Silk Road Ministerial Meeting." U.S. Department of State, September 22, 2011.

Clinton, Hillary Rodham. "Remarks on India and the United States: A Vision for the 21st Century." U.S. Department of State, July 20, 2011.

Cohen, Warren. *East Asia at the Center: Four Thousand Years of Engagement with the World*. New York: Columbia University Press, 2001.

Coy, Peter. "Afghanistan Has Cost the U.S. More Than the Marshall Plan." *Bloomberg Businessweek*, July 31, 2014.

David, Steven R. "Explaining Third World Alignment." *World Politics* 43, no. 2 (January 1991): 233–56.

David, Steven R. *Choosing Sides: Alignment and Realignment in the Third World*. Baltimore, MD: Johns Hopkins University Press, 1991.

De Grazia, Victoria. *Irresistible Empire: America's Advance through Twentieth-Century Europe*. Cambridge, MA: Belknap Press, 2006.

DeLong, J. Bradford, and Barry Eichengreen. "The Marshall Plan: History's Most Successful Structural Adjustment Program." National Bureau of Economic Research no. 3899, 1991.

Deng, Xiaoping. "Liberate Thinking, Seek Truth from Facts and Unite and Look to the Future." Speech delivered December 13, 1978. In *Selected Works of Deng Xiaoping, Volume II*. Beijing, Foreign Languages Press, 1995.

Deng, Yong. "China: The Post-Responsible Power." *Washington Quarterly* 37 (2014): 117–32.

Denton, Kirk A. *Exhibiting the Past: Historical Memory and the Politics of Museums in Postsocialist China*. Honolulu: University of Hawaii Press, 2014.

d'Hooghe, Ingrid. *China's Public Diplomacy*. Leiden: Brill, 2015.

Dillon, Michael, ed. *Encyclopedia of Chinese History*. New York: Routledge, 2017.

Dirlik, Arif. "The Idea of a 'Chinese Model': A Critical Discussion." *China Information* 26, no. 3 (November 2012): 277–302.

Djankov, Simeon, and Sean Miner. "China's Belt and Road Initiative: Motives, Scope, and Challenges." Peterson Institute for International Economics Briefing, March 2016.

Dong, Feng, and Cong Wang. "India Appears Threatened by Chinese Projects in Sri Lanka: Experts." *Global Times*, December 24, 2017.

Douzinas, Costas. *Syriza in Power: Reflections of an Accidental Politician*. Cambridge, England: Polity, 2017.

Downs, Erica S., and Suzanne Maloney. "Getting China to Sanction Iran." Brookings, February 23, 2011.

Drahokoupil, Jan, ed. *Chinese Investment in Europe: Corporate Strategies and Labour Relations*. Brussels: ETIU, 2017.

Dreher, Axel, Andreas Fuchs, Bradley Parks, Austin M. Strange, and Michael J. Tierney. "Aid, China, and Growth: Evidence from a New Global Development Finance Dataset." *AidData*. October 10, 2017.

Dreyer, Edward L. *Zheng He: China and the Oceans in the Early Ming Dynasty 1405–1433*. London: Pearson Education, 2007.

Dutton, Peter A., and Ryan D. Martinson, eds. *Beyond the Wall: Chinese Far Seas Operations*. Newport, RI: CMSI Red Books, 2015.

Economy, Elizabeth C. "History with Chinese Characteristics: How China's Imagined Past Shapes Its Present." *Foreign Affairs*, July 2017.

Economy, Elizabeth, and Michael Levy. *By All Means Necessary: How China's Resource Quest Is Changing the World*. New York: Oxford University Press, 2014.

Edney, Kingsley. "Soft Power and the Chinese Propaganda System." *Journal of Contemporary China* 21 (July 2012): 899–914.

Edwards, Paul M. *United Nations Participants in the Korean War: The Contributions of 45 Member Countries*. Jefferson, NC: MacFarland & Company, 2013.

Ehteshami, Anoush. "The Rise and Impact of Iran's Neocons." Stanley Foundation Policy Analysis Brief, April 2008.

Ehteshami, Anoushiravan, Niv Horesh, and Ruike Xu. "Chinese-Iranian Mutual Strategic Perceptions." *China Journal* 79 (2018): 1–5.

Elinaza, Abduel. "Home Port for East African Prosperity." *China Daily*, August 29, 2014.

Erdbrink, Thomas. "For China's Global Ambitions, 'Iran Is at the Center of Everything'." *New York Times*, July 25, 2017.

Erickson, Andrew S. "China's Naval Modernization: The Implications of Seapower." *World Politics Review* (2014).

Erickson, Andrew S. "Numbers Matter: China's Three 'Navies' Each Have the World's Most Ships." *National Interest*, February 26, 2018.

Erickson, Andrew S., and Lyle J. Goldstein, eds., *China, the United States, and 21st-Century Sea Power: Defining a Maritime Security Partnership*. Annapolis, MD: Naval Institute Press, 2012.

Erickson, Andrew S. and Lyle J. Goldstein, eds., *Chinese Aerospace Power: Evolving Maritime Roles*. Annapolis, MD: Naval Institute Press, 2012.

Erickson, Andrew S. and Ryan D. Martinson, eds., *China's Maritime Gray Zone Operations*. Annapolis, MD: Naval Institute Press, 2019.

Erickson, Andrew S., and Austin M. Strange. "China's Blue Soft Power: Antipiracy, Engagement, and Image Enhancement." *Naval War College Review* 68, no. 1 (Winter 2015): 71–91.

Eriksen, Stein Sundstøl. "Tanzania: A Political Economy Analysis." Norwegian Institute of International Affairs, March 2018.

Evera, Stephen Van. "The Cult of the Offensive and the Origins of the First World War." *International Security* 9, no. 1 (1984): 58–107.

Faiola, Anthony. "Greece Is Tapping China's Deep Pockets to Help Rebuild Its Economy." *Washington Post*, June 9, 2010.

Fairbank, John King, ed. *The Chinese World Order: Traditional China's Foreign Relations*. Cambridge, MA: Harvard University Press, 1968.

Fallon, Theresa. "The New Silk Road: Xi Jinping's Grand Strategy for Eurasia." *American Foreign Policy Interests* 37, no. 3 (2015): 140–47.

Fallows, James. *China Airborne: The Test of China's Future*. New York: Knopf, 2012.

Faucon, Benoit. "China Pulls Out of Giant Iranian Gas Project." *Wall Street Journal*, October 6, 2019.

Federal Reserve Bank of St. Louis. "Credit to Government and State-Owned Enterprises to GDP for Sri Lanka." Updated September 21, 2018.

Feng, Coco. "Belt and Road Helps China Offload Overcapacity, According to Moody's Credit Officer." *Caixin*, November 16, 2017.

Ferchen, Matt, "Can China Help Fix Venezuela?" Carnegie–Tsinghua Center for Global Policy, July 24, 2017.

Ferdinando, Shamindra. "No Funds for H'tota port—Hakeem." *The Island*, October 10, 2010.

Foteinos, Fotis. "Crash Test Gia Tin Kivernisi O OLP" [PPA a Crash Test for the Government]. *Enet*, January 14, 2014.

Foteinos, Fotis. "Prosgeiosi Kinezon Sto El. Venizelos" [Chinese Land at El. Venizelos]. *Enet*, April 19, 2013.

Fouere, Marie-Aude. *Remembering Nyerere in Tanzania: History, Memory, Legacy*. Dar es Salaam: Mkuki na Nyota, 2015.

Frankopan, Peter. *The New Silk Roads: The Present and Future of the World*. New York: Bloomsbury, 2018.

Frankopan, Peter. *The Silk Roads: A New History of The World*. New York: Vintage, 2015.

Fravel, Taylor M. "China's Strategy in the South China Sea." *Contemporary Southeast Asia* 33, no. 3 (2011): 292–319.

Fravel, Taylor M. "International Relations Theory and China's Rise: Assessing China's Potential for Territorial Expansion." *International Studies Review* 12, no. 4 (December 2010): 505–32.

Freeden, Michael. *Ideology. A Very Short Introduction*. New York: Oxford University Press, 2003.

French, Howard. *China's Second Continent: How a Million Migrants Are Building a New Empire in Africa*. New York: Knopf, 2014.

French, Howard. *Everything Under the Heavens: How the Past Helps Shape China's Push for Global Power*. New York: Knopf, 2017.

Friedberg, Aaron L. "'Going Out': China's Pursuit of Natural Resources and Implications for the PRC's Grand Strategy." *NBR Analysis* 17, no. 3 (September 2006).

Fu, Mengzi, and Chunhao Lou. "Guanyu 21 shiji 'haishang sichouzhilu' jianshe de ruogan sikao" [Some Reflections on Building the "Maritime Silk Road" of the 21st Century]. *Xiandai Guoji Guanxi* 25 (2015): 1–8, 63.

Furukawa, Mitsuaki. "Management of the International Development Aid System and the Creation of Political Space for China: The Case of Tanzania." JICA Research Institute Working Paper 82, 2014.

Gabuev, Alexander. "A 'Soft Alliance?' Russia-China Relations after the Ukraine Crisis." European Council on Foreign Relations, February 2015.

Gabuev, Alexander. "Belt and Road to Where?" Carnegie Moscow Center, December 8, 2017.

Gabuev, Alexander. "Crouching Bear, Hidden Dragon: 'One Belt One Road' and Chinese-Russian Jostling for Power in Central Asia." *Journal of Contemporary East Asia Studies* 5, no. 2 (2016): 65.

Gabuev, Alexander. "Friends with Benefits? Russian-Chinese Relations after the Ukraine Crisis." Carnegie Endowment for International Peace, June 1, 2016.

Gamache, Lauren, Alexander Hammer, and Lin Jones. "China's Trade and Investment Relationship with Africa." USITC Executive Briefings on Trade, April 2013.

Garver, John W. *China and Iran: Ancient Partners in a Post-Imperial World*. Seattle: University of Washington Press, 2006.

Garver, John. "China and the Iran Nuclear Negotiations: Beijing's Mediation Effort." In *The Red Star & the Crescent: China and the Middle East*, edited by James Reardon-Anderson, 123–48. New York: Oxford University Press, 2018.

Garver, John W. *China's Quest: The History of the Foreign Relations of the People's Republic of China*. New York: Oxford University Press, 2016.

Garver, John W. *Protracted Contest: Sino-Indian Rivalry in the Twentieth Century*. Seattle: University of Washington Press, 2002.

Ge, Jianxiong. "History of the Silk Road." *Guangming Daily*, July 9, 2015.

Gerson, Michael S. "The Sino-Soviet Border Conflict Deterrence, Escalation, and the Threat of Nuclear War in 1969." Center for Naval Analyses, November 2010.

Gill, Bates. "Chinese Arms Exports to Iran." *China Report* 34, nos. 3–4 (August 1998): 355–79.

Godement, François, and Agatha Kratz, eds. "'One Belt, One Road': China's Great Leap Outward." European Council on Foreign Relations China Analysis, 2015.

Greenslade, Roy. "Tanzanian Journalists under Attack." *The Guardian*, March 7, 2013.

Gries, Peter Hays. *China's New Nationalism: Pride, Politics, and Diplomacy.* Berkeley: University of California Press, 2004.

Griffiths, Richard T. *Revitalising the Silk Road: China's Belt and Road Initiative.* Leiden: Hipe, 2017.

Groves, Theodore, Yongmiao Hong, John McMillan, and Barry Naughton. "Autonomy and Incentives in Chinese State Enterprises." *Quarterly Journal of Economics* 109, no. 1 (February 1994): 183–209.

Gu, Julia. "The Chongqing-Xinjiang-Europe International Railway." *China Briefing*, February 20, 2012.

Guo, Jiping. "'Chinese Solutions' Will Give the World More Choices." *Economic Daily*, March 9, 2015.

Guo, Tianyong, and Qiong Li. "'Xin sichouzhilu' de maoyi jinrong zhanlüe yiyi" [The Significance of the New Silk Road from Economic, Trade, Financial, and Strategic Perspectives]. *Renmin Luntan Xue Shu Qian Yan* 4 (2015): 64–70.

Gupta, Anubhav. "Pakistan Confirms the Bugs in the Architecture of China's 'Belt and Road.'" Asia Society Policy Institute, September 27, 2018.

Guramani, Nadir. "Reservations Regarding CPEC Echo in Senate." *Dawn*, November 24, 2017.

Hadid, Diaa. "In Pakistan, Growing Concern over Tensions between Military and Civilian Leaders." National Public Radio, October 10, 2017.

Halper, Stefan. *The Beijing Consensus: How China's Authoritarian Model Will Dominate the Twenty-First Century.* New York: Basic Books, 2010.

Hanemann, Thilo, and Mikko Huotari. "Chinese Investment in Europe: Record Flows and Growing Imbalances." MERICS & Rhodium Group, January 3, 2017.

Hansen, Valerie. *The Silk Road: A New History.* New York: Oxford University Press, 2012.

Harold, Scott and Alireza Nader. "China and Iran: Economic, Political, and Military Relations." RAND Center for Middle East Public Policy, 2012.

Harrison, James P. *The Communists and Chinese Peasant Rebellions: A Study in the Rewriting of Chinese History.* New York: Atheneum, 1969.

Hatzidakis, George. "China's COSCO Eyes Greek Port Investments." *Ekathimerini*, June 5, 2007.

Havnevik, Kjell, and Aida C. Isinika, eds. *Tanzania in Transition: From Nyerere to Mkapa.* Dar es Salaam: Mkuku Na Nyota, 2016.

He, Baogang. "Civic Engagement through Participatory Budgeting in China: Three Different Logics at Work." *Public Administration and Development* 31, no. 2 (2011): 122–33.

He, Baogang. "The Domestic Politics of the Belt and Road and Its Implications." *Journal of Contemporary China* 28, no. 116 (September 2018): 180–95.

He, Baogang. "The Theory and Practice of Chinese Grassroots Governance: Five Models." *Japanese Journal of Political Science* 4, no. 2 (2003/2011): 293–314.

He, Jia. "Zhongguo zhu sililanka dashi yidaiyilu hezuo yicheng sililanka shehui zhuliu gongshi" [Chinese Ambassador to Sri Lanka: OBOR Cooperation Has Become Mainstream Consensus in Sri Lankan Society]. CCTV, September 29, 2018.

Hedin, Sven. *The Silk Road: Ten Thousand Miles through Central Asia.* 1938; New York: Tauris, 2009.

Hedin, Sven, and Folke Bergman. *History of the Expedition in Asia: 1927–1935.* Translated by Donald Burton. 4 vols. Stockholm: Elanders Boktryckeri, 1943–1944.

Heilmann, Sebastian, and Elizabeth J. Perry, eds. *Mao's Invisible Hand: The Political Foundations of Adaptive Governance in China.* Cambridge, MA: Harvard University Asia Center, 2011.

Helleiner, Eric, and Jonathan Kirshner, eds. *The Great Wall of Money: Power and Politics China's International Monetary Relations.* Ithaca, NY: Cornell University Press, 2014.

Heng, Derek. *Sino–Malay Trade and Diplomacy from the Tenth through the Fourteenth Century.* Athens: Ohio University Press, 2009.

Herman, Edward S., and Noam Chomsky. *Manufacturing Consent: The Political Economy of the Mass Media.* New York: Pantheon, 2002.

Hewage, Kithmina. "China in South Asia, Sri Lanka's Strategic Promiscuity." *South Asian Voices,* October 5, 2017.

Hillman, Jonathan. "How Big Is China's Belt and Road?" Center for Strategic and International Studies, April 3, 2018.

Hillman, Jonathan. "Statement on China's Belt and Road Initiative: Five Years Later." Center for Strategic and International Studies, January 25, 2018.

Hobsbawm, Eric and Terence Ranger, eds. *The Invention of Tradition.* New York: Cambridge University Press, 2012.

Hogan, Michael J. "The Search for a 'Creative Peace': The United States, European Unity, and the Origins of the Marshall Plan." *Diplomatic History* 6, no. 3 (Summer 1982): 267–85.

Holbig, Heike. "Ideology after the End of Ideology: China and the Quest for Autocratic Legitimation." *Democratization* 20, no. 1 (2013): 61.

Holt, John C. *Buddha in the Crown: Avalokitesvara in the Buddhist Traditions of Sri Lanka.* New York: Oxford University Press, 1991.

Honan, Edith. "Tanzania Dreams Big with Port Project at Former Slave Harbor." Reuters, March 15, 2015.

Hooi, Alexis, and Ma Wei. "Rail Line Promises to be 'New Silk Road.'" *China Daily,* June 9, 2012.

Horn, Sebastian, Carmen M. Reinhart, and Christoph Trebesch. "China's Overseas Lending." Kiel Institute Working Paper no. 2132, July 2019.

Hornby, Lucy. "Mahathir Mohamad Warns against 'New Colonialism' during China Visit." *Financial Times,* August 20, 2018.

Hu, Huawei. "The Historical Changes and Contemporary Enlightenment of the Silk Road: An Interview with Xing Guangcheng, Director of the Chinese Frontier Institute of the Chinese Academy of Social Sciences." *Guangming Daily,* April 20, 2015.

Huang, Cary. "Who Picks Up the Trillion-Dollar Tab for China's Belt and Road?" *South China Morning Post,* May 14, 2017.

Huang, Yiping. "Understanding China's Belt & Road Initiative: Motivation, Framework and Assessment." *China Economic Review* 40 (2016): 314–21.

Hui, Ning, and Shidi Yang. "Sichouzhilu jingji dai de neihan jieding, hezuo neirong ji shixian lujing" [The Connotation, Cooperation Contents, and Path of the Silk Road Economic Belt]. *Yanan daxue xuebao* 36 (August 2014): 60–66.

Hurley, John, Scott Morris, and Gailyn Portelance. "Examining the Debt Sustainability Implications of the Belt and Road Initiative from a Policy Perspective." Center for Global Development Policy Paper, 2018.

Husain, Khurram. "Exclusive: CPEC Master Plan Revealed." *Dawn*, June 21, 2017.

International Crisis Group. "Central Asia: Border Disputes and Conflict Potential." *ICG Asia Report*, 2002.

Jaipragas, Bhavan. "'Chinese by Nature Are Very Good Businesspeople': Malaysian Prime Minister Mahathir Mohamad's Exclusive Interview in Full." *South China Morning Post*, March 8, 2019.

Jakobson, Linda, and Ryan Manuel. "How Are Foreign Policy Decisions Made in China?" *Asia & the Pacific Policy Studies* 3, no. 1 (2016): 101.

Jansz, Frederica. "Seaport Study in Stormy Seas." *Sunday Leader*, December 7, 2003.

Jia, Qingguo. "Disrespect and Distrust: The External Origins of Contemporary Chinese Nationalism." *Journal of Contemporary China* 14, no. 42 (2005): 11–21.

Johnson, Christopher K. *Decoding China's Emerging "Great Power" Strategy in Asia.* Washington, DC: Center for Strategic & International Studies, 2014.

Johnston, Alastair I. "How New and Assertive Is China's New Assertiveness?" *International Security* 37, no. 4 (2013/2014): 7–48.

Joy-Perez, Cecilia, and Derek Scissors. "A Close Look at OBOR Reveals Overstated Gains." American Enterprise Institute, May 2017.

Kairuki, Mbelwa. "Message from the Ambassador of United Republic of Tanzania in People's Republic of China." Embassy of the United Republic of Tanzania Beijing, China, n.d. Accessed November 18, 2019.

Kamilali, Thanos. "Ti Sta Alitheia Prosferei I COSCO Gia Ton OLP" [What COSCO Is Really Offering for OLP]. Press Project, January 21, 2016.

Kang, David. *East Asia before the West: Five Centuries of Trade and Tribute.* New York: Columbia University Press, 2012.

Karaganov, Sergey, ed. "Toward the Great Ocean-3: Creating Central Eurasia." Valdai Discussion Club, June 10, 2015.

Karrar, Hasan Haider. "The New Silk Road Diplomacy: A Regional Analysis of China's Central Asian Foreign Policy, 1991–2005." PhD diss., McGill University, 2006.

Karrar, Hasan Haider. *The New Silk Road Diplomacy: China's Central Asian Foreign Policy Since the Cold War.* Vancouver: University of British Columbia Press, 2010.

Kassenova, Nagis. "More Politics than Substance: Three Years of Russian and Chinese Economic Cooperation in Central Asia." Foreign Policy Research Institute, October 24, 2018.

Kassimi, Aleksandra. "Meso Thriaseiou i Anaptiksi Gia OSE" [OSE Will Develop via Thriasio]. *Kathimerini*, April 22, 2012.

Kaufman, Robert G. "To Balance or to Bandwagon? Alignment Decisions in 1930s Europe." *Security Studies* 1, no. 3 (Spring 1992): 417–47.

Kay, Chris, and Iain Marlow. "Military Tightens Grip on Pakistan's Media ahead of Polls." Bloomberg, July 16, 2018.

Kelemen, Paul. "Planning for Africa: The British Labour Party's Colonial Development Policy, 1920–1964." *Journal of Agrarian Change* 7, no. 1 (2007): 76–98.

Kennedy, John. "Xi Jinping's Opposition to Political Reforms Laid Out in Leaked Internal Speech." *South China Morning Post*, January 28, 2013.

Kennedy, Scott. "The Myth of the Beijing Consensus." *Journal of Contemporary China* 19, no. 65 (June 2010): 461–77.

Kennedy, Scott, and Christopher K. Johnson. "Perfecting China, Inc.: China's 13th Five-Year Plan." Center for Strategic and International Studies, 2016.

Kiani, Khaleeq. "Chinese Firms to Get Contracts for Two CPEC Projects." *Dawn*, August 13, 2015.

Kikwete, Jakaya. "Transcript: Tanzania's Transformation and Vision 2025: Governing Economic Growth for Social Gain." Chatham House, March 31, 2014.

Kinfe, Abraham. *China Comes to Africa: The Political Economy and Diplomatic History of China's Relation with Africa*. Addis Ababa: EIIPD HADAD Ethiopia, 2005.

King, Gary, Robert O. Keohane, and Sidney Verba. *Designing Social Inquiry: Scientific Inference in Qualitative Research*. Princeton, NJ: Princeton University Press, 1994.

Kirui, Dominic. "African Countries Take Bold Step to Cancel Chinese Investment Projects." *Epoch Times*, August 23, 2019.

Kissinger, Henry. *On China*. New York: Penguin Books, 2012.

Kleine-Ahlbrandt, Stephanie, and Andrew Small. "China's New Dictatorship Diplomacy: Is Beijing Parting with Pariahs?" *Foreign Affairs* 87, no. 1 (2008): 38–56.

Kley, Dirk, van der. "China's Security Activities in Tajikistan and Afghanistan's Wakhan Corridor." National Bureau of Asian Research 80, September 2019.

Kong, Deming. "'Yidaiyilu' xuanchuan zhong de ba xiang zhuyi" [Eight Notes on OBOR Propaganda]. *Renmin Wang*, January 8, 2016.

Kontogiannis, Dimitris. "OLP Kai COSCO" [PPA and COSCO]. *Enet*, May 26, 2011.

Kornai, János. "The Soft Budget Constraint." *Kyklos* 39, no. 1 (1986): 3–30.

Kornai, Janos, Eric Maskin, and Géard Roland. "Understanding the Soft Budget Constraint." *Journal of Economic Literature* 41, no. 4 (2003): 1095–1136.

Koronaiou, Paschalis. "Ksafnikos Erotas me to Yuan" [Suddenly in Love with the Yuan]. *Enet*, March 20, 2011.

Kostecka, Daniel J. "The Chinese Navy's Emerging Support Network in the Indian Ocean." *Naval War College Review* 64, no. 1 (Winter 2011): 59–78.

Kostecka, Daniel. "Hambantota, Chittagong, and the Maldives—Unlikely Pearls for the Chinese Navy." *China Brief* 10, no. 23 (November 19, 2010).

Kostopoulos, Tassos, Dimitris Trimmis, Anta Psarra, and Dimitris Psarras. "To Kryfo Mnimonio" [The Secret Memorandum]. *Enet*, May 29, 2010.

Kouroumplis, Panayiotis. "Greek Government Has Offered All Forms of Support to Shipping Sector, at the Highest Political Level." *Naftemporiki*, June 1, 2018.

Kratz, Agatha. "One Belt, One Road: What's in It for China's Economic Players?" In *'One Belt, One Road': China's Great Leap Outward*, edited by François Godement and Agatha Kratz. European Council on Foreign Relations, June 10, 2015.

Kratz, Agatha, Allen Feng, and Logan Wright. "New Data on the 'Debt Trap' Question." Rhodium Group, April 29, 2019.

Kucera, Joshua. "Clinton's Dubious Plan to Save Afghanistan with a 'New Silk Road.'" *The Atlantic*, November 2, 2011.

Kuhn, Dieter, and Helga Stahl, eds. *Perceptions of Antiquity in Chinese Civilization*. Heidelberg: University of Heidelberg Press, 2008.

Kuik, Cheng-Chwee. "Making Sense of Malaysia's China Policy: Asymmetry, Proximity, and Elite's Domestic Authority." *Chinese Journal of International Politics* 6 no. 4 (Winter 2013): 429–67.

Kunz, Diane B. "The Marshall Plan Reconsidered: A Complex of Motives." *Foreign Affairs* 76, no. 3 (1997): 162–70.

Kurlantzick, Joshua. *Charm Offensive: How China's Soft Power Is Transforming the World*. New Haven, CT: Yale University Press, 2008.

Kynge, James, Chris Campbell, Amy Kazmin, and Farhan Bokhari. "How China Rules the Waves." *Financial Times*, January 12, 2017.

Ladduwahetty, Ravi. "Hambantota Port Will Attract 36,000 ships Annually—Ananda Kularatne." *Daily News*, June 18, 2002.

Lancaster, Kirk, Michael Rubin, and Mira Rapp-Hooper. "What the COVID-19 Pandemic May Mean for China's Belt and Road Initiative." Council on Foreign Relations, March 17, 2020.

Lardy, Nicholas R. *Markets over Mao: The Rise of Private Business in China*. New York: Columbia University Press, 2014.

Lardy, Nicholas R., and Arvind Subramanian. *Sustaining China's Economic Growth after the Global Financial Crisis*. Washington, DC: Peterson Institute for International Economics, 2011.

Large, Daniel. "Beyond 'Dragon in the Bush': The Study of China–Africa Relations." *African Affairs* 107, no. 426 (January 2008): 45–61.

Laruelle, Marlene, ed. *China's Belt and Road Initiative and Its Impact in Central Asia*. Washington, DC: George Washington University Press, 2018.

Lasswell, Harold D. *Propaganda Technique in the World War*. New York: Peter Smith, 1927.

Law 2688 1999 (Gov. 40 Α/ 1999) "Metatropi tou Organismou Limenos Piraios Kai Thessalonikis se Anonymes Etairies" [Conversion of the Piraeus Port Authority and the Port Authority of Thessaloniki into Limited Liability Companies]. Ypourgeio Nautilias kai Nisiotikis Politikis [Ministry of Maritime and Island Policy]. Accessed February 25, 2019.

Le Corre, Philippe. "China's Rise as a Geoeconomic Influencer: Four European Case Studies." *Carnegie Endowment for International Peace*, October 15, 2018.

Lee, Christopher J. *Making a World after Empire: The Bandung Moment and Its Political Afterlives*. Athens: Ohio University Press, 2010.

Lee, Raymond. "The Strategic Importance of Chinese-Pakistani Relations." Al Jazeera Centre for Studies, August 3, 2016.

Lerski, George J. "Sri Lanka Turns East." *Asian Affairs: An American Review* 1, no. 3 (1974): 187.

Li, Dongdong. "Hongyang Zheng He jingshen wei jiakuai Ningxia fazhan zuo gongxian" [Proclaim the Spirit of Zheng He, Contribution to Accelerating Ningxia's Development]. *Journal of Hui Muslim Minority Studies* 1 (2005).

Li, Haixia, and Mengyong Weng. "Jiaotong hezuo shi sichouzhilu jingji dai de xianxing he zhongyao jichu [Transportation is the Prerequisite and Foundation for the Silk Road Economic Belt]. *Renmin Wang,* July 2, 2014.

Li, Jing. "Sri Lanka." Belt and Road Portal, n.d. Accessed February 28, 2018.

Li, Shaomin and Jun Xia. "The Roles and Performance of State Firms and Non-State Firms in China's Economic Transition." *World Development* 36, no. 1 (January 2008): 39–54.

Li Xiao and Xue Li. "The 21st Century Maritime Silk Road: Security Risks and Countermeasures." *Pacific Journal* 23 no. 7 (2015): 50–64.

Lieberthal, Kenneth, Li Cheng, and Keping Lu. *China's Political Development: Chinese and American Perspectives.* Washington, DC: Brookings Institution Press, 2014.

Lies, Elaine. "Malaysia Wants to Be Friendly, Not Indebted, to China, Says Mahathir." Reuters, June 11, 2018.

Lin, Christina. "China's New Silk Road to the Mediterranean: The Eurasian Land Bridge and Return of Admiral Zheng He." *ISPSW* 165 (2011): 1–23.

Lin, Christina. "China's Silk Road Strategy in AfPak: The Shanghai Cooperation Organization." *ISPSW,* 2011.

Lin, Kun-Chin. "Protecting the Petroleum Industry: Renewing Government Aid to Fossil Fuel Producers." *Business Politics* 16, no. 4 (December 2014): 549–78.

Liow, Joseph Chin Yong. "Malaysia-China Relations in the 1990s: The Maturing of a Partnership." *Asian Survey* 40, no. 4 (July–August 2000): 672–91.

Liu, Alan P. L. "Rebirth and Secularization of the Central Party School in China." *China Journal* 62 (July 2002): 105–25.

Liu, Cigui. "Fazhan haiyang hezuo huoban guanxi, tuijin 21 shiji haishang sichouzhilu jianshe de ruogan sikao" [Reflections on Maritime Partnership: Building the 21st Century Maritime Silk Road]. *Guoji Wenti Yanjiu* [China International Studies] 4 (2014): 1–8, 31.

Liu, Lulu. "NYT Sees Chinese Investment in Greece through Western Centrist Lens." *Global Times,* August 31, 2017.

Liu, Weidong. "'Yi Dai Yi Lu' Zhanlue de Renshi Wuqu" [Misunderstandings of "One Belt One Road" Strategy]. *Guojia Xingzheng Xueyuan Xuebao* 1 (2016): 30–34.

Liu, Xiaoming. "New Silk Road Is an Opportunity Not a Threat." *Financial Times,* May 24, 2015.

Liu, Ying, Zhongping Chen, and Gregory Blue, eds. *Zheng He's Maritime Voyages (1405–1433) and China's Relations with the Indian Ocean World: A Multilingual Bibliography.* New York: Brill, 2014.

Liu, Yue. "Yearender: Belt and Road Gains Momentum in 2017." Belt and Road Portal. Accessed February 28, 2018.

Lockman, Shahriman. "The 21st Century Maritime Silk Road and China-Malaysia Relations." *ISIS Focus* (May 2015): 1–5.

Lu, Bingyang, and Yelin Mo. "China-Backed Rail Project Steams Ahead in Russia." *Caixin*, September 24, 2017.

Lü, Youqing. "Tansangniya xin zongtong Magufuli de zhizheng fengge" [Governing Style of New Tanzanian President Magufuli]. *Sina*, December 28, 2015.

Lü, Youqing. "Tanzania: The Belt and Road Initiative and China-Tanzania Relations." Forum on China-Africa Cooperation, May 11, 2017.

Lü, Youqing. "Xi jinping waijiao sixiang zai tansangniya de chuanbo" [The Spread of Xi Jinping Diplomatic Thought in Tanzania]. *Sina*, December 4, 2017.

Lu, Yuling. "Zhongguo dui sililanka shexia zhaiwu xianjing sililanka he wo dashiguan bochi meimei mohei baodao" [Has China Laid a Debt Trap for Sri Lanka? Sri Lanka and Our Embassy Refute U.S. Media Reports]. *Guancha*, July 2, 2018.

Lu, Zhenhua. "'Pro-China' Boris Johnson 'Enthusiastic' about Belt and Road Plan." *South China Morning Post*, July 24, 2019.

Lundestad, Geir. "Empire by Invitation? The United States and Western Europe, 1945–1952." *Journal of Peace Research* 23, no. 3 (September 1986): 263–77.

Lynch, David. *After the Propaganda State: Media, Politics, and "Thought Work" in Reformed China*. Stanford, CA: Stanford University Press, 1999.

Ma, Damian, and Neil Thomas. "In Xi We Trust: How Propaganda Might Be Working in the New Era." *MacroPolo*, September 12, 2018.

Maçães, Bruno. *Belt and Road: A Chinese World Order*. London: Hurst, 2018.

Maçães, Bruno. *The Dawn of Eurasia: On the Trail of the New World Order*. New Haven, CT: Yale University Press, 2018.

Macan-Markar, Marwaan. "Sri Lanka Attempts Tricky Maritime Balancing Act." *Nikkei Asian Review*, October 13, 2016.

MacDonald, Juli. *Energy Futures in Asia: Final Report*. McLean, VA: Booz-Allen & Hamilton, 2004.

Mackenzie, Peter. "A Closer Look at China-Iran Relations: Roundtable Report." Center for Naval Analyses China Studies, September 2010.

Mackinder, H. J. *Democratic Ideals and Reality: A Study in the Politics of Reconstruction*. Washington, DC: National Defense University Press, 1996.

Mackinder, Halford J. "The Geographical Pivot of History." *Geographical Journal* 23, no. 4 (April 1904): 421–37.

Mackoki, Michal, and Nicu Popescu. "China and Russia: An Eastern Partnership in the Making?" *Chaillot Papers* 140 (December 2016): 38.

Mahr, Krista. "Sri Lanka to Start Tally of Civil-War Dead." *Time*, November 28, 2013.

Maltezou, Renee. "China Hints at Purchase of Greek Bonds, Reiterates Targets." Reuters, June 19, 2014.

Marat, Erica. "National Ideology and State-Building in Kyrgyzstan and Tajikistan." Central Asia-Caucasus Institute and Silk Road Studies Program, 2008.

Mauk, Ben. "Can China Turn the Middle of Nowhere into the Center of the World Economy?" *New York Times*, January 30, 2019.

Maull, Hans W. "The Politics of the EU: China's Relationship with Europe." *Asian Journal of Comparative Politics* 2, no. 1 (March 2017): 55–69.

McGarr, Paul M. *The Cold War in South Asia: Britain, the United States and the Indian Subcontinent, 1945–1965.* New York: Cambridge University Press, 2013.

Mearsheimer, John J. "Can China Rise Peacefully?" *National Interest* 25 (2014): 23–37.

Medeiros, Evan S. "Strategic Hedging and the Future of Asia-Pacific Stability." *Washington Quarterly* 29, no. 1 (2005): 145–67.

Melhuish, Charles. "Tanzania Transport Sector Review." African Development Bank, September 2013.

Meng, Jie. "Vision for Maritime Cooperation under the Belt and Road Initiative." Xinhua, June 20, 2017.

Menon, Shivshankar. *Choices: Inside the Making of India's Foreign Policy.* Washington, DC: Brookings Institution Press, 2016.

Miller, Alice L. "The New Party Politburo Leadership." *China Leadership Monitor*, no. 40 (January 2013).

Miller, Alice L. "Some Things We Used to Know about China's Past and Present (But Now, Not So Much)." *Journal of American-East Asian Relations* 16, nos. 1–2 (Spring–Summer 2009): 41–68.

Minde, Nicodemus. "Opposition Politics in Tanzania and Why the Country will Benefit from a Strong Unified Opposition." Africa at LSE Blog, June 29, 2015.

Ministry of Education. *Zhongguo gudaishi: Quanrizhi putong gaoji zhongxue jiaokeshu (xuanxiu)* [Ancient Chinese History: Full-time Normal High School Textbooks (Elective) 中国古代史: 全日制普通高级中学教科书 选修]. Beijing: People's Education Press, 2003.

Ministry of Education. *Zhongguo lishi: Yiwu jiaoyu kecheng biaozhun shiyan jiaokeshu* [Chinese History: Compulsory Education Curriculum Standard Experimental Textbook 中国历史: 义务教育课程标准实验教科书]. Beijing: People's Education Press, 2001.

Ministry of Education. *Zhongguo lishi: Yiwu jiaoyu kecheng biaozhun shiyan jiaokeshu qinianji shangce* [Chinese History: Compulsory Education Curriculum Standard Experimental Textbook, Grade 7 Volume 1 中国历史: 义务教育课程标准实验教科书 七年级 上册]. Beijing: People's Education Press, 2016.

Ministry of Education and Ma Shili, eds. *Lishi di er ce bixiu: Putong gaozhong kecheng biaozhun shiyan jiaokeshu* [History II Compulsory: Normal Senior Secondary School Curriculum Experimental Textbook, Volume 2 历史第二册必修: 普通高中课程标准实验教科书]. Beijing: People's Education Press, 2005.

Mirondo, Rosemary. "Govt. Halts Building of Bagamoyo Port." *Citizen*, January 8, 2016.

Mitter, Rana. "Behind the Scenes at the Museum: Nationalism, History and Memory in the Beijing War of Resistance Museum, 1987–1997." *China Quarterly* 161 (2000): 279–93.

Mohamad, Mahathir. "Regional Co-operation: Challenges and Prospects." Speech, Tsinghua University, November 1985. Quoted in Joseph Chin Yong Liow, "Malaysia-China Relations in the 1990s: The Maturing of a Partnership," *Asian Survey* 40, no. 4 (July–August, 2000): 672–91.

Mokry, Sabine. "Decoding Chinese Concepts for the Global Order: How Chinese Scholars Rethink and Shape Foreign Policy Ideas." MERICS, October 4, 2018.

Morou, Argyros. "Foniki Epidrome" [Deadly Raid]. *Enet*, May 6, 2010.

Mpardounias, Nikos. "Eksigiseis gia to Forologiko Kathestos tis COSCO Zitoun oi Vrikselles" [Brussels Asks for Clarifications on COSCO's Tax Regime]. *Kathimerini*, October 11, 2012.

Mpardounias, Nikos. "Katalitiki I Eisodos tis COSCO gia ta Thetika Oikonomika Megethi ston Piraia" [COSCO's Arrival at the Port Catalyzed Positive Financial Indicators at Piraeus]. *Kathimerini*, February 12, 2012.

Mpardounias, Nikos. "O OLP Plironei 82 Ek, Gia 320 Ergazomenous Kai Tha Eksoikonomisei 11 Ek." [PPA Pays 82 Million to 320 Employees to Save 11 Million]. *Kathimerini*, Dec 16, 2009.

Mpellos, Ilias. "Allagi Montelou Gia OLP Kai OLTH" [A Change of Model for PPA and THPA]. *Kathimerini*, July 1, 2012.

Msuya, Elias. "China, Tanzania zatofautiana ujenzi Bandari ya Bagamoyo" [China, Tanzania Disagree on Construction of Bagamoyo Port]. *Mainichi*, February 18, 2017.

Mu, Xuequan. "Oman Pledges to Support Tanzania's Industrial Drive." Xinhua, October 19, 2017.

Murdoch, Lindsay. "Thailand's Kra Canal Plan Would Link Indian, Pacific Oceans, Benefiting China." *Sydney Morning Herald*, August 8, 2017.

Mustafa, Khalid. "China Has Provided $5 BN Loan, $2 BN Grant for CPEC, Senate Body Told." *News International*, September 4, 2018.

Naughton, Barry. "China's Distinctive System: Can It Be a Model for Others?" *Journal of Contemporary China* 19, no. 65 (2010): 437–60.

Naughton, Barry J. *The Chinese Economy: Adaptation and Growth*. Cambridge, MA: MIT Press, 2018.

Naughton, Barry. "The Current Wave of State Enterprise Reform in China: A Preliminary Appraisal." *Asian Economic Policy Review* 12, no. 2 (July 2017): 282–98.

Netherlands Enterprise Agency. "Scoping Project: Tanzania's Potential for Integrated Agriculture-Infrastructure Solutions." Ministry of Foreign Affairs of the Netherlands, February 2018.

Ngarabali, Julieth. "Ujenzi wa bandari, viwanda kuathiri mazingira Bagamoyo" [Construction of Ports, Industry Affects Environment of Bagamoyo]. *Mainichi*, November 30, 2015.

Niyas, M. R. M. "Hambantota Port Project: Canadian Experts Here for Feasibility Studies Next Month." *Daily News*, July 23, 2002.

Nolan, Peter. *Chinese Firms, Global Firms: Industrial Policy in the Age of Globalization*. New York: Routledge 2013.

Nolan, Peter. *Is China Buying the World?* Cambridge: Polity, 2013.

Nolan, Peter, and Xiaoqiang Wang. "Beyond Privatization: Institutional Innovation and Growth in China's Large State-Owned Enterprises." *World Development* 27, no. 1 (March 1999): 169–200.

Nonini, Donald M. *"Getting By": Class and State Formation among Chinese in Malaysia*. Ithaca, NY: Cornell University Press, 2015.

Nouwens, Meia, and Helena Legarda. "Emerging Technology Dominance: What China's Pursuit of Advanced Dual-Use Technologies Means for the Future of Europe's Economy and Defence Innovation." International Institute for Strategic Studies, December, 2018.

Nyaluke, David, and Eileen Connolly. "The Role of Political Ideas in Multi-Party Elections in Tanzania: Refuting Essentialist Explanations of African Political Systems." *Irish Studies in International Affairs* 24 (2013): 41–57.

Nye, Joseph S., Jr. "Public Diplomacy and Soft Power." *Annals of the American Academy of Political and Social Science* 616 no. 1 (2008): 94–109.

OECD. "FDI Stocks: Outward/Inward, % of GDP, 2018 or latest available." OECD, 2018.

Office of the Secretary of Defense. "Annual Report to Congress: Military and Security Developments Involving the People's Republic of China 2019." Office of the Secretary of Defense, May 2, 2019.

Osnos, Evan. "Making China Great Again." *New Yorker*, January 8, 2018.

Page, Jeremy, Gordon Lubold, and Rob Taylor. "Deal for Naval Outpost in Cambodia Furthers China's Quest for Military Network." *Wall Street Journal*, July 22, 2019.

Pallotti, Arrigo. "Lost in Transition? CCM and Tanzania's Faltering Democratisation Process." *Journal of Contemporary African Studies* 35, no. 4 (2017): 544–64.

Pannier, Bruce. "Putin Offers Russian Help to Build Kazakh Nuclear Plant." Radio Free Europe, April 6, 2019.

Papaconstantinou, George. *Game Over: The Inside Story of the Greek Crisis.* Scotts Valley, CA: CreateSpace, 2016.

Papadiochou, K. P. "Kritiki Apo ton Papandreou gia ton Neo Kapodistria" [Papandreou Critiques the "New Kapodistrias" Reform]. *Kathimerini*, November 26, 2008.

Papadopoulos, Tassos. "To Thema Itan Kai Einai Na Lithei Sosta to Kypriako" [The Point Was and Still Is to Solve the Cypriot Issue the Right Way]. *Rizospastis*, August 24, 2005.

Papahelas, Alexis. "O Piraias, Proto Limani tis Mesogeiou" [Piraeus, the First Port of the Mediterranean]. *Kathimerini*, May 21, 2010.

Papastathopoulou, Christina. "COSCO kai Thriaseio" [COSCO and Thriasio]. *Enet*, March 5, 2011.

Papastathopoulou, Christina. "Tichodioktes Pou Prin Katigkeilan Ti COSCO" [The Opportunists Who Used to Denounce COSCO]. *Enet*, May 25, 2011.

Pape, Robert A. "Soft Balancing against the United States." *International Security* 30, no. 1 (2005): 7–45.

Parker, Sam, and Gabrielle Chefitz. "Debtbook Diplomacy." Belfer Center for Science and International Affairs, Harvard Kennedy School, May 24, 2018.

Patnaik, Sivananda, and Sanjeeb K. Haldar. "Sino-Sri Lanka Economic Relations: An Appraisal." *China Report* 16, no. 6 (1980): 19–31.

Pauley, Logan. "China Takes the Lead in UN Peacekeeping." *The Diplomat*, April 17, 2018.

Pehrson, Christopher J. "String of Pearls: Meeting the Challenge of China's Rising Power across the Asian Littoral." Strategic Studies Institute, July 2006.

Pei, Minxin. *China's Trapped Transition: The Limits of Developmental Autocracy.* Cambridge, MA: Harvard University Press, 2008.

Perera, Amantha. "Life in the Limbo Zone." *Sunday Leader*, April 10, 2005.

Perlez, Jane. "China Looks West as It Bolsters Regional Ties." *New York Times*, September 7, 2013.

Perlez, Jane, and Yufan Huang. "Behind China's $1 Trillion Plan to Shake Up the Economic Order." *The New York Times*, May 13, 2017.

Perry, Elizabeth J. *Challenging the Mandate of Heaven: Social Protest and State Power in China*. New York: Routledge, 2015.

Perry, Elizabeth J. "Cultural Governance in Contemporary China: 'Re-Orienting' Party Propaganda." *Harvard-Yenching Institute Working Paper Series* (2013): 1–36.

Phillips, Tom. "The $900 BN Question: What Is the Belt and Road Initiative?" *The Guardian*, May 12, 2017.

Pieke, Frank. *The Good Communist. Elite Training and State Building in Today's China*. New York: Cambridge University Press, 2009.

Plafker, Ted. "A Year Later, China's Stimulus Package Bears Fruit." *New York Times*, October 22, 2009.

Poling, Gregory B., et al. *Defusing the South China Sea Disputes*. Washington, DC: Center for Strategic and International Studies, 2018.

Pomfret, John. "China Debt Traps around the World Are a Trademark of Its Imperialist Ambitions." *Washington Post*, August 27, 2018.

Press Trust of India. "Pakistan Government Plans to Renegotiate Agreements Reached under China's Belt and Road Initiative: Report." *Firstpost*, September 10, 2018.

Pu, Yunqiao, ed. "Xiangying yidaiyilu zhuyou jiudian jituan tisheng jingzheng shili" [Responding to OBOR, Sumitomo Hotel Group Enhances its Competitive Strength]. Xinhua, May 15, 2017.

Putnam, Robert D. "Diplomacy and Domestic Politics: The Logic of Two-Level Games." *International Organization* 42 (1988): 427–60.

Reconnecting Asia. "Methodology." Center for Strategic and International Studies, n.d. Accessed January 31, 2020.

Renshon, Jonathan. *Fighting for Status: Hierarchy and Conflict in World Politics*. Princeton, NJ: Princeton University Press, 2017.

Richthofen, Ferdinand von. *Baron Richthofen's Letters, 1870–1872*. Shanghai: North China Herald, 1903.

Rithmire, Meg. "Varieties of Outward Chinese Capital: Domestic Politics Status and Globalization of Chinese Firms." Harvard Business School Working Paper, 2019.

Rolland, Nadège. "China's 'Belt and Road Initiative': Underwhelming or Game-Changer?" *Washington Quarterly* 40, no. 1 (2017): 127–42.

Rolland, Nadège. "China's New Silk Road." National Bureau of Asian Research, February 12, 2015.

Roy, Denny. "Southeast Asia and China: Balancing or Bandwagoning?" *Contemporary Southeast Asia: A Journal of International and Strategic Affairs* 27, no. 2 (2005): 305–22.

Rubin, Michael. "Iran: IRGC Training in China." American Enterprise Institute, September 6, 2017.

Russell, Daniel. "The Coronavirus Will Not Be Fatal for China's Belt and Road Initiative but It Will Strike a Heavy Blow." *South China Morning Post*, March 19, 2020.

Ryall, Julian. "Japan Commits to China's 'One Belt, One Road' Initiative." *Deutsche Welle*, July 17, 2017.

Safi, Mariam, and Bismellah Alizada. "Integrating Afghanistan into the Belt and Road Initiative: Analysis and Prospects." *Friedrich Ebert Stiftung*, August 2018.

Sakamoto, Kōichi. *Japan and China: A Contest in Aid to Sub-Saharan Africa*. Singapore: World Scientific, 2018.

Saqafi, Ameri N. "In Search of New Horizons in the Foreign Policy of Iran: The Policy of Look to the East." Center for Strategic Research, 2006.

Sauvant, Karl P., and Victor Zitian Chen. "China's Regulatory Framework for Outward Foreign Direct Investment." *China Economic Journal* 7, no. 1 (February 2014): 141–63.

Schneider, Florian. *Visual Political Communication in Popular Chinese Television Series*. Leiden: Brill, 2012.

Schoenhals, Michael. *Doing Things with Words in Chinese Politics: Five Studies*. Berkeley, CA: Institute of East Asian Studies, 1992.

Schurmann, Franz. *Ideology and Organization in Communist China*. Berkeley: University of California Press, 1968.

Schwartz, Benjamin. "The Chinese Perception of World Order, Past and Present." In *The Chinese World Order: Traditional China's Foreign Relations*, edited by John K. Fairbank, 276–88. Cambridge, MA: Harvard University Press, 1968.

Sen, Tansen. *India, China, and the World: A Connected History*. New York: Rowman and Littlefield, 2017.

Sevastopulo, Demetri. "Trump Gives Glimpse of 'Indo-Pacific' Strategy to Counter China." *Financial Times*, November 10, 2017.

Shaba, Richard. "State of Politics in Tanzania." *Konrad-Adenauer-Stiftung*, July 9, 2009.

Shambaugh, David. "China's Propaganda System: Institutions, Processes and Efficacy." *China Journal* 57 (2007): 25–58.

Shambaugh, David. "Training China's Political Elite: The Party School System." *China Quarterly* 196 (2008): 827–44.

Shanghai Cooperation Organization. Charter of the Shanghai Cooperation Organization, Article II. June 2001.

Shangwe, Muhidin J. "China's Soft Power in Tanzania: Opportunities and Challenges." *China Quarterly of International Strategic Studies* 3, no. 1 (2017): 79–100.

Shen, Weizhong. "One Road for Many Itineraries—Bucharest Forum October 2–4, 2014." YouTube, October 17, 2014.

Shepard, Wade. "Beijing to the World: Don't Call the Belt and Road Initiative OBOR." *Forbes*, August 1, 2017.

Shi, Yaqiao, and Jing Wang, eds. "'Yidaiyilu' meiti hezuo luntan" [Samsung Electronics Unveils "OBOR" Media Cooperation Forum]. *Renmin Ribao*, November 8, 2018.

Shih, Victor C. *Factions and Finance in China: Elite Conflict and Inflation*. New York: Cambridge University Press, 2009.

Shih, Victor, Christopher Adolf, and Mingxing Liu. "Getting Ahead in the Communist Party: Explaining the Advancement of Central Committee Members in China." *American Political Science Review* 106, no. 1 (February 2012): 166–87.

Shirk, Susan. *China: Fragile Superpower*. New York: Oxford University Press, 2008.

Shirk, Susan. *The Political Logic of Economic Reform in China*. Berkeley: University of California Press, 1993.

Shuvalov, Igor. "Rossiya gotova k sovmestnoy rabote s Kitaem v formate EAES" [Russia Is Ready to Work with China in the EAEU Framework]. Speech, Boao Forum, March 26, 2015.

Simitis, Costas. *The European Debt Crisis: The Greek Case.* Manchester: Manchester University Press, 2014.

Simtowe, Aurea. "Ujenzi Bandari ya Bagamoyo kuanza Januari, Serikali yataja wabia" [Construction of Bagamoyo Harbor Will Start in January, Government Tells Partners]. *Mainichi*, November 24, 2017.

Sivaram, Karthik. "'Locked-In' to China: The Colombo Port City Project." Stanford Leadership Academy for Development, 2016.

Sivasundaram, Sujit. *Islanded: Britain, Sri Lanka, and the Bounds of an Indian Ocean Colony.* Chicago: University of Chicago Press, 2013.

Slavin, Barbara. *Iran Turns to China, Barter to Survive Sanctions.* Washington: Atlantic Council, 2011.

Smith, Jeff. "China's Belt and Road Initiative: Strategic Implications and International Opposition." *Heritage Foundation*, August 2018.

Solana, Javier. "Remarks at the Southern Corridor-New Silk Road Summit." May 8, 2009.

Soltaninejad, Mohammad. "Iran and Southeast Asia: An Analysis of Iran's Policy of 'Look to the East.'" *International Journal of Asia Pacific Studies* 13, no. 1 (2017): 29–49.

Song, Lifang. "What Is 'Belt and Road Initiative'?" Belt and Road Portal, October 22, 2016. Accessed February 28, 2018.

Song, Shuangshuang. "Zai 'yidaiyilu' zhanlüe xia kuoda duiwai nongye hezuo' [Expand External Agricultural Cooperation under the Banner of the "OBOR" Strategy]. *Guoji jingji hezuo* 9 (2014): 63–66.

Soysa, David. "China's Silicon Sea Route via Thailand Boon to Hambantota, But Threat to Singapore." *The Island*, September 14, 2008.

Spector, Regine A. "The Transformation of Askar Akaev, President of Kyrgyzstan." Berkeley Program in Soviet and Post-Soviet Studies Working Paper Series, 2004.

Sri Lanka Ports Authority Annual Reports, 2010–2015. Parliament of Sri Lanka. Accessed February 22, 2018.

Sridharan, E. *International Relations Theory and South Asia: Security, Political Economy, Domestic Politics, Identities, and Images.* Oxford: Oxford University Press, 2015.

Ssebwami, Javira. "Magufuli Suspends Bagamoyo Port Construction, Says Conditions Set by Investor Amount to Selling Tanzania to China." *PML Daily*, June 16, 2019.

Staalesen, Atle. "More Nuclear Power for Russia's Icebreaker Fleet." *Barents Observer*, November 29, 2018.

Stanley, Jason. *How Propaganda Works.* Princeton, NJ: Princeton University Press, 2016.

Steinmetz, George. *The Devil's Handwriting: Precoloniality and the German Colonial State in Qingdao, Samoa, and Southwest Africa.* Chicago: University of Chicago Press, 2007.

Stockmann, Daniela. *Media Commercialization and Authoritarian Rule in China.* New York: Cambridge University Press, 2008.

Strange, Austin M., Axel Dreher, Andreas Fuchs, Bradley C. Parks, and Michael J. Tierney. "Tracking Underreported Financial Flows: China's Development Finance and the Aid-Conflict Nexus Revisited." *Journal of Conflict Resolution* 61, no. 5 (2017): 935–63.

Strauss, Julia C. "The Past in the Present: Historical and Rhetorical Lineages in China's Relations with Africa." *China Quarterly* 199 (September 2009): 777–95.

Studwell, Joe. *How Asia Works: Success and Failure in the World's Most Dynamic Region.* New York: Grove, 2013.

Sued, Hilal K. "Tazara: How the Great Uhuru Railway Was Built." Embassy of the People's Republic of China in the United Republic of Tanzania, November 4, 2012.

Sukumaran, Tashny. "Mahathir, the Malaysian Dictator Who Became a Giant Killer." *South China Morning Post*, May 10, 2018.

Sun, Lichao. "Zhong-ou ban lie ji paomo" [A Bubble Is Emerging in China-Europe Rail Trade]. *Zhongguo jingying bao* [China Business News], July 26, 2019.

Sun, Tianren. "Piraeus Port Project a Role Model for Sino-Greek Cooperation." *People's Daily*, May 14, 2017.

Swaine, Michael D. "Beijing's Tightrope Walk on Iran." *China Leadership Monitor* 33 (June 2010): 1–19.

Swaine, Michael D. "Chinese Views and Commentary on Periphery Diplomacy." *China Leadership Monitor* 44, no. 1 (2014): 1–43.

Swaine, Michael D. "Chinese Views and Commentary on the "One Belt, One Road" Initiative." *China Leadership Monitor* 47 (July 14, 2015): 1–24.

Talbot, Ian. *Pakistan: A Modern History*. London: Hurst, 2009.

Talbott, Strobe, and Will Moreland. *The Marshall Plan and the Shaping of American Strategy*. Washington, DC: Brookings Institution Press, 2017.

Tan, Desai. "Gongtong dazao jiankang sichouzhilu" [Jointly Building a Health Silk Road]. World Health Organization, August 18, 2017.

Tanzania Ports Authority. "Dar es Salaam and Central Coast Sea Ports." N.d.

Terzis, G. P. "I Symfonia tou Karamanli to 2006" [Karamanlis' Agreement in 2006]. *Kathimerini*, July 1, 2016.

Thampi, Madhavi, Bernhard Vogel, Rudolf Dolzer, and Matthias Herdegen. *India and China in the Colonial World*. New York: Berghahn Books, 2005.

Thucydides. *History of the Peloponnesian War*. Translated by Richard Crawley. New York: Dent, 1910.

Tonchev, Plamen. "China's Road: Into the Western Balkans. European Union Institute for Security Studies (EUISS), 2017.

Trebesch, Christoph, Michael G. Papaioannou, and Udaibir S. Das. "Sovereign Debt Restructurings 1950–2010: Literature Survey, Data, and Stylized Facts." IMF Working Paper no. 203, August 2012.

Trenin, Dmitri V. *The End of Eurasia: Russia on the Border between Geopolitics and Globalization*. Washington, DC: Carnegie Endowment for International Peace, 2002.

Tsamopoulos, Minas. "OLP: Kleidi o Tropos Pou Tha Ginei I Polisi Ton Metochon" [The Way the Shares Will Be Sold Is Essential]. *Proto Thema*, May 31, 2011.

Tse, Kwan-Choi T. "Creating Good Citizens in China: Comparing Grade 7–9 School Textbooks, 1997–2005." *Journal of Moral Education* 40, no. 2 (2011): 161–80.

Tsebelis, George. "Lessons from the Greek Crisis." *Journal of European Public Policy* 23, no. 1 (2016): 25–41.

Tsimplakis, Antonis. "Entono Paraskinio Diapragmateuseon Gia Ton OLP" [Intense Happenings Behind the Scene for PPA]. *Naftemporiki*, January 15, 2016.

Tsimplakis, Antonis. "Megales Zimies Gia to Ependitiko Fileto tou OLP Apo ton Provlita I" [Pier I Induces Greater Losses for the Investable "Filet" of PPA]. *Naftemporiki*, January 30, 2014.

Tsimplakis, Antonis. "Pur Omathon Stin Kivernisi Gia Ton OLP" [Volleys inside the Government over OLP]. *Naftemporiki*, February 28, 2014.

Tsimplakis, Antonis. "Stin Yperdeksameni Tis COSCO Pnigontai Ta Ellinika Napigeia" [Greek Ship Shipyards Are Drown in COSCO's Tank]. *Naftemporiki*, November 9, 2016.

Tsimplakis, Antonis. "Stous Kinezous to Megalo Limani Me Symfonia Pou Ftanei to 1,5 Dis" [The Big Port Goes to the Chinese with a Deal Reaching 1,5 Billion Euros]. *Naftemporiki*, January 21, 2016.

Tsubura, Machiko. "'Umoja ni Ushindi (Unity Is Victory)': Management of Factionalism in the Presidential Nomination of Tanzania's Dominant Party in 2015." *Journal of Eastern African Studies* 12, no. 1 (2017): 63–82.

Tuch, Hans. *Communicating with the World: U.S. Public Diplomacy Overseas*. Washington, DC: Institute for the Study of Diplomacy, Georgetown University, 1990.

Unger, Jonathan, ed. *Using the Past to Serve the Present: Historiography and Politics in Contemporary China*. New York: Routledge, 1993.

Van Der Putten, Frans-Paul. "Chinese Investment in the Port of Piraeus, Greece: The Relevance for the EU and the Netherlands." *Clingendael*, February 14, 2014.

Varoufakis, Yanis. *Adults in the Room: My Battle with Europe's Deep Establishment*. London: Vintage, 2018.

Varoufakis, Yanis. *And the Weak Suffer What They Must?: Europe's Crisis and America's Economic Future*. New York: Nation Books, 2016.

Vogel, Ezra. *Deng Xiaoping and the Transformation of China*. Cambridge, MA: Harvard University Press, 2011.

Wafula, Paul. "Tanzania Building Electric Rail at Half Price of Kenya's Diesel Standard Gauge Railway Line." *Standard Media*, October 8, 2017.

Wain, Barry. *Malaysian Maverick: Mahathir Mohamad in Turbulent Times*. New York: Springer, 2009.

Waldron, Arthur. "China's New Remembering of World War II: The Case of Zhang Zizhong." *Modern Asian Studies* 30, no. 4 (1996): 945–78.

Walt, Stephen. "Alliance Formation and the Balance of World Power." *International Security* 9, no. 4 (Spring, 1985): 3–43.

Walt, Stephen M. *The Origins of Alliance*. Ithaca, NY: Cornell University Press, 1990.

Waltz, Kenneth N. *Theory of International Politics*. New York: Waveland Press, 2010.

Wang, Fei-Ling, and Esi A. Elliot. "China in Africa: Presence, Perceptions and Prospects." *Journal of Contemporary China* 23, no. 90 (April 2014): 1012–32.

Wang, Gungwu. "Ming Foreign Relations: Southeast Asia." In *The Cambridge History of China, Volume 8: The Ming Dynasty, 1368–1644, Part 2*, edited by Denis Twitchett and Frederick Mote, 301–32. Cambridge: Cambridge University Press, 1998.

Wang, Gungwu. *Only Connect!: Sino-Malay Encounters*. Singapore: Marshall Cavendish, 2002.

Wang, Hongliang. "China Opens Space Station: 'Space Silk Road' Shows Eastern Wisdom." *The Paper*, June 30, 2018.

Wang, Huning. *Meiguo Fandui Meiguo* [America against America]. Shanghai: Shanghai Literature and Art Press, 1991.

Wang, Jisi. "International Relations Theory and the Study of Chinese Foreign Policy: A Chinese Perspective." In *Chinese Foreign Policy: Theory and Practice*, edited by Thomas W. Robinson and David L. Shambaugh, 481–505. Oxford: Clarendon Press, 1994.

Wang, Jisi. "'Marching Westwards': The Rebalancing of China's Geostrategy." In *The World in 2020 According to China: Chinese Foreign Policy Elites Discuss Emerging Trends in International Politics*, edited by Binghong Shao, 129–36. Leiden: Brill, 2014.

Wang, Jisi. "'Xijin': zhongguo diyuan zhanlue de zaipingheng" ["Marching Westwards": The Rebalancing of China's Geostrategy]. *Huanqiu Shibao*, October 17, 2012.

Wang Liping and Xia Shi. "He anquan beijing xia de yilang he wenti yu zhongguo waijiao zhanlüe xuanze" [The Iranian Nuclear Issue and China's Strategic Foreign Policy Options against the Background of Nuclear Security]. *Lingdao kexue* (June 2010): 58–60.

Wang, Simin. "Moving from Top-Level Design to Pragmatism: Voices from the 'Vision and Action' Seminar." *Guangming Daily*, April 11, 2015.

Wang, Yiwei. *The Belt and Road: What Will China Offer the World in Its Rise*. Beijing: New World Press, 2016.

Wang, Yiwei. "'Yidaiyilu' juefei zhongguoban 'maxie'er jihua'" ["OBOR" Is By No Means the Chinese Version of the "Marshall Plan"]. *Qiushi*, June 15, 2015.

Wang, Yong. "Offensive for Defensive: The Belt and Road Initiative and China's New Grand Strategy." *Pacific Review* 29, no. 3 (2016): 455–63.

Wang, Zheng. *Never Forget National Humiliation: Historical Memory in Chinese Politics and Foreign Relations*. New York: Columbia University Press, 2014.

Weatherley, Robert, and Coirle Magee. "Using the Past to Legitimise the Present: The Portrayal of Good Governance in Chinese History Textbooks." *Journal of Current Chinese Affairs* 47, no. 1 (2018): 41–69.

Weinstein, Laura. "The Politics of Government Expenditures in Tanzania, 1999–2007." *African Studies Review* 54, no. 1 (2011): 33–57.

Wen, Jiabao. "Zaichuang sichouzhilu xin huihuang" [Create the New Glory of the Silk Road]. *China Daily*, September 4, 2012.

Wen, Philip, and Drew Hinshaw. "China Asserts Claim to Global Leadership, Mask by Mask." *Wall Street Journal*, April 1, 2020.

Westad, Odd Arne. *The Global Cold War: Third World Interventions and the Making of Our Times*. Cambridge: Cambridge University Press, 2005.

White House. "President Donald J. Trump's Visit to Japan Strengthens the United States-Japan Alliance and Economic Partnership." White House, November 6, 2017.

White House Office of Trade and Manufacturing Policy. "How China's Economic Aggression Threatens the Technologies and Intellectual Property of the United States and the World." White House, June, 2018.

Wickramasinghe, Kamanthi. "'I Am Not a Person Who Goes After Portfolios': Arjuna Ranatunga." *Daily Mirror*, April 27, 2017.

Wijedasa, Namini. "Four of Seven Berths in Hambantota Port Development Project—Phase 2 to Be Given to Chinese Joint Venture." *Sunday Times*, September 21, 2014.

Wijedasa, Namini. "Hambantota Port Phase II: China to Get Four of the Seven Berths." *Sunday Times*, September 21, 2014.

Wissenbach, Uwe, and Yuan Wang. "African Politics Meets Chinese Engineers: The Chinese-Built Standard Gauge Railway Project in Kenya and East Africa." *China Africa Research Initiative*, no. 2017/13 (2017): 1–33.

Womack, Brantly. "Asymmetry and China's Tributary System." *Chinese Journal of International Politics* 5 (2012): 37–54.

Wood, Robert Everett. *From Marshall Plan to Debt Crisis: Foreign Aid and Development Choices in the World Economy*. Berkeley: University of California Press, 1986.

Wu, Haiying. "Zheng He jingshen ji qi dangdai yiyi" [The Spirit of Zheng He and Its Contemporary Significance]. *Journal of Hui Muslim Minority Studies* 1 (2005).

Wu, Hongyuran, and Fran Wang. "Central Bank Chief Says China Will Guard against Belt and Road Debt Risks." *Caixin*, April 25, 2019.

Wu, Po-Kuan, and Mads Dagnis Jensen. "Examining the EU-China Relationship in the Aftermath of the Economic Crisis." *International Journal of Public Administration* 40, no. 14 (April 2017): 1223–36.

Wu, Xiao An. *Chinese Business in the Making of a Malay State, 1882–1941: Kedah and Penang*. Singapore: National University of Singapore Press, 2010.

Wu, Zelin. "Tanxi ouya liangzhong butong de quyu hezuo moshi" [Exploring Europe and Asia's Two Different Models of Regional Cooperation]. *Zhongguo Guoqing Guoli* 3 (2016): 68–71.

Wübbeke, Jost, Mirjam Meissner, Max J. Zenglein, Jaqueline Ives, and Björn Conrad. "Made in China 2025: The Making of a High-Tech Superpower and Consequences for Industrial Countries." MERICS, December 2016.

Xiang, Qiu. "Ban yiliu pingan saishi zonglv kejia bei 'yidaiyilu' guoji zuqiu yaoqingsai ni qidai ma" [Hold a First-Class, Safe Event! Are You Looking Forward to the Palm, Hakka Cup, "One Belt, One Road" International Football Invitational Match?]. *Ping'an Meizhou*, December 28, 2018.

Xie, Guifang. "The Potential Dual Use of Support Facilities in the Belt and Road Initiative." National Bureau of Asian Research 80, September 2019.

Xie, Jing. "Yidaiyilu" yu Zhongguo: dongmeng hulian hutong de Yindu yinsu [India Factor in "The Belt and Road" and China-ASEAN Connectivity]. *Dongnanyan zongheng* (2015): 38–41.

Xu, Fangqing. "'One Belt One Road' Case: 'Replicating' China's Reform and Opening Up in Piraeus Port, Greece." *China News Weekly*, May 14, 2017.

Xu, Rui. "Speech by Chinese President Xi Jinping to Indonesian Parliament." ASEAN-China Centre, October 2, 2013.

Xu, Zhong. "Why China's Reform Documents Are Often Ambiguous." *Caixin*, February 19, 2019.

Xue, Li, and Yanzhuo Xu. "China Needs Great Power Diplomacy in Asia." *The Diplomat*, March 12, 2015.

Yan, Xuetong. *Ancient Chinese Thought, Modern Chinese Power*. Princeton, NJ: Princeton University Press, 2013.

Yan, Xuetong. "Chinese Values vs. Liberalism: What Ideology Will Shape the International Normative Order?" *Chinese Journal of International Politics* 11, no. 1 (March 2018): 1–22.

Yan, Xuetong. "From Keeping a Low Profile to Striving for Achievement." *Chinese Journal of International Politics* 7, no. 2 (June 2014): 153–84.

Yan, Xuetong. "Strategic Challenges for China's Rise." Carnegie Tsinghua Center for Global Policy, February 23, 2017.

Yang, Huaizhong. "Zoujin Zheng He" [Approaching Zheng He]. *Journal of Hui Muslim Minority Studies* (2005).

Yang, Mi. "The Challenges and Opportunities of 'One Belt One Road' in Southeast Asia." *Guangming Daily*, August 19, 2015.

Yang, Yang. "Belt and Road Initiative Warmly Welcomed in Australia's Northern Territory." *China Daily*, July 16, 2018.

Yang, Yi. "China Fully Committed to Iran Nuclear Deal: Chinese Delegate." Xinhua, June 29, 2019.

Yang, Youming. "China and Zambia, We Grow Up Together." Embassy of the People's Republic of China in Zambia, October 27, 2014.

Yfanti, P. D., and Michalis Gelantalis. "Fernoun Pelateia, Dinoume Foroapallages" [They Bring Customers, We Give Tax Exemptions]. *Enet*, February 7, 2010.

Yi, Ling. "Ammar's Silk Road Dream." China.org, March 13, 2017.

Yong, Deng. *China's Struggle for Status: The Realignment of International Relations.* Cambridge: Cambridge University Press, 2008.

Yu, George. "China Development in Africa: Looking Backwards and Forwards." Central European University School of Public Policy, March 7, 2016.

Yu, Jiangwei, ed. "Qianming zhongwai keshang qi xianxue, Yidaiyilu liantong guojia xuemai" [Thousands of Chinese and Foreign Businessmen Donate Blood, OBOR to Connect the Blood of Nations]. *Fenghuang Wang Zhejiang*, July 15, 2017.

Yu, Ying-shih. *Trade and Expansion in Han China: A Study in the Structure of Sino-Barbarian Economic Relations.* Berkeley: University of California Press, 1967.

Yung, Christopher D., and Ross Rustici. "'Not an Idea We Have to Shun': Chinese Overseas Basing Requirements in the 21st Century." National Defense University Press, October 2014.

Zaidi, Akbar S. "Has China Taken Over Pakistan?" *News on Sunday*, June 18, 2017.

Zaidi, Akbar S. *Issues in Pakistan's Economy: A Political Economy Perspective.* New York: Oxford University Press, 2015.

Zainul, Intan Farhana. "Business as Usual for East Coast Rail Line." *The Star*, May 16, 2018.

Zarif, Mohammad Javad. "Shared Vision Binds Iran-China Relations." *Global Times*, August 26, 2019.

Zeng, Xianghong. "Zhongguo de zhongya waijiao yu sichouzhilu jingji dai de goujian" [China's Central Asian Diplomacy and the Construction of the Silk Road Economic Belt]. *Shanghai Jiaotong Daxue Xuebao (Zhexue Shehui Kexue Ban)* 3 (2015): 5–14.

Zhang, Hong. "Beyond 'Debt-Trap Diplomacy': The Dissemination of PRC State Capitalism." *China Brief* 19, no. 1 (January 2019): 8–12.

Zhang, Wenxian, Ilan Alon, and Christoph Lattemann, eds. *China's Belt and Road Initiative: Changing the Rules of Globalization.* New York: Palgrave, 2018.

Zhang, Xiaomin, and Chunfeng Xu. "The Late Qing Dynasty Diplomatic Transformation: Analysis from an Ideational Perspective." *Chinese Journal of International Politics* 1 (2007): 405–45.

Zhang, Yongjin. "China and Liberal Hierarchies in Global International Society: Power and Negotiation for Normative Change." *International Affairs* 92, no. 4 (2016): 795–816.

Zhang, Yongjin. "Introduction: Dynamism and Contention: Understanding Chinese Foreign Policy under Xi Jinping." *International Affairs* 92, no. 4 (2016): 769–72.

Zhao, Ena, Shuo Zhang, Yasong Ding. "Rang dang de qizhi zai gaoxiao gaogao piaoyang gaoxiao dang de jianshe yu sixiang zhengzhi gongzuo zongshu" [Let the Party's Flag Fly High in Colleges and Universities—A Summary of the Work on Party Building, Ideological and Political in Colleges and Universities]. *Renmin Ribao*, January 15, 2019.

Zhao, Huaipu. "Zhongou guanxi" [Sino-EU Relations]. *Zhongguo Wang*, July 28, 2009.

Zhao, Lei. "Projects Promote Fairness as Supreme Value." *China Daily*, April 24, 2015.

Zheng, Bijian. "China's 'Peaceful Rise' to Great-Power Status." *Foreign Affairs* (September–October 2005): 18–24.

Zheng, Sarah. "China, Tanzania in Talks to Get US$10 Billion Bagamoyo Port Project Back on Track, Ambassador Says." *South China Morning Post*, July 11, 2019.

Zheng, Yongnian. *The Chinese Communist Party and Organizational Emperor: Culture, Reproduction and Transformation*. New York: Routledge, 2010.

Zheng, Yongnian, and Fook Lye Liang. "China's Foreign Policy: Balancing Its International Responsibility and National Interest." *East Asian Policy* 8, no. 1 (2016): 55–70.

Zheng, Yongnian, Lye Liang Fook, and Chen Gang. "China's Foreign Policy: Responding to the US Pivot to Asia and Managing Differences with its Neighbours." *East Asia Policy* 5, no. 1 (2013): 14–31.

Zheng, Yu, and Chris Smith. "New Voyages in Search of Treasure: China Ocean Shipping Company (COSCO) in Europe." In *Chinese Investment in Europe: Corporate Strategies and Labour Relations*, edited by Jan Drahokoupil, 231–50. Brussels: ETIU, 2017.

Zhong, Sheng. "Epoch-Making Significance of 'Silk Road Economic Belt and 21st Century Maritime Silk Road' Proposal." *People's Daily*, February 25, 2014.

Zhong, Sheng. "New Vitality and New Heights." *People's Daily*, September 8, 2013.

Zhong, Sheng. "Open Up Bright Prospects through Active Action." *People's Daily*, February 17, 2015.

Zhong, Sheng. "A Staunch Force for Pushing Forward Global Economic Governance." *People's Daily*, November 19, 2014.

Zhong, Sheng. "Writing a New Chapter on the Silk Road." *People's Daily*, June 28, 2014.

Zhou, Laura. "How a Chinese Investment Boom Is Changing the Face of Djibouti." *South China Morning Post*, May 1, 2017.

Zhou, Shuchun. "Gongtong de qinghuai—zhenxing 'sichou zhilu'—xiezai lipeng zongli jieshu fangwen zhongya siguo zhiji" [Common Feelings—Revitalize the "Silk Road"—Written at the End of Premier Li Peng's Visit to Four Countries in Central Asia]. *Renmin Ribao*, April 29, 1994, 6.

Zikou, Zeta. "O Epomenos Igetis tis Kinas tha Einai o Gkorpatsof Tis?" [Will China's Next Leader Be Its Gorbachev?]. *Kathimerini*, October 14, 2012.

Zuenko, Ivan. "Kak proidet kitajskiy Shelkoviy put I kto na nem zarabotaet" [Which Road Will the Chinese Silk Road Take and Who Will Win?]. Carnegie Moscow Center, April 21, 2016.

Index

Page numbers for figures, maps, and tables are in italics.

Harvard East Asian Monographs
(most recent titles)